Programming in ANSI C

Programming in ANSI C

Ram Kumar

Late, Professor, University of Udaipur, Udaipur
Late, Professor, Motilal Nehru Regional Engineering
College, Allahabad

Rakesh Agrawal

IBM Almaden Research Center, San Jose, California

West Publishing Company
St. Paul   New York   Los Angeles   San Francisco

Production credits
Copyediting: Martha Knutson
Composition: Professional Book Center
Text Design: Lois Stanfield
Cover Design: Elaine Saint-Marie

Library of Congress Cataloging-in-Publication Data

Kumar, Ram.
    Programming in ANSI C / Ram Kumar, Rakesh Agrawal
        p.   cm.
    Includes bibliographical references and index.
    ISBN 0-314-89563-9 (soft)
    1. C (Computer program language) I. Agrawal, Rakesh. II. Title.
QA76.73.C15K86 1992
005.26'2--dc20   91-26474
                                                     CIP

For Mrs. Urmila Agrawal
with love and gratitude

 # Notices

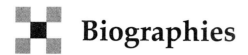 # Biographies

RAM KUMAR

Dr. Ram Kumar was Professor and Head of the Department of Mathematics, University of Udaipur, Udaipur, and Motilal Nehru Regional Engineering College, Allahabad. He was a noted scholar and was engaged in research and teaching for over 40 years. He wrote several books, including the highly popular *Programming with FORTRAN 77*.

He was a holder of both Ph.D. and D.Sc. degrees. On his D.Sc. thesis, he was awarded the Bonarjee Research Prize by the University of Lucknow for the best research production of 1963. He was a Fellow of the National Academy of Sciences, India.

RAKESH AGRAWAL

Dr. Rakesh Agrawal is a Research Staff Member at the IBM Almaden Research Center, San Jose, California. He was a member of Technical of Staff at the AT&T Bell Laboratories, Murray Hill, New Jersey from September 1983 to December 1989. He holds M.S. and Ph.D. degrees in Computer Science from the University of Wisconsin, Madison. He has published extensively in technical journals and conferences. He is a co-designer of O++, a database programming language based on C++. He is an Editor of the *IEEE Data Engineering* and the *Database Technology*, and was a Program Chairman of the *2nd International Symposium on Databases in Parallel and Distributed Systems*. He is a Senior Member of IEEE and a Member of ACM.

 **Preface**

C has emerged as the most widely used programming language for software development. It is a small, yet powerful language. It features modem control flow and data types that allow the development of well-structured programs. Its data types and control structures are directly supported by most computers, resulting in the construction of efficient programs. It is independent of any particular machine architecture or operating system, which makes it easy to write portable programs. It is this combination of rich control structures and data types, ability to get close to computer hardware, efficiency, portability, and conciseness that has contributed to the popularity of C.

Audience

This book teaches computer programming using C. It does not presume prior knowledge of some other programming language, and teaches C from first principles. At the same time, it is a complete description of C. Even knowledgeable C programmers should find the examples and exercises interesting and challenging. This book can be used either as a textbook for a course on programming, as a source book for a training course on C, as a guide for self-teaching C, or as a reference by software professionals.

Approach

The text is designed in such a way that it gradually introduces new concepts, gives examples based on the concepts introduced so far, and then builds on what you have already assimilated. *There is a strong emphasis on examples*. The book is full of illustrative programs that exemplify how different language constructs can be put together to solve a given problem. Examples in each chapter have been chosen so that they not only embody the various language constructs introduced in that chapter, but also use the ideas learned in previous chapters. In this way, concepts are reinforced and covered at a deeper level in each new context. In several instances, the same problem has been solved using different language constructs to clarify differences between them. Concepts are first introduced informally through one or more motivating example programs in order for you to develop an intuitive understanding of them. They are then rigorously discussed in the remainder of the chapter. Each chapter ends with a set of exercises that allow you to review and test your understanding of the new material. Examples and exercises have been 'selected from various disciplines and application domains, including business, engineering, science, mathematics, and statistics. Illustrative programs have been run and tested under both UNIX and DOS environments.

Organization

We begin with an overview of the computer organization in Chapter 1. The principal components of computer hardware — memory, control unit, arithmetic-logic unit, and input/output devices — are described. We then discuss computer software and programming languages, explaining the differences between machine, assembly, and higher level languages. A brief history of the evolution of C is also given. We then describe the programming process: problem definition, program design, program coding, program compilation and execution, program testing and debugging, and program documentation. Algorithm development, which is the heart of computer programming, is also discussed in this chapter.

We start learning the specifics of C in Chapter 2. A useful starting point for understanding computer programming is that all programs can be written using just three logical structures: sequential, selective, repetitive, or a combination thereof. We first discuss the sequential structure, which consists of one operation followed by another, and then introduce some C constructs sufficient to write simple sequential programs. In particular, we examine the main function, the C character set, various data types, variables and constants, arithmetic operators, assignment statements, input and output functions, type conversions, and simple macros.

The selective structure, which consists of a test for a condition followed by alternative paths that the program can follow, is discussed in Chapter 3. Selection among alternative processing is programmed with certain decision-making constructs: conditional statement, nested conditional statement, multiway conditional statement, and constant multiway conditional statement. Besides introducing these constructs, we also examine the relational, logical, and conditional expression operators necessary for understanding these constructs.

The repetitive structure, also known as the iterative or loop structure, allows a set of program statements to be executed several times even though they appear only once in the program. This topic is discussed in Chapter 4. The constructs presented include while loop, do-while loop, for loop, and nested loops. The facilities for loop interruption are also discussed.

A C program is usually developed by dividing it into logically coherent functional components, each of which carries out a specific task. We discuss the user-defined functions in Chapter 5. In particular, we look at how a function is defined and called, function prototypes, block structure, external variables, storage classes, separate compilation and data abstraction, and recursion.

Arrays, which enable a user to organize and process a set of ordered data items, are the subject of Chapter 6. We discuss array type declaration, array initialization, and how array elements are accessed. We also study arrays as function arguments.

We examine in Chapter 7 one of the most sophisticated features of C: pointers. After introducing the basics of pointers, such as pointer type declaration, pointer assignment, pointer initialization, pointer arithmetic, pointer comparison, and pointer conversion, we discuss the relationship between functions and pointers, arrays and pointers, strings and pointers, and multidimensional arrays and pointers. We then look at pointer arrays, pointers to functions, and dynamic memory management.

Structures allow a fixed number of data items, possibly of different types, to be treated as a single object, whereas unions allow a number of different types of grouped data items to be referred to using the same name. These topics form the subject matter of Chapter 8. Besides introducing the techniques for defining and using structures and unions, we discuss the scope rules for structure definitions, structures as function arguments, structures as function values, nested structures, arrays of structures, structures containing arrays, structures containing pointers, and self-referential structures.

Systems programs frequently require the capability to manipulate individual bits of a word. C provides four operators, called bitwise logical operators, for masking operations on bits, and two operators, called the bitwise shift operators, for shifting bits in a word. In addition, C allows a word to be partitioned into groups of bits, called bit-fields, and names to be assigned to them. We study these features in Chapter 9.

C does not provide language constructs for input/output (I/O) operations. However, ANSI C has defined a rich set of functions to provide a standard I/O system for C programs. We discuss in Chapter 10 the functions available in the standard I/O library and their use in writing applications involving file processing that require large amount of data to be read, processed, and saved for later use.

The C preprocessor, which can conceptually be thought of as a program that processes the source text of a C program before it is compiled, is the subject of Chapter 11. The three major functions of the C proeprocessor discussed are macro replacement, conditional inclusion, and file inclusion. Macro replacement is the replacement of one string by another, conditional inclusion is the selective inclusion and exclusion of portions of source text on the basis of a computed condition, and file inclusion is the insertion of the text of a file into the current file. In addition, the line, error, pragma, and null directives, and the predefined macro names are also described.

We discuss some additional C features in Chapter 12. In particular, we describe the type definition facility, which allows synonyms to be defined for existing data types; the type qualification facility, which permits greater control over program optimization; the enumeration type, which provides the facility to specify the possible values of a variable by meaningful symbolic names; the facility to define functions that take variable number of arguments; the storage class specifier register, which can speed up programs by specifying to the compiler the heavily used variables to be kept in machine registers; facilities for alternative representation of characters; and the goto statement, which can be used to branch around one or more statements.

The book contains six appendices. Appendix A describes functions included in the standard library but not presented in the text earlier. Appendix B summarizes C operators together with their precedence and associativity. Appendix C explains the main differences between ANSI C and the version of C as described in Kernighan and Ritchie's 1978 book "The C Programming Language." Those of you who still have pre-ANSI C compilers will find this appendix particulary useful. Appendix D reviews the decimal, binary, octal, and hexadecimal number systems, discusses how numbers in any one of these systems can be converted into numbers in the others, and describes how numbers and characters are represented inside the computer. Appendix E gives a table of ASCII and EBCDIC character codes and equivalent representations of some decimal numbers in the binary, octal, and hexadecimal systems. Appendix F lists some classical references on programming and C.

We believe that the best way to learn programming is by reading, writing, and experimenting with programs. To increase your understanding of C, we encourage you to read and re-read the example programs given in the book and to solve as many exercises as you can. We also encourage you to experiment with the programs by running them with different test inputs, by modifying them to use alternate constructs, and by enhancing them with error checking and additional functionality. The source code for the programs given in the illustrative examples has been made available on a compainion diskette to aid this process.

We hope that this text will make problem solving on computers an exciting and rewarding endeavor, and that you will find computer programming a fun experience. We appreciate receiving suggestions for improvements and ideas for additional illustrative examples and exercises.

Acknowledgments

We have been fortunate to have had the advise and criticism of many talented people who reviewed earlier drafts of this book. In particular, we would like to mention Stephen J. Allan, Utah State University; Eric P. Bloom, Bentley College; John L. Carroll, San Diego State University; John Crenshaw, Western Kentucky University; Grady Early, Southwest Texas State University; Maurice L. Eggen, Trinity University; Rhonda Ficek, Moorhead State University; Robert C. Gann, Hartwick College; Gordon Hoagland, Ricks College; Peter C. Isaacson, University of Northern Colorado; Keith E. Jolly, Chabot College; William Jones, California State University, Dominquez Hills; Lyndon Marshall, College of Great Falls; Eric Nagler, De Anza, Mission, and Ohlone Colleges; Kenneth Pierce, University of Mary Hardin-Baylor; Arline Sachs, Northern Virginia Community College; Peter Schleppenbach, Los Angeles Pierce College; and Jack van Luik, Mount Hood Community College.

We have had a pleasant relationship with West. Rick Mixter believed in this project from day one and kept us focused on students. Keith Dodson put in a great deal of effort in bringing this project to fruition. Tom Modl enthusiastically experimented with many new ideas in the production of this book. Martha Knutson helped us smooth many language wrinkles. Liz Grantham was instrumental in the promotion of the book. We thank them and others at West.

This book would not have completed without the support and patience of our family. They are the ones who had to constantly endure our "Not this weekend, I have to work on the book" answers.

Ram Kumar
Rakesh Agrawal

Contents

1 Computers and Programming

To be able to program well, in addition to mastering the details of a programming language, you need to understand the nature of computers and the process of developing computer programs. We summarize the basic concepts of computers and their programming in this chapter.

We first discuss computer hardware and software. *Hardware* refers to the physical equipment that makes up a computer. *Software* refers to programs that make computers do useful work. A computer *program* is a sequence of instructions that a computer follows to solve a particular problem. We then describe different types of programming languages and the place of the programming language C in this spectrum. Finally, we discuss the *programming process*, that is, the steps involved in developing a computer program.

1.1 HARDWARE

A computer is composed of five principal components: *(i) input* device, *(ii) memory, (iii) control unit, (iv) arithmetic-logic unit*, and *(v) output device*. The control and arithmetic-logic units are collectively referred to as the *central processing unit*. Figure 1.1 shows the logical organization of the principal components of a computer. The arrows in the figure represent information flow within the computer.

The input device converts information from a form suitable to human users into one suitable for a computer. The control unit manages the computation and directs the computer-usable information provided by the input device to the appropriate units for processing. The memory stores the information as directed by the control unit. The arithmetic-logic unit performs arithmetic operations and conducts comparisons of stored information to make logical decisions. After the completion of a computation, the control unit directs the results of the computation to the output device; it may also direct that the results be stored back in memory for future use. The output device converts the results into a form convenient for human users.

We will now look into these components and their interactions in some detail.

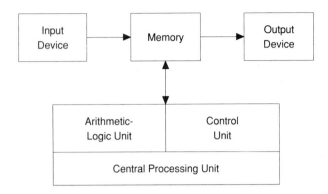

Figure 1.1.   Principal components of a computer system

1.1.1 Memory

Memory is used to store both data and program instructions. It also holds intermediate and final results of a computation.

Memory can be visualized as an ordered sequence of *storage locations*, or *cells*, labeled from zero upwards. The label of a location is called its *address*; each location is called a *word* and consists of *bits*. A bit is a computer abbreviation for a *binary digit* and can contain either a 0 or 1. Eight adjacent bits are referred to as a *byte*. A word usually consists of 8, 16, or 32 bits. A 16-bit word is usually divided into 2 bytes and a 32-bit word into 4 bytes. Figure 1.2 gives a visual representation of a 16-bit word-addressable computer memory.

When some information is stored in a memory location, the previous contents of that location are overwritten. The contents of a location remain unaltered when information is retrieved from it.

1.1.2 Control Unit

The control unit fetches, interprets, and controls the execution of the program instructions stored in computer memory. It also directs and coordinates all other units of a computer.

We briefly describe the execution of a program instruction. A program instruction specifies the operation and the operands (data) on which the operation is to be performed. Associated with the control unit are some special storage locations, called *registers*, that have very fast access time. The memory address of the instruction to be executed is first placed in a special register, called the *program counter*, from where it is transferred to the *memory address register*. A memory-read operation is then performed that copies the instruction from memory into the *memory buffer register*. From the memory buffer register, the instruction is transferred to the *instruction register*, where it is decoded to identify the operation and the operands. The control unit then causes the operation indicated by the instruction to be executed. Operations requiring arithmetic or logical computations are carried out using special registers and circuits of the arithmetic-logic unit.

Address	Word		
	Byte		Byte	
0			
1			
2			
3			
4			
5			
6			

Figure 1.2. Visual representation of computer memory

Every time an instruction is moved into the instruction register, the program counter is automatically incremented, so that after the execution of the instruction, the program counter contains the memory address of the next instruction. It is also possible to load the program counter with a memory address other than the next one in sequence.

1.1.3 Arithmetic-Logic Unit

The arithmetic-logic unit performs arithmetic operations and conducts comparisons of data to make logical decisions. This unit contains the necessary components, such as *adders*, *multipliers*, *counters*, and *comparators*, for carrying out these operations.

The arithmetic-logic unit, like the control unit, also contains several registers, the most important being the *accumulator* in which the results of arithmetic and logical operations are produced. Typical instructions will load the accumulator with a data value from memory, add to it another data value, store the result back in memory, clear the accumulator to zero, shift its contents left or right, or complement its contents.

1.1.4 Input and Output Devices

Input and output (I/O) devices are the means of communication between human users and a computer. An input device is used to enter data to be manipulated into memory and an output device is used to display or record the results of this manipulation. Some important I/O devices are: (i) *terminal*, (ii) *printer*, (iii) *magnetic tape* unit, and (iv) *magnetic disk* unit.

Terminal

A computer terminal provides both input and output capability. Input is accomplished by keying information on a keyboard. Output is displayed on a *video monitor*. Some terminals are equipped with graphic capabilities. With some graphic terminals, the user can communicate with a computer by pointing at information displayed on the screen using a *mouse*. A mouse is a small object, containing one to three buttons, that moves a pointer on the video monitor when it is rolled on the desk.

Printer

A printer is an output device capable of accepting information from computer's memory and producing a corresponding printed record on paper, sometimes called the *hard copy*. A great variety of printers are available, including line printers, matrix printers, laser printers, and ink-jet printers. They differ in speed, cost, reliability, and the quality of output.

Magnetic Tape Unit

Magnetic tape units have the dual capacity of reading (input) and writing (output) by either sensing (reading) the magnetized spots or by magnetizing (writing) areas in parallel tracks along the length of a magnetic tape. Magnetic tape units come in a variety of sizes ranging from the larger reel tape units to units no bigger than a portable cassette tape unit.

A magnetic tape unit is a *sequential* device: to access a specific area of the magnetic tape, the entire earlier portion of the tape must be scanned first.

Magnetic Disk Unit

A magnetic disk unit is an I/O device with the capability to read or write data *sequentially* as well as *randomly*. Random access permits access to any specific portion of information without accessing the preceding information.

A magnetic disk is a thin disk of metal coated with magnetic recording material. A stack of disks mounted on a common spindle is called a *disk pack*. Data is stored as magnetized spots on concentric circles called *tracks* that are numbered and divided into *sectors*. A group of all the tracks with the same number on all the surfaces of a disk pack is called a *cylinder*. Data is read and written using an *access mechanism* that consists of read/write heads, one for each of the recording surfaces.

A *floppy disk* (also called *diskette*) consists of a plastic disk coated with magnetic material and comes in two sizes — 3.5 inch and 5.25 inch. The floppy disks operate much the same way as the hard magnetic disks, but have relatively less capacity, larger access time, and are less expensive. The main advantage of the floppy disks is that they are *portable* — they can be used to transfer information from one computer to another.

1.2 SOFTWARE

A finite sequence of instructions that a computer follows to solve a particular problem is called a *computer program*. Some programs, called *systems programs*, direct the internal operations of a computer, such as controlling input and output devices or managing storage areas within the computer. Others, called *application programs*, direct a computer to solve user-oriented problems, such as preparing electricity bills, determining the rate of return for a proposed project, or calculating the stress factors for a building structure. Collectively, the group of programs that a computer uses is referred to as *software*.

1.2.1 Programming Languages

Every computer has its own language, called *machine language*, that depends on the specific hardware of the computer. A program written in a machine language is machine-dependent and is good only for that particular type of a computer. An instruction for a computer specifies precisely the operation to be performed. In machine language, it consists of a given number of bits; each bit, or a group of contiguous bits, signifies some required action. Thus, a machine-language programmer must know the numeric codes of various operations and must keep track of the address of each data item in memory.

Programming in machine language is cumbersome and error-prone. It is difficult to make modifications to a machine-language program because to move even a single data item, all instructions that manipulate it must be changed to reflect the new address of the memory cell containing this data item.

These difficulties may be alleviated somewhat by writing programs in *assembly language*, wherein the sequences of 1's and 0's are replaced by symbols. Data items are referred to by descriptive names, such as gross or tax, and operations are specified in symbolic codes, such as ADD or HALT. However, since a computer does not "understand" assembly language, an assembly language program is first translated into machine-language instructions by a systems program, called an *assembler*, before it can be executed.

Programming in assembly language is relatively convenient as the programmer does not have to keep track of as many details as with the machine language. However, the programmer is still concerned with tedious details, such as indexing and storage locations, in addition to writing a complex sequence of instructions. Furthermore, assembly language programs written for one computer generally will not execute on another. It is for these reasons that languages known as *higher-level languages* have been developed.

Higher-level languages are akin to our written languages. They relieve programmers from the burden of low-level details and allow them to concentrate on the problem being solved. Higher-level language programs contain very few of the machine-dependent details required in machine or assembly language programs, and they may be used with little or no modification on a variety of computers. They are also much easier to maintain and update.

A higher-level language program also needs to be translated into machine language instructions before it can be executed. This translation, called the *compilation*, is performed by a systems program called a *compiler*. The original program is called the *source program* and its translation the *object program*.

As an illustration of the difference between machine, assembly, and higher-level languages, given below are three versions of a program that adds the numbers B and C stored in two different memory locations and stores the result A in a third memory location:

Machine Language Version			Assembly Language Version			Higher-Level Language Version
016767	000012	000014	GO:	MOV	B A	B = 100
066767	000006	000006		ADD	C A	C = 150
000000				HALT		A = B + C
000100			B	.WORD	100	
000150			C	.WORD	150	
000000			A	.WORD	0	
				.END	GO	

You are not expected to understand these programs. However, the higher-level language program is obviously more readable.

C is a higher-level language, but provides several powerful operations such as bit manipulations that are typically found only in assembly languages. Some other popular higher-level languages include BASIC, FORTRAN, COBOL, PL/1, Algol, Pascal, and Ada.

1.2.2 C

C belongs to the "Algol family" of programming languages and gets its name from being the successor to the B language. It was designed by Dennis Ritchie in about 1972 as the systems language for the UNIX operating system on a PDP-11 computer at the AT&T Bell Laboratories. C was developed as an alternative to the systems Language B, developed by Ken Thompson in about 1970 for the first UNIX operating system on a PDP-7 at the Bell Laboratories. B was an offspring of BCPL, developed by Martin Richards in 1969 at the Cambridge University. The earlier languages belonging to this ancestry are Cambridge's CPL (1963) and Algol 60 (1960).

C has acquired an immense following in recent times, and many commercial implementations of C exist on a variety of machines. Initially the book *The C Programming Language* by Brian Kernighan and Dennis Ritchie served as the standard language reference. To propose a standard for C, a technical subcommittee on C language standardization, X3J11, was formed by the American National Standards Institute (ANSI) in 1982. The goal of this committee was to produce an unambiguous and machine-independent standard definition of C, while retaining its original spirit. After considerable debate and deliberation, the standard was finalized in 1989 as the American National Standard for Information Systems–Programming Language C, X3.159-1989. This book is based on C as defined by this standard.

1.3 PROGRAMMING PROCESS

The process of developing a computer program to solve a specific problem involves the following steps:

1. Problem Definition
2. Program Design
3. Program Coding

4. Program Compilation and Execution
5. Program Testing and Debugging
6. Program Documentation

Although listed as distinct, these steps tend to blend into each other. The later steps sometimes feed back into the previous ones, making the whole process iterative.

1.3.1 Problem Definition

A precise definition of the problem that the program is meant to solve is an essential prerequisite for a successful program. Defining a problem involves obtaining answers to the following questions:

- What must the program do?
- What outputs are required and in what form?
- What inputs are available and in what form?

Consider, for example, the generation of an inventory report. When the quantity for an item in stock falls below the reorder level, a replenishment order is placed. The amount of the order, called the economic order quantity EOQ, is given by

$$EOQ = (2AO/CI)^{1/2}$$

where A is the annual usage of the item, O the ordering cost, C the unit cost, and I the interest rate for carrying inventory. The reorder level R is given by

$$R = L \times W$$

where L is the lead time — time between placing an order and the arrival of the item — in weeks, and W is the weekly usage. The purpose of the inventory program can be stated as follows:

> The inventory program must provide the order quantity for each item whose current stock has fallen below the reorder level.

We now have to specify the outputs of the program. This step usually requires interaction with the potential users of the program outputs. We assume that the output of the inventory program is required to be in the form of an inventory report as shown in Figure 1.3. The report heading consists of the report title followed by the column names. The report body contains the item code, the current stock, the reorder level, and the order quantity for each item that needs to be reordered. The relative position and the largest value of each of the data items in the report have also been shown in the figure.

Is this a complete specification of the program outputs? Consider the following additional questions that should also be answered:

- How many pages can there be in the inventory report? Do pages need to be numbered? If the report is more than one page, do we need to repeat the title and the column names on every page, or do we require them only on the first page, or do we need only the column names on subsequent pages?

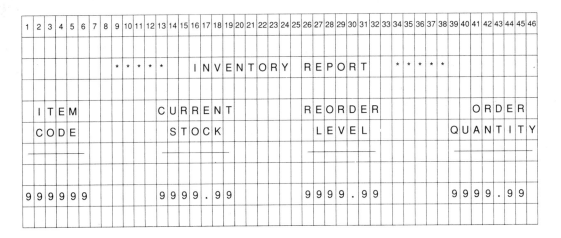

Figure 1.3.   The output format for the inventory problem

- How should the program respond to exceptions? What should be printed if the value of a data item turns out to be larger than the specified largest value? What if the report has more pages than the anticipated maximum?
- Should the items be printed in any particular order? In ascending or descending order of item code? In descending order of order quantity? In ascending order of current stock? Or is the ordering not important?

One could add several other questions to this list. Should the program also save information about the items reordered on a disk file for feeding as input to a purchase monitoring program? Should the report be dated? However, many times it is best to start with answers to a reasonably complete set of questions, initiate the design, and then revisit the output specification to make it firm. The key point to remember is that the assumptions at every iteration must be documented as part of the problem definition, as they crucially affect the program design. If any of the assumptions become invalid, the program may have to be modified to reflect the new reality.

The output specification is followed by an investigation of what inputs are required to generate the desired outputs and how the inputs will be made available to the program. Inputs can be free-format in which the data items are separated by some special character (usually a space), or in a stylized form in which every data item has a fixed position on the data line. They may be supplied interactively by the user in response to prompts from the program, or they may be prepared in advance specifically for the use of the program, or they may be the outputs of some other program.

For the inventory program, we assume that the input consists of a line of data for each item in the stock, as shown in Figure 1.4. The largest value of each data item has also been specified.

We need to answer some additional questions for a complete input specification:

1	2	3	4	5	6	7	8	9	10	11	12	13	14	15	16	17	18	19	20	21	22	23	24	25	26	27	28	29	30	31	32	33	34	35	36	37
Item Code						Ordering Cost						Unit Cost						Rate				Weekly Usage						Lead Time		Current Stock						
9	9	9	9	9	9	9	9	9	9	.	9	9	9	9	9	9	.	9	9	.	9	9	9	9	9	.	9	9	9	9	9	9	9	9	.	9	9

Figure 1.4. The input format for the inventory problem

- Is there a fixed number of stock items that need to be processed, or is it a variable number?
- In what order, if any, do the stock items appear in input?
- Can there be errors in input (alphabetic characters in an item code, for example) or has the input been validated by some other program?

Once again, answers to these and other relevant questions should be documented as part of the problem definition.

The complete set of requirements and assumptions constitute the problem definition.

1.3.2 Program Design

Having defined a problem, the next step in the programming process involves devising an *algorithm*, or a sequence of steps, by which a computer can produce the required outputs from the available inputs. An algorithm for solving a problem can be devised by starting with the problem and dividing it into major subtasks. Each subtask can then be further divided into smaller tasks. This process is repeated until each task reduces to one that is easily doable and does not require further subdivision. This process of designing an algorithm by successive division of a problem into subtasks is known as the *top-down design*, and each successive subdivision is referred to as a *stepwise refinement*.

We illustrate the top-down design by devising an algorithm for solving the inventory problem. For simplicity, we assume that the inventory report contains no more than one page, the stock items may be printed in any arbitrary order, and the data is perfect so that no error checking is necessary.

The problem of printing the inventory report can be divided into two subtasks:

   1. Print inventory report:
      1.1 Print heading
      1.2 Print body

The task of printing the heading can be further divided into two subtasks:

   1.1 Print heading:
      1.1.1 Print title
      1.1.2 Print column names

The task of printing the body can also be decomposed into two subtasks: *(i)* reading data for a stock item, and *(ii)* printing a report line for the item, if necessary. These subtasks must be performed for every stock item. Thus, the following is a refinement of the task of printing the body:

   1.2 Print body:
      For each stock item, do 1.2.1 and 1.2.2
      1.2.1 Read data for the item
      1.2.2 Print a report line for the item (if necessary)

The italicized statement controls the number of times the two subtasks are performed. It is a *control construct*, not a subtask. Thus, the refinement of a task consists of its decomposition into subtasks and constructs to control their execution.

The task of printing a report line for a stock item can be further decomposed into the following subtasks: *(i)* computation of the reorder level for the item, *(ii)* computation of the economic order quantity for the item, and *(iii)* printing of the data line for the item, if necessary. Subtasks *(ii)* and *(iii)* are performed only for an item whose current stock is below its reorder level. Thus, the following is a refinement of the task of printing a report line:

   1.2.2 Print a report line for the item (if necessary):
      1.2.2.1 Compute the reorder level for the item
      Only if the current stock for the item is less than the reorder level, do 1.2.2.2 and 1.2.2.3
      1.2.2.2 Compute the economic order quantity for the item
      1.2.2.3 Print the data line for the item

The italicized statement is another control construct that allows some subtasks of a task to be conditionally performed.

Figure 1.5 is a graphic representation of the top-down decomposition of the problem of printing the inventory report. The following is a complete description of the algorithm for solving this problem:

   1. Print inventory report:
      1.1 Print heading:
         1.1.1 Print title
         1.1.2 Print column names
      1.2 Print body:
         For each stock item, do 1.2.1 and 1.2.2
         1.2.1 Read data for the item
         1.2.2 Print a report line for the item (if necessary):

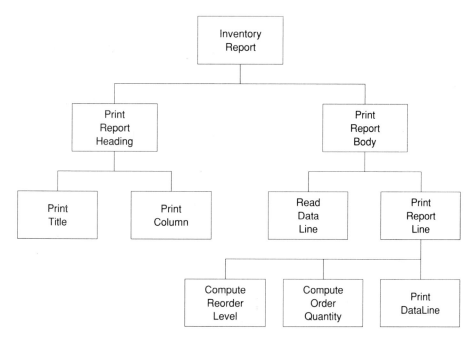

Figure 1.5. A top-down decomposition of the inventory problem

1.2.2.1 Compute the reorder level for the item
*Only if the current stock for the item is less than the reorder level,
do 1.2.2.2 and 1.2.2.3*
1.2.2.2 Compute the economic order quantity for the item
1.2.2.3 Print the data line for the item
1.3 Stop

The problem definition has a significant impact on the algorithm development. Reconsider the inventory problem, but redefine the output specifications to allow more than one page of report and require that the report heading be printed on every page. An algorithm for solving this modified problem is as follows:

1. Print inventory report:
   For each stock item, do 1.1 and 1.2
   1.1 Read data for the item
   1.2 Print a portion of the report (if necessary):
       1.2.1 Compute the reorder level for the item
       *Only if the current stock for the item is less than the reorder level,
       do 1.2.2 through 1.2.5*
       1.2.2 Compute the economic order quantity for the item
       1.2.3 Print heading (if necessary):
       *Only if it is the beginning of the report or the line count is not less than
       the data lines allowed on a page, do 1.2.3.1 through 1.2.3.3*
           1.2.3.1 Print title
           1.2.3.2 Print column names

        1.2.3.3 Set the line count to 0
     1.2.4 Print the data line for the item
     1.2.5 Increment the line count by 1
  1.3 Stop

Many subtasks in the revised algorithm are the same as in the original algorithm. However, the report heading is now printed only after an item to be reordered has been found, which has the desirable consequence that no page is printed with only heading and no data lines on it. A line counter keeps track of the number of data lines printed on the current page, and the heading is printed after the permissible number of data lines have been printed on the page.

1.3.3 Program Coding

Program coding is the process of expressing the algorithm developed for solving a problem as a computer program in a programming language. An algorithm developed using the top-down design methodology can be directly coded in C. Every higher-level task is coded as a separate *function*. Functions corresponding to higher-level tasks contain program statements, or calls to functions corresponding to tasks directly below in the top-down decomposition. Tasks at the lowest level are coded either as one or more C statements or as separate functions, depending upon the complexity of the task.

We encourage *structured programming* to code individual C functions. Structured programming entails the simplification of program control logic so that what a program does to data is more easily understood. A basic fact about structured programming is that all programs can be written using a combination of only three control structures: *sequential*, *selective*, and *repetitive*. The sequential structure consists of a sequence of program statements that are executed one after another in order. The selective structure consists of a test for a condition, followed by alternative paths that the program can follow. The repetitive structure consists of program statements that are repeatedly executed while some condition holds. C provides constructs to directly represent these control structures. These constructs are described in Chapters 2 through 4, and Chapter 5 discusses how a function is defined and interfaced with another function.

To illustrate program coding, we give below a computer program for the inventory problem. This program implements the first algorithm, which assumes that the inventory report cannot be longer than one page. You are not expected to understand all the details of the program at this stage. However, you should be able to see the direct correspondence between the algorithm and the C program.

```
/*
 *   Program to print the order quantity for those inventory items
 *   whose current stocks are below their reorder levels.
 */

#include <math.h>
#include <stdio.h>
```

```
void print_heading(void);
void print_title(void);
void print_column_names(void);
void print_body(void);
int  read_data(void);
void print_report_line(void);

int    item_code, lead_time;
float  order_cost, unit_cost, interest_rate, weekly_use,
       current_stock;
/* Main Task 1 */
int main(void)
  {
    print_heading();              /* calling 1.1 */
    print_body();                 /* calling 1.2 */
    return 0;
  }

/* Task 1.1 */
void print_heading(void)
  {
    print_title();               /* calling 1.1.1 */
    print_column_names();        /* calling 1.1.2 */
  }

/* Task 1.1.1 */
void print_title(void)
  {
    printf("        *****  INVENTORY REPORT  *****\n\n");
  }

/* Task 1.1.2 */
void print_column_names(void)
  {
    printf(
     " ITEM          CURRENT       REORDER        ORDER\n");
    printf(
     " CODE          STOCK         LEVEL       QUANTITY\n");
    printf(
     "_____      _____      _____      _____");
    printf("\n\n");
  }

/* Task 1.2 */
void print_body(void)
  {
    /* repetitive structure: for each stock item, do 1.2.1 and 1.2.2 */
    while (read_data())           /* calling 1.2.1 */
        print_report_line();    /* calling 1.2.2 */
  }
```

```
/* Task 1.2.1 */
int read_data(void)
  {
    return scanf("%6d %6f %7f %3f %6f %2d %7f",
        &item_code, &order_cost, &unit_cost,
        &interest_rate, &weekly_use,
        &lead_time, &current_stock) != EOF ? 1 : 0;
  }

/* Task 1.2.2 */
void print_report_line(void)
  {
    float reorder_level, order_qty;

    /* Task 1.2.2.1: compute the reorder level */
    reorder_level = lead_time * weekly_use;

    /* selective structure: only if the current stock for the item
        is less than the reorder level, do 1.2.2.2 and 1.2.2.3 */
    if (current_stock < reorder_level)
      {
        /* Task 1.2.2.2: compute the economic order quantity */
        order_qty =
            sqrt((2 * 52 * weekly_use * order_cost)
                / (unit_cost * interest_rate));
        /* Task 1.2.2.2: print data line */
        printf("%6d %12.2f %12.2f %12.2f\n", item_code,
            current_stock, reorder_level, order_qty);
      }
  }
```

1.3.4 Program Compilation and Execution

As mentioned in Section 1.2.1, a program written in a higher-level language like C must be translated into machine language instructions before it can be executed. C implementations do this translation in two steps: *compilation* and *linking*. The compilation step converts your source program into an intermediate form, called *object code*, and the linking step combines this object code with other code to produce an executable program. The advantage of this two-step approach is that you may split a large program into more than one file, compile these files separately, and then combine them later into one executable program. Another advantage is that it becomes possible to build libraries of useful functions, such as the functions sqrt, scanf, and printf used in the inventory program given in the previous section. The linker extracts the object code for the library functions used in your program from the library and combines it with the object code for your program.

The exact details of compiling and executing a program depend on the computer system being used. We illustrate this step for an IBM PC running the MS-DOS operating system, and for a machine running the UNIX System V Release 4 operating system.

IBM PC

First, you need to enter the statements that make up your program into a file using a text editor. You may use the editor EDLIN that comes with MS-DOS for this purpose. You may also use any word processor such as WordStar, Word-Perfect, or Microsoft Word, but you must take care to create simple ASCII files. The text-formatting information added by the word processors in the default file formats used by them is not understood by the compiler. Some compilers, such as the Borland Turbo C and Microsoft C compilers, provide an editor specifically designed for programming. These editors are more convenient to use than a general purpose text editor. A discussion of how to use a text editor is beyond the scope of this book. If you are not familiar with text editors, read the user's guide or contact a local guru. By convention, the extension .c is used for C program file names. Thus, the program for the inventory problem may be keyed into a file named inventory.c.

Assuming that your PC has the Microsoft C compiler, the program stored in the file inventory.c can be compiled by invoking the compiler with the command:

```
cl inventory.c
```

The compiler first produces an object file having the same base name as the source file, but with the extension .obj. Thus, the object file will have the name inventory.obj in our example. It then invokes the link program to combine the object file produced with the object code of the necessary library functions to produce the file containing the executable code. The executable file also has the same base name as the source file, but has the extension .exe. Thus, the executable file inventory.exe will be produced.

You may now execute the inventory program by typing

```
inventory
```

This execution will expect you to provide the input for the program by typing data for the inventory items on the terminal. If the inventory data is available in a file named inventory.inp, you may provide it to the inventory program using the command:

```
inventory < inventory.inp
```

The output of the program will be printed on the terminal. You may store the program output in a file named inventory.out using the command:

```
inventory < inventory.inp > inventory.out
```

Figure 1.6 summarizes the compilation and execution of a C program on an IBM PC using the Microsoft C compiler.

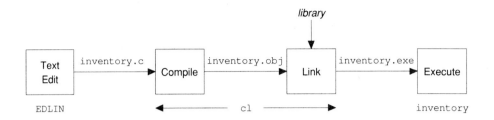

Figure 1.6. Compilation and execution of a program on an IBM PC

UNIX

With the UNIX operating system, you must first create a source file using a text editor. The two most popular text editors on the UNIX machines are `vi` and `emacs`. The source file is suffixed with the extension `.c`. Thus, you may enter the inventory program in the file `inventory.c`.

You may compile this program by using the command

```
cc inventory.c
```

The `cc` command first converts the source program into the object program and then links it with the object code of the necessary library functions to produce the executable file. By default, `cc` searches only some of the C libraries. If your program uses a mathematical function, such as `sqrt` used by the inventory program, you must explicitly instruct `cc` to search the math library by specifying the name of the library with the `-l` option of the `cc` command:

```
cc inventory.c -lm
```

The object file has the same base name as the source file, but has the extension `.o`. However, you will not find `inventory.o` in your directory after the completion of this command, since `cc` removes the object file once the executable file has been produced.

Any executable file produced by `cc` gets the name `a.out` by default. Since the name `a.out` is not a meaningful name, you may supply an appropriate name for the executable version of the program by using the `-o` option when compiling the program:

```
cc -o inventory inventory.c -lm
```

This command produces an executable program file named `inventory` that you may execute as

```
inventory
```

This execution will expect input from the terminal and will print the output on the terminal. You may give the command

```
inventory < inventory.inp > inventory.out
```

to read input from the file `inventory.inp` and store the output in the file `inventory.out`.

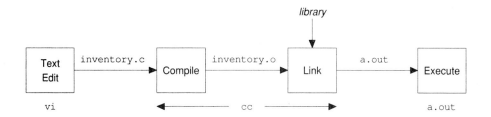

Figure 1.7. Compilation and execution of a program on a UNIX machine

Figure 1.7 summarizes the compilation and execution of a C program on a UNIX machine.

1.3.5 Program Testing and Debugging

No matter how simple or complex, programs usually do not execute success-fully for the first time; they contain a few errors or *bugs*. A program is, there-fore, debugged and errors are removed until the program executes successfully. There are four levels of debugging:

1. The programmer locates and corrects as many errors as possible by eyeing the program before compiling it. This process is referred to as *desk checking*.

2. Errors in the syntax of the program, such as incorrect punctuations or misspelling of key words, are usually detected during the compilation of the program, and are called the *compile-time errors*. Some of these prove fatal and make it impossible to complete the compilation, while others generate *diagnostics*, or error messages, that show the sources of errors within the program, but the compilation continues.

3. Errors such as an attempt to divide an arithmetic expression by zero will be detected only while the program is executing. Such errors are called the *run-time*, or *execution-time*, errors. When such errors are detected, the program execution is aborted and an error message is displayed.

4. *Logical* errors that arise in the design of the algorithm, or in the coding of the program that implements the algorithm, cannot be detected automatically since such a program is syntactically correct. For exam-ple, if the statement

    ```
    if (n == 1)   return 1;
    ```

    in a function to calculate factorials is mistakenly written as

    ```
    if (n = 1)   return 1;
    ```

    with the equality symbol (==) replaced by the assignment symbol (=), the program would be compiled and executed with no error mes-sages. However, the results produced by the program would be incorrect, since the function would now compute the factorial of any number as 1.

Logical errors are the most difficult to diagnose and remove from a program. A program is tested by executing it with a set of test inputs for which the results are already known, and verifying that it produces the same results. The test data should be such that it exercises all fragments of the program.

A buggy program produces incorrect output, or it halts before producing the complete output. Locating where the bug is involves *tracing* the execution of the program and *dumping* the state of the program at significant points. One may employ debugging tools, such as symbolic debuggers, available on some computers, or manually insert print instructions at appropriate points in the source program for this purpose. By examining the output so produced, the programmer can use inductive reasoning to explain why the achieved result is different from the expected result, which leads to the source of the bug.

1.3.6 Program Documentation

Documentation for a program refers to a collection of information about the program that specifies what is being done and how. It includes detailed requirements of the program, the layout of all output reports and input data, the top-down decomposition, the algorithm for each component, the source listing created during the last compilation of the program, the input data used for testing and the output of the test run, and finally a user's guide that provides procedural instructions for installing and executing the program.

Program documentation should be generated as the program is being developed, and not as an afterthought. Every effort should be made to make programs self-documenting. The following programming practices are particularly useful in this regard:

1. *Meaningful variable names suggestive of the entity represented should be used.* For example, the statement

   ```
   value = principal * (1 + rate) * years;
   ```

   should be used to implement the formula

   $$v = p\,(1 + r)\,n$$

   for finding the value accumulated after n years by the deposit of a given amount p at the simple interest rate r.

2. *Comments to provide information helpful in understanding the program should be included within the program.* Comments should be used liberally throughout the program to explain the purpose of the sections of the program that are not self-evident. Assumptions made in the various sections should also be included as comments within the program. Comments should be meaningful and to the point.

Most computer programs are used, maintained, and updated by someone other than the original writer of the program. A program without proper documentation soon becomes unusable.

1.3.7 Illustrative Examples

We now give some examples to further illustrate the process of algorithm development.

Example 1

The tax rate is 10% of the first $1000 and 20% of all additional income. Design an algorithm for printing the gross pay, the tax withheld, and the net pay of an employee, given the number of hours worked and the hourly wage rate.

The desired algorithm is as follows:

1. Print salary information:
   1.1 Read `hours worked` and `wage rate`
   1.2 Do computations:
      1.2.1 Compute `gross pay`:
         `gross pay = hours worked × wage rate`
      1.2.2 Compute `tax`:
         If `gross pay` is less than `1000` then
            `tax = 0.1 × gross pay`
         otherwise
            `tax = 100 + 0.2 × (gross pay – 1000)`
      1.2.2 Compute `net pay`:
         `net pay = gross pay – tax`
   1.3 Print `gross pay`, `tax`, and `net pay`
   1.4 Stop

Example 2

Design an algorithm to find the value of `n!`, *where* `n` *is zero or any positive integer.*

By definition,

   $n! = 1 \times 2 \times 3 \times \ldots \times n > 0$, and $0! = 1$.

The desired algorithm is as follows:

1. Computation of `n!`:
   1.1 `n` less than `0`:
      1.1.1 Report error
      1.1.2 Stop
   1.2 `n` equals `0`:
      1.2.1 Print `factorial = 1`
      1.2.2 Stop
   1.3 `n` greater than `0`:
      1.3.1 Let the initial value of `factorial` be 1
      1.3.2 Let the initial value of `number` be 1

1.3.3 Compute `factorial`:
     While number *is not greater than* n, *do 1.3.2.1 and 1.3.2.2*
     1.3.3.1 Multiply the current value of `factorial` and the current value of number **giving the new value of** `factorial`
     1.3.3.2 Increment the current value of number **by** 1 **giving the next integer** number
1.3.4 Print the final value of `factorial`
1.3.5 Stop

Exercises 1

1. Informatics employees are paid at the overtime rate of one and a half times the base rate for hours worked above 40 hours in a week. Informatics desires a payroll program that reads, for every employee, the base pay rate and the number of hours worked and prints their weekly wages. It should also print the total of weekly wages paid by Informatics. Develop an algorithm to solve this problem.

2. Each data line of a file contains four numbers. The first number represents a student id and the remaining three indicate the scores in three tests. Design an algorithm to compute for each student the average of three tests, the average score in each test for the whole class, and the average class score over all tests.

3. Design an algorithm to convert a given number of pennies into dollars, quarters, dimes, nickels, and pennies.

4. Design an algorithm to find the largest of a given set of numbers.

5. Design an algorithm to arrange six numbers in descending order of magnitude.

6. Design algorithms to find the sum of the following series:

    a. $1 + x + x^2 + x^3 + \ldots + x^{50}$

    b. $x - \dfrac{x^2}{2!} + \dfrac{x^3}{3!} - \dfrac{x^4}{4!} + \ldots - \dfrac{x^{12}}{12!}$

2 Sequential Structure

Now that we have acquired some background in the nature of computers and the process of developing computer programs, we will start learning the specifics of C. A basic fact about computer programming is that all programs can be written using a combination of only three control structures: *sequential*, *selective*, and *repetitive*. The sequential structure consists of a sequence of program statements that are executed one after another in order, the selective structure consists of a test for a condition followed by alternative paths that the program can follow, and the repetitive structure consists of program statements that are repeatedly executed while some condition holds. In this chapter, we introduce C constructs sufficient to write simple sequential programs. Selective and repetitive structures will be introduced in Chapters 3 and 4 respectively.

The sequential structure can be pictorially represented as shown in Figure 2.1.

Figure 2.1. Sequential structure

2.1 OVERVIEW

We begin by analyzing two simple sequential programs. Our intent is to give you an overview of the various components of a C program so that you develop a feel for the language. In the subsequent sections, we will discuss in detail the concepts introduced informally through these examples.

Example 1

We first consider a program for printing Victor Hugo's famous quotation: `Knowledge is Power`. The algorithm for solving this problem is trivial — it consists of a single step of printing the specified sequence of characters.

Here is the program:

```c
#include <stdio.h>
int main(void)
  {
    printf("Knowledge is Power\n");
    return 0;
  }
```

Let us examine the various components of this program.

All C programs are made up of one or more *functions*, each performing a particular task. Every program has a special function named `main`. It is special because the execution of any program starts at the beginning of its `main` function. This example program consists of only one function — the `main` function.

When a function is called, it is usually provided a list of values, called *arguments*. For example, if you are calling the function `sqrt`, you must provide the value whose square root is to be computed. The arguments that a function expects are specified in a parenthesized *parameter list* following the function name. The *keyword* `void` enclosed within a pair of parentheses in

```c
main(void)
```

indicates that this `main` expects no arguments.

An opening brace { following a function name and its parameter list marks the beginning, and the corresponding closing brace } the end, of the *function body*. A function body may contain zero or more *variable declarations* and *statements*. Statements specify the computing operations necessary to achieve the desired result, and variables hold values during the computation. The `main` function in this program contains two statements, but no variable declarations.

The first statement

```c
printf("Knowledge is Power\n");
```

is a call to the *standard library* function `printf`. There are several commonly used computations that are required in many programs. Instead of requiring every programmer to write code for such computations, C provides a standard library of commonly used functions. Appendix A contains a comprehensive description of the standard C library. When a program uses a function that is not coded as part of the program, the compiler searches through the standard library for the missing function. If the compiler finds the function, it adds the necessary code for that function to the program.

A function is called by following its name with a parenthesized list of arguments. A sequence of characters enclosed within double quotation marks is called a *string constant*, or simply a *string*. When `printf` is supplied with a string as argument, it prints the characters between the double quotation marks. Thus, the `printf` statement in this program causes Hugo's quotation to be printed. The sequence \n represents the *newline* character and it causes the output to advance to the left margin on the next line. If we did not include \n in the string, the quotation would still be printed, but without a line advance in the output. The semicolon ; terminates the statement.

Information relevant to the functions in the standard library is grouped into *standard header* files, and a program calling such a function must include the appropriate header file using the `#include` directive. Information about the `printf` function is contained in the header file <stdio.h> and the first line of this program

```
#include <stdio.h>
```

includes it in the program.

A C function may return a value to its caller using a `return` statement. The `main` function is like any other C function, except that it is called by the environment in which the program is executed, and it should return its completion status to the environment. The keyword `int` before `main` in the line

```
int main(void)
```

indicates that `main` returns an integer value. By convention, a 0 is returned to indicate normal completion of the program, whereas a nonzero return value indicates abnormal termination. The second statement of this program will be executed after `printf` has completed successfully. We therefore return a 0 in the second statement

```
return 0;
```

to signal successful completion of the program.

The following transcript shows a sample execution of this program on a Unix System V Release 4 machine, where the program text is available in a file named `hugo.c`:

```
unix-> cc -o hugo hugo.c
unix-> hugo
Knowledge is Power
unix->
```

This particular computer uses the prompt `unix->` to indicate that it is ready to accept commands from the user. The first command invokes the C compiler, compiles the program, and creates an executable program named `hugo`. The next command executes this program. The third line shows the output generated by the program. The last line indicates that the program execution is complete and the computer is ready to accept the next command.

The following transcript shows the execution of this program on an IBM PC using the Microsoft C compiler:

```
C> cl hugo.c
C> hugo
Knowledge is Power
C>
```

Example 2

We now consider a program that computes the total interest earned on an investment that pays a fixed rate of simple interest when the principal remains invested for a specified number of years. Here is an algorithm for solving this problem:

1. Read the amount of principal, interest rate (as a percentage), and the number of years for which the principal is to be invested.
2. Convert the percentage rate read into a decimal fraction.
3. Compute the total interest earned using the formula

   interest = principal × rate × years.

4. Print interest.

Here is the program:

```
/*
 * This program computes the total interest accrued on an
 * investment that pays simple interest at a fixed rate when the
 * principal is invested for the specified number of years.
 */

#include <stdio.h>

int main(void)
  {
    /* variable declarations */
    float    principal, rate, interest;
    int      years;

    /* prompt the user to provide input values */
    printf("principal, rate, and years of investment? ");

    /* read the input values */
    scanf("%f %f %d", &principal, &rate, &years);

    /* compute interest */
    rate = rate / 100;   /* convert percentage into fraction */
    interest = principal * rate * years;
```

```
    /* print interest */
    printf("interest = %f\n", interest);

    /* successful completion */
    return 0;
}
```

The first new feature to note in this program is the use of *comments* to explain different segments of the program. The character sequence /* starts a comment and the sequence */ ends the comment. As shown, a comment may occupy part of a line, all of a line, or several lines. Comments may include any characters, but a comment cannot be placed inside another comment. Comments are ignored by the compiler. They should be used liberally to improve the readability of the program.

This program uses two functions from the standard library: scanf and printf. The program, therefore, includes the header file <stdio.h> in the line

```
#include <stdio.h>
```

The line

```
int main(void)
```

indicates that this main does not expect any argument and it returns an integer value to its execution environment.

The next new feature introduced in this program is the *variable declarations*. All the variables used in a function are usually declared at the beginning of the function body. The main function of this program uses four variables: principal, rate, years, and interest. They store the values of the principal amount, the rate of interest, the number of years the principal remains invested, and the interest earned respectively.

A variable declaration, besides specifying that this variable is being used, also specifies the properties of the variable. In particular, it specifies the *type* of the variable. The type of a variable is a characteristic that restricts the variable to assume a particular set of values. For example, the type int specifies that the corresponding variable can only assume integer values, whereas the type float allows the variable to have real values. Thus, the declarations

```
float    principal, rate, interest;
int      years;
```

establish the variables principal, rate, and interest to be of type float, and the variable years to be of type int.

The first executable statement of main

```
printf("principal, rate, and years of investment? ");
```

calls the function printf, which prints a message asking the user to provide values for principal, interest rate, and the number of years of investment.

The next statement

```
scanf("%f %f %d", &principal, &rate, &years);
```

calls `scanf`, another function provided in the standard library. It reads the input values typed in by the user and assigns them to the variables `principal`, `rate`, and `years` respectively.

The next statement

```
rate = rate / 100;   /* convert percentage into fraction */
```

is an *assignment statement* that causes the value of the variable `rate` to be divided by 100 and the result to be assigned as the new value of the variable `rate`. The previous value of `rate` is destroyed in the process.

In `rate / 100`, the symbol `/` represents *arithmetic division* and it is one of the C *arithmetic operators*. An *operator* is a symbol that causes specific mathematical or logical manipulations to be performed. Other examples of arithmetic operators include + (*addition*), - (*subtraction*), and * (*multiplication*). 100 is an *integer constant*. A *constant* is an entity whose value does not change during program execution. Other examples of constants include `3.14159265`, a *floating-point constant*, `'C'`, a character constant, and `"Knowledge is Power"`, a *string constant*. A combination of constants and variables together with the operators is referred to as an *expression*. The expression `rate / 100` is an *arithmetic expression* as it involves only floating-point and integer data and an arithmetic operator.

The next statement

```
interest = principal * rate * years;
```

causes the expression `principal * rate * years` to be evaluated, and the result is assigned to the variable `interest`. The next statement

```
printf("interest = %f\n", interest);
```

prints the value of `interest`. Finally, the statement

```
return 0
```

terminates the execution of the program, returning 0 to its execution environment.

The following transcript shows an execution of this program:

```
unix-> cc -o simplint simplint.c
unix-> simplint
principal, rate, and years of investment? 7500  8.75  5
interest = 3281.250000
unix->
```

The program was keyed into a file named `simplint.c`. The first command creates the executable `simplint` and the second command initiates its execution. The program prompts the user to provide values for principal, interest rate, and years of investment. The user-entered data has been italicized. The program then calculates interest and prints the fourth line. The program execution is now complete and the computer prompts the user for a new command.

By now you should have developed some feel for the various building blocks that make up a sequential C program. We will now study them in detail.

2.2 CHARACTER SET

The set of characters that may appear in a legal C program is called the *character set* for C. This set includes some *graphic* as well as *non-graphic* characters. The graphic characters, shown in Table 2.1, are those that may be printed. The non-graphic characters, shown in Table 2.2, are represented by escape sequences consisting of a backslash \ followed by a letter. The character set also includes a *null* character, represented as \0.

The graphic characters, other than decimal digits, letters, and blank, are referred to as *special* characters. Blank, horizontal and vertical tabs, newlines, and formfeeds are called *whitespace* characters. When necessary for clarity, we will represent the blank character as ⌀.

The C compiler groups characters into *tokens*. A token is a sequence of one or more characters that have a uniform meaning. For instance, the token -> has a meaning that is quite distinct from that of the characters that make it up and is independent of the context in which -> appears. Some tokens, such as /, *, -, >, and =, are only one character long; others, such as ->, ==, >=, comments, and variable names, are several characters long. When collecting characters into tokens, the compiler always forms the longest token possible.

Table 2.1. C character set (graphic characters)

Character	Meaning	Character	Meaning
0,1,. . .,9	Decimal digits	:	Colon
A,B,. . .,Z	Uppercase letters	;	Semicolon
a,b,. . .,z	Lowercase letters	<	Less than
!	Exclamation point	=	Equal to
"	Double quotation mark	>	Greater than
#	Number/pound sign	?	Question mark
$	Dollar sign	@	"At" sign
%	Percent sign	[	Left bracket
&	Ampersand sign	\	Backslash
'	Apostrophe/single quotation mark	]	Right bracket
		^	Caret/circumflex
(	Left parenthesis	_	Underscore
)	Right parenthesis	`	Accent grave/back quotation mark
*	Asterisk		
+	Plus	{	Left brace
,	Comma	|	Vertical bar
-	Minus/hyphen	}	Right brace
.	Period	~	Tilde
/	Slash	⌀	Blank/space

Table 2.2. C character set (non-graphic characters)

Character	Meaning	Character	Meaning
\a	Audible alert (bell)	\b	Back space
\f	Form feed	\n	New line
\r	Carriage return	\t	Horizontal tab
\v	Vertical tab		

C is a *free-format language*, meaning that tokens can go anywhere on a page and can be separated by any number of whitespaces. Thus, the program fragment

```
int main(void)
  {
    printf("Knowledge is Power\n");
    return 0;
  }
```

can equivalently be written as

```
int main(void){printf("Knowledge is Power\n");return 0;}
```

However, as a matter of programming style, the latter form is never used. Programs are written with every statement starting on a new line and with proper indentation to bring out the program structure. We encourage you to study the style used in the example programs in the book and use it in your programs.

2.3 DATA TYPES

Data is differentiated into various *types*. The type of a data element restricts the data element to assume a particular set of values. For example, on some machines, a data element of type `int` may only have integer values in the range –32,768 to +32,767. The basic C data types are:

char	a character in the C character set
int	an integer
float	a single-precision floating-point number
double	a double-precision floating-point number

The qualifiers `short` and `long` may be applied to some of the above data types. Thus we have the following additional data types:

short int	also abbreviated as `short`
long int	also abbreviated as `long`
long double	an extended-precision floating-point number

The qualifiers `signed` and `unsigned` may be applied to `char`, `short int`, `int`, or `long int`. `unsigned` variables can only have nonnegative values, while `signed` variables can have both positive and negative values. In the absence of explicit `unsigned` specification, `int`, `short int`, and `long int` are considered to be `signed`. The default signedness of `char`, however, is implementation-dependent.

Many implementations represent a `char` in 8 bits, a `short` in 16 bits, an `int` in 16 or 32 bits, and a `long` in 32 bits. The width for `float` is often 32 bits and that of `double` 64 bits. These bit widths have not been specified by the C language, but have become traditional. All that C specifies is that the range of `int` may not be smaller than `short`, and the range of `long` may not be smaller than `int`. The magnitudes of `float`, `double`, and `long double` depend on the method used to represent the floating-point numbers, but a `long double` is at least as precise as a `double`, and a `double` at least as precise as a `float`. The particular bit widths for an implementation are specified in that implementation's standard header files `<limits.h>` and `<float.h>`.

You may be wondering why C provides so many data types. The primary use for smaller data types, such as `short int`, is to economize on storage. For example, if you know that the largest value that your integer variable may assume is 1000, and a `short int` is represented in 16 bits whereas an `int` takes 32 bits, you may specify it to be of type `short int`. Similarly, `char` is sometimes used as a small integer type, as `char` normally takes only 8 bits. However, using a smaller integer type may increase program execution time as values of these types are converted into `int` before they are used in a computation. Unsigned integers are used to squeeze an extra bit for representing larger numbers when the sign bit is not needed. For example, the largest positive number that can be represented in a 16-bit `signed int` is 32,767, whereas 65,534 can be represented in a 16-bit `unsigned int`.

All types of integers and characters are collectively referred to as of *integral* type, and the types `float`, `double`, and `long double` as of *floating-point* type. The term *arithmetic* type is used to refer collectively to the integral and floating-point types.

2.4 CLASSES OF DATA

A computer program manipulates two kinds of data — variables and constants.

2.4.1 Variables

A *variable* is an entity used by a program to store values used in the computation. Every variable in C has a type and it must be declared before it is used.

Declarations

A *declaration* consists of a type name followed by a list of one or more variables of that type, separated by commas. Thus, the declarations

```
int     mint;
char    cherry;
double  trouble;
float   swim, snorkel;
```

declare the variable `mint` to be of type `int`, the variable `cherry` to be of type `char`, the variable `trouble` to be of type `double`, and the variables `swim` and `snorkel` to be of type `float`. The variables `swim` and `snorkel` could have been equivalently declared in two separate declarations:

```
float   swim;     /* time spent swimming in minutes */
float   snorkel;  /* time spent snorkeling in hours */
```

As shown, the latter form is useful for adding comments immediately after the declarations, explaining the purpose of the variables being declared.

It is possible to assign an initial value to a variable in its declaration by following its name with an equal sign and the value. Thus, the declaration

```
float start = -1.0, final = 1.0, increment = 0.1;
```

declares the variables `start`, `final`, and `increment` to be of type `float` and also initializes them to `-1.0`, `1.0`, and `0.1` respectively.

All declarations within a function are usually put together at the beginning of the function body before any executable statement.

Names

C places some restrictions on what can be a *variable name*. The following are the rules for naming a variable:

1. A variable name must begin with a letter or underscore, and may be made up of any combination of letters, underscores, or the digits 0–9. Whitespace characters are not permitted within a name. Thus,

   ```
   foo       r2d2       Agent707       ANSI_C       _mvBytes
   ```

   are valid names, whereas the following are not, for the reasons indicated:

`4ever`	The first character is not a letter or underscore.
`x2.5`	Period (.) is not allowed in a variable name.
`ANSI C`	Embedded spaces are not permitted.

2. A variable name may use uppercase letters, lowercase letters, or both. Changing the case of even one character makes a different name. For example, the variable names

   ```
   interest             Interest             INTEREST
   ```

   are all recognized to be different. However, it is bad programming style to have distinct names that differ only in the case of their letters.

3. The number of characters that can be used in a variable name is compiler-dependent. The original description of C specified that only the first eight characters of a variable name were significant, and hence names like `average_weight` and `average_width` would be indistinguishable since they are identical up to the first eight characters. ANSI C permits at least 31 significant characters in variable names, and hence accidental name collision rarely becomes a problem.

4. C reserves certain names, called *keywords*, for specific meanings, and they cannot be used as variable names. The 32 standard keywords are:

   ```
   auto       break      case       char       const      continue
   default    do         double     else       enum       extern
   float      for        goto       if         int        long
   register   return     short      signed     sizeof     static
   struct     switch     typedef    union      unsigned   void
   volatile   while
   ```

Variable names are traditionally written in lowercase letters. It is absolutely desirable to use meaningful names suggestive of the entity they represent. This practice increases the readability of a program and pays off handsomely during the debugging and maintenance of the program.

Technically, a variable name is an identifier. *Identifiers* are names given to various program entities. Examples of identifiers other than variable names include function names, enumeration constants, symbolic constants, etc. The rules discussed above for naming variables apply to all identifiers.

2.4.2 Constants

A *constant* is an entity whose value does not change during program execution. Constants are of five different types: integer, floating-point, character, string, and enumeration. The first four will be discussed here; enumeration constants will be discussed in Chapter 12.

Integer Constants

An *integer constant* is a number that has an integer value. Integer constants may be specified in decimal, octal, or hexadecimal notation. (See Appendix D for a review of these number systems.)

A *decimal* integer constant consists of a sequence of one or more decimal digits 0 through 9. The first digit of the sequence cannot be 0, unless the decimal integer constant is 0. Thus,

```
0        255      32767      32768      65535      2147483647
```

are valid decimal integer constants.

An *octal* integer constant consists of the digit 0, followed by a sequence of one or more octal digits 0 through 7. Thus,

```
012      037      0177      01000      077777      0100000
```

are valid octal integer constants corresponding to the decimal integer constants

```
10        31        127        4096        32767        32768
```

respectively.

A *hexadecimal* integer constant consists of the digit 0, followed by one of the letters x or X, followed by a sequence of one or more hexadecimal digits 0 through 9, or letters a through f, or letters A through F. Thus,

```
0x1f      0X1F      0xff      0xABC      0x10000      0x7FFFFFFF
```

are valid hexadecimal integer constants corresponding to the decimal integer constants

```
31        31        255        2748        65536        2147483647
```

respectively.

Commas and spaces are not allowed in integer constants. Thus, the following are not valid integer constants for the reasons indicated:

```
10,000          Contains a comma.
8 4141          Contains a space.
```

The type of an integer constant is normally `int`. However, if the value of a decimal integer constant exceeds the largest positive integer that can be represented in type `int`, its type instead is `long`. The type of an octal or hexadecimal integer constant, whose value exceeds the largest integer that can be represented in type `unsigned int`, is likewise taken to be `long`. An integer constant followed by the letter l or L, such as `123456789L`, is an explicit `long` type. It is also possible to explicitly express `unsigned` constants. An explicit `unsigned` integer constant is written by suffixing the constant with an u or U, as in `123U`, and an `unsigned long` integer constant by suffixing the constant with an ul or UL, as in `123456789UL`.

Floating-Point Constants

A *floating-point* constant is a number that has a real value. The *standard decimal form* of a floating-point constant is a number written with a decimal point. Thus,

```
1.0     1.      .1      0.      .0
```

are valid floating-point constants, whereas the following are not for the reasons indicated:

```
1               Contains no decimal point.
1,000.0         Contains a comma.
1 000.0         Contains a space.
```

The *scientific notation* is often used to express numbers that are very small or very large. Thus, 0.000000011 is written as 1.1×10^{-8} and 20000000000 as 2×10^{10}. C provides an *exponential form* for such numbers that is related to the scientific notation as follows:

$$(coefficient) \text{ e } (integer) = (coefficient) \times 10^{integer}$$

The part appearing before e is called the *mantissa* and the part following e is called the *exponent*. The uppercase E can also be used instead of the lowercase e. Thus, 1.1×10^{-8} is written as `1.1e-8` and 2×10^{10} as `2e10`.

The type of a floating-point constant is `double`, unless suffixed. The suffixes f or F indicate a `float` constant, and l or L a `long double` constant. Thus, `1.23F` is a floating-point constant of type `float`, whereas `1e-10L` is a floating-point constant of type `long double`.

Character Constants

A *character constant* consists of a single character enclosed within apostrophes. For example,

```
'0'     'a'     'Z'     '?'     '%'
```

are all valid character constants. The first represents the character 0, the second the lowercase letter *a*, the third the uppercase letter Z, the fourth a question mark, and the fifth a percent sign.

Character constants are of type int. The value of a character constant is the numeric value of the character in the machine's character set, and hence depends on whether the machine uses the ASCII or EBCDIC character set. (See Appendix D for more on internal representation of characters.) Appendix E gives a complete table of the decimal values of the character constants in the ASCII and EBCDIC character sets. The following are the decimal values of the character constants given above in the two character sets:

Character Constant	ASCII	EBCDIC
'0'	48	240
'a'	97	129
'Z'	90	233
'?'	63	111
'%'	37	108

If the apostrophe or the backslash is to be used in a character constant, it must be preceded by a backslash as shown below:

'\''   '\\'

Non-graphic characters may also be used to form character constants. Thus, the following are valid character constants:

'\a' (Audible alarm) '\b' (Back space)   '\f' (Form feed)
'\n' (New line)   '\r' (Carriage return) '\t' (Horizontal tab)
'\v' (Vertical tab)

In addition, an arbitrary byte-sized bit pattern can be used to specify the value of a desired character constant by writing

'\ooo'

where the escape \ooo consists of a backslash followed by 1, 2, or 3 octal digits. The bit pattern may also be expressed in hexadecimal by writing

'\xhh'

where the escape \xhh consists of a backslash, followed by an x and 1 or 2 hexadecimal digits. Here are some examples:

Character Constant		Decimal Value	ASCII Character	EBCDIC Character
Octal	Hexadecimal			
'\100'	'\x40'	64	'@'	' '
'\135'	'\x5d'	93	']'	')'
'\176'	'\x7e'	126	'~'	'='

A special case of the above construction is \0, which represents the character with the value zero, that is, the null character.

String Constants

A *string constant*, or simply a *string*, consists of zero or more characters enclosed within double quotation marks. Non-graphic characters may also be used as part of a character string. Here are some examples:

```
"Madam, I'm Adam"
"Programming in C is fun\n"
"\n\n\t\t***** inventory report *****\n\n"
```

The double quotation marks are not part of the string; they only serve to delimit it. If the double quotation mark is required to be one of the characters of the string, it must be preceded by a backslash (\). If the backslash is required to be a character of the string, it must be preceded by another backslash. Thus, the string constant I'm a " and I'm a \ is written as

```
"I'm a \" and I'm a \\"
```

The length of a string is the number of characters that form the string. There is no limit on the length of a string. A string can be continued by putting a backslash (\) at the end of the line as in:

```
"Great things are not done by impulse,\
 but by a series of small things brought together"
```

Adjacent string constants are concatenated at compile time. Thus, the last string can equivalently be written as

```
"Great things are not done by impulse,"
" but by a series of small things brought together"
```

or

```
"Great things are not done by impulse,"
" but by a series of small things"
" brought together"
```

The compiler automatically places the null character \0 at the end of each string so that a program scanning a string can find its end. The physical storage required is thus one byte more than the number of characters enclosed within double quotation marks. When the compiler concatenates two string constants, it puts the null character at the end of the resultant concatenated string and not after each individual string.

Note that a character constant, say 'Z', is not the same as the string that contains the single character "Z". The former is a single character and the latter a character string consisting of characters Z and \0.

2.5 ARITHMETIC OPERATORS

An *operator* is a symbol that causes specific mathematical or logical manipulations to be performed. We discuss here the *arithmetic* operators, *addition* (+), *subtraction* (−), *multiplication* (*), *division* (/), *remainder* (%), *unary plus* (+), and *unary* *minus* (–). Two other arithmetic operators, *increment* (++) and *decrement* (––), will be discussed in Section 2.7.1. All these operators, except remainder (%), operate on operands of any arithmetic type. The remainder operator (%) takes only integral operands.

The first five arithmetic operators are *binary* operators and require two operands. The result of addition (+), subtraction (–), multiplication (*), and division (/) is the same as in mathematics, except that when division is applied to integer data, the result is truncated to the integer value. The operator % obtains the remainder when one integer is divided by another. Thus, we have

```
12 + 9 = 21         12. + 9. = 21.
12 - 9 = 3          12. - 9. = 3.
12 * 9 = 108        12. * 9. = 108.
12 / 9 = 1          12. / 9. = 1.33
12 % 9 = 3
```

The unary minus is a *unary* operator and requires only one operand. The result of the unary minus applied to an operand is the negated value of the operand.

The unary plus is also a *unary* operator. The result of the unary plus applied to an operand is the value of the operand.

2.6   EXPRESSIONS

A combination of constants and variables together with the operators is referred to as an *expression*. Balanced parentheses may be used in combining constants and variables with the operators. Constants and variables by themselves are also considered expressions. An expression that involves only constants is called a *constant* expression.

We will, for the present, restrict ourselves to the arithmetic operators and the corresponding expressions, called *arithmetic expressions*. In an arithmetic expression, integer, character, or floating-point type of data can participate as operands. Thus, the following are valid arithmetic expressions:

```
012                 '\n'            i           -x
12.3 / 45.6         -(i + 1)        i % j       32 + 1.8 * c
```

2.6.1 Evaluation of an Expression

Every expression has a value that can be determined by first binding the operands to the operators and then evaluating the expression. If an expression contains more than one operator and parentheses do not explicitly state the binding of operands, it may appear that an operand may be bound to either of the operators on its two sides. For example, apparently the expression $32 + 1.8 *$ c may be interpreted as $(32 + 1.8) * c$ or as $32 + (1.8 * c)$. C uses a *precedence and associativity rule* and a *parentheses rule* to specify the order in which operands are bound to operators.

Table 2.3.   Precedence and associativity of the arithmetic operators

Operators	Type	Associativity
+ –	Unary	Right to left
* / %	Binary	Left to right
+ –	Binary	Left to right

Every operator in C has been assigned a precedence and an associativity. The *precedence and associativity rule* states that the operator precedence and associativity determine the order in which operands are bound to operators. Operators receive their operands in order of decreasing precedence. If an expression contains two or more operators of equal precedence, their associativity determines their relative precedence. If the associativity is "left to right", then the operator to the left in the expression has the higher precedence; if it is "right to left", then the operator to the right has higher precedence.

Appendix B contains a complete table of the precedence and associativity of the C operators. Table 2.3 summarizes the precedence and associativity of the basic arithmetic operators. In this table, an operator in a higher row has a higher precedence when compared to an operator in a lower row. Operators that are in the same row have the same precedence and associativity. Thus, the expression 32 + 1.8 * c is interpreted as 32 + (1.8 * c) because * has precedence over the binary +.

The following table shows the evaluation of some arithmetic expressions using the precedence and associativity rule:

Expression	Equivalent Expression	Value
2 – 3 + 4	(2 – 3) + 4	3
2 * 3 – 4	(2 * 3) – 4	2
2 – 3 / 4	2 – (3 / 4)	2
2 + 3 % 4	2 + (3 % 4)	5
2 * 3 % 4	(2 * 3) % 4	2
2 / 3 * 4	(2 / 3) * 4	0
2 % 3 / 4	(2 % 3) / 4	0
– 2 + 3	(–2) + 3	1
2 * – 3	2 * (–3)	–6
– 2 * – 3	(–2) * (–3)	6

As a further illustration of the precedence and associativity rule, consider the evaluation of the expression

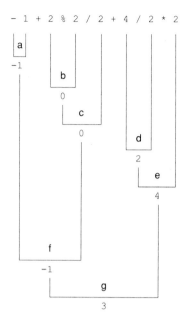

The order in which the expression is evaluated is indicated by the sequence of lowercase letters.

Parentheses can be used to alter the order of precedence; they force an operation, or set of operations, to have a higher precedence level. The *parentheses rule* states that the operation will be performed in the innermost set of parentheses, using the precedence and associativity rule where appropriate, and then in the next outer set, etc., until all operations inside the parentheses have been performed. The remaining operations in the expression are then carried out according to the precedence and associativity rule.

As an illustration of the parentheses rule, consider the evaluation of the following expression, obtained after adding a few parentheses to the expression evaluated above:

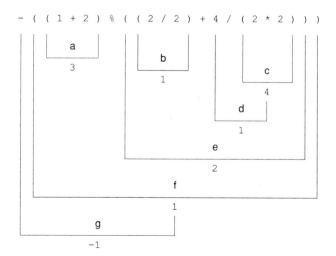

2.7 ASSIGNMENT STATEMENTS

An *assignment expression* is of the form

> *variable = expression*

An assignment expression when followed by a semicolon becomes an *assignment statement*.

The "equals" symbol (=) in an assignment should not be interpreted in the same sense as in mathematics. It is an operator that assigns the value of the expression on its right side to the variable on its left side. Thus, the two statements

```
x = y;
```

and

```
y = x;
```

produce very different results. The first assigns the value of y to x leaving y unchanged, whereas the second assigns the value of x to y leaving x unchanged. Thus, if x and y have the values shown in (a) in Figure 2.2, the values produced by the two assignment statements would be as shown in (b) and (c) of the same figure.

To further illustrate the assignment statement, consider the statement

```
sum = sum + item;
```

This statement causes the value of the variable item to be added to the current value of the variable sum, and the result is assigned as the new value of the variable sum. The previous value of sum is destroyed in the process. If sum and item have values as shown in (a) in Figure 2.3, the effect of the assignment would be as shown in (b) of the same figure. The value 10 of the variable sum is destroyed in the process.

(a)   (b)   (a)   (c)

Figure 2.2. Effect of assignment statements

(a)   (b)

Figure 2.3. Effect of an assignment statement

The precedence of the assignment operator is lower than that of the arithmetic operators. Thus,

```
sum = sum + item;
```

is interpreted as

```
sum = (sum + item);
```

and not

```
(sum = sum) + item;
```

It is mandatory that the left operand of the assignment operator be an *lvalue*: an expression that refers to an object that can be examined as well as altered. A variable name is an example of an lvalue. An expression that permits examination but not alteration is called an *rvalue*. A constant is an example of an rvalue. Thus,

```
15 = n;
x + 1.0 = 2.0;
```

are not valid assignment statements because 15 and x + 1.0 are not lvalues. Note that x + 1.0 evaluates to a value, depending upon the current value of x, which can be examined and used but not altered, and hence is an rvalue.

2.7.1 Increment and Decrement Operators

Two common forms of assignments found in programs are those that increment or decrement the value of a variable by 1. C provides two operators, *increment* (++) and *decrement* (--), for this purpose. Increment (++) and decrement (--) are unary operators, and require only one operand. They are of equal precedence and their precedence is the same as the other unary operators.

These operators can be used both as *prefix*, where the operator occurs before the operand, and *postfix*, where the operator occurs after the operand, in the following manner:

++variable
variable++
--variable
variable--

Both in the prefix and the postfix form, ++ adds 1 to its operand and -- subtracts 1 from its operand. However, in the prefix form, the value is incremented or decremented by 1 *before* it is used. In the postfix form, the value is incremented or decremented by 1 *after* the use. For example, if i were 1,

```
n = ++i;
```

first increments the value of i to 2, and then sets n to the current value of i making n equal to 2, but

```
n = i++;
```

first sets n to 1, and then increments the value of i to 2. Similarly,

```
n = --i;
```

first decrements the value of i to 0, and then sets n to 0, but

```
n = i--;
```

first sets n to 1, and then decrements the value of i to 0.
Thus, the statement

```
n = ++i;
```

is equivalent to the two assignment statements

```
i = i + 1;
n = i;
```

and the statement

```
n = i++;
```

is equivalent to the two assignment statements

```
n = i;
i = i + 1;
```

Similarly, the statements

```
n = --i;
```

and

```
n = i--;
```

are respectively equivalent to

```
i = i - 1;
n = i;
```

and

```
n = i;
i = i - 1;
```

The following table further illustrates the increment and decrement operators:

Assignment	Before Values	After Values
k = i++;	i = 1	k = 1, i = 2
k = ++i;	i = 1	k = 2, i = 2
k = i--;	i = 1	k = 1, i = 0
k = --i;	i = 1	k = 0, i = 0
k = 5 - i++;	i = 1	k = 5 - 1 = 4, i = 2
k = 5 - ++i;	i = 1	k = 5 - 2 = 3, i = 2
k = 5 + i--;	i = 1	k = 5 + 1 = 6, i = 0
k = 5 + --i;	i = 1	k = 5 + 0 = 5, i = 0
k = i++ + --j;	i = 1, j = 5	k = 1 + 4 = 5, i = 2, j = 4
k = ++i + j--;	i = 1, j = 5	k = 2 + 5 = 7, i = 2, j = 4

2.7.2 Compound Assignment Operators

C provides ten compound assignment operators

```
+=        -=        *=        /=        %=
<<=       >>=       &=        |=        ^=
```

for the *compression* of assignment statements. The meaning of the last five of these operators will become clear when we study the bit operators in Chapter 9.

If we let *op=* denote the compound assignment operator, the compressed form of the assignment statement

variable op= expression ;

is equivalent to the simple assignment statement

variable = variable op expression;

Thus, the compressed form of

```
           i = i + 1;          is     i += 1;
           i = i - a;          is     i -= a;
       i = i * (a + 1);        is     i *= a + 1;
       i = i / (a - b);        is     i /= a - b;
         i = i % 101;          is     i %= 101;
         i = i << 1;           is     i <<= 1;
         i = i >> j;           is     i >>= j;
         i = i & 01;           is     i &= 01;
         i = i | 0xf;          is     i |= 0xf;
   i = i ^ (07 | 0xab);        is     i ^= 07 | 0xab;
```

All the compound assignment operators have equal precedence, which is the same as that of the simple assignment operator (=) but lower than that of the arithmetic operators. Thus, in the preceding example

```
i *= a + 1;
```

is equivalent to

```
i = i * (a + 1);
```

and not

```
i = (i * a) + 1;
```

The following table further illustrates the compound assignment operators:

int i = 2, j = 2, k = 3;		
Assignment	Equivalent Statement	Values After Assignment
k -= i;	k = k - i;	k = 3 - 2 = 1
k += i - 1;	k = k + (i - 1);	k = 3 + (2 - 1) = 4
k /= i + 1;	k = k / (i + 1);	k = 3 / (2 + 1) = 1
k *= i - j;	k = k * (i - j);	k = 3 * (2 - 1) = 3
k %= i * j;	k = k % (i * j);	k = 3 % (2 * 1) = 1

Compound assignment operators are convenient short-hands and lead to more concise, more readable, and more efficient code.

2.7.3 Nested Assignments

C permits multiple assignments in one statement, and the assignments are then said to be *nested*. Assignment operators are right-associative, which allows the nested assignment statements to have the obvious interpretation. Thus, the nested statement

```
i = j = k = 0;
```

is interpreted as

```
i = ( j = ( k = 0 ) );
```

and first assigns 0 to k. The expression k = 0 evaluates to 0, and this value is then assigned to j. The value of the expression j = k = 0 now becomes 0, and hence i also becomes 0.

Similarly, the statement

```
i += j = k;
```

is treated as

```
i += (j = k);
```

and the statement

```
i = j += k;
```

as

```
i = (j += k);
```

Therefore, if i, j and k were originally 1, 2, and 3 respectively, then the first statement would result in i and j being assigned 4 and 3 respectively, whereas the second statement results in both being assigned 5. The value of k remains unchanged.

The following table further illustrates nested assignments:

int i = 9, j = 3, k = 1;		
Assignment	Equivalent Statement	Values After Assignments
i /= j = k+1;	i /= (j = k+1);	k = 1, j = 1+1 = 2, i = 9/2 = 4
i = j /= k+1;	i = (j /= k+1);	k = 1, j = 3/(1+1) = 1, i = 1
i /= j /= k+1;	i /= (j /= k+1);	k = 1, j = 3/2 = 1, i = 9/1 = 9
i /= j /= k++;	i /= (j /= k++);	k = 2, j = 3/1 = 3, i = 9/3 = 3
i /= j /= ++k;	i /= (j /= ++k);	k = 2, j = 3/2 = 1, i = 9/1 = 9

2.8 INPUT AND OUTPUT

C does not provide language constructs for input/output operations. However, ANSI C has defined a rich *standard I/O library*, a set of functions designed to provide a standard I/O system for C programs. We now present some features of only two of these functions: printf, which is used for output operations, and scanf, which is used for input operations. The other functions in the standard I/O library and further details of the printf and scanf functions will be discussed in Chapter 10. A program using these functions must include in it the standard header file <stdio.h> using the directive

```
#include  <stdio.h>
```

2.8.1 printf Function

A call to printf is of the form

```
printf(control  string,  arg1,  arg2,  . . .);
```

The *control string* governs the conversion, formatting, and printing of the arguments of printf. It may consist of *ordinary* characters that are reproduced unchanged on the standard output. For example, the control string in

```
printf("reproduced unchanged");
```

comprises only the ordinary characters, and hence

```
reproduced unchanged
```

is displayed on the standard output.

The control string may also include *conversion specifications* that control the conversion of successive arguments *arg1*, *arg2*, etc., before they are printed. Each conversion specification consists of the character % followed by a *conversion control character*. Some conversion control characters and their effects are given below:

---

d, i	The integer argument is converted to decimal notation of the form [-]*ddd*.
f	The float or double argument is converted to decimal notation of the form [-]*ddd.dddddd*. By default, six digits are printed after the decimal point.
e	The float or double argument is converted to decimal notation of the form [-]*d.dddddd*e[±]*dd*. There is one digit before the decimal point, and the exponent contains at least two digits. By default, six digits are printed after the decimal point.
c	The argument is taken to be a single character.
s	The argument is taken to be a string.

For example, the printf statement

```
printf("%c", \'C\');
```

results in

```
C
```

being displayed on the output. The printf statement

```
int i = 1;
printf("%d\n", 2 * i);
```

results in

```
2
```

being displayed, and then the cursor moves to the next line. The printf statement

```
float r = 100.0;
printf("\n%f\t%e", r, 100.0);
```

first moves the cursor to the next line and then displays

```
100.000000    1.000000e+02
```

on the new line. The two values are separated by a tab caused by the presence of the horizontal tab character \t in the control string. Finally, the printf statement

```
float c = -11.428572;
printf("%f Centigrade = %f %s\n",
       c, 1.8*c+32, "Fahrenheit");
```

displays

```
-11.428572 Centigrade = 11.428571 Fahrenheit
```

The blank characters in the control string are significant. Thus,

```
printf("1 2  3   4    5      end\n");
```

displays

```
1 2  3   4    5      end
```

The conversion specifications and the arguments must match both in number and order. Greater control on the appearance of output can be exercised by providing additional specifications between % and a conversion control character. We will return to the printf function in Chapter 10 to discuss its full capability.

2.8.2 scanf Function

The scanf function is the input analog of the printf function. A call to scanf is of the form

```
scanf (control string, arg1, arg2, ...);
```

The *control string* contains *conversion specifications* according to which the characters from the standard input are interpreted and the results are assigned to the successive arguments *arg1*, *arg2*, etc. The scanf function reads one data item from the input corresponding to each argument other than the control string, skipping whitespaces including newlines to find the next data item, and returns as function value the total number of arguments successfully read. It returns EOF when the end of input is reached.

Each argument, other than the control string, must be a *pointer* to the variable where the results of input are to be stored. We will learn about pointers in detail in Chapter 7. For the present, just remember that if i is a variable, then &i is a pointer to i. Thus, if we want the result of input to be stored in i, we must specify &i as the argument to scanf.

As in the case of printf, a conversion specification consists of the character % followed by a *conversion control character*. Conversion specifications may optionally be separated by whitespace characters, which are ignored. Some of the conversion control characters and their effects are as follows:

d,i	A decimal integer is expected in the input. The corresponding argument should be a pointer to an int.
f,e	A floating-point number is expected in the input. The corresponding argument should be a pointer to a float. The input can be in the standard decimal form or in the exponential form.
c	A single character is expected in the input. The corresponding argument should be a pointer to a char. Only in this case, the normal skip over the whitespaces in input is suppressed.

For example, given the declarations

```
int    i;
float  f1, f2;
char   c1, c2;
```

and the input data

```
10 1.0e1 10.0pc
```

the statement

```
scanf("%d %f %e %c %c", &i, &f1, &f2, &c1, &c2);
```

results in i, f1, f2, c1, and c2 being assigned 10, 10.000000, 10.000000, p, and c respectively.

2.9 TYPE CONVERSIONS

An expression may contain variables and constants of different types. We discuss in this section how such expressions are evaluated.

2.9.1 Automatic Type Conversion

ANSI C performs all arithmetic operations with just six data types: int, unsigned int, long int, float, double, and long double. Any operand of the type char or short is implicitly converted to int before the operation. Conversions of char and short to int are called *automatic unary* conversions

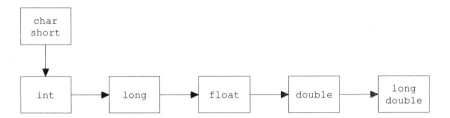

Figure 2.4. Automatic conversion rules (no `unsigned` operands)

to distinguish them from what are called *automatic binary* conversions, which we shall discuss now.

Automatic binary conversions apply to both operands of the binary operators and are carried out after automatic unary conversions. In general, if a binary operator has operands of different types, the "lower" type is promoted to the "higher" type before the operation proceeds. The result is of the higher type. More precisely, for each arithmetic operator, automatic binary conversions are carried out according to the following sequence:

If one operand is `long double` and the other is not, the latter is converted to `long double`, and the result is `long double`;

otherwise, if one operand is `double` and the other is not, the latter is converted to `double`, and the result is `double`;

otherwise, if one operand is `float` and the other is not, the latter is converted to `float`, and the result is `float`;

otherwise, if one operand is `unsigned long int` and the other is not, the latter is converted to `unsigned long int` and the result is `unsigned long int`;

otherwise, if one operand is `long int` and the other is `unsigned int`, then if a `long int` can represent all values of an `unsigned int`, the `unsigned int` is converted to `long int`, and the result is `long int`; if not, both are converted to `unsigned long int`, and the result is `unsigned long int`;

otherwise, if one operand is `long int` and the other is not, the latter is converted to `long int`, and the result is `long int`;

otherwise, if one operand is `unsigned int` and the other is not, the latter is converted to `unsigned int`, and the result is `unsigned int`;

otherwise, both the operands must be `int`, and the result is `int`.

These rules are rather complex. However, if there are no `unsigned` operands, the rules are quite intuitive and have been summarized in Figure 2.4. The vertical line represents the unary conversions that are always performed, and the horizontal lines represent the binary conversions that are performed only when necessary.

Consider, for example, the evaluation of the expression

```
( c / u - l ) + s * f
```

where the types of c, u, l, s, and f are `char`, `unsigned int`, `long`, `short`, and `float` respectively. The following table summarizes the automatic conversions that take place during the evaluation of this expression:

Expression	Conversion	Operand 1	Operand 2	Result
c	unary	char		int
c / u	binary	int	unsigned int	unsigned int
c / u - 1	binary	unsigned int	long int	long int
s	unary	short int		int
s * f	binary	int	float	float
(c / u - 1) + s * f	binary	long int	float	float

C does not specify whether variables of type char are signed or unsigned quantities, and this makes the conversion of a char into an int machine-dependent. On some machines, when converting a char whose leftmost bit is 1 into an int, the *sign extension* takes place, and the result is a negative integer. On others, a char is converted to an int by adding zeros to the left, and thus the result is always positive.

2.9.2 Explicit Type Conversion

Sometimes it is desirable to force a type conversion in a way that is different from the automatic type conversion. C provides a special construct called a *cast* for this purpose. The general form of a cast is

(*cast-type*)   *expression*

where *cast-type* is one of the C data types. For example,

```
(int) 12.8
```

casts 12.8 to an int, which is 12 after truncation.

A cast is a unary operator and has the same precedence as the other unary operators. For example,

```
(int) 12.8 * 3.1
```

casts only 12.8, and not the whole expression 12.8 * 3.1 to int, yielding 37.2 as the value of the expression. If you want to cast the whole expression 12.8 * 3.1, you should write

```
(int) (12.8 * 3.1)
```

yielding 39 as the value of the expression.

A typical use of a cast is in forcing division to return a real number when both operands are of the type int. Thus,

```
(float) sum / n
```

casts sum to a float, and hence causes the division to be carried out as a floating-point division. Without the cast, truncated integer division is performed, if both sum and n are of type int.

2.9.3 Type Conversion in Assignments

When variables of different type are mixed in an assignment expression, the type of the value of the expression on the right side of the assignment operator is automatically converted to the type of the variable on the left side of the operator. The type of the resultant expression value is that of the left operand.

Note that a conversion of a lower-order type, such as `int`, to a higher-order type, such as `float`, only changes the form in which the value is represented; it does not add to the precision or accuracy. On the other hand, a conversion from a higher-order type to a lower-order type may cause truncation and loss of information. For example, the conversion from a 16-bit `int` to a 8-bit `char` results in the loss of the high-order eight bits, and the conversion from a `float` to an `int` means the loss of the fractional part and possibly more.

2.10 SIMPLE MACROS

Consider the following program that determines the surface area and volume of a sphere of a given radius:

```
#include <stdio.h>

int main(void)
   {
      float   radius;

      scanf("%f", &radius);
      printf("surface area = %f\n",
             4 * 3.14 * radius * radius);
      printf("volume = %f\n",
             4 * 3.14 * radius * radius * radius / 3);
      return 0;
   }
```

A problem with this program is that the value of π, 3.14, has been buried in the program statements. If at a later date one wants to get more precise results by providing a more accurate estimate for π, say 3.14159265, one will have to hunt for all occurrences of 3.14 in the program and replace them with the new value. Such transformations could be quite daunting in a large program and susceptible to errors. The same program could also contain a statement such as

```
printf("average home runs = %f\n", 3.14);
```

and one could end up inadvertently modifying this statement. Further, such "magic numbers" convey little information to someone who may have to read the program later.

C provides a `#define` directive to define symbolic names for such constants. The sphere program can be rewritten using a symbolic name `PI` for the value of π as follows:

```
#include <stdio.h>
#define  PI   3.14

int main(void)
  {
    float  radius;

    scanf("%f", &radius);
    printf("surface area = %f\n",
           4 * PI * radius * radius);
    printf("volume = %f\n",
           4 * PI * radius * radius * radius / 3);
    return 0;
  }
```

More precise results can now be obtained by simply changing the definition of PI to

```
#define  PI   3.14159265
```

The #define directive causes a symbolic name to become defined as a *macro* and associates with it a sequence of tokens, called the *body* of the macro. The general form for a *simple* macro definition is

```
#define    macro-name    sequence-of-tokens
```

and it associates with the *macro-name* whatever *sequence-of-tokens* appears from the first blank after the *macro-name* to the end of the line. Note that there is no semicolon at the end of the #define directive. There is no restriction on the sequence of tokens, which can be constants or arbitrary expressions. Previously defined macros can also be used in the definition of a macro.

The #define is actually a directive to the *C preprocessor* that conceptually processes the source text of a C program before the compiler proper parses the source program. The preprocessor replaces every occurrence of a macro name in the program text with a copy of the body of the macro. Macro names are not recognized within comments or string constants.

The rules for naming a macro are the same as for naming a variable described in Section 2.4.1. By convention, macro names are written in upper-case letters. A #define directive can appear anywhere in the program; however, all #define directives are usually collected together at the beginning of the program.

The primary use of simple macros is to define symbolic constants as in

```
#define    OUNCES_PER_GRAM    0.035
#define    GRAMS_PER_OUNCE    1 / OUNCES_PER_GRAM
#define    MAXIMUM_GRAM       1000
#define    STEP_SIZE          10
```

Another important use is in isolating implementation-dependent restrictions as in

```
#define    EOF               -1
#define    MAXINT            2147483647
```

Using symbolic names for constant values helps make programs extendible and portable.

C also provides a *parameterized* version of macro definition that we will study in Chapter 11, along with other preprocessor directives.

2.11 ILLUSTRATIVE EXAMPLES

We now give some examples to further illustrate the concepts introduced in this chapter.

Example 1

Write the C equivalents for the given mathematical expressions, using a minimum number of parentheses.

Mathematical Expression	C Equivalent
$a + b/c - d$	a + b / c - d
$\dfrac{a + b}{c - d}$	(a + b) / (c - d)
$\dfrac{a\,b}{c - d}$	a * b / (c - d)
$\dfrac{a\,b}{c} - d$	a * b / c - d
$\dfrac{a}{c\,d} - b$	a / (c * d) - b
$a + \dfrac{1}{1 + \dfrac{1}{1 + a}}$	a + 1 / (1 + 1 / (1 + a))

Example 2

Determine the value of the following C expression:

```
- 2 * - 3 / 4 % 5 - - 6 + 4
```

At first sight, this expression appears quite formidable, but a strict adherence to the precedence and associativity rule untangles it. In the following figure, the order in which the expression is evaluated is indicated by the sequence of lowercase letters.

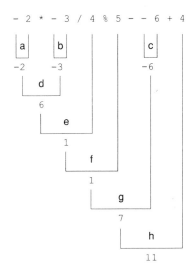

Example 3

Determine the values of i, j, *and* k *after the execution of the following program fragment:*

```
int   i, j, k;
i = j = k = 1;
i -= - j-- - --k;
```

The first nested assignment statement sets i, j and k to 1. In the expression

```
i -= - j-- - --k
```

the compound assignment operator -= has the lowest precedence. In the right-hand side of the assignment, the first - is the unary minus operator, the first -- is the decrement operator in the postfix form, the next - is the binary minus operator, and finally there is a decrement operator -- in the prefix form. The unary minus and decrement operators have higher precedence than the binary minus, and they associate from right to left. We therefore obtain

```
i -= - j-- - (--k)
i -= - (j--) - (--k)
i -= (- (j--)) - (--k)
i -= ((- (j--)) - (--k))
(i -= ((- (j--)) - (--k)))
```

Evaluation from the inside out then gives

```
(i -= ((- (j--)) - 0 ))      and k = 0
(i -= ((- 1) - 0 ))          and j = 0
(i -= (-1) )
(i  = 1 - (-1) )
(i  = 2 )
2                            and i = 2
```

Example 4
Determine the value of the following C expression:

```
- ( 2 * ( - 3 / (double) ( 4 % 10 ) ) ) - ( - 6 + 4 )
```

The subexpressions within parentheses are evaluated first according to the parentheses rule, and we obtain

```
- ( 2 * ( - 3 / (double) 4  ) ) + 2
```

The cast forces conversion of 4 into a `double`, and consequently, before -3 is divided, its type is also converted to a `double`. Thus, the division is no longer an integer division, and we get

```
- ( 2 * - 0.75 ) + 2
```

Further evaluation gives

```
- ( - 1.5 )  + 2
1.5  + 2
3.5
```

Example 5
Determine the values of x, y, and z after the execution of the following program fragment:

```
int   x, z;
float y;
x = 5;
x /= y = z = 1 + 1.5;
```

In the expression

```
x /= y = z = 1 + 1.5
```

there is one arithmetic operator and the rest are assignment operators. The arithmetic operator + has higher precedence than the assignment operators and hence is evaluated first. The simple and compound assignment operators have equal precedence and they associate from right to left. Thus, the operands are bound in the following order:

```
x /= y = z = (1 + 1.5)
x /= y = (z = (1 + 1.5))
x /= (y = (z = (1 + 1.5)))
(x /= (y = (z = (1 + 1.5))))
```

Evaluation proceeds from inside out, and we obtain

```
(x /= (y = (z = 2.5)))
```

The type of the right operand in the assignment z = 2.5 is float, whereas that of the left operand is int, and hence the type of the right operand is automatically converted to int and z becomes 2. Thus, we obtain

```
(x /= (y = 2))
```

Now, y is of type float, and hence before the assignment y = 2, the type of the right operand is automatically converted to float so that y is assigned 2.0, and we obtain

```
(x /= 2.0)
```

which is equivalent to

```
(x = x / 2.0)
```

The current value of x is 5, which is an int. It is converted into a float before the division and the result is 2.5. But since the type of x is int, 2.5 is converted into an int, and 2 is assigned to x.

Thus, the final values of x, y, and z would be 2, 2.0, and 2 respectively.

Example 6

Write an interactive program that computes miles per gallon and cost per mile for the operation of a vehicle based on the miles traveled, gasoline consumed, cost of gasoline, and other operating costs.

The algorithm and program given below provide a solution to the problem.

Algorithm

1. Prompt the user to successively enter the miles traveled miles, gallons of gasoline used gallons, cost of gasoline per gallon gas_price, and other operating costs operating_costs.
2. Compute the miles per gallon miles_per_gallon and the cost per mile cost_per_mile using the formulae:

```
miles_per_gallon = miles / gallons
cost_per_mile = (gas_price × gallons
                 + operating_cost) / miles
```

3. Print results.

Program

```c
#include <stdio.h>

int main(void)
  {
    float   miles, gallons, gas_price, operating_costs;
    float   miles_per_gallon, cost_per_mile;

    printf("miles traveled? ");
    scanf("%f", &miles);

    printf("gallons of gasoline used? ");
    scanf("%f", &gallons);

    printf("price of gasoline per gallon? ");
    scanf("%f", &gas_price);

    printf("other operating costs? ");
    scanf("%f", &operating_costs);

    miles_per_gallon = miles / gallons;
    cost_per_mile = (gas_price * gallons
                      + operating_costs) / miles;

    printf("miles per gallon = %f\n", miles_per_gallon);
    printf("cost per mile = %f\n", cost_per_mile);

    return 0;
  }
```

Sample Execution. The following transcript shows the interaction between the computer and the user:

```
miles traveled? 215
gallons of gasoline used? 6.5
price of gasoline per gallon? 1.39
other operating costs? 5
```

The user-entered data has been italicized. The program now computes the desired quantities and displays

```
miles per gallon = 33.076923
cost per mile = 0.065279
```

Example 7

Write a program that reads the radius of a circle and determines its area, the area of the largest square contained within it, and the ratio of the two.

The algorithm and program given below provide a solution to the problem.

Algorithm

1. Read the radius of the circle, *r*.
2. Compute the area of the circle, πr^2.
3. Compute the area of the largest square contained within the circle, $2 r^2$.
4. Compute the desired ratio.
5. Print results.

Program

```c
#include <stdio.h>
#define   PI   3.14159265

int main(void)
  {
    float   radius;
    float   circle_area, square_area, ratio;

    scanf("%f", &radius);

    circle_area = PI * radius * radius;
    square_area = 2 * radius * radius;
    ratio       = circle_area / square_area;

    printf("area of circle = %f\n", circle_area);
    printf("area of square = %f\n", square_area);
    printf("ratio = %f\n", ratio);

    return 0;
  }
```

Sample Execution. If the input were 2.5, the program would print

```
area of circle = 19.634954
area of square = 12.500000
ratio = 1.570796
```

Example 8
Write a program that determines the difference in the value of an investment after a given number of years when (i) the investment earns simple interest and (ii) the interest is compounded annually at the same rate.

The algorithm and program given below provide a solution to the problem.

Algorithm

1. Read the amount of the principal p, the interest rate r as a percentage, and the number of years y for which the principal is to be invested.
2. Convert the rate read in percentage into a decimal fraction.
3. Compute the value of the investment s if it earns simple interest using the formula

$$s = p(1 + ry)$$

4. Compute the value of the investment c if the interest is compounded annually using the formula

$$c = p(1 + r)^y$$

5. Print the difference in the two values.

Program

```c
#include <math.h>
#include <stdio.h>

int main(void)
  {
    float    principal, rate;
    int      years;
    double   simple, compound;

    scanf("%f %f %d", &principal, &rate, &years);

    rate /= 100;   /* convert percentage into fraction */

    simple   = principal * (1 + rate * years);
    compound = principal * pow((1+rate), (double)years);

    printf("difference = %f\n", compound - simple );

    return 0;
  }
```

Sample Execution. If the `principal` were 7500 and the interest `rate` 8.75%, the program would print

```
difference = 626.699518
```

as the difference in the value of investments after 5 `years`.

   This program uses the function `pow` defined in the standard math library (see Appendix A). We have therefore included `<math.h>` in the program. The function call `pow(x,y)` returns the value of x^y, and the function `pow` expects arguments of type `double`. Since `years` is of type `int`, we have *cast* it into a `double` before calling `pow`.

Example 9
A projectile fired at an angle θ with an initial velocity v travels a distance d given by

$$d = \frac{v^2}{g} \sin 2\,\theta$$

where g is the acceleration constant of 9.8 m/sec². It stays in motion for a time t given by

$$t = \frac{2\,v}{g} \sin \theta$$

and attains a maximum height h given by

$$h = \frac{v^2}{g} \sin \theta$$

Write a program that computes d, t, and h, given v and θ.

The algorithm and program given below provide a solution to the problem.

Algorithm

1. Read the initial `velocity` and the firing angle `theta` entered in degrees.
2. Convert the angle read in degrees into radians, since the function `sin`, defined in the standard math library, expects its arguments in radians.
3. Compute `distance`, `time`, and `height`.
4. Print results.

Program

```
#include <math.h>
#include <stdio.h>
#define  G                  9.8
#define  PI                 3.14159265
#define  RADIANS_PER_DEGREE  (PI/180)

int main(void)
  {
    float    velocity, theta;

    scanf("%f %f", &velocity, &theta);

    /* convert degrees into radians */
    theta *= RADIANS_PER_DEGREE;
```

```
printf("distance = %f\n",
        velocity * velocity * sin(2 * theta) / G);
printf("time = %f\n",
        2 * velocity * sin(theta) / G);
printf("height = %f\n",
        velocity * velocity * sin(theta) / G);

return 0;
}
```

Sample Execution. If the initial velocity were 10 m/sec^2 and the firing angle 30°, the program would print

```
distance = 8.836994
time = 1.020408
height = 5.102041
```

Example 10
Write a program that reads a four-digit number and finds the sum of the individual digits.

The algorithm and program given below provide a solution to the problem.

Algorithm

1. Read the four-digit number.
2. Extract the least significant digit of the four-digit number by taking the *mod* of the number with 10.
3. Determine the three-digit number obtained after truncating the least significant digit of the four-digit number.
4. Determine by a similar procedure the remaining three digits.
5. Obtain the sum of four digits and print the result.

Program

```c
#include <stdio.h>

int main(void)
  {
    int   number, sum;
    int   digit1, digit2, digit3, digit4;

    scanf("%d", &number);

    digit1 = number % 10;
    number /= 10;

    digit2 = number % 10;
    number /= 10;
```

```
        digit3 = number % 10;
        number /= 10;

        digit4 = number;
        sum = digit1 + digit2 + digit3 + digit4;

        printf("sum of the digits = %d\n", sum);

        return 0;
    }
```

Sample Execution. If the four-digit `number` were 8769, the program would calculate

```
    digit1 = 8769 % 10 = 9
    number = 8769 / 10 = 876
    digit2 = 876 % 10  = 6
    number = 876 / 10  = 87
    digit3 = 87 % 10   = 7
    number = 87 / 10   = 8
    digit4 = 8
```

and print

```
    sum of the digits = 30
```

Observe that this program has a simple repetitive pattern for which a concise program can be written. However, we defer it to Chapter 4 till we study some more C constructs.

Exercises 2

1. Which of the following are not acceptable as variable names and why?

    a. `Vax/780`   *b.* `IBM-PC`

    c. `Cray 2`   *d.* `3B20`

    e. `McPaint`   *f.* `__0__`

    g. `integer`   *h.* `union`

2. Which of the following are not acceptable as integer constants and why?

    a. `0L`   *b.* `08`

    c. `0f`   *d.* `0x8f`

    e. `1e0`   *f.* `1.`

    g. `10,000`   *h.* `10 000`

3. Which of the following are not acceptable as floating-point constants and why?

    a. `.1`   *b.* `1.`

    c. `1,000.0`   *d.* `1 000.0`

    e. `1e0`   *f.* `1.e1`

    g. `1e-1`   *h.* `1e1.`

4. Which of the following are not acceptable as character constants and why?

    a. '1'

    b. a

    c. '\'

    d. '\q'

    e. '08'

    f. 'c

    g. '"'

    h. '''

5. Which of the following are not acceptable as string constants and why?

    a. "*&#^%   :-)\n"

    b. "And he said, "Not me !!!""

    c. "And he said, \"Not me !!!\""

    d. "And he said,"   " \"Not me !!!\""

6. Write a C expression corresponding to each of the following mathematical expressions using only the necessary parentheses:

    a. $\dfrac{ab}{a+b}$

    b. $\dfrac{a+b}{ab}$

    c. $a + \dfrac{b}{c^2}$

    d. $\left(\dfrac{a+b}{c-d}\right)^2$

    e. $\dfrac{\frac{a}{b}+c}{a-\frac{b}{c}}$

    f. $\dfrac{ab+bc+ac}{\frac{a+b+c}{abc}}$

7. For each of the following C expressions, find an equivalent expression after deleting superfluous parentheses:

    a. (a * b) / (c - d)

    b. (a * b) - (c / d)

    c. (a * b * c) + ((d * e) % f)

    d. (a * b * c) / ((d * e) % f)

    e. ((a - b) / c) % (d * (e + f))

    f. ((a / b) + (c % d) - (e * (f/g)))

8. Determine the value of each of the following C expressions:

    a. - 1 + 2 * 3 - 4

    b. - (1 + 2) * (3 - 4)

    c. - 1 + 2 % 3 - 4

    d. - ((1 + 2) % 3 - 4)

    e. - 13 / 2 % - 3 * 2

    f. (- 13 / 2) % (- 3 * 2)

9. Determine the value of each of the following C expressions:

    a. 3 + 4.8 * 2

    b. 2.8 - 17 / 5

    c. 2 * (float) 6 / 5

    d. 2 * (int) 6.5 / 5

10. What, if anything, is wrong with the following declarations:

    a. int i j;

    b. int, i, j;

    c. int: i, j;

    d. i, j : int;

11. What, if anything, is wrong with the following assignment statements:

    a. i = ++ - j;

    b. i = --j++;

    c. i = -j++;

    d. i = (-j)++;

e. `i = 1 + j = 1 + k;`   *f.* `i = 1 + (j = 1 + k);`

g. `i =+ 1;`   *h.* `i = j++ = k++;`

i. `i *= j /= k;`   *j.* `i = i * j = j / k;`

12. What, if anything, is wrong with the following input/output statements:

    a. `scanf("%d", i);`   *b.* `scanf("%d", &i, &j);`

    c. `printf("%d %d" i j);`   *d.* `printf("%d %d", 10);`

    e. `printf("%d %d", "i=", i);`   *f.* `printf("%d %d", 1 % 2, 'i');`

13. What, if anything, is wrong with the following program structures:

    a.
    ```
    int main(void)
    {
        printf("bonjour\n");
    };
    ```
    b.
    ```
    int main(void)
    {
        printf("bonjour\n")
    }
    ```
    c.
    ```
    int main(void)
        printf("bonjour\n");
    }
    ```
    d. `int main(void){printf("bonjour\n");}`

14. Assuming x to be of type `float` and i, j, and k to be of type `int`, determine the output of each of the following program fragments:

    a.
    ```
    i = j = k = 1;
    k += - i++ + ++j;
    printf("%d %d %d\n", i, j, k);
    ```
    b.
    ```
    x = 1; i = 2; j = 3; k = 4;
    x -= k *= j /= i %= 5;
    printf("%f %d %d %d\n", x, i, j, k);
    ```
    c.
    ```
    i = 1; j = 2; x = 3;
    x /= j = ++i * 2.5;
    printf("%f %d %d\n", x, i, j);
    ```
    d.
    ```
    i = 1; j = 2; x = 3;
    x /= j = i++ * 2.5;
    printf("%f %d %d\n", x, i, j);
    ```
    e.
    ```
    i = j = 10;
    i %= j = (j = 5) % (i = 3);
    printf("%d %d\n", i, j);
    ```
    f.
    ```
    x = 5; i = 4; j = 3; k = 2;
    x *= 1 + (i %= 1 + (j /= -1 + ++k));
    printf("%f %d %d %d\n", x, i, j, k);
    ```

15. Write assignment statements that result in the computation of the following:

    a. The area a of a cylindrical drum of radius r and height h, given that
    $$a = 2\pi r(r + h)$$

    b. The area a of a triangle that has angle θ between the two sides x and y, given that
    $$a = 1/2\ xy \sin \theta$$

    c. The depreciated value v_n of an asset of initial value v_0 after n years at the depreciation rate r, given that
    $$v_n = v_0(1 - r)^n$$

d. The value v of an investment p after y years at the interest rate r compounded f times in a year, given that

$$v = p\,(1 + r/f)^{yf}$$

e. The annual payment p to repay a loan l for y years at an interest rate r, given that

$$p = l\,\frac{r\,(1 + r)^y}{(1 + r)^y - 1}$$

f. The equivalent parallel resistance R_p of three resistors R_1, R_2, and R_3 in a parallel arrangement, given that

$$R_p = \cfrac{1}{\cfrac{1}{R_1} + \cfrac{1}{R_2} + \cfrac{1}{R_3}}$$

16. Write a program fragment that interchanges the values of x and y so that x has y's value and y has x's value.

17. Write a program to convert a given measurement in feet to an equivalent one in (a) yards, (b) inches, (c) centimeters, and (d) meters.

18. Write a program to convert a given number of seconds into hours, minutes, and seconds.

19. Suppose that a particle gets into motion from rest and has constant acceleration f for t seconds. The distance traveled d by the particle and the final velocity v are given by

$$d = \frac{1}{2} f t^2 \qquad \text{and} \qquad v = f t$$

Write a program that reads f and t, and prints d and v.

20. Write a program that reads three numbers, x_1, x_2, and x_3, and computes their average μ, their standard deviation σ, and the relative percentage RP for each number, where

$$\mu = \frac{x1 + x2 + x3}{3}$$

$$\sigma^2 = \frac{x_1^2 + x_2^2 + x_3^2 - 3\mu^2}{3}$$

$$RP1 = \frac{x_1}{x_1 + x_2 + x_3} \cdot 100$$

and similarly for RP2 and RP3.

21. Assuming $a_1 b_2 - a_2 b_1 \neq 0$, the solution of the linear equations

$$a_1 x + b_1 y = c_1$$

$$a_2 x + b_2 y = c_2$$

is given by

$$x = \frac{b_2 c_1 - b_1 c_2}{a_1 b_2 - a_2 b_1} \qquad y = \frac{a_1 c_2 - a_2 c_1}{a_1 b_2 - a_2 b_1}$$

Write a program that reads the values of a_1, b_1, and c_1 from one data line and those of a_2, b_2, and c_2 from the next data line, and determines the solution pair x, y.

22. The volume v of a sphere of radius r is given by

$$v = (4/3)\,\pi\,r^3$$

Write a program that computes the thickness of a hollow ball, given the total volume occupied by the ball and the volume inside the ball.

23. The distance d between points (x_1, y_1) and (x_2, y_2) is given by

$$d = ((x_1 - x_2)^2 + (y_1 - y_2)^2)^{1/2}$$

and the perimeter p and the area a of a triangle of sides of length u, v, and w are given by

$$p = u + v + w \qquad \text{and} \qquad a = (s(s-u)(s-v)(s-w))^{1/2}$$

where $s = p/2$. Write a program that reads the coordinates of the three points of a triangle and prints its perimeter and area.

24. Students are awarded points toward their grades based upon a weighted average of their quizzes, the midterm examination, and the final examination. The weighting is the average of three quizzes $Q1$, $Q2$, $Q3$, the midterm grade M, and twice the final examination grade F. Write a program that computes total weighted points using $Q1$, $Q2$, $Q3$, M, and F as input.

25. Write a program that helps in visualizing the effect of inflation. Read the inflation rate and print (i) the amount of money needed in four years to buy what $1.00 buys today, and (ii) the amount of money needed four years ago to buy what $1.00 buys today. Note that if the inflation rate is 6%, the two amounts are given by $1.00 \times 1.06 \times 1.06 \times 1.06 \times 1.06$ and $1.00 / (1.06 \times 1.06 \times 1.06 \times 1.06)$ respectively.

⊞ 3 Selective Structure

The sequential structure consists of a sequence of program statements that are executed one after another in order. The *selective structure* allows the usual sequential order of execution to be modified. It consists of a test for a *condition* followed by *alternative paths* that the program can follow. The program selects one of the alternative paths depending upon the result of the test for the condition as illustrated in Figure 3.1.

Selection among alternative processing is programmed with certain decision-making constructs. Before studying these constructs in detail, let us go through an example program to develop an intuitive understanding for them.

3.1 OVERVIEW

Reconsider the program for determining simple interest that we analyzed in Example 2 of Section 2.1. We now assume that the bank offers two interest rates: a bonus rate of 9.75% for those who invest at least $10,000 or keep the

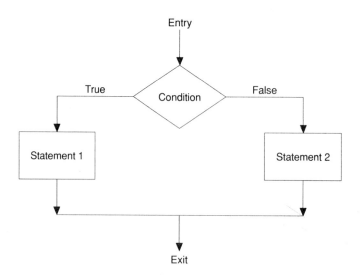

Figure 3.1.   Selective structure

principal invested for more than 5 years, and a regular rate of 8.75% otherwise. Here is an algorithm for solving this problem:

1. Read the amount of principal and the number of years for which the principal is to be invested.
2. Determine the interest rate depending upon the principal and the years of investment.
3. Compute the total interest accrued using the formula

   interest = principal × rate × years.

4. Print interest.

Here is the program:

```
#include <stdio.h>
#define  BONUS     0.0975
#define  REGULAR   0.0875

int main(void)
  {
    float    principal, rate, interest;
    int      years;

    /* prompt the user to provide input values */
    printf("principal and years of investment? ");

    /* read the input values */
    scanf("%f %d", &principal, &years);

    /* determine the interest rate */
    if (principal >= 10000 || years > 5)
        rate = BONUS;
    else
        rate = REGULAR;

    /* compute interest */
    interest = principal * rate * years;

    /* print interest */
    printf("interest = %f\n", interest);

    /* successful completion */
    return 0;
  }
```

The new feature introduced in this program is the if statement:

```
if (principal >= 10000 || years > 5)
    rate = BONUS;
else
    rate = REGULAR;
```

which determines the effective `rate` depending on the values of `principal` and `years`. The expression enclosed within parentheses following the keyword `if`:

```
principal >= 10000 || years > 5
```

is the test that determines whether `rate` is set to BONUS or REGULAR. If the condition is satisfied, i.e., if the expression is *true*, then the statement controlled by `if`:

```
rate = BONUS;
```

is executed; if the condition is not satisfied, i.e., the expression is *false*, then the statement controlled by `else`:

```
rate = REGULAR;
```

is executed. Thus, the program follows one of the two alternative paths depending upon the result of the evaluation of the test condition during the processing of this selective structure. In either case, after this structure has been processed, the program execution continues from the first statement after the structure:

```
interest = principal * rate * years;
```

C does not have Boolean values: *true* and *false*. Instead, integers are used as substitutes for Boolean values. Any nonzero value is interpreted as *true* and zero is interpreted as *false*.

The test expression

```
principal >= 10000 || years > 5
```

consists of two *relational expressions*

```
principal >= 10000
```

and

```
years > 5
```

combined with the *logical OR operator*

```
||
```

into a *logical expression*.

Relational expressions are used for comparing the values of two expressions using a *relational operator*. The relational expression `principal >= 10000` compares `principal` with `10000` using the operator `>=`, and its value is 1 (*true*) if `principal` is greater than or equal to `10000` and 0 (*false*) otherwise. The relational expression `years > 5` compares `years` with `5` using the operator `>`, and its value is 1 (*true*) if `years` is greater than 5 and 0 (*false*) otherwise. The other relational operators are < (less than), <= (less than or equal to), == (equal to), and != (not equal to).

Logical operators are used for combining expressions, usually relational expressions, into logical expressions. The three logical operators are: || (logical OR), && (logical AND), and ! (logical NOT). The value of a logical expression formed by combining two expressions using the logical OR operator is 1 (*true*) if the value of either of the two operands is nonzero (*true*); otherwise, its value is 0 (*false*). Thus, the rate is set to BONUS if principal is at least 10000 or if years is more than 5. Only if both of these conditions are *false*, is the rate set to REGULAR.

More than one action can be specified within an alternative path in a selective structure by grouping statements into a *block*, also called a *compound statement*. A *block* is a sequence of variable declarations and statements enclosed within braces. Moreover, it is not necessary to have an else part in an if statement. Thus, if we wanted to ensure that the values provided by the user for principal and years were nonnegative, we could add the statement

```
if (principal < 0 || years < 0)
  {
    printf("negative values in input\n");
    return 1;
  }
```

after the scanf statement. The block

```
  {
    printf("negative values in input\n");
    return 1;
  }
```

is executed only if the expression

```
principal < 0 || years < 0
```

has a nonzero (*true*) value, and the program terminates abnormally in that case after printing the error message. If the value of this expression is zero (*false*), this block is not executed and the interest is computed and printed as before. Note that there is no semicolon after the closing brace of a block.

C also provides a *conditional expression operator* that is often used to assign one of the two values to a variable depending upon some condition. Using this operator, rate can be set to either BONUS or REGULAR as follows:

```
rate = principal >= 10000 || years > 5 ? BONUS : REGULAR;
```

Here is the complete program that incorporates the validation of input data and the use of the conditional expression operator:

```
#include <stdio.h>
#define  BONUS    0.0975
#define  REGULAR  0.0875

int main(void)
  {
    float    principal, rate, interest;
    int      years;

    /* prompt the user to provide input values */
    printf("principal and years of investment? ");

    /* read the input values */
    scanf("%f %d", &principal, &years);
```

```
/* validate input */
if (principal < 0 || years < 0)
  {
    printf("negative values in input\n");
    return 1;
  }

/* determine the interest rate */
rate = principal >= 10000 || years > 5 ?
            BONUS : REGULAR;

/* compute interest */
interest = principal * rate * years;

/* print interest */
printf("interest = %f\n", interest);

/* successful completion */
return 0;
}
```

We will now study in detail the C constructs for specifying selective structures. We first discuss relational and logical operators and then discuss the conditional expression operator. The various forms of conditional statements — the if statement, the if-else statement, the nested conditional statement, and the multiway conditional statement — are discussed next. Finally, we discuss the switch statement that allows checking for different values of the same expression.

3.2 RELATIONAL OPERATORS

C provides six relational operators for comparing the values of two expressions, and the expression so formed is called a *relational expression*. Table 3.1 gives the relational operators and shows how they can be used to compare two expressions *exp1* and *exp2*.

Relational operators can be applied to operands of any arithmetic type. The result of comparison of two expressions is *true* if the condition being tested is satisfied and *false* otherwise. However, C has no special data type for logically valued quantities. The value of a relational expression, instead, is of type int, and is 1 if the result of comparison is true and 0 otherwise. For example,

15 > 10   has the value 1 (*true*).
15 <= 10   has the value 0 (*false*).

The use of relational operators to compare character values requires special mention. When characters are compared in a relational expression, their relative ordering in the collating sequence (see Appendix D) is used. Therefore, the result of comparison may differ from computer to computer depending upon whether the underlying collating sequence uses ASCII or EBCDIC codes. Thus, the relational expressions

'b' > 'a'
'1' < '2'

Table 3.1. Relational operators

Relational Operator	Name	Relational Expression
<	Less than	*exp1* < *exp2*
<=	Less than or equal to	*exp1* <= *exp2*
>	Greater than	*exp1* > *exp2*
>=	Greater than or equal to	*exp1* >= *exp2*
==	Equal to	*exp1* == *exp2*
!=	Not equal to	*exp1* != *exp2*

are always *true* since 'b' follows 'a' and '1' precedes '2' in any collating sequence. However, the truth or falsity of the relational expressions

```
'A' > '1'
'*' < '('
```

depends on the collating sequence used in a particular computer. The first is *true* and the second *false* for the ASCII code, but both are *false* for the EBCDIC code.

A common programming error is to confuse the equal to operator == with the assignment operator =. The expression

```
x == 10
```

tests if the value of x is equal to 10, whereas

```
x = 10
```

assigns 10 to the variable x. Thus, the statement

```
if (x == 10) printf("tenbagger");
```

will print tenbagger only if x is 10, whereas the statement

```
if (x = 10) printf("tenbagger");
```

will print tenbagger irrespective of the value of x because the value of the assignment expression x = 10 is 10 (*true*).

3.2.1 Precedence and Associativity

Table 3.2 shows the precedence and associativity of the relational operators with respect to the assignment and arithmetic operators. In this table, an operator in a higher row has a higher precedence when compared to an operator in a lower row. Those operators that are in the same row have the same precedence and associativity. Appendix B contains a complete table of the precedence and associativity of the C operators.

Thus, the operators <, <=, >, and >= have equal precedence and associate from left to right. Just below them in precedence are the operators == and != that also have equal precedence and associate from left to right. Therefore, the expressions

Table 3.2.   Precedence and associativity of the relational operators

Operators	Type	Associativity
+ – ++ --	Unary	Right to left
* / %	Binary	Left to right
+ –	Binary	Left to right
< <= > >=	Binary	Left to right
== !=	Binary	Left to right
= *= /= %= += -=	Binary	Left to right

```
5 < n < 10
i == j == 5
p >= q == r >= s
```

are interpreted as

```
(5 < n) < 10
(i == j) == 5
(p >= q) == (r >= s)
```

respectively. The value of the first expression is 1, irrespective of the value of n, since the value of 5 < n is 0 or 1 and either of these two is less than 10. The value of the second expression is always 0, whatever the values of i and j are, since the value of i == j is 0 or 1 and neither of these two is equal to 5. The value of the third expression would be 1 or 0, depending upon whether p >= q and r >= s have the same value or not.

The relational operators have lower precedence than the arithmetic operators but higher than the assignment operator. Thus, the expression

```
a < b + c
```

is interpreted as

```
a < (b + c)
```

However,

```
a = b == c
```

is interpreted as

```
a = (b == c)
```

Finally, the expression

```
a = b + c != d + e
```

is interpreted as

```
a = ( (b + c) != (d + e) )
```

The following table further illustrates the use of precedence and associativity to evaluate relational expressions:

int i = 3, j = 2, k = 1;

Expression	Equivalent Expression	Value
i > j > k	(i > j) > k	(3 > 2) > 1 ≡ 1 > 1 ≡ 0
i >= j >= k	(i >= j) >= k	(3 >= 2) >= 1 ≡ 1 >= 1 ≡ 1
i != j != k	(i != j) != k	(3 != 2) != 1 ≡ 1 != 1 ≡ 0
k < i != k < j	(k < i) != (k < j)	(1<3)!=(1<2) ≡ 1 != 1 ≡ 0
i - k == j * k	(i - k) == (j * k)	(3 - 1) == (2 * 1) ≡ 2 == 2 ≡ 1
i > j == i + k > j + k	(i>j)==((i+k)>(j+k))	1 == (4 > 3) ≡ 1 == 1 ≡ 1
i += j != k	i += (j != k)	i+=(2!=1) ≡ i+=1 ≡ i=4 ≡ 4
i = k != j < k * j	i=(k!=(j<(k*j)))	i=(1!=(2<2)) ≡ i=(1!=0) ≡ i=1 ≡ 1

You may, of course, use parentheses to force an order of evaluation different from one yielded by the precedence and associativity rule. You may also freely use redundant parentheses to clarify the order of evaluation in a complex relational expression.

3.3 LOGICAL OPERATORS

C provides three logical operators for combining expressions into *logical expressions*. Table 3.3 gives these operators and their meanings.

The logical operators && and || are binary operators, whereas the logical operator ! is a unary operator. The value of a logical expression is 1 or 0, depending upon the logical values of the operands. The operands may be of any arithmetic type. The type of the result is always int.

3.3.1 Logical AND Operator

The *logical AND* operator combines two expressions into a logical expression and has the following operator formation:

exp1 && *exp2*

An expression of this form is evaluated by first evaluating the left operand. If its value is zero (*false*), the evaluation is short-circuited and the right operand is not evaluated; the value of the logical expression then is 0 (*false*). However, if the value of the left operand is nonzero (*true*), the right operand does get evalu-

Table 3.3. Logical operators

Symbol	Name	Meaning
&&	Logical AND	Conjunction
||	Logical OR	Disjunction
!	Logical NOT	Negation

Table 3.4.   Logical AND operator

exp1	exp2	exp1 && exp2
nonzero (*true*)	nonzero (*true*)	1 (*true*)
nonzero (*true*)	zero (*false*)	0 (*false*)
zero (*false*)	nonzero (*true*)	0 (*false*)
zero (*false*)	zero (*false*)	0 (*false*)

ated. The value of the logical expression is 1 (*true*) if the right operand has non-zero (*true*) value, and 0 (*false*) otherwise. Table 3.4 summarizes the results of the logical AND operation in the form of a truth table.

Thus, given that

```
int a, b, c;
a = b = c = 10;
```

the logical expression

```
a && (b + c)
```

has the value 1 (*true*), since both a and (b + c) are nonzero (*true*), whereas the logical expression

```
a && (b - c)
```

has the value 0 (*false*), since (b - c) is zero (*false*).

A desirable consequence of the short-circuited left to right evaluation of the && operator is that an expression such as

```
(a != 0) && (b/a > 10)
```

can safely be written. The division to the right of && is now guaranteed to be performed only if a is not 0, and the division-by-zero error cannot occur.

3.3.2 Logical OR Operator

The *logical OR* operator, like the logical AND operator, combines two expressions into a logical expression, and has the following operator formation:

exp1 || *exp2*

An expression of this form is evaluated by first evaluating the left operand. If the value of the left operand is nonzero (*true*), the right operand is not evaluated; the value of the logical expression then is 1 (*true*). However, if the value of the left operand is zero (*false*), the right operand is evaluated, and the value of the logical expression is 1 (*true*) if the right operand has a nonzero (*true*) value, and 0 (*false*) otherwise. Table 3.5 summarizes the results of the logical OR operation in the form of a truth table.

Table 3.5.   Logical OR operator

exp1	exp2	exp1 || exp2
nonzero (*true*)	nonzero (*true*)	1 (true)
nonzero (*true*)	zero (*false*)	1 (true)
zero (*false*)	nonzero (*true*)	1 (true)
zero (*false*)	zero (*false*)	0 (false)

Thus, given that

```
int a, b, c;
a = b = c = 10;
```

the logical expression

```
a || (b - c)
```

has the value 1 (*true*), since a is nonzero (*true*), and the logical expression

```
(a - b) || c
```

also has the value 1 (*true*), since c is nonzero (*true*), but the logical expression

```
(a - c) || (b - c)
```

has the value 0 (*false*), since both (a-c) and (b-c) are zero (*false*).

3.3.3 Logical NOT Operator

The *logical NOT* operator inverts the logical value of an expression and has the following operator formation:

```
! exp
```

An expression of this form is evaluated by first evaluating the operand. If its value is zero (*false*), the value of the logical expression is 1 (*true*); if it is nonzero (*true*), the value of the logical expression is 0 (*false*). Table 3.6 summarizes the results of the logical NOT operation in the form of a truth table.

Thus, given that

```
int a, b;
a = b = 10;
```

the logical expression

```
!a
```

has the value 0 (*false*), since a is nonzero (*true*), and the logical expression

```
!(a - b)
```

has the value 1 (*true*), since (a - b) is zero (*false*).

Table 3.6. Logical NOT operator

exp	! exp
nonzero (*true*)	0 (*false*)
zero (*false*)	1 (*true*)

Table 3.7. Precedence and associativity of the logical operators

Operators	Type	Associativity
+ − ++ −− !	Unary	Right to left
* / %	Binary	Left to right
+ −	Binary	Left to right
< <= > >=	Binary	Left to right
== !=	Binary	Left to right
&&	Binary	Left to right
||	Binary	Left to right
= *= /= %= += −=	Binary	Left to right

3.3.4 Precedence and Associativity

Table 3.7 shows the precedence and associativity of the logical operators with respect to the assignment, arithmetic, and relational operators. In this table, an operator in a higher row has a higher precedence when compared to an operator in a lower row. Those operators that are in the same row have the same precedence and associativity. Appendix B contains a complete table of the precedence and associativity of the C operators.

Thus, the logical AND operator has a precedence lower than that of any arithmetic or relational operators but higher than that of the logical OR operator. The logical NOT operator has the same precedence as the unary arithmetic operators, which means that it has higher precedence than all binary arithmetic operators, all relational operators, and the logical operators && and ||. The logical operators associate from left to right, except the unary logical NOT that associates from right to left.

Thus, the expression

```
a || b && c
```

is interpreted as

```
a || (b && c)
```

since && has higher precedence than ||. The expressions

```
! a && b
! a || b
```

are interpreted as

```
(! a) && b
(! a) || b
```

respectively, since ! has higher precedence than both && and ||. Due to the left to right associativity of && and ||, the expressions

```
a && b && c
a || b || c
```

are interpreted as

```
(a && b) && c
(a || b) || c
```

The expressions

```
a < b && c % d
a - b || c == d
```

are interpreted as

```
(a < b) && (c % d)
(a - b) || (c == d)
```

since && and || have lower precedence than the relational and the arithmetic operators. Finally, the expressions

```
! a >= b && c / d
a * b || ! c != d
```

are interpreted as

```
( (!a) >= b ) && (c / d)
(a * b) || ( (!c) != d )
```

since ! has the same precedence as that of unary −, which is higher than that of the relational and the binary arithmetic operators.

The following table further illustrates the use of precedence and associativity to evaluate logical expressions:

int i = 3, j = 2, k = 1;		
Expression	Equivalent Expression	Value
!!k	!(!k)	!(!1) ≡ !0 ≡ 1
! i == ! j	(!i) == (!j)	(!3)==(!2) ≡ 0==0 ≡ 1
k != ! k * k	k != ((!k) * k)	1 != (0 * 1) ≡ 1
i > j && j > k	(i > j) && (j > k)	1 && 1 ≡ 1
i != j && j != k	(i != j) && (j != k)	1 && 1 ≡ 1
i - j - k || k == i / j	(i-j-k) || (k == (i/j))	0 || (1 == (3/2)) ≡ 1
i < j || k < i && j < k	(i<j) || ((k<i)&&(j<k))	0 || (1 && 0) ≡ 0

You may always use parentheses to force a particular order of evaluation, or to clarify the order of evaluation.

3.3.5 Evaluation of Logical Expressions

We just studied how the operands are bound to the operators in a logical expression that contains more than one logical operator and/or other arithmetic or relational operators. For most operators in C, the order of evaluation is determined by their precedence. However, logical AND and logical OR operators are always evaluated conditionally from left to right, and this evaluation rule can make a difference when the expression contains a side effect.

Consider, for example, the expression

```
--a || --b && --c
```

and let a = b = c = 10. Following the precedence rule and binding the operands to the operators, we get

```
( (--a) || ( (--b) && (--c) ) )
```

Hypothetically, if the evaluation order were to follow precedence, && would be evaluated first and we would get

```
( (--a) || ( 9 && (--c) ) )          and   b = 9
( (--a) || (9 && 9) )                and   c = 9
( (--a) || true )
( whatever || true )
  true,   or   1
```

that is, the expression would be *true*, and a = 10, b = 9, and c = 9. Actually, the evaluation proceeds from left to right, although && has higher precedence than ||. Evaluating from left to right, we get

```
( 9 || ( (--b) && (--c) ) )          and   a = 9
( true || ( (--b) && (--c) ) )
( true || whatever )
  true,   or   1
```

That is, the expression is again *true*, but now a = 9, b = 10, and c = 10.

3.4   CONDITIONAL EXPRESSION OPERATOR

The *conditional expression operator*, unlike all other operators in C that are either unary or binary, is a ternary operator and takes three arguments. It has the following operator formation:

> *expression-1 ? expression-2 : expression-3*

where the question mark ? and the colon : are the two symbols that denote this operator. A conditional expression is evaluated by first evaluating *expression-1*. If the resultant value is nonzero (*true*), then *expression-2* is evaluated and the value of *expression-2* becomes the result of the conditional expression. Otherwise, *expression-3* is evaluated and its value becomes the result.

The conditional expression is most often used to assign one of the two values to a variable depending upon some condition. For example, the assignment statement

```
larger = x > y ? x : y;
```

assigns to `larger` the value of x if x is greater than y; otherwise, it assigns the value of y to `larger`.

Precedence of the conditional expression operator is lower than all other operators except the assignment and comma operators. The second operand *expression-2* may even use operators that have lower precedence, since it is effectively bracketed by the tokens ? and :. However, the third operand *expression-3* cannot use an operator of lower precedence without using parentheses. For example, the conditional expression

```
c ? x = a : x = b
```

would be interpreted as

```
(c ? x = a : x) = b
```

due to the lower precedence of the assignment operator. This assignment is illegal, since the conditional expression produces an rvalue. A correct form of this conditional expression is

```
c ? x = a : (x = b)
```

Note that it is not necessary to put parentheses around the second operand x = a. Of course, a better way to write this expression is

```
x = c ? a : b
```

The conditional expression operator is right-associative with respect to its first and third operands, so that

```
a ? b : c ? d : e
```

is interpreted as

```
a ? b : ( c ? d : e )
```

The value of this expression would be b if a is nonzero (*true*); otherwise, the value of the expression would be d if c is nonzero (*true*) and e if c is zero (*false*).

The following table further illustrates the evaluation of expressions containing the conditional expression operator:

int i = 0, j = 1, k = 2, n;		
Expression	After Values	n set to
n = i+1 ? j : k	n=1 i=0 j=1 k=2	j
n = i++ ? j-- : k--	n=2 i=1 j=1 k=1	k--
n = ++i ? --j : --k	n=0 i=1 j=0 k=2	--j
n = i ? j : j ? k - 1 : k * k	n=1 i=0 j=1 k=2	k - 1
n = i ? j : --j ? k - 1 : k * k	n=4 i=0 j=0 k=2	k * k
n = ++i ? j : --j ? k - 1 : k * k	n=1 i=1 j=1 k=2	j

3.5 CONDITIONAL STATEMENTS

A conditional statement allows selective processing of a statement or a group of statements. There are two forms of conditional statements: the `if` statement and the `if-else` statement. The first form begins with the key word `if`, followed by an expression in parentheses, followed by a statement. The second form also begins with the keyword `if`, followed by an expression in parentheses, followed by a statement. In addition, it has appended to it the keyword `else`, followed by another statement. We will now discuss these two forms of conditional statements.

3.5.1 `if` Statement

The `if` statement is used to specify conditional execution of a program statement, or a group of statements enclosed in braces. The general format of this statement is

```
if ( expression )

    statement
```

When an `if` statement is encountered, *expression* is evaluated and if its value is nonzero (*true*), then *statement* is executed. After the execution of *statement*, the statement following the `if` statement is executed next. If the value of *expression* is zero (*false*), *statement* is not executed and the execution continues from the statement immediately after the `if` statement. The `if` statement is pictorially represented in Figure 3.2.

Here are some examples:

1. ```
   if (number < 0)
        number = -number;
   printf("%d\n", number);
   ```

   If the `number` has a negative value, the logical expression `number < 0` evaluates to 1 (*true*), and the assignment statement converts the negative value into a positive value, which is assigned to `number`. If the `number` has nonnegative value, the logical expression evaluates to 0 (*false*), and the assignment statement is not executed. In either case, the `printf` function is executed next and it prints the absolute value of `number`.

2. ```
   if (age > 18  &&  salary < 250)
       {
        unemployed++;
        total_age += age;
        total_salary += salary;
       }
   ```

   If the `age` of the person is more than 18 and the person's `salary` is less than $250, the three statements enclosed in braces are executed. Consequently, the number of `unemployed` is incremented by 1 and this person's `age` and `salary` are added to `total_age` and `total_salary` respectively.

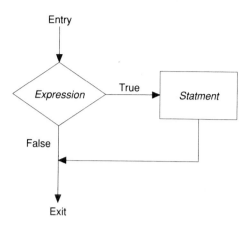

Figure 3.2. `if` statement

Finally, to illustrate the use of the `if` statement, we give a program that prints the larger of the two given integer values:

```
#include <stdio.h>

int main(void)
  {
    int v1, v2, larger;

    scanf("%d %d", &v1, &v2);

    larger = v1;
    if (v2 > v1) larger = v2;

    printf("%d\n", larger);

    return 0;
  }
```

3.5.2 `if-else` Statement

The `if` statement allows conditional execution of a group of statements. However, there are many situations when two groups of statements are given and it is desired that one of them be executed if some condition is true and the other be executed if the condition is false. In such situations, we make use of the `if-else` statement whose general format is:

```
if ( expression )

        statement-1
else
        statement-2
```

When an `if-else` statement is encountered, the value of *expression* is evaluated and if its value is nonzero (*true*), *statement-1* is executed. After the execution of *statement-1*, the program execution continues from the statement immediately after *statement-2*. If the value of *expression* is zero (*false*), *statement-2* is executed. After the execution of *statement-2*, the program execution continues from the statement following *statement-2*. In either case, one of *statement-1* or *statement-2* is executed, but not both.

Statement-1, controlled by `if`, is called the `if`-block, and *statement-2*, controlled by `else`, is called the `else`-block. The `if-else` statement is pictorially represented in Figure 3.3.

Here are some examples:

1. ```
   if (n % 2 == 0)
           n = even;
   else
             n = odd;
   ```

   assigns `even` or `odd` to n, according to whether the remainder resulting from the division of n by 2 is 0 or not. Note that the preceding statement can equivalently be written using the conditional expression operator as

   ```
   n = (n % 2 == 0) ? even : odd;
   ```

2. ```
   if (classification == star_hacker)
      {
         regular_pay  = 2 * regular_rate * regular_hrs;
         overtime_pay = 5 * regular_rate * overtime_hrs;
      }
   else
      {
         regular_pay  = regular_rate * regular_hrs;
         overtime_pay = 2 * regular_rate * overtime_hrs;
      }
   ```

   computes the `regular_pay` and the `overtime_pay` for the employees, but the pay rate depends on the `classification` of the employee.

Finally, to illustrate the use of the `if-else` statement, we give a program that prints the larger of two given integer values:

```c
#include <stdio.h>

int main(void)
   {
      int v1, v2, larger;

      scanf("%d %d", &v1, &v2);

      if (v1 > v2)
          larger = v1;
      else
          larger = v2;
```

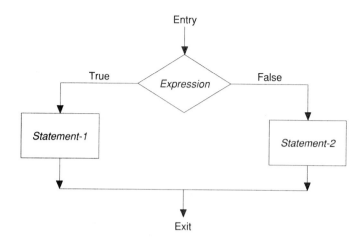

Figure 3.3. `if-else` statement

```
    printf("%d\n", larger);

    return 0;
}
```

Compare this program with the program for the same problem given in the previous section. This program can also be written using the conditional expression operator as

```
#include <stdio.h>

int main(void)
  {
    int v1, v2, larger;

    scanf("%d %d", &v1, &v2);
    larger = (v1 > v2) ? v1 : v2;
    printf("%d\n", larger);

    return 0;
  }
```

Since the only use of `larger` is in printing the result, we can omit the intermediate variable `larger`, and write the program as

```
.#include <stdio.h>

int main(void)
  {
    int v1, v2;

    scanf("%d %d", &v1, &v2);
    printf("%d\n", v1 > v2 ? v1 : v2 );

    return 0;
  }
```

3.6 NESTED CONDITIONAL STATEMENT

In our discussion of the if-else statement, we identified a set of statements as the if-block and another set as the else-block. No restrictions were placed on the kinds of statements that could be included within these blocks. One could, therefore, include another conditional statement in either the if-block or the else-block or both. If this were to happen, the resulting statement is called a *nested conditional* statement. This structure results in one conditional statement being placed inside another conditional statement, and hence the adjective *nested*. The inner conditional statement is said to be *nested* within the outer one. The general format of this statement is

```
if ( expression-1 )
      if ( expression-2 )
            statement-1
      else
            statement-2
else
      if ( expression-3 )
            statement-3
      else
            statement-4
```

Neither *statement-1* nor *statemeni-2* will be executed unless *expression-1* is *true*. Furthermore, neither *statement-3* nor *statement-4* will be executed if *expression-1* is *true*. Note that any of *statement-1*, *statement-2*, *statement-3*, or *statement-4* can itself be a conditional statement, and there is no limit on the depth of nesting. The nested conditional statement is pictorially represented in Figure 3.4.

To illustrate the use of the nested conditional statement, we give a program that reads two integer values and prints Hare Rama! if the first is larger than the second, Hare Krishna! if the second is larger than the first, and Hare Hare! if the two are equal:

```c
#include <stdio.h>

int main(void)
  {
    int v1, v2;

    scanf("%d %d", &v1, &v2);

    if (v1 > v2)
        printf("Hare Rama!\n");
    else
        if (v2 > v1)
            printf("Hare Krishna!\n");
        else
            printf("Hare Hare!\n");

    return 0;
  }
```

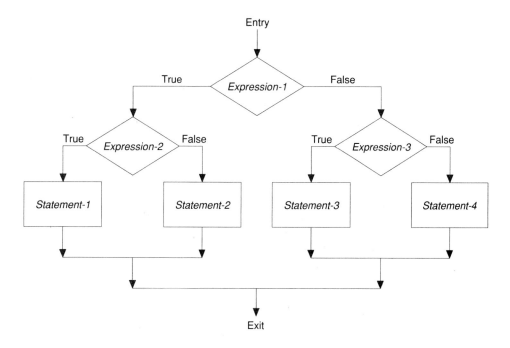

Figure 3.4. Nested conditional statement

The preceding program can be written so that the nesting occurs in the if-block instead of else-block:

```
#include <stdio.h>

int main(void)
  {
    int v1, v2;

    scanf("%d %d", &v1, &v2);

    if (v1 >= v2)
        if (v1 > v2)
            printf("Hare Rama!\n");
        else
            printf("Hare Hare!\n");
    else
        printf("Hare Krishna!\n");

    return 0;
  }
```

In the preceding programs, the nesting occurs either in the if-block or in the else-block. Here is an example of a nested conditional statement in which the nesting occurs both in the if-block and in the else-block:

```
if (x1 > x2)
    if (x1 > x3)
        largest = x1;
    else
        largest = x3;
else
    if (x2 > x3)
        largest = x2;
    else
        largest = x3;
```

This statement assigns the largest of x1, x2, and x3 to largest.

3.6.1 Sequence of Nested ifs

Consider a sequence of nested ifs as in

```
if ( expression-1 )
    if ( expression-2 )
        if ( expression-3 )
                    .
                    .
                    .
            if ( expression-n )
                statement
```

meaning thereby that *expression-2* should be evaluated only if *expression-1* is *true*, *expression-3* should be evaluated only if both *expression-1* and *expression-2* are *true*, and so on, and *statement* should only be executed if all the expressions are *true*. This nested-conditional statement can equivalently be written as

```
if ( expression-1 && expression-2 && ... && expression-n )
        statement
```

This equivalence is possible since C guarantees short-circuited left-to-right evaluation of logical expressions. If any of the expressions in the conjunction becomes *false*, the expressions to the right are not evaluated. Thus,

```
if (r1 != 0)
    if (r2 + 1/r1 != 0)
        if (r3 + 1/(r2+1/r1) != 0)
            r = 1/r1 + 1/(r2+1/r1)
                + 1/(r3+1/(r2+1/r1));
```

can equivalently be written as

```
if ((r1 != 0) && (r2 + 1/r1 != 0)
    && (r3 + 1/(r2+1/r1) != 0))
            r = 1/r1 + 1/(r2+1/r1)
                + 1/(r3+1/(r2+1/r1));
```

3.6.2 Dangling `else` Problem

When conditional statements are nested, it may not be apparent to which of several conditional statements an `else` belongs. The proper indentation helps greatly in understanding the program logic. However, the indentation used to indicate the way a nested conditional statement is intended to be interpreted may not coincide with the way the statement is actually interpreted. For instance, the statement

```
if ( expression-1 )
        if ( expression-2 )
                statement-1
        /* no else-block for the inner if-else statement */
else
        statement-3
```

is not interpreted as intended by the indentation format. Instead, `else` is associated with the closest previous `else`-less `if`, and the statement is interpreted as

```
if ( expression-1 )
        if ( expression-2 )
                statement-1
        else
                statement-3
```

in which the outer `if` has no `else`-block .

The difficulty in such cases in which an innermost `if` does not contain an `else`, but an outer `if` does, can be alleviated by the use of braces for proper association. The braces have the effect of closing the `if` statement. Thus, we can write

```
if ( expression-1 )
    {
        if ( expression-2 )
                statement-1
        /* no else-block for the inner if-else statement */
    }
else
        statement-3
```

for the desired effect.

Here are some examples:

1. An `else` associated with the second `if`.

```
if (i > 1)
    if (j == 2)
        k = 3;
    else
        k = 4;
```

assigns 3 to k when i is greater than 1 and j is equal to 2, but assigns 4 to k when i is greater than 1 and j is not equal to 2. If i is less than or equal to 1, the value of k remains unchanged.

2. An else associated with the first if.

```
if (i > 1)
    {
        if (j == 2)
            k = 3;
    }
else
        k = 4;
```

assigns 3 to k when i is greater than 1 and j is equal to 2, but assigns 4 to k when i is less than or equal to 1. If i is greater than 1 but j is not equal to 2, the value of k remains unchanged.

3. An else associated with each of the ifs.

```
if (i > 1)
        if (j == 2)
            k = 3;
        else
            k = 4;
else
        k = 5;
```

assigns, as in the first example, 3 to k when i is greater than 1 and j is equal to 2 and assigns 4 to k when i is greater than 1 and j is not equal to 2. However, unlike the first example, if i is less than or equal to 1, k is assigned 5.

4. An else associated with a third if.

Consider a slight modification of the sequence of the nested-ifs example considered in Section 3.6.1.

```
if (r1 != 0)
        if (r2 + 1/r1 != 0)
            if (r3 + 1/(r2+1/r1) != 0)
                r = 1/r1 + 1/(r2+1/r1)
                    + 1/(r3+1/(r2+1/r1));
else
        printf("division by zero\n");
```

The intent is that if any of the denominators evaluates to zero, the error message should be displayed. However, the else is paired with the innermost if, and the error message is displayed only if the expression associated with the innermost if is *false*. If either of the expressions associated with the first and second ifs is *false*, the division-by-zero error does not happen, but the error message is not displayed. Note that this statement is not equivalent to

```
if ((r1 != 0) && (r2 + 1/r1 != 0)
        && (r3 + 1/(r2+1/r1) != 0))
                r = 1/r1 + 1/(r2+1/r1)
                    + 1/(r3+1/(r2+1/r1));
```

```
else
      printf("division by zero\n");
```

since the error message is now displayed if any of the denominators is zero, which, of course, was the original intent.

3.7 MULTIWAY CONDITIONAL STATEMENT

There is a special form of the nested conditional statement comprising a sequence of cascaded if-else statements, where each if-else statement but the last has another if-else statement in its else-block. This construction occurs so often in practice that it merits separate discussion, and is often referred to as the *multiway conditional statement*.

The general format of this statement is as follows:

```
if ( expression-1 )
      statement-1
else if ( expression-2 )
      statement-2
else if ( expression-3 )
      statement-3

         .

         .

else if ( expression-(n-1) )
      statement-(n-1)
else
      statement-n
```

In a multiway conditional statement, conditional expressions are evaluated in order. If any of these expressions is found to be *true*, the statement associated with it is executed, and this terminates the whole chain. If none of the expressions is *true* the statement associated with the final else is executed. If no processing is required when none of the expressions is *true*, this else along with the statement associated with it can be omitted, or it may be used for error checking to catch an unanticipated condition. The multiway conditional statement is pictorially represented in Figure 3.5.

To illustrate the use of the multiway conditional statement, we reconsider the problem of printing Hare Rama! if the first of the given integers is larger than the second, Hare Krishna! if the second is larger than the first, and Hare Hare! if the two are equal. The desired program, using the multiway conditional statement, is as follows:

```
#include <stdio.h>

int main(void)
   {
     int v1, v2;

     scanf("%d %d", &v1, &v2);
```

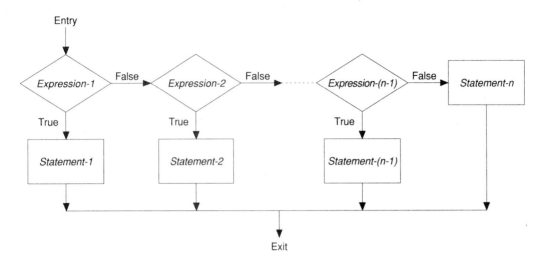

Figure 3.5. Multiway conditional statement

```
if (v1 > v2)
    printf("Hare Rama!\n");
else if (v2 > v1)
    printf("Hare Krishna!\n");
else
    printf("Hare Hare!\n");

return 0;
}
```

Compare this program with the programs for the same problem given in the previous section. This program is identical to the nested conditional version in which the nesting is in the else-block. However, this method of formatting improves the readability and makes it clear that a three-way decision is being made.

3.8   CONSTANT MULTIWAY CONDITIONAL STATEMENT

When each of the tests in a multiway if statement checks for a different value of the same expression, we have a *constant multiway decision*, which is coded using the switch statement. The general format of the switch statement is as follows:

```
switch ( expression )
   {
      case value-1 :
          statement-1
          break;
```

```
        case value-2 :
            statement-2
            break;
                    .
                    .
                    .
        case value-n :
            statement-n
            break;
        default :
            statement-x
            break;
    }
```

Expression must be an integral expression and the `case` values must be constant integral expressions.

When a `switch` statement is encountered, *expression* is evaluated and its value is successively compared with the `case` values *value-1*, *value-2*, ..., and *value-n*. If a `case` value, say *value-m*, matches the *expression* value, the *statement-m* associated with that `case` is executed. The `break` statement signals the end of the particular `case`, and causes the termination of the `switch` statement. If the value of the *expression* does not match any of the `case` values, *statement-x* associated with the `case` label `default` is executed. The label `default` is optional; if it is not there and if none of the `case` values matches, no action takes place. The `default` need not be after the last `case` value; cases and `default` can occur in any order.

The preceding `switch` statement is equivalent to the following `if-else` statement:

```
if ( expression == value-1 )
        statement-1
else if ( expression == value-2 )
        statement-2
                .
                .
                .
else if ( expression == value-n )
        statement-n
else
        statement-x
```

To illustrate the use of the `switch` statement, we give a program to evaluate simple expressions. The program recognizes only the binary operators +, -, *, and /. The program is as follows:

```
#include <stdio.h>

int main(void)
    {
    char    operator;
    float   operand1, operand2;
```

```c
    scanf("%f %c %f", &operand1, &operator, &operand2);

    switch (operator)
      {
        case '+':
            printf("%f\n", operand1 + operand2);
            break;
        case '-':
            printf("%f\n", operand1 - operand2);
            break;
        case '*':
            printf("%f\n", operand1 * operand2);
            break;
        case '/':
            printf("%f\n", operand1 / operand2);
            break;
        default:
            printf("Invalid Operator\n");
            break;
      }

    return 0;
  }
```

Following is the program for the same problem using a multiway if-else statement, instead of a switch statement:

```c
#include <stdio.h>

int main(void)
  {
    char    operator;
    float   operand1, operand2;

    scanf("%f %c %f", &operand1, &operator, &operand2);

    if (operator == '+')
        printf("%f\n", operand1 + operand2);
    else if (operator == '-')
        printf("%f\n", operand1 - operand2);
    else if (operator == '*')
        printf("%f\n", operand1 * operand2);
    else if (operator == '/')
        printf("%f\n", operand1 / operand2);
    else
        printf("Invalid Operator\n");

    return 0;
  }
```

Evidently, the `switch` statement is more convenient and readable than the multiway `if` statement.

No two case values should be the same in a `switch` statement. However, more than one `case` value can be associated with a set of statements by listing multiple `case` values before that particular set of program statements. It is not necessary to terminate each `case` with a `break` statement. Omitting the `break` statement from a particular `case` causes the execution to continue without regard for the `case` values and the `default` label. The `break` statement, although not logically necessary, should also be placed after the statement associated with `default` (or the last `case` value, if `default` is not at the end) as a matter of good programming practice. This practice avoids inadvertent introduction of a bug in the program when a `case` value and associated statements are added later on at the end of a `switch` statement.

To illustrate the above concepts, we extend the calculator program with several features. We will allow the use of _ as the symbol for subtraction, and x and X as the symbols for multiplication. We will perform subtraction by first negating the subtrahend and then adding it to the minuend. We will also ensure that the divisor is not zero in a division operation. The following is the new version of the program:

```c
#include <stdio.h>

int main(void)
  {
    char    operator;
    float   operand1, operand2;

    scanf("%f %c %f", &operand1, &operator, &operand2);

    switch (operator)
      {
        default:
            printf("Invalid Operator\n");
            break;
        case '-':
        case '_':
            operand2 = - operand2;
        case '+':
            printf("%f\n", operand1 + operand2);
            break;
        case '*':
        case 'x':
        case 'X':
            printf("%f\n", operand1 * operand2);
            break;
        case '/':
            if (!operand2)
              {
                printf("Division by Zero\n");
                return 1;
              }
```

```
        else
            printf("%f\n", operand1 / operand2);
        break;
    }

    return 0;
}
```

The alternative symbols for an operator are recognized by simply adding them as alternative `case` values for the same set of statements. Since `break` has been omitted in the `case` for subtraction, after the second operand has been negated, the statements associated with the `case` for addition are also executed and the negated second operand is added to the first operand. The `default` label has been put before any of the `case` values mainly for illustration purposes.

Observe the use of an `if-else` statement to check division by zero. As a matter of fact, any valid C statement can be included in a statement block associated with a `case` value. Thus, it is possible to nest `switch` statements within a `switch` statement. Also, a `switch` statement may be nested within other structures, such as an `if` statement. We will see several examples of such nesting later in the text.

We encourage you to write the preceding program using an `if-else` statement to appreciate the usefulness of the `switch` statement.

3.9   ILLUSTRATIVE EXAMPLES

We now give some programs that use selective structures to further illustrate the concepts introduced in this chapter.

Example 1

Chris and Casey have established the following minimum criteria for persons they will date:

Chris: *6 feet tall and very good looking,*
            or has $50,000 in bank and an imported car,
            or is an engineer or a doctor, and is decent looking.

Casey: *decent looking and owns a car,*
            or isn't broke and is very good looking,
            or is a doctor.

Write a program to decide whether a given person is suitable for dating Chris or Casey.

The relevant data are height, looks, bank balance, car, and job. Assume that this data for a person is keyed on one line as shown below:

height	looks	money	car	job
(inches)	(on a	($)	(0 = none	(0 = unemployed
	1–10		1 = old	1 = lawyer
	scale)		2 = new	2 = engineer
			3 = imported)	3 = doctor
				−1 = programmer)

The following program provides a solution to the problem:

```c
#include <stdio.h>

int main(void)
    {
    int   height, looks, money, car, job, tall,
          verygood_looking, decent_looking, rich,
          broke, any_car, imported_car, engineer,
          doctor, ok_for_Chris, ok_for_Casey;

    /*  Get person's attributes  */

    scanf("%d %d %d %d %d",
        &height, &looks, &money, &car, &job);

    /*  Set person's characteristics  */

    tall              =   height >= 6*12;
    verygood_looking  =   looks >= 9;
    decent_looking    =   looks >= 5;
    rich              =   money >= 50000;
    broke             =   money <= 0;
    any_car           =   car > 0;
    imported_car      =   car == 3;
    engineer          =   job == 2;
    doctor            =   job == 3;

    /*  Check for Chris  */

    ok_for_Chris = tall && verygood_looking ||
        rich && imported_car ||
        (engineer || doctor) && decent_looking;

    /*  Check for Casey  */

    ok_for_Casey = decent_looking && any_car   ||
        !broke && verygood_looking || doctor;
```

```
/* Print Decision */

ok_for_Chris ?
    printf("may date Chris\n") :
    printf("may not date Chris\n");

ok_for_Casey ?
    printf("may date Casey\n") :
    printf("may not date Casey\n");

return 0;
}
```

Sample Execution. If the input data were

```
71   6   40000   2   1
```

the program would print

```
may not date Chris
may date Casey
```

Example 2

A 1000-foot cable for a cable car is stretched between two towers, with a supporting tower midway between the two end towers. The velocity of the cable car depends on its position on the cable. When the cable car is within 30 feet of a tower, its velocity v in ft/sec is given by

$$v = 2.425 + 0.00175 \, d^2$$

where d is the distance in feet from the cable car to the nearest tower. If the cable car is not within 30 feet of a tower, its velocity is given by

$$v = 0.625 + 0.12 \, d - 0.00025 \, d^2$$

Write a program that reads the position of the cable car as the distance in feet from the first tower, and outputs the number of the nearest tower (1 = first, 2 = middle, 3 = end) and the velocity of the cable car.

The following program provides a solution to the problem:

Program

```
#include <stdio.h>

int main(void)
  {
    float   position, distance, velocity;
    int     tower;
    scanf("%f", &position);
```

```
/* Determine the nearest tower and the distance from it */

if (position <= 250)
   {
      tower = 1;
      distance = position;
   }
else if (position <= 750)
   {
      tower = 2;
      distance = position < 500 ?
                  500 - position : position - 500;
   }
else
   {
      tower = 3;
      distance = 1000 - position;
   }

/* Determine velocity */

if (distance <= 30)
      velocity = 2.425
                  + 0.00175 * distance * distance;
else
      velocity = 0.625 + 0.12 * distance
                  - 0.00025 * distance * distance;

printf("Nearest Tower: %d    Velocity: %f\n",
          tower, velocity);

return 0;
}
```

Sample Execution. If the car's position were 700 feet from the first tower, the program would print

```
Nearest Tower: 2    Velocity: 14.625000
```

On the other hand, if the position were 990 feet from the first tower, the program would print

```
Nearest Tower: 3    Velocity: 2.600000
```

Example 3

Write a program that reads the real coefficients a, b, and c (a ≠ 0) of the quadratic equation $ax^2 + bx + c = 0$ and computes its real roots.

The roots of the quadratic equation $ax^2 + bx + c = 0$, when a, b, and c are real and $a \neq 0$, are given by

$$(-b \pm \sqrt{b^2 - 4ac})/2a$$

The roots are real when the *discriminant* $b^2 - 4ac \geq 0$. If $b^2 - 4ac = 0$, the two real roots are equal, each being $-b/2a$.

The following program computes the desired roots:

```c
#include <math.h>
#include <stdio.h>

int main(void)
  {
    float a, b, c;
    float discriminant, root, root1, root2;

    scanf("%f %f %f", &a, &b, &c);

    if (a == 0)
      {
        printf("Not a quadratic equation\n");
        return 1;
      }

    discriminant = b*b - 4*a*c;

    if (discriminant < 0)
        printf("No real roots\n");
    else if (discriminant == 0)
      {
        root = -b / (2*a);
        printf("Two identical roots: %f\n", root);
      }

    else /* discriminant > 0 */
      {
        root1 = (-b + sqrt(discriminant)) / (2*a);
        root2 = (-b - sqrt(discriminant)) / (2*a);
        printf("Two distinct roots: %f %f\n",
                root1, root2);
      }

    return 0;
  }
```

Example 4

Write a program that reads three positive numbers a, b, c and determines whether they can form the three sides of a triangle. If yes, determine whether the triangle will be an obtuse-angle, or a right-angle, or an acute-angle triangle. If the triangle is an acute-angle triangle, determine further whether the triangle is equilateral, isosceles, or scalene.

Recall that

- *a,b,c* can form the three sides of a triangle if each is less than the sum of the other two;
- in an obtuse-angle triangle, if *b* is the side opposite to the obtuse angle, then $b^2 > a^2 + c^2$;
- in a right-angle triangle, if *b* is the side opposite to the right angle, then $b^2 = a^2 + c^2$;
- in an acute-angle triangle, the square of any side is less than the sum of the squares of the other two sides;
- all sides of an equilateral triangle are equal;
- two sides are equal in an isosceles triangle; and
- no sides of a scalene triangle are equal.

The following program provides a solution to the problem:

```
#include <stdio.h>
int main(void)
  {
    float a, b, c;
    int   triangle, obtuse, right_angle,
          equilateral, isosceles;

    scanf("%f %f %f", &a, &b, &c);

    triangle    =  a < b+c  &&  b < a+c  &&  c < a+b;
    obtuse      =  a*a >  b*b + c*c  ||
                   b*b >  a*a + c*c  ||
                   c*c >  a*a + b*b  ;
    right_angle =  a*a == b*b + c*c  ||
                   b*b == a*a + c*c  ||
                   c*c == a*a + b*b  ;
    equilateral =  a == b  &&  b == c;
    isosceles   =  a == b  ||  b == c  || c == a;

    if (! triangle)
        printf("not a triangle\n");
    else if (obtuse)
        printf("obtuse angle triangle\n");
    else if (right_angle)
        printf("right angle triangle\n");
    else
        {
        printf("acute angle triangle\n");
        if (equilateral)
            printf("equilateral triangle\n");
        else if (isosceles)
            printf("isosceles triangle\n");
        else
            printf("scalene triangle\n");
        }

    return 0;
  }
```

Example 5

An electronic component vendor supplies three products: transistors, resistors, and capacitors. The vendor gives a discount of 10% on orders for transistors if the order is for more than $1000. On orders of more than $100 for resistors, a discount of 5% is given, and a discount of 10% is given on orders for capacitors of value more than $500. Assume that the numeric codes 1, 2, and 3 are used for transistors, capacitors, and resistors respectively. Write a program that reads the product code and the order amount, and prints out the net amount that the customer is required to pay after discount.

The program given below provides a solution to the problem.

```c
#include <stdio.h>
#define   TRANSISTOR   1
#define   RESISTOR     2
#define   CAPACITOR    3

int main(void)
   {
     int     code;
     float   order, discount;

     scanf("%d %f", &code, &order);

     switch(code)
       {
         case TRANSISTOR:
             discount = (order > 1000)  ? 0.1  : 0;
             break;
         case RESISTOR:
             discount = (order > 100)   ? 0.05 : 0;
             break;
         case CAPACITOR:
             discount = (order > 500)   ? 0.1  : 0;
             break;
         default:
             printf("Invalid Product Code\n");
             return 1;
       }

     printf("Net Payment = %f\n",
             order - discount * order);

     return 0;
   }
```

Exercises 3

1. For the following sets of values:

    i. i = 3, j = 2, k = 1   *ii.* i = -3, j = -2, k = -1

    iii. i = 1, j = 0, k = 0   *iv.* i = 0, j = 1, k = 0

    what value do the following expressions have?

    a. i >= j >= k

    b. i >= j && j >= k

2. Given that i = 2, j = 3, and k = 6, what value do the following expressions have?

    a. i > j && i*j <= k   *b.* i*j <= k && i > j

    c. !(i > j) && i*j <= k   *d.* !(i*j <= k) && i > j

    e. i > j || i*j <= k   *f.* i*j <= k || i > j

    g. !(i > j) || i*j <= k   *h.* !(i*j <= k) || i > j

    i. !(i > j) && !(i*j <= k)   *j.* !(i > j) || !(i*j <= k)

    k. i > j && i <= k || i*j <= k *l.* i > j && (i <= k || i*j <= k)

3. For the following sets of values:

    i. i = j = 0   *ii.* i = 1, j = -1

    iii. i = 1, j = 0   *iv.* i = 0, j = -1

    what value do the following expressions have?

    a. ((i > 0) && (j < 0)) || (!(i > 0) && !(j < 0))

    b. ((i > 0) && !(j < 0)) || (!(i > 0) && (j < 0))

4. For the following sets of values:

	i	ii	iii	iv	v	vi	vii	viii
u =	0	0	0	0	1	1	1	1
v =	0	0	1	1	0	0	1	1
w =	0	1	0	1	0	1	0	1

    what value do the following expressions have?

    a. --u || --v && --w

    b. --u && --v || --w

    What value will u, v, and w have after each evaluation?

5. For the following sets of values:

	i	ii	iii	iv	v	vi	vii	viii
u =	0	0	1	-1	1	-1	1	-1
v =	1	-1	0	0	-1	1	1	-1

    what value do the following expressions have?

    a. (u > v ? u : v) / (u < v ? (!u ? v : u) : (v ? v : u))

    b. (u < v ? u : v) / (u > v ? (u ? u : v) : (!v ? u : v))

6. For the following sets of values:

	i	ii	iii	iv
u =	0	0	1	1
v =	0	1	0	1

what value do the following expressions have?

a. u ? v ? u++ : v++ : u++

b. v ? v++ : u ? u++ : v++

What value will u and v have after each evaluation?

7. Assuming z to be initially 0, for the following sets of values:

	i	ii	iii	iv
x =	0	0	1	1
y =	0	1	0	1

what value will z have after the execution of each of the following program fragments:

a.
```
if (x)
    if (y)
        z = 1;
    else
        z = 2;
```

b.
```
if (x) {
    if (y)
        z = 1;}
    else
        z = 2;
```

c.
```
if (x);
    if (y)
        z = 1;
    else
        z = 2;
```

d.
```
if (x
    && y)
        z = 1;
    else
        z = 2;
```

8. Consider the nested if statement:

```
if (i)
    if (j)
        if (k) humpty();
        else;
    else;
else
    if (j)
        if (k) dumpty();
        else    bumpty();
    else;
```

Which of the following nested if statements are equivalent to the above statement:

a.
```
if (i && j && k) humpty();
else if (j && k) dumpty();
else bumpty();
```

b.
```
if (i && j && k) humpty();
else if (!i && j && k) dumpty();
else if (!i && j && !k) bumpty();
```

c.
```
if (j)
    if (i && k) humpty();
    else if (!i && k) dumpty();
    else if(!i && !k) bumpty();
```

9. Write a logical expression that is true,

   a. if bug and debug are true and rebug is false.

   b. if bug is true and at least one of debug or rebug is true.

   c. if exactly one of bug and debug is true.

   d. if both bug and debug are true, or both are false.

10. Write a C statement that prints

   a. oof if foo -1 ≤ foo ≤ +1.

   b. oops if a is greater than b and not less than c, or if a is not greater than d and not equal to e .

   c. cannot buy if the car costs more than $25,000 or it gives less than 10 miles per gallon.

   d. hotcar if the car is not more than 2 years old, runs at least 25 miles per gallon, and costs less than $5000.

11. Write a C statement that

   a. classifies a given character as an uppercase letter, a lowercase letter, a digit, or a special character.

   b. determines whether the given year is a leap year. (A year divisible by 4 is a leap year, but if it is also divisible by 100, then it is not, unless it is divisible by 400.)

12. A function f is defined as follows:

   $$f(x) = ax^3 - bx^2 + cx - d, \qquad \text{if } x > k$$
   $$f(x) = 0, \qquad \text{if } x = k$$
   $$f(x) = -ax^3 + bx^2 - cx + d, \qquad \text{if } x < k$$

   Write a program that reads the values of a, b, c, d, k, and x, and prints the value of $f(x)$.

13. Your meteorologist friend has asked you to write a temperature conversion program. The program should read the temperature measured and the type of scale used in the measurement (F for Fahrenheit and C for Celsius), and convert it to the other scale.

14. In a simple thin lens, the optical axis is the line through the center of the lens joining the centers of curvature of the two surfaces. If the lens is used to form an image of an object, then the relation

   $$\frac{1}{a} + \frac{1}{a'} = \frac{1}{f}$$

   holds, when a, the distance from object to lens, a', the distance from image to lens, and f, the principal focal length of the lens, are measured along the optical axis. Note that if $a = \infty$ then $a' = f$, and if $a = f$ then $a' = \infty$.

   Write a program that accepts the focal length of the lens and the position of the object, and prints out the position of the image.

15. A formula for computing the day of the week was developed by a Reverend Zeller. Let m be the month of the year, starting with March as $m = 1$ with January and February being months 11 and 12 of the previous year, d the day of the month, y the year of the century, and c the previous century. For example, for April 1, 1988, $m = 2$, $d = 1$, $y = 88$, and $c = 19$. The day of the week on which a given date falls is computed as follows:

i. Take the integer part of the ratio $(13m - 1)/5$. Call it A.

ii. Take the integer part of the ratio $y/4$. Call it B.

iii. Take the integer part of the ratio $c/4$. Call it C.

iv. Compute $D = A + B + C + d + y - 2c$.

v. Obtain the remainder R of the division of D by 7.

vi. If R is 0, the day is Sunday, if R is 1, the day is Monday, etc.

Write a program that accepts a date as input and determines the day of the week.

16. The Confusion Unlimited has three investment schemes: simple interest of 20%, compound interest of 18% compounded annually, and compound interest of 15% compounded every six months. Write a program that reads the amount and the time for which the money is to be invested, and advises the best choice of scheme.

17. The commission on a salesman's total sales is as follows:

- Sales < \$100 => No commission.
- \$100 ≤ Sales < \$1000 => Commission = 10% of sales.
- Sales ≥ \$1000 => Commission = \$100 + 12% of sales above \$1000.

Write a program that reads sales and prints out the salesman's commission.

18. The Funny Bank offers the following interest rates for fixed deposits:

- Deposit < \$1000 for 5 or more years => rate is 6% compounded annually.
- Deposit ≥ \$1000 for 5 or more years => rate is 7% compounded annually.
- Deposit ≥ \$5000 for 5 or more years => rate is 8% compounded annually.
- Deposit > \$10,000 => rate is 10% compounded annually.
- Deposit for more than 10 years => rate is 10% compounded every six months.
- \$5000 ≤ Deposit ≤ \$10,000 for less than 5 years => rate is 5% compounded annually.
- Deposit < \$5000 for less than 5 years => rate is simple annual interest of 5%.

Write a program that reads a customer's deposit and the number of years for which the deposit is being made, and computes the interest that the customer will earn from this investment.

19. Anonymous Inc. has classified its employees into four categories, and has the following salary policy:

Class 1:	\$10 per hour for regular hours and no overtime.
Class 2 or 3:	\$7 per hour for regular hours, and overtime hours at the rate of 1.5 times the rate for the regular hours.
Class 4:	\$5 per hour for regular hours, and overtime hours at the rate of 2.0 times the rate for the regular hours for overtime hours, up to a time equal to regular hours. The rate is 2.5 times the regular rate for excess overtime hours.

Write a program that reads an employee's classification and regular and overtime hours and prints the employee's pay. An error message should be printed if a classification number other than 1, 2, 3, or 4 is read.

20. A semiconductor manufacturer sells three types of microprocessors: 8-bit, 16-bit, and 32-bit. It differentiates between three types of customers: industrial, government, and university. It has the following discount policy that depends on the type of microprocessor, the amount of the order, and the type of customer:

For 32-bit microprocessors, if the order is for less than \$50,000, allow 5% discount to industrial customers and 6.5% discount to government agencies. If the order is \$50,000 or more, discounts of 7.5% and 8.5% are given to industrial customers and government agencies respectively. A discount of 10% is given to both industrial customers and government agencies if the order is more than $100,000. Universities get a discount of 7.5% irrespective of the amount of order. For 16-bit microprocessors, no discount is given for orders less than $10,000. For orders of $10,000 or more, 5% discount is given to industrial customers and universities, and 6% discount to government agencies. For 8-bit microprocessors, a flat discount of 10% is given to all three types of customers for any order.

Write a program that reads the type of the customer, the type of the product, and the amount of the order, and prints the net amount payable by the customer.

4 Repetitive Structure

We have discussed so far the first two of the three control structures: sequential, selective, and repetitive. The third structure, namely the *repetitive structure*, also known as the *iterative structure* or *program loop*, is introduced in this chapter.

The repetitive structure allows a sequence of program statements to be executed several times even though those statements appear only once in the program. It consists of an *entry point* that may include initialization of certain variables, a *loop continuation condition*, a *loop body*, and an *exit point*, as illustrated in Figure 4.1.

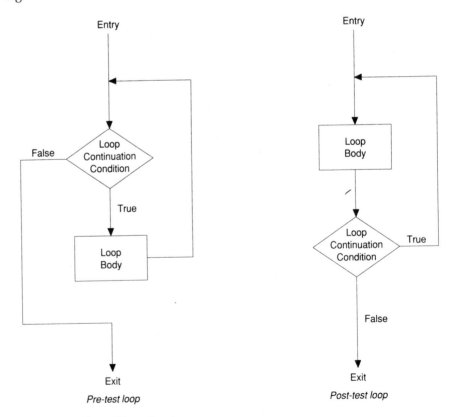

Figure 4.1. Repetitive structure

A repetitive structure must always be entered at the entry point to ensure that the appropriate initialization takes place. The loop body consists of statements that are normally executed several times. The exit point is the first statement following the loop body.

The number of repetitions in a repetitive structure is controlled by a *loop continuation condition*, which is tested once for each execution of the loop body. This condition normally involves testing the value of a *loop control variable* whose value is changed every time the loop body is executed. For example, if the statements to be repetitively executed consist of reading input data, processing it, and writing out the results, then the repetitive execution may be terminated by checking for the end-of-file condition. Another example is the use of a counter to control the number of times a loop body is executed. The value of the counter is changed, usually by 1, for every execution of the loop body, and when the counter attains a predetermined value, the repetition is terminated.

The loop continuation condition may be tested before the loop body is executed, in which case the loop is referred to as a *pre-test* loop, or the condition may be tested after the execution of the loop body, in which case the loop is referred to as a *post-test* loop. Note that the body of a post-test loop is always executed at least once; the body of a pre-test loop may possibly never be executed.

4.1 OVERVIEW

Consider the program for finding the sum of the first *n* terms of the series

$$\frac{1}{1} + \frac{1}{2} + \frac{1}{3} + \frac{1}{4} + \cdots$$

Here is an algorithm for solving this problem:

1. Read the value of *n*.
2. Initialize an accumulator *sum* to 0.
3. Repeat step (4) *n* times.
4. In the *i*th iteration, determine the value of the term $1/i$, and add it to *sum*. Thus, $1/1$ is added to *sum* in the 1st iteration, $1/2$ in the 2nd iteration, $1/3$ in the 3rd iteration, etc.
5. Print *sum*.

Here is a program for this problem that uses a `while` loop for iteration:

```
#include <stdio.h>

int main(void)
   {
    int     i, n;
    float   sum;

    scanf("%d", &n);   /* read n */
    i = 1;             /* initialize the loop control variable i */
    sum = 0;           /* initialize the accumulator sum */
```

```
   while (i <= n)      /* iterate n times */
     {
       sum += 1.0/i;/* add the ith term to sum */
       i++;             /* increment the loop control variable i */
     }

   printf("sum = %f\n", sum); /* print sum */

   return 0;           /* successful completion */
  }
```

The first three statements

```
scanf("%d", &n);     /* read n */
i = 1;               /* initialize the loop control variable i */
sum = 0;             /* initialize the accumulator sum */
```

read the value of n, initialize the loop control variable i to 1, and set the accumulator sum to 0. These statements must be executed before the loop execution for proper initializations.

The parenthesized expression following the keyword while

```
i <= n
```

is the loop continuation condition. The loop body enclosed within braces and consisting of the statements

```
sum += 1.0/i;      /* add the ith term to sum */
i++;               /* increment the loop control variable i */
```

is repeatedly executed as long as the loop continuation condition is true, i.e., as long as i is not more than n. In the ith execution of the loop body, the ith term of the series $1/i$ is added to sum. Thus, after i iterations, sum contains the sum of the first i terms of the given series.

Every execution of the loop body also increments the value of the loop control variable i by 1. Eventually, i becomes n+1, the loop continuation condition becomes false, and the loop execution is terminated. Thus, the loop body is executed a total of n times, and the terms $1/1, 1/2, \ldots, 1/n$ are accumulated in sum in successive iterations, giving the desired sum of the series.

Once the loop continuation condition becomes false, the program control transfers to the first statement following the loop body

```
printf("sum = %f\n", sum);/* print sum */
```

and sum is printed.

Besides the while loop, C also provides do-while and for loops to express repetitive structures. Here is the program for the same problem, written using a for loop.

```
#include <stdio.h>

int main(void)
  {
    int    i, n;
    float  sum;
```

```
scanf("%d", &n);

for (i = 1, sum = 0; i <= n; i++)
    sum += 1.0/i;

printf("sum = %f\n", sum);

return 0;
}
```

We will now study the various looping constructs in detail.

4.2 `while` LOOP

The `while` loop is a pre-test loop, whose general form is:

loop initialization

```
while ( expression )
        statement-1
```

statement-2

The *loop initialization* defines the entry point of the structure. In the `while` statement, *expression* provides the loop continuation condition, and *statement-1* is any valid simple or compound C statement that constitutes the loop body. *Statement-2* is the exit point of the structure.

When the `while` statement is encountered, *expression* is evaluated. If *expression* evaluates to a nonzero value (*true*), *statement-1* is executed. *Expression* is then again evaluated, and if the result of this evaluation is nonzero, *statement-1* is again executed. This process continues until the result of *expression* evaluation becomes zero (*false*). The iteration is then terminated and the program execution continues from *statement-2*. If the result of *expression* evaluation is zero at the very outset, *statement-1* is not executed at all and the program control immediately transfers to *statement-2*.

Suppose we are interested in reading one character at a time from the standard input and echoing it on the standard output. At the end, we also want to output the total number of characters echoed. The standard I/O library provides a function `getchar` that reads a character from the standard input, and another function `putchar` that writes it to the standard output (see Chapter 10). Here is a `while` loop that uses these functions and accomplishes the desired task:

```
int ch, count;

count = 0;
ch = getchar();
```

```
while (ch != EOF)
  {
    putchar(ch);
    count++;
    ch = getchar();
  }

printf("total characters echoed = %d\n", count);
```

We begin by initializing to zero a counter `count` in which we will accumulate the count of the characters echoed, and use `getchar` to read the first character from the standard input into the loop control variable `ch`. These two statements together are the loop initialization statements.

Immediately following the keyword `while` is the loop continuation condition that tests the value of the loop control variable `ch` to determine whether the last `getchar` has resulted in a successful read from input or whether the end of input was reached. As long as a character has been successfully read, the loop body is repetitively executed. The loop body consists of echoing the last character read using `putchar`, incrementing `count`, and getting the next character from input into `ch` using `getchar`. When the end of input is reached, `getchar` returns `EOF` (end-of-file), the loop continuation condition becomes false, and the control transfers to the `printf` statement, which is the exit point of this repetitive structure. The `printf` statement outputs the total number of characters echoed.

The preceding `while` loop contains the duplicated code: `ch = getchar();`. Here is a better alternative:

```
int ch, count;

count = 0;

while ((ch = getchar()) != EOF)
  {
    putchar(ch);
    count++;
  }

printf("total characters echoed = %d\n", count);
```

This version avoids code duplication by embedding the call to `getchar` in the loop continuation condition. This form of embedding is a popular C idiom, and it works because assignment is an expression whose value is the same as that of the variable on the left of the assignment operator after the assignment. The parentheses surrounding the assignment expression `ch = getchar()` are necessary since the precedence of the assignment operator is lower than that of the relational operators.

The function `getchar` returns an `int`, and not a `char`. The reason for it has to do with detecting the end of input. When the end of input is detected, `getchar` returns `EOF`, the conventional value for which is -1. Since C does not require that a `char` be able to hold a signed quantity, `getchar` is made to return an `int`. For the same reason, a variable that holds the value returned by getchar, such as ch in the example, is declared to be of type int. The end of input in a data file is reached when the file runs out of data. The end of input on a terminal can be signaled by typing *ctrl-d* on a UNIX machine and *ctrl-z* on a DOS machine.

4.2.1 Infinite Loop

If one is not careful, one could write a loop that never terminates — an *infinite loop*. Consider, for example, the following while loop that determines the sum of integers from 1 to n for a user-specified value of n:

```
int n, sum = 0;

scanf("%d", &n);
while (n != 0)
   {
     sum += n;
     n--;
   }
printf("sum = %d\n", sum);
```

This loop correctly determines the desired sum as long as the user provides a nonnegative value for n. However, if a negative value is provided as input, n will keep decreasing and never become zero. Consequently, the loop continuation condition will not become false and the loop body will be repeatedly executed until interrupted by the user. Program interruption is system-dependent — on some machines, typing *cntrl-c* interrupts the executing program, while others use the delete, rubout, or break key for this purpose.

There are several ways in which you can guard against the possibility of an infinite loop. In the preceding example, you may test that the user has provided a positive value for n immediately after reading it. Another alternative is to change the loop continuation condition to

```
n >= 0
```

The sum of the first n integers will now be printed as 0 for any negative value of n.

A similar problem could arise if the loop continuation condition is a floating-point expression. Consider the following while loop that prints a temperature conversion table from degrees Celsius into degrees Fahrenheit:

```
float celsius = 0;
while (celsius != 1.0)
   {
     printf("%f  %f\n", celsius, 1.8 * celsius + 32);
     celsius += 0.005;
   }
```

The problem here is that a floating-point value such as 0.005 is represented inside a computer as an approximation of 0.005, and may not exactly equal 0.005. The loop continuation test in this example can be made more robust by changing it to

```
celsius <= 1.0
```

A common programming error that leads to an infinite loop is the inadvertent use of the assignment operator = in place of the equality operator == in the loop continuation condition. A loop such as

```
while(more = 1)
    {
            .
            .
            .
        more = should_i_continue();
    }
```

will never terminate because, irrespective of the value assigned to more by should_i_continue, the loop continuation condition more = 1 is always satisfied since its value is 1.

Forgetting to change the value of the loop continuation variable inside the loop body is another common error that results in an infinite loop. Thus, the loop

```
int i = 0, sum = 0, n;
while(i < 25)
    {
        scanf("%d", &n);
        sum += n;
    }
```

will never terminate because the loop body does not change the value of i.

Infinite loops of the form

```
while ( 1 )
```

   statement

are sometimes deliberately used. In Section 4.6.1, we will see the use of such constructions.

We have used only while loops in the preceding examples to illustrate infinite looping, but infinite loops also occur in do-while or for loops for identical reasons.

4.2.2 Illustrative Examples

We now give some programs to illustrate the use of while loops.

Example 1
Write a program that determines what fraction of a given text consists of vowels.

The following program provides a solution to the problem:

```
#include <stdio.h>

int main(void)
  {
    int   c, vowel, vowelcnt, charcnt;

    vowelcnt = charcnt = 0;

    while ((c = getchar()) != EOF)
      {
        /* if c is an uppercase letter,
            convert it into a lowercase letter */
        c = (c >= 'A' && c <= 'Z') ?
              (c - 'A' + 'a') : c;

        /* test if c is a vowel */
        vowel = c == 'a' || c == 'e' ||
                c == 'i' || c == 'o' || c == 'u';

        if (vowel) vowelcnt++;
        charcnt++;
      }

    printf("vowels = %f\n",
            (float)vowelcnt/charcnt);

    return 0;
  }
```

One character at a time is read from input until the end of file is reached. If the character read is an uppercase letter, it is converted into a lowercase letter. This conversion simplifies the test that the character read is a vowel, in that the test now becomes a disjunction of five, rather than ten, relational expressions. If the character read is indeed a vowel, the count of vowels vowelcnt is incremented. The count of total characters read charcnt is incremented in either case. After the complete text has been processed, vowelcnt is divided by charcnt to determine the fraction of vowels in the input text.

Example 2

Write a program that determines the greatest common divisor of two positive integers using the Euclidean algorithm.

The Euclidean algorithm begins by dividing the first number by the second and retaining the remainder. At each successive stage, the previous divisor is divided by the previous remainder. The algorithm terminates when the remainder becomes zero. The greatest common divisor is the last nonzero remainder, or the last divisor. For example, the algorithm finds 7 to be the greatest common divisor of 119 and 35 as follows:

i	j	remainder(i, j)
119	35	14
35	14	7
14	7	0

The following program implements the Euclidean algorithm:

```
#include <stdio.h>
int main(void)
  {
    int dividend, divisor, remainder;

    scanf("%d %d", &dividend, &divisor);
    if (dividend <= 0 || divisor <= 0)
      {
        printf("non-positive values in input\n");
        return 1;
      }

    while((remainder = dividend % divisor) != 0)
      {
        dividend = divisor;
        divisor = remainder;
      }

    printf("%d\n", divisor);

    return 0;
  }
```

4.3 `do-while` LOOP

The `do-while` loop is a post-test loop, whose general form is:

loop initialization

```
do
```
    statement-1
```
while ( expression );
```

statement-2

As with the `while` loop, the *loop initialization* statement defines the entry point of the structure, *expression* provides the loop continuation condition, *statement-1* is any valid simple or compound C statement that constitutes the loop body, and *statement-2* is the exit point of the structure.

When the keyword do is encountered, *statement-1* is executed, followed by an evaluation of *expression*. If the result of the expression evaluation is nonzero, *statement-1* is again executed. This process continues until the result of the expression evaluation becomes zero. The iteration is then terminated and the program execution continues from *statement-2*. If the result of the expression evaluation is zero at the very outset, the program control transfers to *statement-2*. Thus, in this case, *statement-1* is executed only once.

Consider, for example, the following do-while loop:

```c
int number, digits, sum;

digits = sum = 0;
scanf("%d", &number);

do
  {
    sum += number % 10;
    number /= 10;
    digits++;
  }
while (number > 0);

printf("number of digits = %d  sum = %d\n",
        digits, sum);
```

Here we are interested in determining the number of digits and their sum in a nonnegative decimal integer of arbitrary length. These two quantities will be accumulated in variables digits and sum respectively, which are initially set to zero. Then the number is read. These two statements constitute the loop initialization.

The keywords do and while bracket the loop body. In each iteration of the loop, first the right-most digit of the number is extracted and added to sum, and then this digit is truncated from the number. Finally, the count of number of digits is incremented. The test that the number has not become zero provides the loop continuation condition. Thus, number is the loop control variable in this structure. Note that the loop would be executed as many times as the number of digits in number.

Once the loop continuation condition becomes false, the program control transfers to the printf statement, which is the exit statement of the structure. The printf statement outputs the desired values.

. Observe that the preceding program fragment computes the correct results when the input number is 0. Try writing this program using a while loop, and you would discover that you may have to resort to special processing to handle the case of 0 correctly.

4.3.1 Illustrative Examples

We now give some programs to illustrate the use of do-while loops.

Example 1

The present populations of two countries, Curvedland and Flatland, are 817 million and 1.088 billion respectively. Their rates of population growth are 2.1% and 1.3% respectively. Write a program that determines the number of years until the population of Curvedland will exceed that of Flatland.

The following program provides a solution to the problem:

```
#include <stdio.h>
#define   CURVED_POPULATION   0.817
#define   FLAT_POPULATION     1.088
#define   CURVED_GROWTH       1.021
#define   FLAT_GROWTH         1.013

int main(void)

  {
    float   curvedland, flatland;
    int     years;

    curvedland = CURVED_POPULATION;
    flatland = FLAT_POPULATION;
    years = 0;

    do
      {
        curvedland *= CURVED_GROWTH;
        flatland *= FLAT_GROWTH;
        years++;
      }
    while (curvedland <= flatland);

    printf("%d\n", years);

    return 0;
  }
```

Example 2

Mega Minis sells a laptop computer for $1000, or on monthly installments of $47.08 till the principal and interest are fully paid. Every month, 1% interest is charged on the unpaid principal. The monthly installment is first used towards the payment of interest, and the remaining money is used for decreasing the principal. The following table shows some sample calculations:

Month	Interest Paid	Principal Paid	Unpaid Principal
1	10.00	37.08	962.92
2	9.63	37.45	925.47
3	9.25	37.83	887.64

Write a program to compute the number of monthly installments and the total interest till the principal is fully paid.

The following program provides a solution to the problem:

```c
#include <stdio.h>

int main(void)
  {
    float   principal, installment, rate,
            interest, total_interest;
    int     months;

    scanf("%f %f %f", &principal, &installment, &rate);
    if (installment <= principal*rate)
      {
        printf("Installment must exceed interest\n");
        return 1;
      }

    total_interest = months = 0;

    do
      {
        interest = rate * principal;
        principal -= installment - interest;
        total_interest += interest;
        months++;
      }
    while (principal > 0);

    printf("Number of Installments = %d\n", months);
    printf("Total Interest = %f\n", total_interest);

    return 0;
  }
```

What could happen if we did not check before the loop execution that `installment` was more than `principal*rate`?

4.4 `for` LOOP

The `for` loop is a very flexible and powerful repetitive structure. The general format of this structure is:

for (*expression-1; expression-2; expression-3*)
        statement-1

statement-2

Expression-1 defines the entry point of the structure and is used to perform loop initializations. *Expression-2* provides the loop continuation condition. *Statement-1* is any valid simple or compound C statement, whose execution is followed by an evaluation of *expression-3*. *Statement-1* together with *expression-3* constitute the loop body. *Statement-1* is also referred to as the *scope* of the `for` statement. *Expression-3* is the *reinitialization expression,* and is generally used to alter the value of the loop variables before the next iteration begins. *Statement-2* is the exit point of the structure.

Consider, for example, the following `for` loop:

```
int i, sum = 0;

for (i = 1; i <= n; i++)
    sum += i;

printf("%d\n", sum);
```

We wish to determine the `sum` of integers from 1 to n. The loop control variable i is used to successively generate integers from 1 to n. First, the integer 1 is generated by initializing i to 1. Before executing the loop body, it is checked that i has not become greater than n. In each execution of the loop body, the current value of i is added to sum, and i is incremented to the next integer. The loop terminates when i becomes n+1, and the control transfers to the exit point of the structure that prints the desired result.

A `for` loop is equivalent to the following `while` loop:

```
expression-1;

while ( expression-2 )
   {
     statement-1
     expression-3;
   }

statement-2
```

Thus, the preceding `for` loop for determining the sum of integers from 1 to n is equivalent to the following `while` loop:

```
i = 1;

while (i <= n)
   {
     sum += i;
     i++;
   }

printf("%d\n", sum);
```

All the three expressions within parentheses in the `for` loop are optional and hence may be omitted. However, the two semicolons separating the expressions and the parentheses surrounding them must be provided. *Expression-2*, when omitted, is assumed to evaluate to true, and the resulting loop is infinite, presumably to be broken by some statement within the loop body. *Expression-1* is omitted when initialization is not required, or is made before the loop is entered. *Expression-3* is omitted when the reinitialization required for the next execution of the loop body is done as part of *statement-1*. Thus, the preceding for loop can also be written as

```
i = 1;
for ( ;  i <= n; )
   {
      sum += i;
      i++;
   }

printf("%d\n", sum);
```

Similarly,

```
for ( ; ; )
      statement
```

sets up an infinite loop because *expression-2* has been omitted and hence the loop continuation condition is always true.

A do-while loop of the form

```
do
   {
      statement
   }
while ( expression );
```

can be simulated by a for loop of the form

```
for ( x=1; x; x=(expression) )
      statement
```

where x is a dummy variable of the same type as the type of the *expression* that is initially set to nonzero, causing a first iteration, and then set to the loop continuation expression of the do-while at the end of each iteration. The variable x should not be otherwise used in the program. For example, consider the following do-while loop used in the previous section for determining the number of digits and their sum in a nonnegative decimal integer:

```
do
   {
      sum += number % 10;
      number /= 10;
      digits++;
   }
while (number != 0);
```

It can be equivalently written as

```
for (i = 1; i; i = (number != 0) )
  {
    sum += number % 10;
    number /= 10;
    digits++;
  }
```

The previous `for` loop can be further simplified to

```
for (i = 1; i; i = number)
  {
    sum += number % 10;
    number /= 10;
    digits++;
  }
```

4.4.1 Illustrative Examples

We now give some programs to illustrate the use of `for` loops.

Example 1

Write a program that reads a positive integer and classifies it as being deficient, perfect, or abundant.

The *proper* divisors of a positive integer N are those integers that are less than N and divide N evenly. A positive integer is said to be a *deficient, perfect,* or *abundant* number as the sum of its proper divisors is less than, equal to, or greater than the number. For example, 4 is deficient since its divisors are 1 and 2, and 1+2 < 4; 6 is perfect since 1+2+3 = 6; 12 is abundant since 1+2+3+4+6 > 12.

The following program provides a solution to the problem:

```
#include <stdio.h>

int main(void)
  {
    int n, i, divisor_sum = 0;

    scanf("%d", &n);

    for (i=1; i < n; i++)
        if (n % i == 0)  divisor_sum += i;

    if (divisor_sum < n)
        printf("%d is deficient\n", n);
    else if (divisor_sum > n)
        printf("%d is abundant\n", n);
    else
        printf("%d is perfect\n", n);

    return 0;
  }
```

Example 2

Write a program that reads an integer N and computes N!.

The following program provides a solution to the problem:

```c
#include <stdio.h>

int main(void)
  {
    int  number, factorial;

    do
      {
        printf("nonnegative number please\n");
        scanf("%d", &number);
      }
    while (number < 0);

    for (factorial = 1; number > 0; number--)
        factorial *= number;

    printf("%d\n", factorial);

    return 0;
  }
```

The program insists that the user provide a nonnegative integer before proceeding to calculate its factorial. Note that if `number` is 0, the body of the `for` loop would not be executed, and the program would correctly output 1 as the value of 0!.

4.5 NESTED LOOPS

Several loops may be used within the same program. Loops may follow one another as we have seen in the previous illustrative example. Loops may also be *nested*; that is, a loop may contain other loops within its body. There is no limit on the number of loops that can be nested or the depth of nesting.

When nesting one loop inside another, the inner loop must be entirely contained within the body of the outer loop and each loop must have its own unique loop continuation expression. However, the loops may have the same exit point. The inner loop is indented with respect to the outer loop for better readability.

As an example, consider the problem of printing the interest table for the simple interest formula `interest = principal * rate * years`, where the `principal` amount is specified as the symbolic constant `PRINCIPAL`, the `rate` of annual interest ranges from 10 to 15 percent in increments of 0.5 percent, and the number of `years` of the loan ranges from 1 to 5 years in increments of 1 year. The entries for different interest rates are required to be separated by a blank line.

The kernel of a program for this problem using nested loops is as follows:

```
for (rate = 10; rate <= 15; rate += 0.5)
  {
    for (years = 1; years <= 5; years++)
      {
        interest = PRINCIPAL * (rate/100) * years;
        printf("%f %f %d %f\n",
               PRINCIPAL, rate, years, interest);
      }
    printf("\n"); /* exit point for the inner years loop */
  }

/* exit point for the outer rate loop */
```

The program involves two `for` loops; the inner is nested in the outer one. When the first `for` is encountered, the value of `rate` is set to 10. The loop continuation condition of the outer `rate` loop is tested, and is found to be true, and the execution of its loop body begins. The inner `for` is encountered, and the value of `years` is set to 1. Next, the loop continuation condition of the inner `years` loop is tested, and is found to be true, and the execution of its loop body begins. Thus, the `interest` is computed and the first table entry gets printed. The program control now returns to the reinitialization expression of the inner loop, causing `years` to be incremented by 1. The loop continuation expression of the inner loop is still true, and one more table entry gets printed. This process continues until `years` becomes 6 and the table entries for $1000 for the interest rate of 10% for 1 through 5 years have been printed. At this stage, the loop continuation expression of the inner loop becomes false, and the program control transfers to the exit point of the inner loop, causing a blank line to be printed.

The printing of a blank line is the last statement within the scope of the outer `for`, and therefore the reinitialization expression of the outer loop is evaluated next, so that `rate` is increased by 0.5. The loop continuation expression of the outer loop is still true, and hence the body of the outer loop is again executed. This means that once again the inner loop becomes active, its loop variable `years` is reset to 1, and the inner loop prints five more table entries, this time for the interest rate of 10.5% for 1 through 5 years. A blank line is then printed, the interest rate is reinitialized, and the execution of the outer loop continues as before. Eventually, the `rate` increases to 15.5 and the outer loop terminates.

Let us determine the number of table entries and blank lines printed during the whole process. For one complete execution of the inner loop, 5 table entries are printed. The outer loop is executed 11 times, and in each execution of the outer loop, the inner loop is executed once followed by a printing of a blank line. Thus, a total of 55 table entries and 11 blank lines are printed.

As an example of a triply nested loop, let us extend the previous problem to additionally require that the interest table is to be printed for `principal` amounts ranging from $1000 to $10,000 in increments of $1000. As before, the `rate` of annual interest ranges from 10 to 15 percent in increments of 0.5 percent, and the number of `years` of the loan ranges from 1 to 5 years in increments of 1 year. The entries for different interest rates for the same principal amount are required to be separated by a blank line, and for different principal amounts by two blank lines.

The kernel of a program for this problem is as follows:

```
for (principal = 1000;
     principal <= 10000; principal += 1000)
  {
    for (rate = 10; rate <= 15; rate += 0.5)
      {
        for (years = 1; years <= 5; years++)
          {
            interest = principal * (rate/100) * years;
            printf("%f %f %d %f\n",
                    principal, rate, years, interest);
          }
        printf("\n"); /* exit point for the inner years loop */
      }
    printf("\n"); /* exit point for the middle rate loop */
  }

/* exit point for the outer principal loop */
```

The program now involves three for loops: inner, middle, and outer; the inner loop is nested in the middle one, which itself is nested in the outer one. When the first for is encountered, the value of principal is set to 1000, the loop continuation condition of the outer loop is tested and is found to be true, and the execution of its loop body begins. The nested loops considered in the previous problem comprise the first statement in the loop body of the outer loop. Thus, all the table entries for $1000 for different interest rates and numbers of years are printed. The program control now transfers to the exit statement of the rate loop, and one more blank line is printed, separating the entries for different principal amounts by two blank lines. Since this statement is the last statement in the scope of the outer for, the loop variable of the outer loop — that is, principal — is reset to 2000, and all the steps described for the value 1000 of the variable principal are repeated for this value. This process continues until finally principal becomes 11000 and the loop continuation expression of the outer loop becomes false.

The outer loop is executed 10 times, and each time the outer loop is executed, 55 table entries and 11 blank lines are printed due to the execution of the middle and inner loops, followed by the printing of one more blank line. Thus, a total of 550 table entries and 120 blank lines are printed.

In the preceding example, for loops were nested within another for loop. Other types of loops may similarly be nested, or different types of loops may be nested within one another. The following example shows how the preceding nested structure may be written equivalently by nesting a while loop within a for loop, and a do-while loop within the while loop:

```
for (principal = 1000;
     principal <= 10000; principal += 1000)
  {
    rate = 10;
```

```
      while (rate <= 15)
        {
          years = 1;
          do
            {
              interest = principal * (rate/100) * years;
              printf("%f %f %d %f\n",
                      principal, rate, years, interest);
              years++;
            }
          while (years <= 5);

          printf("\n");/*exit point for inner do-while loop*/
          rate += .5;
        }

      printf("\n");/*exit point for the middle while loop*/
    }

/* exit point for the outer for loop */
```

4.5.1 Illustrative Examples

We now give some programs to illustrate the use of nested loops.

Example 1

Four different tests are given to a class of ten students. The test data is arranged so that each student's ID is followed by the student's scores in the four tests. Write a program that calculates the average score of every student and the class average over all tests.

The following program provides a solution to the problem:

```
#include <stdio.h>
#define   TOTAL_STUDENTS   10
#define   TOTAL_TESTS       4

int main(void)
  {
    int   student_id, score;
    float total_score, grand_total;
    int   i, j;

    grand_total = 0;

    for (i = 1; i <= TOTAL_STUDENTS; i++)
      {
        total_score = 0;
        scanf("%d", &student_id);
```

```
        for (j = 1; j <= TOTAL_TESTS; j++)
          {
            scanf("%d", &score);
            total_score += score;
          }

        printf("%d    %f\n",
                student_id, total_score/TOTAL_TESTS);
        grand_total += total_score;
      }

    printf("Class Average = %f\n",
            grand_total/(TOTAL_STUDENTS*TOTAL_TESTS));

    return 0;
  }
```

The program contains two nested loops. The outer loop, executed once for each of the ten students, consists of reading `student_id` and `score` in each of the four tests, calculating the student's average score, and adding the student's `total_score` to the `grand_total` for the class. The inner loop reads the four scores for a student and accumulates them in `total_score`.

Example 2

Three positive integers a, b, and c, such that a < b < c, form a Pythagorean triplet if $a^2 + b^2 = c^2$. Write a program that generates all Pythagorean triplets a, b, c, where a, b ≤ 25.

The following program provides a solution to the problem:

```
#include <math.h>
#include <stdio.h>
#define  LIMIT         25

int main(void)
  {
    int    a, b, c, c_sqr;

    for (a = 1; a < LIMIT; a++)
        for (b = a+1; b <= LIMIT; b++)
          {
            c_sqr = a * a + b * b;
            c = sqrt(c_sqr); /* truncate fraction */
            if (c * c == c_sqr)
                printf("%d %d %d\n", a, b, c);
          }

    return 0;
  }
```

We start with $a = 1$ and find the values of b from 2 through 25 such that $c = (a^2 + b^2)^{1/2}$ is an integer. This process is repeated for $a = 2$ through 24.

The above program is error prone. Consider what will happen when a is 2, b is 3, and sqrt(25.0) turns out to be 4.999999, instead of 5.0. How would you fix this problem?

4.6   LOOP INTERRUPTION

It is sometimes desirable to control loop exits other than by testing a loop termination condition at the top or the bottom of the loop. Similarly, it is sometimes desirable that a particular iteration be interrupted without exiting the loop. We will now study the facilities provided by C for this purpose.

4.6.1 break Statement

When a break statement of the form

```
break;
```

is encountered within a loop body, the execution of the loop body is interrupted, and the program control transfers to the exit point of the loop. Reconsider, for example, the problem of computing simple interest discussed in Section 2.1. However, the interest is now required to be computed for a set of values of principal, rate, and years of investment. The following loop accomplishes this task:

```
while (1)
  {
    printf(
      "principal, rate, and years of investment? ");

    if (scanf("%f %f %d", &principal, &rate, &years)
        == EOF) break;

    interest = principal * rate / 100 * years;
    printf("interest = %f\n", interest);
  }
```

We have deliberately set up an infinite loop by providing a loop continuation condition that is always true. In each iteration of the loop, the user is prompted to provide principal, rate, and years, their values are read, and interest is computed and printed. When the user provides the end-of-file indication, the break statement is executed, and the loop is exited without computing and printing interest.

When a break is located within a nested loop structure, the only loop that gets interrupted is the innermost one whose body contains the break statement. The statement that is executed after the break is the one which is the exit point of the loop in which the break occurs. Consider, for example, the following program fragment that determines the sum of prime numbers between 10 and 100:

```
for (i = 10; i <= 100; i++)
  {
    /* check if i is prime */

    for (j = 2; j <= sqrt(i); j++)
        if (i % j == 0)   /* i is not prime */
            break;

    if (j > sqrt(i))        /* i is prime */
        sum += i;
  }
```

A number is prime if its only positive divisors are 1 and itself. The outer `for` loop successively tests every number between 10 and 100 to determine whether it is a prime. The test is performed in the inner `for` loop using a very simple algorithm. This algorithm successively divides the given number i by integers from 2 to `sqrt(i)`, and declares the number to be not a prime if any of these numbers divides i evenly; otherwise i is prime. The `break` statement breaks the inner loop as soon as the first divisor is found, but the iteration continues in the outer loop for the next value of i. Once `break` has been executed in the inner loop, j is not incremented; instead, the conditional statement in the outer loop is executed next. This statement determines whether the program control has reached this point due to a `break` in the inner loop or after the inner loop was fully executed. The complete execution of the inner loop signals that i under consideration is a prime number, and only then is i added to `sum`.

We saw in Section 3.8 that the `break` statement is also used to terminate the processing of a particular `case` within `switch` statements. If a `switch` statement is included in a loop body, any `break` that terminates the processing of a `case` does not cause loop interruption.

It is illegal to use the `break` statement outside a loop body or a `switch` statement.

4.6.2 `continue` Statement

The `continue` statement is another loop interruption statement, but unlike `break`, it does not terminate a loop; it only interrupts a particular iteration. The `continue` statement is of the form

```
continue;
```

When a `continue` statement is encountered within the loop body of a `while` or `do-while` loop, all the remaining statements in the loop body following the `continue` statement are skipped and the loop continuation condition is evaluated next. Thus, the repetition behaves as if the last statement of the loop body has just been completed. In the case of a `continue` in the body of a `for` loop, any statements following the `continue` in the scope of the particular `for` statement are skipped, and the reinitialization expression (third expression) is evaluated next. The execution of the repetition continues thereafter as normal.

For example, reconsider the problem of determining the sum of integers from 1 to n, with the added constraint that 5 and integers divisible by 5 not be included in the sum. The following program fragment obtains the desired sum:

```
for (i = 1; i <= n; i++)
  {
    if (i % 5 == 0) continue;
    sum += i;
  }
```

Following the execution of the continue statement, the assignment statement, which adds i to sum, is skipped, but the reinitialization expression that increments i is still executed. Note that in the presence of a continue statement, a while loop may not be equivalent to the for loop. If the preceding program were written as follows, using a while loop,

```
i = 1;
while (i <= n)
  {
    if (i % 5 == 0) continue;
    sum += i;
    i++;
  }
```

then the loop would not terminate for n ≥ 5, since i would get stuck at 5. How would you modify the above program to obtain the desired result?

The continue statement is generally used for checking abnormal conditions at the beginning of the loop and skipping the rest of the loop if such conditions arise. It is possible to avoid most uses of the continue statement by using an appropriate if statement. The condition of the if statement would be the opposite of the condition that would have caused the continue statement to be executed. Thus, the program for obtaining the sum of integers from 1 to n, excluding those divisible by 5, can be rewritten without using a continue as follows:

```
for (i = 1; i <= n; i++)
    if (i % 5 != 0)
        sum += i;
```

Indiscriminate use of continue statements may render a program difficult to understand. As a rule of thumb, use a continue primarily to avoid excessive nesting within a loop.

It is invalid to use the continue statement outside a loop body.

4.6.3 Illustrative Examples

We now give some example programs to further illustrate the concepts introduced in this section.

Example 1

Write a program fragment equivalent to the following that does not use break *or* continue *statements:*

```
count = 0;
while ((c = getchar()) != EOF)
    {
    if (c != '\t' && c != '\n') continue;
    if (c == '\n') break;
    if (c == '\t') count++;
    }
```

The only effective action that takes place inside the loop is that count is incremented, provided that the necessary conditions are satisfied. The break statement provides an alternative condition for exiting the loop, but since this break condition is tested before the condition for incrementing count, the break statement can be avoided altogether by adding the negation of the break condition to the loop continuation condition. We then have:

```
count = 0;
while ((c = getchar()) != EOF && c != '\n')
    {
    if (c != '\t' && c != '\n') continue;
    if (c == '\t') count++;
    }
```

The second condition of the first if statement, that is c != '\n', is now also a loop continuation condition, and hence must always be true whenever the loop is entered. Therefore, we can simplify this condition to get:

```
count = 0;
while ((c = getchar()) != EOF && c != '\n')
    {
    if (c != '\t') continue;
    if (c == '\t') count++;
    }
```

It is now apparent that the continue and the associated if test are redundant, and we can write:

```
count = 0;
while ((c = getchar()) != EOF && c != '\n')
    if (c == '\t') count++;
```

This program fragment can be written more compactly as:

```
for (count = 0;
    (c = getchar()) != EOF && c != '\n'; )
        if (c == '\t') count++;
```

This `for` loop makes it obvious that this program fragment is counting the number of tab characters in a line. The original program fragment also accomplishes the same task, but is relatively harder to understand. This example clearly brings out that, while there are several alternative ways in which a program can be written, the choice of right constructs makes a program much more readable.

Example 2

Two measures of interest in statistics are the arithmetic mean and variance defined for a set of numbers $x_1, x_2, \ldots, x_n$ as follows:

$$arithmetic\ mean\ =\ \frac{1}{n} \sum_{i=1}^{n} x_i$$

$$variance\ =\ \frac{1}{n} \sum_{i=1}^{n} x_i^2 - \frac{1}{n^2} \left(\sum_{i=1}^{n} x_i \right)^2$$

Write a program that reads a set of numbers and prints the above statistics on them. The program should ignore any number that is greater than 100 or less than –100.

The following program computes the desired statistics:

```c
#include <stdio.h>
#define   THRESHOLD    100

int main(void)
  {
     int    n;
     float  x, sum, sum_sqr;

     sum = sum_sqr = n = 0;

     for( ; ; )
       {
          if (scanf("%f", &x) == EOF)  break;

          if (x > THRESHOLD  ||  x < -THRESHOLD)
             continue;

          n++;
          sum += x;
          sum_sqr += x * x;
       }
```

```
        printf("arithmetic mean = %f\n", sum/n);
        printf("variance = %f\n",
                sum_sqr/n - (sum * sum)/(n * n));

        return 0;
    }
```

Rewrite this program without using break or continue statements.

4.7 NULL STATEMENT

C permits a statement consisting of a solitary semicolon to be placed wherever a program statement can appear. This statement, known as the *null* statement, is of the form

```
    ;
```

Execution of a null statement has no effect, and hence may seem quite useless. Its use, however, becomes necessary when, although no action is desired, the language syntax requires a statement. Consider, for example, the following iterative statement:

```
    for (count=0; getchar() != EOF; count++)
        ;
```

This statement counts the number of characters in input. A null statement had to be supplied, as the syntax rules require a for to have a statement following the right parenthesis.

It is a good programming practice to place the null statement on a line by itself after proper indentation.

4.8 COMMA OPERATOR

The comma operator (,) is used to combine two related expressions into one, making programs more compact. The compound expression so formed is evaluated from left to right, and the type and value of the result are the type and value of the right operand. The value of the left operand is discarded; it is evaluated only for side effects. The comma operator has the lowest precedence of any other operator, and hence can safely be used to turn any list of expressions into a single expression. For example, given that

```
    int i;
    float x;
```

the expressions

```
    i = 1
```

and

```
    x = i + 1
```

can be combined by the comma operator into a single expression as

```
i = 1, x = i + 1
```

The left operand of the comma operator assigns 1 to i, and is discarded. The right operand is then evaluated, and its type (float) and value (2) become the type and value of the compound expression. Similarly, the assignment statements

```
t = x;
x = y;
y = t;
```

that interchange the values of x and y, can be combined into a single statement as

```
t = x, x = y, y = t;
```

The assignments are made from left to right; first x is assigned to t, then y to x, and finally t to y.

When writing a for loop, very often, more than one variable requires initialization. Similarly, sometimes one likes to have more than one variable controlling a for loop, and all these loop variables require reinitialization before the next iteration begins. The comma operator is specially useful in such situations as it can group several expressions into a single expression. For example, the for statement

```
for (x = .85, y = 1.05, z = 0;
     x <= y;  x *= 1.06, y *= 1.04)   z++;
```

initializes the values of x, y, and z to 0.85, 1.05, and 0 respectively before the loop begins, and increases the value of x to 1.06 times its current value and that of y to 1.04 times its current value after each execution of the loop body. Note that this for loop is a one-line version of the do-while loop used in the population program in Section 4.3.1.

The comma operator is frequently used to issue a prompt before an input request. Using the comma operator, the loop considered in Section 4.6.1 can be rewritten without using a break as:

```
while (printf(
        "principal, rate, and years of investment? "),
        scanf(
        "%f %f %d", &principal, &rate, &years) != EOF)
  {
    interest = principal * rate / 100 * years;
    printf("interest = %f\n", interest);
  }
```

The test for end-of-file still controls the loop termination, since the operands are evaluated from left to right.

The comma operator can also be used to eliminate embedded assignments from tests. For example,

```
while ((c = getchar()) != EOF)  putchar(c);
```

can be rewritten as

```
while (c = getchar(), c != EOF)  putchar(c);
```

separating the reading of the character from testing the end-of-file.

4.8.1 Illustrative Example

We now give a program that uses the comma operator to initialize multiple variables in a `for` loop.

Example

A small test rocket is being designed for use in testing a retrorocket that is intended to permit "soft" landings. The designer believes that the following equations predict the performance of the test rocket:

$$\text{Acceleration in ft/sec}^2 = 4.25 - 0.015\, t^2 + \frac{6.07\, t^{2.751}}{9995}$$

$$\text{Velocity in ft/sec} \quad = 4.25\, t - \frac{0.015\, t^3}{3} + \frac{6.07\, t^{3.751}}{3.751 \cdot 9995}$$

$$\text{Height in ft/sec} \quad = 90 + \frac{4.25\, t^2}{2} - \frac{0.015\, t^4}{12} + \frac{6.07\, t^{4.751}}{4.751 \cdot 37491}$$

where t is the time elapsed in seconds. The first term (90) in the equation for Height is the height in feet above ground level of the launch platform.

To check the predicted performance, the flight of the rocket is to be simulated for a maximum of 100 seconds. Increments of time are to be 2 seconds from launch through the ascending and descending portions of the trajectory until the rocket descends to within 75 feet of ground level. Below 75 feet, the time increments are to be 0.05 seconds. If the rocket impacts prior to 100 seconds, the simulation should be stopped immediately after impact. At each time increment, the simulator should print the elapsed time, the acceleration, the velocity, and the height above ground level.

The following program provides a solution to the problem:

```
#include <math.h>
#include <stdio.h>
#define   STEP1         2.0
#define   STEP2         0.5
#define   TOTALTIME     100
#define   THRESHOLD     75
#define   YES           1
#define   NO            0
```

```
int main(void)
  {
    double  t, acceleration, velocity, height,
            step, previous_height;
    int     descending;

    for (t=0, step=STEP1, descending=NO,
         previous_height=0; t <= TOTALTIME; t += step)
      {
    .   acceleration = 4.25 - 0.015 * t * t +
            (6.07 * pow(t,2.751)) / 9995;
        velocity = 4.25 * t - (0.015 * t * t * t) / 3 +
            (6.07 * pow(t,3.751)) / (3.751 * 9995);
        height = 90 + (4.25* t * t) / 2 -
            (0.015 * pow(t,4.0)) / 12 +
            (6.07 * pow(t,4.751)) / (4.751 * 37491);

        if (height <= 0)
          {
            printf(
              "rocket impacted at or before %f\n", t);
            break;
          }
        else
            printf("%f %f %f %f\n",
                    t, acceleration, velocity, height);

        if (height < previous_height)
            descending = YES;
        else
            previous_height = height;

        if (descending && height <= THRESHOLD)
            step = STEP2;

      }

    return 0;
  }
```

Note that the program determines that the rocket is in the descending portion of its trajectory, if the current height of the rocket is less than its height at the previous observation.

Exercises 4

1. How many times will the loops defined by the following `for` statements be executed?

   a. `for(i=10; i<=10; i++);`   *b.* `for(i=10; i<10; i++);`

   c. `for(i=10; i>=1; i-=4);`   *d.* `for(i=10; i==1; i-=4);`

   e. `for(x=.1; x<=.5; x=.2);`   *f.* `for(x=.1; x<=.5; x-=.2);`

2. What will be the output of the following program fragment?

```
for (sum = 0, i = 2; i <= 8; i += 2)
  {
    j = i;
    while (j < 4)
      {
        k = j;
        do
          {
            sum++;
            k += 2;
          }
        while (k <= 3);

        j++;
      }
  }
printf("%d %d %d %d\n", sum, i, j, k);
```

3. What will be the output of each of the following program fragments?

   a.
```
for (j=2,i=3; i <= 8; i += 2)
  {
    j += i;
  }
printf("%d %d\n", i, j);
```
   b.
```
for (j=2,i=3; i <= 8; i += 2)
  {
    j += i;
    if (j > 6)  break;
  }
printf("%d %d\n", i, j);
```
   c.
```
for (j=2,i=3; i <= 8; i += 2)
  {
    if (j == 5)  continue;
    j += i;
  }
printf("%d %d\n", i, j);
```

4. Rewrite the following program fragments without using any `continue` or `break` statements:

a.
```
while (go_on)
    {
    if (interrupt) continue;
    do_some_work();
    }
```

b.
```
do
    {
    if (!go_on) continue;
    else do_some_work();
    do_more_work();
    }
while (go_on);
```

c.
```
while ((c=getchar()) != EOF)
    {
    if (c=='\n') continue;
    if (c=='\t') continue;
    if (c==' ') continue;
    if (c<'0') {special++;continue;}
    if (c<='9') {digit++;continue;}
    if (c<'A') {special++;continue;}
    if (c<='Z') {alpha++;continue;}
    if (c<'a') {special++;continue;}
    if (c<='z') {alpha++;continue;}
    special++;
    }
```

d.
```
i = 1;
j = over = 0;
while (!over)
    {
    if (i == n) break;
    if (n % i)
        {i++; continue;}
    j += i++;
    if (j > MAXJ) over++;
    }
```

5. Write a program that reads numbers until a negative number is read, and prints the number of values read, the largest value, the smallest value, and the range.

6. A perfect square is an integer which is the square of another integer. Write a program that reads a number and computes the first perfect square larger than this number.

7. Write a program that reads numbers from input and prints `yes` if the numbers read are in increasing order (latest number read is larger than the one immediately before).

   Modify the program so that it keeps track of the length of subsequences of the input numbers that are in increasing order, and prints the length each time such a subsequence terminates.

8. Write a program to print the first ten partial sums of the continued fraction

$$1 + \cfrac{1}{1 + \cfrac{1}{1 + \cfrac{1}{1 + \cdots}}}$$

given that if S_k is the kth partial sum, then

$$S_1 = 1, \quad S_2 = 1 + \frac{1}{1}, \quad S_3 = 1 + \cfrac{1}{1 + \cfrac{1}{1}}, \quad \cdots$$

9. Adam has invested $1000 at 10.0% simple interest, whereas Smith has invested $750 at 7.5% interest compounded annually. Write a program to determine the number of years it will take for the value of Smith's investment to exceed that of Adam's.

10. If there are 23 people in a room, the probability is a little more than half that two will have the same birthday. Do you find it surprising? Pick a person. This eliminates one birthday, and the probability that the next person you pick will have a different birthday is 365/366 (includes February 29 birthdays). This eliminates two birthdays. The probability that the third person will have yet another birthday is 364/366. For the fourth person, the probability is 363/366, and so on. Thus, the probability that at least two of them have the same birthday is

$$1 - \frac{365}{366} \cdot \frac{364}{366} \cdot \frac{363}{366} \cdots \frac{366 - 23 + 1}{366}$$

Write a program that reads the number of people in a room and computes the probability of at least two people having the same birthday. Use your program to find the number of people it takes to make the probability 0.9 or better.

11. Here is an ecological simulation of wolf and rabbit populations. Rabbits eat grass and wolves eat rabbits. There is plenty of grass; therefore, wolves are the only obstacle to the rabbits' population increasing. The wolf population increases with the population of rabbits. The day-by-day changes in the rabbit population R and the wolf population W can be expressed by the following formulas:

$R[\text{tomorrow}] = (1+a) \cdot R - c \cdot R \cdot W$ [today]

$W[\text{tomorrow}] = (1-b) \cdot W + c \cdot d \cdot R \cdot W$ [today]

$a = 0.01$ Fractional increase in rabbit population without competition from wolves

$b = 0.005$ Fractional decrease in wolf population without rabbits to eat

$c = 0.00001$ Likelihood that a wolf will encounter and eat a rabbit

$d = 0.01$ Fractional increase in wolf population attributed to a devoured rabbit

Assume that initially there are 10,000 rabbits and 1000 wolves. Write a program to calculate populations of rabbits and wolves over a 1000-day period. Have the program print the populations every 25 days. See what happens when you start with 500 wolves instead of 1000. Try starting with 2000 wolves too.

12. Capital assets are depreciated for tax purposes on a year-by-year basis. One way of calculating depreciation is by the straight-line method. Each year the asset is depreciated by an amount equal to cost of the asset divided by its expected life, and the book value of the asset is decreased by this amount.

Another way of calculating depreciation is by the sum-of-digit methods. For example, suppose that a microcomputer costing $1000 is to be depreciated over five years. The sum of the years' digits, *sum*, in this case is

$$sum = 1 + 2 + 3 + 4 + 5 = 15$$

According to this method, 5/15 of $1000 may be depreciated in the first year, 4/15 the second year, 3/15 the third year, and so on.

Write a program that reads the cost and expected life of an asset, and prints the depreciation and the book value each year, over the expected life of the asset, by the above two methods of depreciating assets.

13. Super-Duper Micros currently sells 100 Super-Dupers per month at a profit of $500 per Super-Duper. They have a fixed operating cost of $10,000 that does not depend on the volume of sales. They currently spend $1000 per month on advertising. A marketing consultant advised them that if they double the amount spent on advertising, sales would increase by 20%. Write a program that begins with the company's current status, and successively doubles the amount spent on advertising until the net profit begins to decline. Have the program print the number of Super-Duper sales, the advertising budget, and the net profit just before the profit begins to decline.

14. Write a program to approximate the area under the curve $f(x) = x^3$ from $x = 0$ to $x = 1$ using the following trapezoidal rule:

$$area = \frac{h}{2} [f(0) + 2f(h) + 2f(2h) + 2f(3h) + \ldots + 2f(1-h) + f(1)]$$

The step size h should be such that $1/h$ is an integer. Compute the area for $h = 0.1$, $0.01, 0.001$, and 0.0001 and compare the results.

15. The equation $x^2 + y^2 = r^2$ represents a circle with center at the origin and radius r. Write a program that reads r and determines the number of points with integer coordinates that lie within the circle.

16. Write a program that, for all positive integers $i, j, k,$ and l from 1 through 1000, determines all combinations of $i, j, k,$ and l such that $i + j + k = l$ and $i < j < k < l$.

17. Write a program that reads a positive integer N and determines the smallest integer n such that $n > N$ and $x^2 + y^3 + z^4 = n$, where $x > y > z$, and x, y, z are positive integers.

18. Write a program using nested loops to generate the following pattern:

```
zyxwvwxyz
 zyxwxyz
  zyxyz
   zyz
    z
```

5 Functions

A C program is usually made up of many small functions, each performing a particular task, rather than one large `main` function. A program is usually kept in more than one source file, each file consisting of closely related functions. Source files may be compiled separately and loaded together, possibly along with previously compiled library functions. Once a function has been designed, its result can be used in complex computations without concern for details of how the result was obtained. Functions can be developed, tested, and debugged independently and possibly concurrently by different members of a programming team. They avoid duplication of effort as the same processing may be needed more than once in a program or in more than one program. Separating a program into functions also aids in maintenance and enhancement of programs by localizing the effects of changes.

In this chapter, we discuss how functions are defined and used.

5.1 OVERVIEW

Let us consider a function that computes the sum of the cubes of the digits of a given positive integer. The function is defined as follows:

```
int cubesum(int number)
  {
    int sum, residue, digit;

    residue = number;
    sum = 0;

    do
      {
        digit = residue % 10;/* rightmost digit */
        sum += digit * digit * digit;
        residue /= 10;/* after removing this digit */
      }
    while (residue != 0);

    return sum;
  }
```

The *type* of this function is `int` as indicated by the type specification just before the *function name*, `cubesum`. The function name is followed by the *parameter declarations* enclosed in parentheses. This function has only one *parameter*, `number`, which is of type `int`. The opening brace { following the parameter declarations marks the beginning of the *function body*. The function body consists of the declarations of *local variables* and *function statements*. There are three local variables: `sum`, `residue`, and `digit`. These variables are only accessible in the body of `cubesum`, and not in any other function. The function statements following the variable declarations compute the sum of the cubes of the digits of `number`. The `return` statement terminates the execution of function and communicates the value `sum` computed by the function to the calling function. The closing brace } marks the end of the function body.

All that a calling function has to know about `cubesum` is that it can compute the sum of the cubes of the digits of a given number; the calling function does not have to know the details of how this sum is computed. Any function that requires this sum can call `cubesum`.

We will use the function `cubesum` to determine narcissistic cubes. *Narcissistic cubes* are positive integers that equal the sum of the cubes of their digits. For example, 153 is a narcissistic cube since

$$153 = 1^3 + 5^3 + 3^3.$$

Besides 153, only four other narcissistic cubes exist: 1, 370, 371, and 407. The following program finds all of them:

```
#include <stdio.h>
#define  MAX        5

int main(void)
  {
    int i, count;
    int cubesum(int number);

    for(i=1, count=0;  count < MAX; i++)

        if (i == cubesum(i))
          {
            printf("%d\n", i);
            count++;
          }
    return 0;
  }
```

The declaration of `cubesum` in `main` is the *function prototype* for `cubesum`. This specifies that `cubesum` can be called with one argument of type `int`, and it returns a value of type `int`. Function prototypes have been introduced by ANSI C, and they help the compiler check whether or not the function has been called correctly.

A function is called by specifying the name of the function followed by a list of *arguments* enclosed in parentheses. Thus, within the body of `main`, `cubesum(i)` is the call to the function `cubesum` with the current value of `i` as the argument. When a function is called, its parameters are *initialized* to the *value* of the arguments supplied with the function call. The function body is then executed. On encountering a `return` statement in the function body, the program control returns to the calling function, and the value returned by the function is substituted for the function call in the calling function. Thus, this program repeatedly checks whether the sum of the cubes of the digits of the candidate number `i` equals `i` itself, till all the narcissistic cubes have been found.

We now discuss in detail various aspects of a function definition and its use.

5.2   FUNCTION DEFINITION

A *function definition* introduces a new function by declaring the type of value it returns and its parameters, and specifying the statements that are executed when the function is called. The general format of the function definition is:

function-type function-name (parameter-declarations)
```
{
```
   variable-declarations

   function-statements
```
}
```

Function-type specifies the type of the function and corresponds to the type of value returned by the function. Functions in C are used not only to determine values, but also to group together related actions, such as printing the headers of a report. A function that does not return any value, but only causes some side effects, is declared to be of type `void`. The specification of function type is optional; if it is omitted, it is taken to be `int`.

Function-name is the name of the function being defined. *Parameter-declarations* specify the types and names of the *parameters* (also called *formal parameters*) of the function, separated by commas. If a function does not have any parameters, the keyword `void` is written in place of parameter declarations. The rules for naming functions and parameters are the same as for naming variables discussed in Section 2.4.1.

Thus, the function definition

```
float interest (float prin, float rate, int yrs)
   {
      . . .
   }
```

defines `interest` to be a function that returns a value of type `float`, and has three parameters: `prin` and `rate`, which are of type `float`, and `yrs`, which is of type `int`; the function definition

```
void initialize(void)
  {
    . . .
  }
```

defines `initialize` to be a function that neither returns any value nor takes any arguments; and the function definition

```
quotient(int i, int j)
  {
    . . .
  }
```

defines `quotient` to be a function that returns an integer value and has two integer parameters `i` and `j`. Note that the type of `quotient` is taken to be `int`, since its type has not been explicitly specified.

The *function-body* consists of *variable-declarations* followed by *function-statements*, enclosed within the opening brace { and the matching closing brace }. *Variable-declarations* specify types and names of the variables that are local to the function. A *local variable* is one whose value can only be accessed by the function in which it is declared. Variables declared local to a function supersede any identically named variables outside the function. Parameters are treated as if they were declared at the top of the function body. Thus, functions may be developed independently, without any concern for variable names used in other functions. For example, the functions `lcm` and `gcd`

```
int lcm(int m, int n)
  {
    int i;
    . . .
  }
int gcd(int m, int n)
  {
    int i;
    . . .
  }
```

have identically named parameters and local variables, but any reference to `m`, `n`, or `i` in `gcd` has nothing to do with `m`, `n`, or `i` in `lcm`.

Function-statements can be any valid C statements that are to be executed when the function is called. The execution of the function terminates when either the execution reaches the closing brace at the end of the function body, or a `return` statement is encountered.

5.2.1 `return` Statement

A `return` statement can be of one of the following two forms:

```
return expression;
return;
```

If the `return` statement is of the first form, the value of the *expression* is returned to the calling function. For example, the function `smaller`

```
double smaller(double x, double y)
    {
      return  x < y ? x : y;
    }
```

returns the value of the smaller of the two arguments in the function call. If the type of the *expression* does not match the type of the function, it is converted to the type of the function. For example, in the function

```
int trunc(void)
    {
      return  1.5;
    }
```

the `return` statement is equivalent to

```
return (int) 1.5;
```

and returns 1 to the calling function.

The `return` statement of the second form returns no value to the calling function. This form of the `return` statement should be used only when the function is of type `void`; otherwise, the value returned is unpredictable. If a function is declared to be of type `void`, it is an error to supply an expression in any `return` statement in the function. Flowing off the end of a function, without encountering a `return` statement, is equivalent to executing a `return` statement of the second form as the last statement of the function. More than one `return` statement can be used in the same function, as is the case with the following function definition:

```
int factorial(int n)
    {
      int i, result;

      if (n < 0) return -1;

      if (n == 0) return 1;

      for (i = 1, result = 1; i <= n; i++) result *= i;

      return result;
    }
```

The first executed `return` statement terminates the execution of the function, and the rest of the function body is not executed. Thus, if `factorial` is called with argument 0, the function will return with the value 1, and the `for` loop will not be executed.

5.3   FUNCTION CALL

A function call is an expression of the form

function-name (*argument-list*   )

where *function-name* is the name of the function called, and *argument-list* is a comma-separated list of expressions that constitute the *arguments* (also called *actual arguments*) to the function. Thus, the expression

```
cubesum(i)
```

is a function call that invokes the function named `cubesum` with the argument `i`.

The type of a function-call expression is the same as the type of the function being called, and its value is the value returned by the function. A function call can occur in any place where an expression can occur, such as in

```
if (i == cubesum(i))  printf("%d\n", i);
```

A function call, followed by a semicolon, becomes an expression statement. Thus, the expression in the statement

```
printf("hello there");
```

is a call to the function named `printf` with the argument `"hello there"`.

Function calls can be embedded in other function calls. Thus, the statements

```
t = cubesum(i);
j = cubesum(t);
```

are equivalent to

```
j = cubesum( cubesum(i) );
```

Another example of an embedded function call is the statement

```
printf("sum of the cube of the digits of %d = %d",
        i, cubesum(i));
```

in which the call to `cubesum` is embedded in `printf`.

Parentheses must be present in a function call even when the argument list is empty. Thus,

```
initialize();
```

is a call to the function named `initialize`, which does not take any argument.

The commas that separate function arguments are not comma operators, but a separate syntactic entity. In such contexts, expressions involving the comma operator must be enclosed in parentheses. For example,

```
f((a=0, a+=1), b)
```

has two arguments, the first of which has the value 1.

The function in which the function call is contained is said to be the *calling* function and the function named in the call is said to be the *called* function. A function call alters the sequential execution of the program. Upon call, the program control passes from the calling function to the called function, and execution begins from the first executable statement of the called function. The called function is executed until a `return` or the closing brace of the function is encountered, at which point the control passes back to the point after the function call. The calling function may choose to ignore the value returned by the called function.

When a function is called, parameters in the called function are bound to the corresponding arguments supplied by the calling function. The names of the parameters need not be identical to those of the arguments. The difference between parameters and arguments can be understood by drawing an analogy with the proof of a theorem in elementary geometry. Such a proof is written in terms of angles and lengths. These angles and lengths correspond to the parameters of a function. If we replace angles and lengths in the proof by particular values, such as 60° and 10 inches, every statement of the proof would still be true, and we would have proved a particular case of the theorem. This process is analogous to providing arguments to a function. As a proof is true for a class of figures, a function represents a class of computations. A call to a function performs a specific computation belonging to the corresponding class of computations.

C only provides *call by value* parameter passing, meaning thereby that the called function is only provided with the current values of the arguments, but not their addresses, and the corresponding parameters are assigned these values. Since the addresses of the arguments are not available to the called function, any change in the value of a parameter inside the called function does not cause a change in the corresponding argument. This form of parameter passing is different from the *call by reference* parameter passing supported by some languages, such as FORTRAN. In call by reference, the address of the argument is supplied to the called function, and any change in the value of a parameter is automatically reflected in the corresponding argument. The following program illustrates parameter passing by value:

```
#include <stdio.h>

int main(void)
  {
    int i = 1, j = 2;
    void exchange(int, int);

    printf("main     :  i = %d  j= %d\n", i, j);
    exchange(i,j);
    printf("main     :  i = %d  j= %d\n", i, j);
    return 0;
  }

void exchange(int i, int j)
  {
    int t;

    t = i, i = j, j = t;
    printf("exchange:  i = %d  j= %d\n", i, j);
  }
```

The following is the output of this program:

```
main      :   i = 1   j= 2
exchange:   i = 2   j= 1
main      :   i = 1   j= 2
```

The change in the value of the parameters is not reflected in the arguments and they retain their values. Thus, the parameters can be treated as initialized local variables in the called function. This feature many times avoids extraneous variables in the program. For instance, the function cubesum in the narcissistic cubes example, given in Section 5.1, can be rewritten without using the local variable residue as follows:

```
int cubesum(int n)
   {
     int sum, digit;

     sum = 0;

     do
        {
          digit = n % 10;  /* rightmost digit of n */
          sum += digit * digit * digit;
          n /= 10;  /* n without the rightmost digit */
        }
     while (n != 0);

     return sum;
   }
```

What if the programmer wants the called function to modify the values of the variables supplied as arguments to the called function, such as in the call to the function exchange in the preceding example? There are two possible solutions. The calling function may explicitly pass the address of the variable (called the *pointer* to the variable) as the argument, and the called function can then use this address to manipulate the value of the variable. We will discuss this approach in detail after we have introduced pointers in Chapter 7. The other approach is to make such variables *external* to both calling and called functions. External variables are global in nature, and they can be changed by any function that has access to them. We will discuss communication between functions through external variables in Section 5.6.

5.4 FUNCTION PROTOTYPES

Before calling a function, it must be declared with a prototype of its parameters. The general form for a function declaration is

function-type function-name (parameter-type-list) ;

where the *function-type* and *function-name* are type and name respectively of the function being declared. The *parameter-type-list* is the comma-separated list of pairs of type and name of the parameters of the function. Thus, the function declaration

```
int cubesum(int n);
```

in the narcissistic cubes program in Section 5.1 is a function prototype. Similarly, the function declaration of `interest` contained in the following `main` function to compute the interest earned is a function prototype:

```
int main(void)
  {
    int prin, yrs;
    float rate, intr;
    float interest (float prin, float rate, int yrs);

    scanf("%d %f %d,"0prin,0rate,0yrs);
    intr = interest(prin, rate, yrs)
    printf("%f\n", intr);
    return 0;
  }
```

The prototype of a function must agree with the function definition and its use. However, the parameter names in the prototype can be different from the names used in the function definition. These names are effectively treated as comments, and may even be omitted. Thus, the preceding prototypes could have been equivalently written as

```
int cubesum(int);
float interest (float, float, int);
```

When a function for which a prototype has been specified is called, the arguments to the function are converted, as if by assignment, to the declared types of the parameters. Thus, the call

```
interest (prin, rate, yrs)
```

where `prin` and `yrs` are of type `int` and `rate` is of type `float`, is equivalent to

```
interest ((float) prin, rate, yrs)
```

and no explicit casting is necessary. It is an error if the number of arguments in the call is different from the number in the prototype, or if their types are not the same as or convertible to the types in the prototype.

. At the time of a function call, if there is no prototype for this function, the function is implicitly declared to be of type `int`, and the result can be meaningless computation if the function actually returns a value of a different type. Thus, if a source file looks as follows

```
int main(void)
  {
    ...
    interest (1000, 0.075, 5);
    ...
  }
```

```
float interest (float principal, float rate, int yrs)
   {
     ...
   }
```

then while processing `main`, `interest` will be implicitly declared as

```
int interest (int, float, int);
```

which is inconsistent with its subsequent definition. If `main` and `interest` are defined in separate files, there is no way for a compiler to detect such inconsistencies. We strongly encourage you, therefore, to ensure before calling a function that its prototype is available.

A function definition in the prototype form serves as a prototype for any subsequent call to the function in the same source file. For example, a prototype would not be necessary for `interest` if the source file were organized as

```
float interest (float principal, float rate, int yrs)
   {
     ...
   }

int main(void)
   {
     ...
     interest (1000, 0.075, 5);
     ...
   }
```

A program may contain more than one declaration of a function; however, all these declarations must be consistent.

5.4.1 Illustrative Examples

We now give some example programs to consolidate the concepts introduced in this chapter so far.

Example 1

Write a program to determine the positive integer that has the largest persistence among two-digit integers.

Multiplying the digits of an integer and continuing the process gives the surprising result that the sequence of products always arrives at a single-digit number. For example,

$$36 \to 18 \to 8$$
$$39 \to 27 \to 14 \to 4$$

The number of products necessary to reach the single digit is called the *persistence number* of that integer. Thus, the persistence number of 36 is 2 and that of 39 is 3. There is only one two-digit integer, 77, with a persistence number greater than 3. The following program determines this integer.

```c
#include <stdio.h>
#define   START       10
#define   END         99

int main(void)
  {
    int n, p, number, maxp;

    /* computes the persistence number of n */
    int p_number(int n);

    for(n = START, maxp = 0; n <= END; n++)
      {
        p = p_number(n);

        if (p > maxp) /* save values */
          {
            maxp = p;
            number = n;
          }
      }

    printf("number = %d  persistence = %d\n",
            number, maxp);
    return 0;
  }


int p_number(int n)
  {
    int p;

    /* computes the product of the digits of n */
    int digitprod(int n);

    /* loop while the digit product does not
       become a single-digit number */
    for(p = 0; n/10 != 0; p++)
        n = digitprod(n);

    return p;
  }
```

```
int digitprod(int n)
  {
    int digit, prod;

    prod = 1;

    do
      {
        digit = n % 10;/* rightmost digit */
        prod *= digit;
        n /= 10;/* number after deleting rightmost digit */
      }
    while (n != 0);

    return prod;
  }
```

Example 2
Write a program for a consumer service organization that will help people bargain for a low price while purchasing a personal computer. The program will take as input the list price for the basic configuration, the list price for the desired options, and an indication whether it is an imported model. It will output the lowest price that the dealer would accept. The buyer can then hold out for this price.

The consumer service organization knows that dealers will accept a price that is 20% above the cost to the dealer of the basic configuration plus options. The wholesale cost to the dealer is half the list price, but the dealers pay a 10% surcharge on the imported models. The desired program is as follows:

```
#include <stdio.h>

#define   MARKUP     0.2 /* 20% over cost */
#define   WHOLESALE  0.5 /* wholesale is 50% of list price */
#define   SURCHARGE  0.1 /* 10% surcharge on imported models */

int main(void)
  {
    float base_price;/* list price of the basic configuration */
    float options;    /* list price of the options */
    int imported;/* nonzero value implies an imported model */
    float lowest_price(float, float, int);

    scanf("%f %f %d",
        &base_price, &options, &imported);
    printf("Lowest Price = %f",
        lowest_price(base_price, options, imported));
    return 0;
  }
```

```
float lowest_price(float base_price,
                   float options, int imported)
  {
    float dealer_cost(float base_price,
                      float options, int imported);

    return (1 + MARKUP) *
          dealer_cost(base_price, options, imported);
  }

float dealer_cost(float base_price,
                  float options, int imported)
  {
    float base_cost, options_cost;

    base_cost = imported ?
         (1 + SURCHARGE) * WHOLESALE * base_price :
         WHOLESALE * base_price;
    options_cost = WHOLESALE * options;

    return base_cost + options_cost;
  }
```

5.5 BLOCK STRUCTURE

A *block* is a sequence of variable declarations and statements enclosed within braces. C does not allow a function to be defined inside another function, but it is permissible to nest blocks and to declare variables and initialize them at the beginning of any block. The *scope* of a variable declared in a block extends from its point of declaration to the end of the block. Such a declaration hides any identically named variable in the outer blocks.

Consider, for example, the `factorial` function given in Section 5.2. It can be rewritten as

```
int factorial(int n)
  {
    if (n < 0)
        return -1;
    else if (n == 0)
        return 1;
    else
      {
        int i, result = 1;

        for (i = 1; i <= n; i++) result *= i;
        return result;
      }
  }
```

In this version, the variables i and result are declared inside the block associated with the second else, rather than at the beginning of the function block. This version is more readable as these variables are now declared near the place of their use.

As another example, reconsider the problem of determining the sum of prime numbers between two given numbers, discussed in Section 4.6.1. The code for determining this sum can be rewritten as

```
#include <math.h>

int primesum(int from, int to)
   {
     int i, j, sum = 0;

     for (i = from; i <= to; i++)
       {
         int sqrt_i = (int) sqrt(i);

         for (j = 2; j <= sqrt_i; j++)
             if (i % j == 0)   /* i is not prime */
                 break;

         if (j > sqrt_i)         /* i is prime */
             sum += i;
       }

     return sum;
   }
```

Rather than computing the square root of i for every iteration of the inner loop, it is computed only once for a given value of i and saved in sqrt_i, a variable declared local to the block associated with the outer for.

5.6 EXTERNAL VARIABLES

Local variables can only be accessed in the function in which they are defined; they are unknown to other functions in the same program. Even if variables in different functions have the same name, they are not related in any way.

Data must often be shared between functions. One safe way to accomplish this sharing is to use function parameters to pass data among functions. We have seen several examples of this method in the previous sections. This method, however, becomes quite cumbersome if a large number of variables have to be shared.

An alternative is to set up variables that are available across function boundaries. If a variable is defined outside any function at the same level as function definitions, it is available to all the functions defined below in the same source file, and is called an *external* variable. Technically, that part of the program within which a name can be used is called its *scope*. The scope of a local variable is the function in which its has been defined, whereas the scope of an external variable is the rest of the source file starting from its definition. Note that the scope of external variables defined before any function definition will be the whole program, and hence such variables are sometimes referred to as *global* variables.

External variables can be used instead of long parameter lists to communicate data among functions, since their scope spans function boundaries. The following program fragment illustrates the definition and use of external variables:

```
int i, j; /* external variables accessible in
              ' input, compute, and output */

void input (void)
   {
     scanf("%d %d", &i, &j);
   }

int k; /* external variable accessible in compute and output */

void compute (void)
   {
     k = power(i,j);
   }

void output (void)
   {
     printf("i = %d   j = %d   k = %d", i, j, k);
   }
```

A local variable definition supersedes that of an external variable. If an external variable and a local variable have identical names, all references to that name inside the function will refer to the local variable. Thus, the following definition of the function power can be inserted between the functions compute and output without affecting i in output:

```
int power(int base, int exponent)
   {
     int i, result;

     for (i = 1, result = 1; i <= exponent; i++)
         result *= base;
     return result;
   }
```

The variable i defined in power is local to power and has nothing to do with the external variable i defined before input. Thus, any change in i in power is not reflected in the external i, and output remains unaffected.

You may have noticed that all the functions considered so far in the text returned only one value. What if a function has to return two or more values? External variables can be used for this purpose, as shown in the following example:

```
    float root1, root2;

int roots(float a, float b, float c)
    {
      float discriminant;

      if (a == 0)
        {
          printf("not a quadratic equation\n");
          return 1;
        }

      discriminant = b*b - 4*a*c;

      if (discriminant < 0)
        {
          printf("equation has no real roots\n");
          return 1;
        }

      root1 = (-b + sqrt(discriminant)) / (2*a);
      root2 = (-b - sqrt(discriminant)) / (2*a);
      return 0;
    }
```

This function returns the two roots of a quadratic equation in external variables root1 and root2. In Chapter 7, we will study an alternative way of returning more than one result from a function computation.

You may ask at this stage why external variables should not always be used if some data is to be shared between functions, as they certainly appear somewhat convenient. The heavy use of external variables hides the relationship between different parts of the program, and leads to programs that are harder to understand and modify. Such programs are prone to errors as changes in one part of the program may affect some other part in unexpected ways. For instance, in the first example, a change of names of external variables i, j, and k to, say, base, exponent, and result would require a careful study of the whole program, as changes are not localized. Moreover, embedding the names of external variables in the function body destroys the generality of the function. Any program that uses roots, for example, has to make sure that it uses variable names root1 and root2 for obtaining the results of calling roots. External variables, therefore, must be used with utmost discretion.

5.6.1 Illustrative Examples

We now give some example programs to further illustrate the concept of external variables.

Example 1
Rewrite the computer bargaining program given in Section 5.4.1, using external variables.

The desired program is as follows:

```
#include <stdio.h>

#define  MARKUP    0.2 /* 20% over cost */
#define  WHOLESALE 0.5 /* wholesale is 50% of list price */
#define  SURCHARGE 0.1 /* 10% surcharge on imported models */

/* external variables */
float base_price;/* list price of the basic configuration */
float options;   /* list price of the options */
int   imported;  /* nonzero value implies an imported model */

/* function prototypes */
float lowest_price(void);
float dealer_cost(void);

int main(void)
  {
    scanf("%f %f %d",
          &base_price, &options, &imported);
    printf("Lowest Price = %f\n", lowest_price());
    return 0;
  }

float lowest_price(void)
  {
    return (1 + MARKUP) * dealer_cost();
  }

float dealer_cost(void)
  {
    float base_cost, options_cost;

    base_cost = (imported) ?
        (1 + SURCHARGE) * WHOLESALE * base_price :
        WHOLESALE * base_price;
    options_cost = WHOLESALE * options;
    return base_cost + options_cost;
  }
```

Example 2
Write a program for transforming rectangular coordinates to polar coordinates.

The polar coordinates (r,θ) corresponding to the rectangular coordinates (x,y) of points other than the origin are given by

$$r = (x^2 + y^2)^{\frac{1}{2}}, \qquad \tan \theta = y/x, \ -\pi < \theta \leq \pi \, .$$

The desired program is as follows:

```
#include <math.h>
#include <stdio.h>
#define  PI            3.1415927

float  r, theta;
void  polar(float x, float y);

int main(void)
  {
    float x, y;

    scanf("%f %f", &x, &y);
    printf("x = %f, y = %f\n", x, y);
    polar(x, y);
    printf("r = %f, theta = %f\n", r, theta);
    return 0;
  }

void polar(float x, float y)
  {
    if (x == 0 && y == 0)   /* origin */
        r = theta = 0;
    else
      {
        r = sqrt(x*x + y*y);
        theta = atan2(y,x);
      }
  }
```

The function atan2(y,x), defined in the standard math library, computes the value of arctangent of y/x (see Appendix A).

5.7 STORAGE CLASSES

A variable belongs to one of the two storage classes: *automatic* and *static*. The storage class determines the lifetime of the storage associated with the variable.

5.7.1 Automatic Variables

A variable is said to be *automatic* if it is allocated storage upon entry to a segment of code, and the storage is deallocated upon exit from this segment. A variable is specified to be automatic by prefixing its type declaration with the storage class specifier auto in the following manner:

    auto   *type*   *variable-name*;

Variables can be declared to be automatic only within a block. If the storage class has not been explicitly specified, a variable declared within a block is taken to be `auto`. Thus, the declarations of the variables `i` and `result` in

```
int factorial(int n)
    {
      int i, result;
      ...
    }
```

are equivalent to

```
int factorial(int n)
    {
      auto int i, result;
      ...
    }
```

and declare `i` and `result` to be automatic variables of type integer.

An automatic variable may be initialized at the time of its declaration by following its name with an equal sign and an expression. The expression is evaluated and its value is assigned to the automatic variable each time the block is entered. Thus, the `auto` variable `result`, when initialized as

```
int factorial(int n)
    {
      int i, result = 1;
      ...
    }
```

will be set to 1 each time `factorial` is called. The function parameters can also be used in the initialization expression. Thus, the `auto` variable `last` when initialized as

```
int sort(int n)
    {
      int last = n - 1;
      ...
    }
```

is set to one less than the value of the actual argument supplied with a call to `sort`.

In the absence of explicit initialization, the initial value of an automatic variable is undefined.

5.7.2 Static Variables

A variable is said to be *static* if it is allocated storage at the beginning of the program execution and the storage remains allocated until the program execution terminates. Variables declared outside all blocks at the same level as function definitions are always static. Within a block, a variable can be specified to be static by prefixing its type declaration with the storage class specifier `static` in the following manner:

```
static   type   variable-name;
```

Thus, the declaration of `i` in

```
int f(void)
  {
    static int i;
    . . .
  }
```

specifies that `i` is a static variable of type integer.

Variables declared `static` can be initialized only with constant expressions. Unlike with `auto` variables, the initialization takes place only once, when the block is entered for the first time. If not explicitly initialized, `static` variables are assigned the default initial value of zero. The values assigned to `static` variables are retained across calls to the function in which they have been declared.

The following program illustrates the difference between `auto` and `static` variables:

```
#include <stdio.h>

int main(void)
  {
    int i;
    void incr(void);

    for (i = 0; i < 3; i++)  incr();
    return 0;
  }

void incr(void)
  {
    int auto_i = 0;
    static int static_i = 0;

    printf("auto = %d   static = %d\n",
            auto_i++, static_i++);
  }
```

The output generated by this program is:

```
auto = 0   static = 0
auto = 0   static = 1
auto = 0   static = 2
```

The output shows the value of `auto_i` as 0 for each line of display, and that of `static_i` incremented by 1 from 0 through 2. This is what is expected, for while `auto_i` is assigned the value 0 each time the function `incr` is called, `static_i` is assigned the value 0 only once, when `incr` is first executed, and its value is retained from one function call to the next.

The choice between an automatic variable and a static variable depends upon the intended use of the variable. An automatic variable is the logical choice when the value of a variable must be initialized at the beginning of each function call. However, if the value of a variable local to a function is to be retained from one function call to the next, a static variable is the obvious choice.

5.7.3 Illustrative Example

We now give an example to further illustrate the concept of static variables.

Example

Write a program to simulate the outcome of the following betting game: Two coins are tossed. The bettor wins if the outcome is two heads, and loses if it is two tails. The coins are tossed again if the outcome is one head and one tail. This time, the bettor wins if the outcome is two heads, but loses otherwise. Assume that the bettor started with $10,000 and played 10,000 games, and each bet is for $1.

Simulation programs usually require a *random number generator* that produces a sequence of numbers selected at random from a given range. A commonly used method to generate random numbers is the *linear congruential method*. In this method, each number r_k in the sequence of random numbers is calculated from its predecessor r_{k-1} using the formula

$$r_k = (multiplier \times r_{k-1} + increment) \% modulus$$

where *multiplier*, *increment*, and *modulus* are appropriately chosen constants. The sequence generated by this formula is really *pseudo-random*, since the value of r_k can always be predicted, given r_0. However, pseudo-random sequences are sufficient for most purposes.

The program given below uses a pseudo-random number generator `rand`, based on the linear congruential method. This generator generates 65536 pseudo-random numbers in the range 0 through 1 before repeating itself, and will work correctly on a computer for which *maxint* $\geq 2^{31}$.

```
#include <stdio.h>
#define    MULTIPLIER    25173
#define    INCREMENT     13849
#define    MODULUS       65536
#define    SEED          21973
#define    KITTY         10000
#define    GAMES         10000

/*  returns 2 if both coins have a head;
    returns 1 if one coin has a head and the other a tail;
    returns 0 if both coins have a tail  */
int     play(void);
```

```c
/*  returns outcome of one toss: 'H' (head) or 'T' (tail)  */
char    toss(void);

/*  pseudo-random number generator  */
double rand(unsigned int seed0);

int main(void)
   {
     int i, heads, balance;

     for (i = 1, balance = KITTY; i <= GAMES; i++)
        {
          heads = play();
          if (heads == 1)  /* toss again */
               heads = play();
          heads == 2 ? balance++ : balance --;
        }

     printf("kitty = %d; take home = %d\n",
             KITTY, balance);
     return 0;
   }

int play(void)
   {
     char flip1, flip2;

     flip1 = toss();
     flip2 = toss();

     if (flip1 == 'H' && flip2 == 'H')  return 2;
     if (flip1 == 'T' && flip2 == 'T')  return 0;
     return 1;
   }

char toss(void)
   {
     return  rand(SEED) < 0.5 ? 'H' : 'T';
   }


double rand(unsigned int seed0)
   {
     static unsigned int number;
     static int initialized = 0;

     if (!initialized)
        {
          number = seed0 % MODULUS;
          initialized = 1;
        }
```

```
       number = (MULTIPLIER * number + INCREMENT)
               % MODULUS;
       return (double) number / (MODULUS - 1);
}
```

The first time `rand` is called, the variable `initialized` is set to 0. Therefore, `number` is initialized to `seed0`, and `initialized` is set to 1. Since both `number` and `initialized` are `static` variables, their values are preserved across function calls, and the variable `initialized` is initialized only once. Consequently, `number` is also initialized with `seed0` only once, and every call to `rand` generates a new pseudo-random value using the previous value saved in `number`.

Note that the argument `seed0`, although required only in the first call, is supplied in every call to `rand`. The next section contains a more pleasing version of this program.

5.8 SEPARATE COMPILATION AND DATA ABSTRACTION

A large program is developed by partitioning it into logically related functions, called *modules*, each of which can reside in a separate file. These files can be compiled separately, and linked later to form an executable program. Hence, if a compilation error is found, only the file in which the error occurs needs to be corrected and recompiled. The program can also be tested module-by-module by writing small driver programs that test the functions contained within a single file.

Abstract data objects can be implemented through a careful use of modules. An *abstract data object* is one that can be manipulated using only the operations supplied by the definer of the object. Details of how an abstract data object is implemented are hidden from the user. This design prevents objects from becoming dependent on specific implementation details of other objects, allowing local changes to an object without affecting the others. The designer of a module may allow only certain functions defined in a file to be referenced from other functions. Implementation details of these functions, such as the data structures used and shared by them, can be hidden from the users of the module.

We will first discuss how a function can access a variable defined in another file, and then describe the facilities provided in C to realize information hiding.

5.8.1 `extern` Declaration

We studied in Section 5.6 that if a variable is defined outside any function, it can be accessed by any statement following this definition in the rest of the source file by simply naming the variable. However, if this variable is needed in another file, or in the same file but at a point earlier than that at which it has been defined, it must be declared with the keyword `extern` before it can be used. An `extern` declaration is of the form

```
extern type identifier;
```

At this stage, it will be useful to understand the distinction between the *declaration* and the *definition* of an external variable. The declaration of an external variable, specified using the keyword `extern`, declares for the rest of the source file the type of the variable, but does not allocate any storage for the variable. On the other hand, the definition of an external variable, specified without the keyword `extern`, causes the storage to be allocated, and also serves as the declaration for the rest of that source file. An external variable can be initialized only at the time of its definition. There must be only one definition of an external variable; all other files that need access to this variable must contain an `extern` declaration for this variable.

All function names are considered global and are visible in any part of the program, be it the file in which the function has been defined or any other file that is part of the source for the program. Thus, a file need not contain `extern` declarations for functions external to it.

The following example program shows the definition, declaration, and use of external variables. The program consists of two modules, residing in files `main.c` and `compute.c`.

```
/********************   main.c   ********************/

#include <stdio.h>

extern int i;      /* extern declaration of i in the same file */
void mod(void);

int main(void)
  {
    scanf("%d", &i);
    mod();
    return 0;
  }

int i;             /* definition of i */

extern j;          /* extern declaration of j */

void output(void)
  {
    printf("%d %d\n", i, j);
  }

/******************   compute.c   ******************/

#include <stdio.h>
#define  MODULUS  10

extern int i;    /* extern declaration of i in a different file */
void output(void);

int j = MODULUS; /* declaration and definition of j */
int k;           /* external variable used only in compute.c */
```

```
void input(void)
  {
    scanf("%d", &k);
  }

void mod(void)
  {
    input();
    i %= j+k;
    output();
  }
```

The declarations common to more than one module are usually collected in a single file, known as the *header file*. These are then copied into the modules that use them by means of the #include facility. By convention, the names of the header files are suffixed with .h. For instance, the preceding program can be rewritten by collecting constants and external declarations in a file named global.h as follows.

```
/******************** global.h ********************/
#include <stdio.h>
#define  MODULUS  10
extern int i, j;
void mod(void), output(void);

/******************** main.c ********************/
#include "global.h"

int main(void)
  {
    scanf("%d", &i);
    mod();
    return 0;
  }

int i;

void output(void)
  {
    printf("%d %d\n", i, j);
  }

/******************** compute.c ********************/
#include "global.h"

int j = MODULUS;
int k;

void input(void)
  {
    scanf("%d", &k);
  }
```

```
void mod(void)
  {
    input();
    i %= j+k;
    output();
  }
```

For a very large program, there may be more than one header file; each module then includes only those header files that contain information relevant to it. However, the larger the number of header files, the more difficult it becomes to maintain them. For programs of up to moderate size, therefore, often only one header file, containing everything to be shared between any two parts of the program, is used.

Each module of a large program is separately compiled. Separate compilation speeds up debugging, as the whole program does not have to be recompiled if the changes are confined to one module. If your IBM PC has the Microsoft C compiler, you may compile a module by using the /c option with the cl command. Thus, the two modules of the preceding program can be separately compiled using the commands:

```
cl /c main.c
cl /c compute.c
```

Successful compilation of main.c and compute.c produces the files main.obj and compute.obj respectively. These .obj files are then linked together using the command

```
cl /Femod main compute
```

that produces the executable file named mod.exe. The Fe option allows you to give a name of your choice to the executable file produced. Without the Fe option, cl gives the base name of the first file on the command line, plus the extension .exe to the executable file it creates. Thus, the command

```
cl main compute
```

will create main.exe.

On a Unix System V Release 4 machine, you may compile a module by providing the -c flag with the cc command:

```
cc -c main.c
cc -c compute.c
```

Successful compilation of main.c and compute.c produces the files main.o and compute.o respectively. These .o files are then linked together using the command

```
cc -o mod main.o compute.o
```

that produces an executable title named mod.

5.8.2 Information Hiding

Information hiding is accomplished by defining external variables and functions with the prefix static as follows:

static *type identifier*;

Such a declaration limits the scope of the declared object to the rest of the source file being compiled. These objects then become invisible in other files, although they can be shared in the file they have been defined in. For instance, the designer of the program given in Section 5.8.1 may decide that the external variable k and the function input defined in the file compute.c should not be visible in the file main.c. This can be achieved by rewriting compute.c as follows.

```
/******************   compute.c   *******************/
#include "global.h"

int j = MODULUS;        /* j can be accessed from other files */
static int k;           /* k cannot be accessed from other files */

static void input(void)/* input cannot be accessed
           from other files */
  {
    scanf("%d", &k);
  }

void mod(void)          /* mod can be accessed from other files */
  {
    input();
    i %= j+k;
    output();
  }
```

Note that the effect of prefixing an external variable declaration with the keyword static is different from that of making a variable static within a block. The former is a device for realizing information hiding, whereas the latter provides private permanent storage within a function.

5.8.3 Illustrative Example

We now give an example to further illustrate the concepts of separate compilation and information hiding.

Example
Rewrite the simulation of the betting game, given in Section 5.7.3, by partitioning it into separate files.

We will organize the betting game program into four files, according to the following:

1. `global.h`: symbolic constants and external declarations.
2. `main.c`: the `main` function and the initialization of the pseudo-random number generator.
3. `simulate.c`: simulation routines.
4. `random.c`: pseudo-random number generator.

The desired program is as follows:

```
/******************** global.h ******************/

#include <stdio.h>
#define   SEED      21973
#define   KITTY     10000
#define   GAMES     10000

void    srand(unsigned int seed0);
double  rand(void);
int     simulate(int kitty, int games);

/******************** main.c ******************/

#include "global.h"
static void initialize(void);

int main(void)
  {
    int balance;

    initialize();
    balance = simulate(KITTY, GAMES);
    printf("kitty = %d; take home = %d\n",
            KITTY, balance);

    return 0;
  }

static void initialize(void)
  {
    srand(SEED);
  }

/******************** simulate.c ******************/

#include "global.h"
static int  play(void);
static char toss(void);
```

```
int simulate(int kitty, int games)
  {
    int i, heads, balance;

    for (i = 1, balance = kitty; i <= games; i++)
      {
        heads = play();
        if (heads == 1)  /* toss again */
            heads = play();

        (heads == 2) ? balance++ : balance --;
      }

    return balance;
  }

static int play(void)
  {
    int flip1, flip2;

    flip1 = toss();
    flip2 = toss();

    if (flip1 == 'H' && flip2 == 'H')  return 2;
    if (flip1 == 'T' && flip2 == 'T')  return 0;
    return 1;
  }

static char toss(void)
  {
    return  rand() <= 0.5 ? 'H' : 'T';
  }

/******************  random.c  ******************/
#include "global.h"
#define  MULTIPLIER  25173
#define  INCREMENT   13849
#define  MODULUS     65536

static unsigned int number = 1; /* default seed */

void srand(unsigned int seed0)
  {
    number = seed0 % MODULUS;
  }

double rand()
  {
    number = (MULTIPLIER * number + INCREMENT)
                % MODULUS;
    return (double) number / (MODULUS - 1);
  }
```

The pseudo-random number generator, contained in the file `random.c`, uses an external variable `number` to keep track of the last number generated. The variable `number` has been made `static` so that any function not in `random.c` may not access it. The file `random.c` really implements an *abstract data object*. The pseudo-random number generator in `random.c` can only be accessed using the functions, `srand` and `rand`: the first initializes the pseudo-random number generator, and the second returns a new pseudo-random number every time it is called. The user of this pseudo-random number generator does not have to know which algorithm has been used to implement the random number generation. The advantage of this approach is that the implementor of the pseudo-random number generator may use a different random number generation algorithm, without affecting the rest of the program, as long as the current interface to the pseudo-random number generator is preserved; that is, the function prototypes for `srand` and `rand` specified in `global.h` are not changed. Only `random.c` will require recompilation and linking with the compiled versions of other source files. Note that we kept the symbolic constants MULTIPLIER, INCREMENT, and MODULUS in the file `random.c`, rather than `global.h`, since these constants are closely tied to the current algorithm being used for random number generation.

The file `simulate.c` contains the routines that implement the simulation of the betting game. In contrast to the program given in Section 5.7.3, a new function `simulate` has been added in this version of the program. The advantage of this approach is that if the rules of the game were changed in any way, only the file `simulate.c` would need modifications. The functions `play` and `toss` are local to this module, and they have been made `static` so that they cannot be called by functions outside this module. Note that the function prototypes of `play` and `toss` have not been included in `global.h`.

The file `main.c` contains the `main` function. We have chosen to provide two parameters to `simulate`, rather than burying the symbolic constants in the body of `simulate`, for the simple reason that if we later decide to modify the program to read as input parameters the size of the kitty and the number of games for which the simulation should be run, it could be accomplished by adding a call to `scanf` in `initialize` without having to modify `simulate`. In general, you should strive to design programs in such a way that they are amenable to additions and improvements. The decoupling of the modules by communicating values to functions across modules only through parameters goes a long way toward achieving this goal.

Finally, the file `global.h` contains some symbolic constants and the prototypes of the functions that are called across modules. One could argue that these symbolic constants should have been part of `main.c` as that is the only file where they are used. Our viewpoint is that these constants represent external properties of the program, and putting them in `global.h` helps in the documentation of the program. The disadvantage of this choice is that a redefinition of any of these constants will force the recompilation of not only `main.c` but all other source files that include `global.h`.

5.9 RECURSION

Recursion is the process whereby a construct operates on itself. In C, functions may be defined recursively; that is, a function may directly or indirectly call itself in the course of its execution. If the call to a function occurs inside the function itself, the recursion is said to be *direct*. However, if a function calls another function, which in turn makes a call to the first one, the recursion is said to be *indirect*. The chain of calls may be more involved; there may be several intermediate calls before the original function is called back.

The factorial function, defined as

factorial(0) = 1
factorial(n) = n * factorial(n-1), $n > 0$

is the classic example of recursion. This function can be coded as

```
int factorial(int n)
   {
      if (n == 0)
          return 1;              /* termination condition */
      else
          return n * factorial(n-1);/* recurse */
   }
```

or more succinctly as:

```
int factorial(int n)
   {
      return n == 0 ? 1 : n * factorial(n-1);
   }
```

Figure 5.1 provides a visual representation of the recursive evaluation of `factorial(3)`.

Note that if `factorial` were called with a negative value, it would never terminate. Why? One way to ensure termination is to write the function `factorial` as follows:

```
int factorial(int n)
   {
      if (n > 0)
          return n * factorial(n-1);
      else if (n == 0)
          return 1;
      else
         {
            printf("no factorial for negative values\n");
            return -1;
         }
   }
```

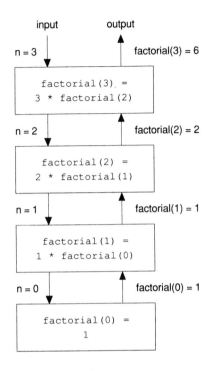

Figure 5.1. Recursive evaluation of `factorial(3)`

As another example of recursion, consider the Fibonacci sequence of numbers

1, 1, 2, 3, 5, 8, 13, 21, . . .

defined by

fib(0) = fib(1) = 1
fib(n) = fib (n-1) + fib(n-2), $n > 1$

This recursive definition can be translated into a recursive C function in a straightforward manner as

```
int fib(int n)
   {
      return n == 0 || n == 1 ?
               1 :  fib(n-1) + fib(n-2);
   }
```

Note that `fib` contains two calls to itself in its body. Figure 5.2 provides a visual representation of the recursive evaluation of `fib(3)`.

5.9.1 Recursion Versus Iteration

In theory, any recursive function can be transformed into an iterative function. We have given a nonrecursive function for computing factorials in Section 5.5.

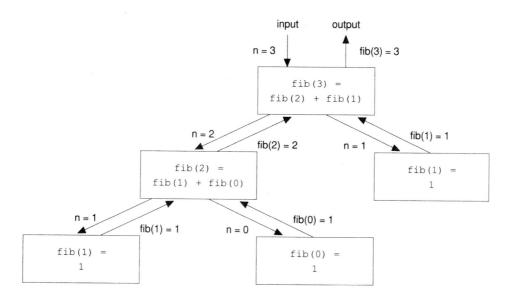

Figure 5.2. Recursive evaluation of `fib(3)`

The following is a nonrecursive function for computing the *n*th Fibonacci number:

```
int fib(int n)
  {
    int i, result, n_minus1 = 1, n_minus2 = 1;

    if (n == 0 || n == 1)   return 1;

    for (i = 2; i <= n; i++)
      {
        result = n_minus1 + n_minus2;
        n_minus2 = n_minus1;
        n_minus1 = result;
      }

    return result;
  }
```

It is obvious that the recursive versions of these functions are more concise and understandable than their iterative counterparts, and their correctness can easily be verified by appealing to the corresponding mathematical definitions. Why would then one ever want to use iterative versions of these functions? The problem with the recursive solutions is that, compared to their iterative versions, they can be far more inefficient. Iterative versions are generally faster as they avoid the overhead of passing arguments and returning values in a series of function calls and returns. The other source of inefficiency in recursive solutions is redundant computations. For example, in calculating `fib(3)`, fib(1) is calculated two times, and in calculating fib(4), fib(2) is calculated two times, fib(1) three times, and fib(0) two times. As n increases, this duplication of calculation increases exponentially, resulting in prohibitive execution time.

5.9.2 Illustrative Example

We now give an example of a problem whose recursive solution is rather straightforward, but an iterative solution is quite cumbersome.

Example
Write a program to solve the Tower of Hanoi puzzle.

The Tower of Hanoi puzzle was quite popular in Europe toward the late nineteenth century. Part of its popularity is attributed to the following legend that accompanied the puzzle:

> In the great temple at Benares, beneath the dome that marks the center of the world, rests a brass plate in which are fixed three diamond needles, each a cubit high and as thick as the body of the bee. On one of these needles, at the creation, God placed sixty-four disks of pure gold, the largest disk resting on the brass plate and the others getting smaller and smaller up to the top one. This is the Tower of Brahma. Day and night unceasingly, the priests transfer the disks from one diamond needle to another according to the fixed and immutable laws of Brahma, which require that the priest on duty must not move more than one disk at a time, and that he must place this disk on a needle so that there is no smaller disk below it. When all the sixty-four disks shall have been thus transferred from the needle on which at the creation God placed them to one of the other needles, the tower, the temple and the priests alike will crumble into dust, and with a thunderclap the world will vanish.

The promoters of the puzzle renamed the Tower of Brahma as the Tower of Hanoi, and it is by this name that the puzzle is now popularly known.

If the needles have been numbered 1, 2, and 3, and the priests are moving the tower of 64 disks from needle 1 to needle 2, using needle 3 as the spare needle, this task can be represented as

move(64, 1, 2, 3)

The insight that leads to a simple solution is to think about the bottom disk on needle 1 rather than the top one. The task *move(64, 1, 2, 3)* can then be seen to be equivalent to the following sequence of subtasks:

move(63, 1, 3, 2)
move a disk from needle 1 to 2
move (63, 3, 2, 1)

that is, first move the tower of the top 63 disks from needle 1 to needle 3, then move the 64th disk on needle 1 to needle 2, and finally move the tower of 63 disks from needle 3 to needle 2. We can thus write the program to solve the puzzle as:

```c
#include <stdio.h>

/*
 *   Move n disks from tower x to tower y,
 *   where z is the third tower
 */

void move(int n, int x, int y, int z)
  {
    if (n == 1)
        printf("move the top disk on %d to %d\n",
                x, y);
    else
      {
        /* move the top n-1 disks on tower x to tower z */
        move(n-1, x, z, y);

        /* move the bottommost disk on tower x to tower y */
        printf("move the top disk on %d to %d\n",
                x, y);

        /* now move the n-1 disks on tower z to tower y */
        move(n-1, z, y, x);
      }
  }

int main(void)
  {
    int disks;

    scanf("%d", &disks);
    move(disks, 1, 2, 3);
    return 0;
  }
```

The following is the solution of the puzzle for 3 disks:

```
move the top disk on 1 to 2
move the top disk on 1 to 3
move the top disk on 2 to 3
move the top disk on 1 to 2
move the top disk on 3 to 1
move the top disk on 3 to 2
move the top disk on 1 to 2
```

Do not try to run this program for 64 disks. The 64-disk game, at a million moves per second, would require something like 584,542 years of CPU time. It shows that the existence of an algorithm to perform a task does not necessarily mean that the task can really be performed (which might be good in this case, just in case the legend was really true).

Exercises 5

1. Analyze the output of the following programs:

   a.
   ```c
   #include <stdio.h>

   int i = 0;

   void f(void)
     {
       int i;
       i = 1;
     }

   void g(void)
     {
       i = 2;
     }

   void h(int i)
     {
       i = 3;
     }

   int main(void)
     {
       {
         int i = 4;
         printf("%d\n", i);
       }
       printf("%d\n", i);
       f();
       printf("%d\n", i);
       g();
       printf("%d\n", i);
       h(i);
       printf("%d\n", i);
       return 0;
     }
   ```

   b.
   ```c
   #include <stdio.h>

   void hill(int n)
     {
       printf("%d ", n);
       if (n <= 100)
         {
           hill(3*n - 1);
           printf("%d ", n);
         }
     }

   int main(void)
     {
       hill(1);
       return 0;
     }
   ```

c.
```
#include <stdio.h>

void flathill(int n)
  {
    printf("%d ", n);
    if (n <= 100) flathill(3*n - 1);
    printf("%d ", n);
  }

int main(void)
  {
    flathill(1);
    return 0;
  }
```

d.
```
#include <stdio.h>

int g(int n, int x, int y)
  {
    return n == 0 ? x : g(n-1, y, x+y);
  }

int f(int n)
  {
    return g(n, 0, 1);
  }

int main(void)
  {
    int i;

    for (i = 1; i <= 10; i++)
        printf("%d\n", f(i));
    return 0;
  }
```

e.
```
#include <stdio.h>

void print(void)
  {
    int c;

    if ((c = getchar()) != '\n') print();
    else return;
    putchar(c);
  }

int main(void)
  {
    print();
    putchar('\n');
    return 0;
  }
```

Input: ABLE WAS I ERE I SAW ELBA

2. Define a function to calculate

$$(x^2 + y^2 + z^2)^{1/2}$$

and use it to calculate

$$\alpha = 1/(u^2 + v^2 + w^2)^{1/2}, \quad \beta = (u^4 + v^4 + w^4)^{1/2},$$

$$\gamma = (4u^2 + 9v^2 + 25w^2)^{1/2}, \quad \delta = (3u^2)^{1/2}(12v^2)^{1/2}(27w^2)^{1/2}$$

where u, v, and w are read from input.

3. Two positive integers are said to be *buddies* if each one is equal to the sum of the divisors of the other and the divisors include 1 but exclude the number itself. For example, the numbers 220 and 284 are buddies since:

divisors of 220: 1+2+4+5+10+11+20+22+44+55+110 = 284

divisors of 284: 1+2+4+71+142 = 220

Write a program to find all the pairs of buddies in a given range of numbers.

4. When Professor Ramanujam was presenting to his mathematics class the interesting property of the integer 8833 that $8833 = 88^2 + 33^2$, Shakunthala observed that the time in her digital clock, viewed as a number without the colon, had the same property, that is, the square of the hours digits plus the square of the minutes digits equaled the number she saw. Write a program to determine the time that Shakunthala observed.

5. The *zero* of a function f is defined to be the value k such that $f(k) = 0$. The *Newton-Raphson* method finds the zero of a function by successive approximations, using the relationship

$$x_{i+1} = x_i - \frac{f(x_i)}{f'(x_i)}$$

where

$\quad x_i$ = the current estimate of *zero*

$\quad x_{i+1}$ = the next estimate

$\quad f(x_i)$ = the function evaluated at x_i

$\quad f'(x_i)$ = the first derivative of the function evaluated at x_i

An initial estimate x_0 is required to initiate the process, and the process terminates when $|x_{i+1} - x_i| < \varepsilon$, where ε is a small value such as 0.00001. Write a program to locate a zero of the function $f(x) = x^3 - 3x^2 + 1$, using the Newton-Raphson method.

6. The *power series*

$$1 + x + \frac{x^2}{2!} + \frac{x^3}{3!} + \cdots = \sum_{n=0}^{\infty} \frac{x^n}{n!}$$

converges to e^x for all values of x. Write a function that uses this series to calculate e^x to six-place accuracy by adding terms from the series up to the first term that is less than 10^{-6} in absolute value. Use this function to print a table of values for the functions

$$sinh(x) = \frac{e^x - e^{-x}}{2}$$

and

$$cosh(x) = \frac{e^x + e^{-x}}{2}$$

for $x = -1$ to 1 in increments of 0.1.

7. Write a program to calculate the partial sums of the harmonic series

$$1 + \frac{1}{2} + \frac{1}{3} + \cdots + \frac{1}{n} .$$

The result is to be expressed in the form of a rational number, that is, a number of the form

$$\frac{numerator}{denominator} ,$$

where *numerator* and *denominator* are integers with no common factors. A method by which common factors can be eliminated is to divide the numerator and denominator by their greatest common divisor.

8. When his teacher asked Sleepy to simplify the fraction $26/65$, he simply canceled the digit 6 both from the numerator and denominator. To the teacher's amazement, Sleepy's cancellation technique produced the correct result:

$$\frac{2\cancel{6}}{\cancel{6}5} = \frac{2}{5}$$

Write a program to determine all the fractions with two-digit numerators and denominators for which Sleepy's technique works correctly.

9. *Twin primes* are defined to be two consecutive odd numbers which are both primes. For example, 11 and 13 are twin primes. Write a program to generate all the twin primes in a given range of numbers.

10. To understand the relationship between two sets of data, a straight line is often fitted to the data using the method of *least squares*, which minimizes the squares of the differences between actual and fitted function values. The general equation for a straight line is

$$y = mx + c$$

The values of m and c are computed from a set of n paired observations of x and y as

$$m = \frac{n\sum xy - \left(\sum x\right)\left(\sum y\right)}{n\sum x^2 - \left(\sum x\right)^2}$$

$$c = \bar{y} - m\bar{x}$$

where $\bar{y}$ and $\bar{x}$ are the arithmetic means of their respective data sets.

Instead of a straight line, one may also fit a curve of the form

$$y = cx^m$$

Taking logarithms, this equation takes the form

$$\log y = \log c + m \log x$$

which, on substituting $Y = \log y$, $X = \log x$, and $C = \log c$, takes the form

$$Y = mX + C$$

and, thus, m and C in this equation can be computed using the equations for m and c for the straight line, modified for logarithms.

Write a program that reads pairs of values of x and y and computes m and c for the equations of the straight line and curve given above.

11. The mean $\bar{x}$ and standard deviation σ of a set of numbers $x_1, x_2, \ldots, x_n$ are defined as:

$$\bar{x} = \frac{\displaystyle\sum_{i=1}^{n} x_i}{n}$$

$$\sigma^2 = \frac{n \displaystyle\sum_{i=1}^{n} x_i^2 - \left(\displaystyle\sum_{i=1}^{n} x_i\right)^2}{n(n-1)}$$

Write a function that calculates the mean and standard deviation of a set of numbers, and then use this function in a program that reads a set of test scores and assigns letter grades to each of these scores using the following grading scheme, commonly called "grading on a curve":

x = numeric score	Letter Grade
$x \geq \bar{x} + 1.5\sigma$	A
$\bar{x} + 0.5\sigma \leq x < \bar{x} + 1.5\sigma$	B
$\bar{x} - 0.5\sigma \leq x < \bar{x} + 0.5\sigma$	C
$\bar{x} - 1.5\sigma \leq x < \bar{x} - 0.5\sigma$	D
$x < \bar{x} - 1.5\sigma$	F

12. In the following number puzzles:

```
    I            IS
 +AM          +IT
 ———          ———
  OK           OK
```

the letters take the place of digits and each distinct letter represents a different digit. Write a program for each of the above puzzles to determine all possible combinations of digits for the letters such that the addition holds.

13. In the game of Nim, there are three piles of sticks and two players take turns making moves. A move consists of picking up as many sticks as the player desires, subject to the constraints that the sticks must be picked up from the same pile, and a player must pick up at least one stick. The player who picks up the last stick loses. Write a program to play Nim with the user. The program should use the linear congruential random number generator discussed in Section 5.7.3 to choose the size of three piles, subject to the constraint that the three piles must be of different sizes and must contain at least 2 and at most 10 sticks.

14. The *squaring* or the *inner product* method for generating a sequence of *pseudo-random numbers* is as follows: Take a number having a given number of digits, say five, square it, and pick out the central five digits of the product as a random number. The five-digit random number is now squared, etc. For example, starting with 54321, the random numbers 50771, 77694, 36357, 21831, 65925, 46105, . . . are generated as

$$54321^2 = 29\ \underline{50771}\ 041$$

$$50771^2 = 25\ \underline{77694}\ 441$$

$77694^2 = 60\ \underline{36357}\ 636$

$36357^2 = 13\ \underline{21831}\ 449$

$21831^2 = 47\ \underline{65925}\ 61$

$65925^2 = 43\ \underline{46105}\ 625$

Use this pseudo-random number generator to write a program to play a simplified roulette. The roulette selects a number between 0 and 35 at random. The player can place a bet on a particular number or can place an even or odd bet. A winning bet on a particular number is paid off at 35 to 1. A winning even or odd bet is paid off at 2 to 1, except that any even or odd bet loses if the roulette selects 0.

15. If an irregular figure I is enclosed within a regular figure R, then the probability that a random point inside R is also inside I is given by the ratio of the area of I to the area of R. Thus, the area of I can be estimated by generating random points in R and counting those that fall inside I. Write a program that uses this technique to estimate the area of a circle of unit radius by enclosing it in a square. Then use the formula $area = \pi r^2$ to get an estimate of π.

The program should use the following *power residue* method for generating pseudo-random numbers: To obtain five-digit random numbers, form the product of a starting value that is neither even nor ends in a 5 with a special constant multiplier, and pick out the low-order five digits as the random number. The five-digit random number is now multiplied with the constant multiplier, etc. Thus, starting with 54321, the random numbers 69137, 06289, 10033, 73201, 00497, 48209, . . . are generated as

$54321 \times 97 = 52\ \underline{69137}$

$69137 \times 97 = 67\ \underline{06289}$

$06289 \times 97 = 6\ \underline{10033}$

$10033 \times 97 = 9\ \underline{73201}$

$73201 \times 97 = 71\ \underline{00497}$

$00497 \times 97 = \ \underline{48209}$

16. Write a recursive function to print an integer as a string.

17. Write a recursive definition for the following sawtooth function:

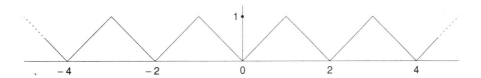

18. Write a recursive function for calculating values of *Ackermann's function*, $Ack(m,n)$, defined for $m \geq 0$ and $n \geq 0$ by

$Ack(0,n) = n + 1$ for $n \geq 0$

$Ack(m,0) = Ack(m-1,1)$ for $m \geq 1$

$Ack(m,n) = Ack(m-1,Ack(m,n-1))$ for $m \geq 1, n \geq 1$

Convince yourself that

$Ack(1,n) = n + 2,$ $Ack(2,n) = 2n + 3,$ $Ack(3,n) = 2^{n+3}$

$Ack(4,0) = 13,$ $Ack(4,1) = 65533,$ $Ack(4,2) = 2^{65536} - 3$

19. Write iterative and recursive functions for calculating values of the following polynomials:

Chebyshev polynomial:

$$C_n(x) = \begin{cases} 1 & \text{for } n = 0 \\ 2 & \text{for } n = 1 \\ 2xC_{n-1}(x) - C_{n-2}(x) & \text{for } n > 1 \end{cases}$$

Hermite polynomial:

$$H_n(x) = \begin{cases} 1 & \text{for } n = 0 \\ 2x & \text{for } n = 1 \\ 2xH_{n-1}(x) - 2(n-1)H_{n-2}(x) & \text{for } n > 1 \end{cases}$$

Legendre polynomial:

$$L_n(x) = \begin{cases} 1 & \text{for } n = 0 \\ x & \text{for } n = 1 \\ ((2n-1)L_{n-1}(x) - (n-1)L_{n-2}(x))/n & \text{for } n > 1 \end{cases}$$

20. Given a_0 and b_0, a_n and b_n are defined as follows:

$a_n = a_{n/2} + b_{n/3}$

$b_n = a_{n/3} \times b_{n/2} + 1$

Write a program to print a table of values of a_j and b_j for j from 1 to an input value n.

6 Arrays

Very often, one needs to process a collection of related data items, such as test scores of students in a university, a set of measurements resulting from an experiment, income tax tables, etc. One way of handling such a situation would be to invent a new variable name for each of these data items. This approach obviously is quite cumbersome, if not altogether impossible.

A notation, called *subscript notation*, exists in mathematics to handle such situations. For example, prices of 10 items are represented as

$$P_1, P_2, P_3, \ldots, P_{10}$$

where P is the group name for all prices and the subscript $(1, 2, 3, \ldots, 10)$ identifies the price of a specific item. Thus, P_i represents the price of the ith item. C provides a capability similar to the subscript notation that enables you to structure and process a set of ordered data items.

6.1 BASICS OF ARRAYS

An ordered finite collection of data items, each of the same type, is called an *array*, and the individual data items are its *elements*. Only one name is assigned to an entire array, and individual elements are referenced by specifying a *subscript*. A subscript is also called an *index*. In C, subscripts start at 0, rather than 1, and cannot be negative. The single group name and the subscript are associated by enclosing the subscript in square brackets to the right of the name. Thus, if prices have been stored in an array named `price`, then `price[0]` refers to the price of the first item, `price[4]` to the price of the fifth item, etc.

An array has the following properties:

1. The *type* of an array is the data type of its elements.
2. The *location* of an array is the location of its first element.
3. The *length* of an array is the number of data elements in the array.
4. The *size* of an array is the length of the array times the size of an element.

Arrays whose elements are specified by one subscript are called *single-subscripted*, *linear*, or *one-dimensional* arrays. Analogous arrays whose elements are specified by two and three subscripts are called *double-subscripted* or *two-dimensional* and *triple-subscripted* or *three-dimensional* arrays respectively. For most

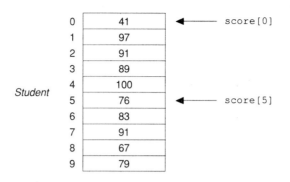

Figure 6.1. One-dimensional array `score`

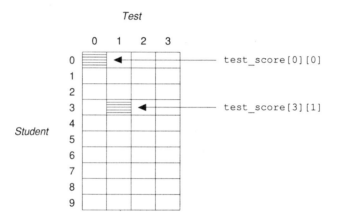

Figure 6.2. Two-dimensional array `test_score`

applications, one-, two-, or three-dimensional arrays are adequate, although C allows arrays of any number of dimensions. Here are examples of these arrays:

1. Test scores of ten students can be arranged in a one-dimensional array, often called a *vector*, as shown in Figure 6.1. If `score` is used to denote the array, the score of student 1 is identified as the array element `score[0]`, the score of student 6 as the array element `score[5]`, etc.

2. Four test scores of ten students can be arranged in a two-dimensional array, often called a *matrix*, having 10 rows and 4 columns, as shown in Figure 6.2. An element of a two-dimensional array is referred to by specifying two subscripts, the first designating row and the second column. Thus, if `test_score` is the name of the array, the score of student 1 in test 1 is identified as the matrix element `test_score[0][0]` and the score of student 4 in test 2 as the matrix element `test_score[3][1]`.

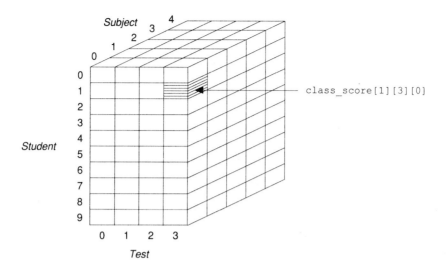

Figure 6.3. Three-dimensional array `class_score`

Note that in C the notation `test_score[i][j]`, rather than `test_score[i, j]`, is used to refer to the element in row `i` and column `j`.

3. Scores of ten students in four tests each in five subjects can be arranged in a three-dimensional array, say `class_score`, having 10 rows, 4 columns, and 5 levels, as shown in Figure 6.3. An element of this array is referenced by specifying the name of the array, `class_score`, together with the three subscripts listed in the order of row, column, and level. Thus, the score of student 2 in test 4 of subject 1 is identified as the array element `class_score[1][3][0]`.

The capability to represent a collection of related data items by a single array enables the development of concise and efficient programs. As an illustration of the use of arrays, consider the following program that reads test scores into the array `score`, adds them, and prints their average.

```
#include <stdio.h>
#define   STUDENTS   10

int main(void)
  {
    int i, sum;
    int score[STUDENTS];

    for (i = 0; i < STUDENTS; i++)
        scanf("%d", &score[i]);

    for (sum = 0, i = 0; i < STUDENTS; i++)
        sum += score[i];
```

```
    printf("average score = %f\n",
           (float)sum/STUDENTS);

    return 0;
}
```

The declaration

```
int score[STUDENTS];
```

specifies that `score` is a one-dimensional array of `STUDENTS`, that is, 10 integer elements. The first `for` loop reads test scores one at a time and assigns them to the successive elements of `score`. The second `for` loop steps through the elements of `score` and accumulates into `sum` the value of each score. The `printf` statement prints the average score.

We will now look into array declaration, access to array elements, and array initialization in detail.

6.1.1 Array Declaration

Arrays, like simple variables, need to be declared before use. An array declaration is of the form

type   array-name[*expr-1*] [*expr-2*] $\cdots$ [*expr-n*];

where *array-name* is the name of the array being declared, *type* is the type of the elements that will be contained in the array, and *expr–i* is a constant integral expression specifying the number of elements in the *i*th dimension of the array. For example, the declaration

```
int    score[10];
```

declares `score` to be an array containing 10 integer elements; the declaration

```
float   test_score[10][4];
```

declares the array `test_score` to be a two-dimensional array with 10 rows, 4 columns, and $10 \times 4 = 40$ single-precision floating point elements; and the declaration

```
double   class_score[10][4][5];
```

declares the array `class_score` to be a three-dimensional array with 10 rows, 4 columns, 5 levels, and $10 \times 4 \times 5 = 200$ double-precision floating point elements.

Since any constant integral expression may be used to specify the number of elements in an array, symbolic constants or expressions involving symbolic constants may also appear in array declarations. For example, the declarations

```
#define   CHARS_PER_LINE   80
#define   TOTAL_LINES      100
char   line[CHARS_PER_LINE];
char   text[CHARS_PER_LINE * TOTAL_LINES];
```

declare `line` and `text` to be one-dimensional character arrays of 80 and 8000 elements respectively.

Besides specifying the amount of storage that must be allocated, an array declaration also places bounds on the valid values for the subscripts of the array. For example, given the declaration

```
float   price[100];
```

the valid range of values for the subscript of `price` is 0 through 99.

While declaring an array, the type can be prefixed with `auto`, `static`, or `extern`. We can therefore write

```
auto int score[10];
static float test_score[10][4];
extern double class_score[10][4][5];
```

The length may be omitted in an `extern` declaration of a one-dimensional array, since this declaration does not allocate storage but refers to an object defined elsewhere. The `extern` declaration of an n-dimensional array ($n > 1$), however, must include the last $n-1$ dimensions so that the accessing algorithm can be determined. Thus, the following are legal declarations:

```
extern int score[];
extern float test_score[][4];
extern double class_score[][4][5];
```

6.1.2 Accessing Array Elements

A particular element of an array can be accessed by specifying appropriate subscripts with the array name. Any integral expression can be used as a subscript. Thus, if `score` has been declared to be a one-dimensional array and `offset` an `int`, the following are all valid references to the elements of `score`:

```
score[offset]
score[3*offset]
score[offset/5]
```

Subscripts should not have values outside the array bounds. C does not automatically check subscripts to lie within the array bounds. It is imperative, therefore, that you check the value of a subscript before using it to access an array element whenever the characteristics of a program make it possible for the subscript to have a value outside the array bounds. The omission of bounds checking is among the most common causes of error in C programs.

An individual array element can be used anywhere that a simple variable could be used. For example, we can assign a value to it, display its value, or perform arithmetic operations on it. Thus, the assignment statement

```
matrix[0][5] = 1;
```

assigns 1 to the element at row 0 and column 5, that is, to the element defined by the first row and sixth column of `matrix` ; the assignment statement

```
p = (price[0] + price[9]) / 2;
```

assigns the average `price` of the first and the tenth item to p; and the statement

```
--matrix[0][5];
```

decrements the contents of `matrix[0][5]` by 1. Further, the assignment statements

```
i = 5;
p = price[++i];
```

assign the value of `price[6]` to p, whereas the statements

```
i = 5;
p = price[i++];
```

assign the value of `price[5]` to p, since i is incremented before use in the first case, but after use in the second case.

An array cannot be copied into another array by assigning it to the other array. Thus, an array `from` declared as

```
int from[10];
```

cannot be copied into an array `to` declared as

```
int to[10];
```

by writing assignment statements such as

```
to = from;       /* illegal */
```

or

```
to[] = from[]; /* illegal */
```

It should be copied element-by-element through individual assignments by setting up an appropriate loop such as

```
for(i = 0; i < 10; i++) to[i] = from[i];
```

6.1.3 Array Initialization

Elements of an array, be it an external, static, or automatic array, can be assigned initial values by following the array definition with a list of initializers enclosed in braces and separated by commas. For example, the declaration

```
int  score[5]  = { 41, 97, 91, 89, 100 };
```

defines the array `score` to contain five integer elements and initializes `score[0]` to 41, `score[1]` to 97, `score[2]` to 91, `score[3]` to 89, and `score[4]` to 100. Similarly, the declaration

```
char letter[3] = { 'a', 'b', 'c' };
```

defines the array `letter` to contain three character elements and initializes `letter[0]` to 'a', `letter[1]` to 'b', and `letter[2]` to 'c'.

Multi-dimensional arrays are initialized analogously, with initializers listed by rows. Brace pairs are used to separate the list of initializers for one row from the next, and commas are placed after each brace (except for the last row) that closes off a row. Thus, to define and initialize the two-dimensional array `test_score` to the values shown below

	0	1	2	3
0	95	98	97	96
1	79	89	79	85
2	99	98	99	99
3	90	89	83	86
4	70	72	79	69

the following declaration can be used:

```
int test_score[5][4] =
    {
       { 95, 98, 97, 96 },
       { 79, 89, 79, 85 },
       { 99, 98, 99, 99 },
       { 90, 89, 83, 86 },
       { 75, 72, 79, 69 }
    };
```

The inner pairs of braces are optional. Thus, the above declaration can equivalently be written as

```
int test_score[5][4] =
    {
       95, 98, 97, 96, 79, 89, 79, 85, 99, 98,
       99, 99, 90, 89, 83, 86, 75, 72, 79, 69
    };
```

A three-dimensional array can be initialized as

```
int sales[4][2][3] =
    {
       { { 5, 8, 7 }, { 6, 7, 7 }  },
       { { 9, 9, 9 }, { 9, 9, 8 }  },
       { { 9, 8, 9 }, { 8, 8, 7 }  },
       { { 4, 5, 3 }, { 5, 3, 3 }  }
    };
```

A possible interpretation of this sales array can be that it gives the sales figures for four salesmen. Each salesman has been assigned two territories and sells three products. Thus, the first line corresponds to the sales data for the first salesman. Sales figures for the two territories have been separated by inner braces. Within a territory, sales figures for the three products have been listed consecutively separated by commas. The above declaration can equivalently be written as

```
int sales[4][2][3] =
  {
    5, 8, 7, 6, 7, 7, 9, 9, 9, 9, 9, 8,
    9, 8, 9, 8, 8, 7, 4, 5, 3, 5, 3, 3
  };
```

Some special rules govern array initialization:

1. If the number of initializers is less than the number of elements in the array, the remaining elements are set to zero. Thus, the initializations

    ```
    int score[5] = { 41, 97, 91 };

    int test_score[5][4] =
      {
        {  0, 98 },
        { 79, 89, 79 },
        {  0,  0,  0, 99 },
        { 90 },
      };
    ```

    are equivalent to

    ```
    int score[5] = { 41, 97, 91, 0, 0 };

    int test_score[5][4] =
      {
        {  0, 98,  0,  0 },
        { 79, 89, 79,  0 },
        {  0,  0,  0, 99 },
        { 90,  0,  0,  0 },
        {  0,  0,  0,  0 }
      };
    ```

    It is an error to specify more initializers than the number of elements in the array.

2. If initializers have been provided for an array, it is not necessary to explicitly specify the array length, in which case the length is derived from the initializers. For example,

    ```
    float  sqroot[]  = { 0, 1.0, 1.414, 1.732, 2.0 };
    ```

    is equivalent to

    ```
    float  sqroot[5] = { 0, 1.0, 1.414, 1.732, 2.0 };
    ```

3. A character array may be initialized by a string constant, resulting in the first element of the array being set to the first character in the string, the second element to the second character, and so on. The array also receives the terminating '\0' in the string constant. Thus,

    ```
    char os[4]       = "AIX";
    char computer[]  = "sierra";
    ```

    are equivalent to

```
char os[4]          = { 'A', 'I', 'X', '\0' };
char computer[7] =
    { 's', 'i', 'e', 'r', 'r', 'a', '\0' };
```

It is also possible to initialize a character array with an explicit length specification by a string constant with exactly as many characters. The array does not receive the terminating ' \0' in that case. For example,

```
char os[3]          = "AIX";
```

is equivalent to

```
char os[3]          = { 'A', 'I', 'X' };
```

However, the string constant must not have more characters than the length of the character array being initialized. Thus, it is an error to initialize os as

```
char os[3]          = "ultrix";
```

C does not provide a mechanism to specify a repetition count for initializing several elements of an array to the same value. Consequently, if you want to initialize all the 100 elements of some array observations to 1, then you must either explicitly provide all the 100 ones in the list of initializers in the declaration, or set up an appropriate for loop of the form

```
for (i = 0; i < 100; i++)  observations[i] = 1;
```

in the function body.

6.2   ARRAYS AS FUNCTION ARGUMENTS

You can pass an array element or an entire array as argument to a function. Passing an entire array as argument is quite different from passing its individual elements as arguments.

6.2.1 Passing Array Elements as Arguments

To pass an array element to a function, the array element is specified in the function call just as a simple variable is specified. For example, given the function definition

```
#include <math.h>
double cuberoot(double x)
  {
    return pow(x, 1.0/3.0);
  }
```

and the declarations

```
double z[10];
double zzz[10][5][20];
```

the function call

```
cuberoot(z[5])
```

returns the cube root of the value of the element z[5], and the function call

```
cuberoot(zzz[5][0][10])
```

returns the cube root of the value of the element zzz[5][0][10].

Individual array elements, like simple variables, are passed by value. Their values are copied into the corresponding parameters and cannot be changed by the called function. If the type of the array element is different from the argument type expected by the function, the same conversion rules as for simple variables apply.

6.2.2 Passing Arrays as Arguments

Functions can be defined to take arrays as arguments. For example, here is a definition of a function array_cuberoot that takes an array containing 10 elements of type double as argument:

```
void array_cuberoot(double x[10])
  {
    int i;

    for(i = 0; i < 10; i++)
        x[i] = cuberoot(x[i]);
  }
```

To pass an entire array to a function, just the name of the array, without any subscripts or brackets, is specified as the argument in the function call. Thus, the array z, defined as

```
double z[10];
```

can be passed to array_cuberoot as

```
array_cuberoot(z);
```

This function call will alter every element of z to the cube root of its current value.

Did you notice that we just now said something quite different from what we had been saying all along about parameter passing? How could array_cuberoot alter the elements of the argument array z by altering its parameter array x? Didn't we say earlier that the parameters are passed by value in C and changes to formal parameters do not affect actual arguments? The explanation is that the passing of arrays as arguments is the only exception to the rule of parameter passing by value. When an array is passed as argument, the address of the beginning of the array is passed; the elements of the array are not copied into the parameter array. Any references to the parameter array inside the called function refer to the appropriate elements of the argument array. Thus, an assignment to x[i] inside array_cuberoot actually results in an assignment to z[i].

Since only its starting address is provided when an array is passed as argument, we only need to indicate that an array is expected and can omit the declaration of the number of elements in the parameter array. This feature can be used to generalize functions that manipulate arrays. For example, the function array_cuberoot, as defined above, cannot be used to determine the cube roots of the elements of an array y declared as

```
double y[100];
```

since array_cuberoot can only handle arrays of 10 elements. This function can be generalized by not specifying the number of elements in the declaration of the parameter array x, but making the number of elements an additional parameter. The function array_cuberoot can then be written as

```
void array_cuberoot(double x[], int length)
  {
     int i;

     for(i = 0; i < length; i++)
         x[i] = cuberoot(x[i]);
  }
```

The new parameter length is bound to the number of elements in the argument array at the time of the function call. The function array_cuberoot can now be used to compute the cube roots of the elements of z as well as y by invoking it as

```
array_cuberoot(z, 10);
```

and

```
array_cuberoot(y, 100);
```

respectively.

When declaring a multi-dimensional array as a parameter, it is necessary to specify the lengths of all but the first dimension. Thus, the prototype of a function to compute the cube root of every element of a two-dimensional array can be written as

```
void matrix_cuberoot(double xx[10][5]);
```

or as

```
void matrix_cuberoot(double xx[][5], int rows);
```

but not as

```
void matrix_cuberoot(double xx[][],
                     int rows, int cols);
```

6.3 ILLUSTRATIVE EXAMPLES

We now give some programs to illustrate the use of arrays.

Example 1
Write a program that cyclically permutes the elements of a given sequence.

Given a sequence $x_1, x_2, x_3, \ldots, x_n$, its cyclic permutation is defined to be the sequence $x_2, x_3, \ldots, x_n, x_1$. The desired program is as follows.

```
#include <stdio.h>
#define   LAST   10

int main(void)
    {
      float   array[LAST], temp;
      int     i;

      /* read array */
      for (i = 0; i < LAST; i++)
          scanf("%f", &array[i]);

      /* permute array */
      temp = array[0];
      for (i = 1; i < LAST; i++)
          array[i-1] = array[i];
      array[LAST-1] = temp;

      /* output the permuted array */
      for (i = 0; i < LAST; i++)
          printf("%f\n", array[i]);

      return 0;
    }
```

The first element of `array` is saved in `temp`. The second element is then assigned to the first, the third element to the second, and so on. Finally, the last element of `array` is set to the value saved in `temp`. Thus, given the sequence

```
3 4 2 4 3 9 7 8 0 2
```

the program prints

```
4 2 4 3 9 7 8 0 2 3
```

How would you generalize the preceding program so that the sequence is cyclically permuted by a user-specified number of elements?

Example 2

Four tests are given to a class of ten students. Write a program that calculates the average score of each student, the class average in each test, and the class average over all tests.

Test scores are stored in a matrix `score` of size `TESTS+1` × `STUDENTS+1`. The scores in test i are stored in row i, and the scores of student j are stored in column j. Thus, the element (i,j), for $i, j > 0$, contains the score in test i of student j. We will use row 0 and column 0 for accumulating intermediate results. The element $(0,j)$ in row 0 will be used to accumulate the total score of student j over all tests. The element $(i, 0)$ in column 0 will be used to accumulate the total score of all students in test i. The scores of all students over all tests will be accumulated in the element $(0,0)$.

The desired program is as follows.

```c
#include <stdio.h>
#define  TESTS      4
#define  STUDENTS   10

int main(void)
  {
    int score[TESTS+1][STUDENTS+1] =
      {
        {0, 0, 0, 0, 0, 0, 0, 0, 0, 0, 0},
        {0, 4, 3, 4, 2, 1, 0, 3, 4, 1, 0},
        {0, 4, 4, 3, 3, 2, 1, 2, 3, 1, 2},
        {0, 4, 3, 4, 3, 2, 2, 2, 3, 0, 1},
        {0, 4, 3, 4, 4, 1, 3, 3, 3, 1, 2}
      };
    int  i, j;

    for (i = 1; i <= TESTS; i++)
        for (j = 1; j <= STUDENTS; j++)
          {
            /* total for a test */
            score[i][0] += score[i][j];
            /* total for a student */
            score[0][j] += score[i][j];
            /* total for the class */
            score[0][0] += score[i][j];
          }

    for (j = 1; j <= STUDENTS; j++)
        printf("student %d: average score = %f\n",
                j, (float)score[0][j]/TESTS);

    for (i = 1; i <= TESTS; i++)
        printf("test %d: average score = %f\n",
                i, (float)score[i][0]/STUDENTS);

    printf("class average = %f\n",
            (float)score[0][0]/(STUDENTS*TESTS));

    return 0;
  }
```

Compare this problem to that in Example 1 of Section 4.5.1. How would you modify the program of that problem if you were also required to calculate the average score in each test as in this problem?

Example 3
Income data for people in different states has been recorded so that each line of input contains the state number and the income of a person in that state. Thus, there are as many input lines for a state as the number of people in the state. However, input is not in any particular order. Write a program that computes and prints the average income for each state and for the whole nation.

Assuming all states have been coded from 1 to STATES, each line of input is a pair <state, individual_income>, where state is the state number, and individual_income is the income of an individual in that state. We create an array, state_income, and accumulate income values for state *i* in element *i* of this array. Another array, people, is used to count the number of people in every state whose income values have been accumulated. Both state_income and people are of size STATES+1. The state number read from input provides the subscript for accessing appropriate elements from state_income and people. Elements of these arrays with a subscript of 0 are used to accumulate the values of total income and total number of people in the nation.

The desired program is as follows.

```c
#include <stdio.h>
#define  STATES  50
#define  NATION  0

void zeroize(float state_income[], int people[]);
void accumulate(float state_income[], int people[]);
void print(float state_income[], int people[]);

int main(void)
  {
    float   state_income[STATES+1];
    int     people[STATES+1];

    zeroize(state_income, people);
    accumulate(state_income, people);
    print(state_income, people);
    return 0;
  }

void zeroize(float state_income[], int people[])
  {
    int state;

    for (state = 0; state <= STATES; state++)
        state_income[state] = people[state] = 0;
  }
```

```
void accumulate(float state_income[], int people[])
  {
    int state;
    float individual_income;

    while (scanf("%d %f", &state, &individual_income)
            != EOF)
        if (state >= 1 && state <= STATES)
          {
            state_income[state] += individual_income;
            people[state]++;
          }
  }

void print(float state_income[], int people[])
  {
    int state;

    /*  print state averages  */

    for (state = 1; state <= STATES; state++)
        if (people[state])
          {
            printf("state %d: %f\n", state,
                state_income[state]/people[state]);

            /*  accumulate values for the national average  */
            state_income[NATION] +=
                state_income[state];
            people[NATION] += people[state];
          }
        else
            printf("state %d: no data\n", state);

    /*  print the national average  */

    if (people[NATION])
        printf("national average = %f\n",
            state_income[NATION]/people[NATION]);
    else
        printf("no data\n");
  }
```

Note that the test

```
state >= 1 && state <= STATES
```

in `accumulate` ensures that the subscript `state` is within the bounds of the `state_income` and `people` arrays. If a data line contains an invalid state number, the program simply ignores this line.

Example 4
Write a program that reads two matrices and determines their product matrix.

Let M_1 be an $l \times m$ matrix and M_2 an $m \times n$ matrix. The product P of M_1 with M_2 is an $l \times n$ matrix, whose element $P(i,j)$ is the sum of the products of the elements in row i of M_1 with the elements of column j of M_2; that is,

$$P(i,j) = M_1(i,1) \times M_2(1,j) + M_1(i,2) \times M_2(2,j) + \ldots + M_1(i,m) \times M_2(m,j)$$

For example, if

$$M_1 = \begin{bmatrix} 1 & 2 & 3 \\ 3 & 2 & 1 \end{bmatrix} \quad \text{and} \quad M_2 = \begin{bmatrix} 1 & 2 & 3 & 4 & 5 \\ 2 & 5 & 3 & 1 & 4 \\ 5 & 4 & 3 & 2 & 1 \end{bmatrix}$$

then

$$P = \begin{bmatrix} 20 & 24 & 18 & 12 & 16 \\ 12 & 20 & 18 & 16 & 24 \end{bmatrix}$$

The desired matrix multiplication program is as follows.

```c
#include <stdio.h>
#define  MAXROWS    10
#define  MAXCOLS    10

void readm(float matrix[][MAXCOLS],
           int rows, int cols);
void writem(float matrix[][MAXCOLS],
            int rows, int cols);
void multiply(float matrix1[][MAXCOLS],
              int rows1, int cols1,
              float matrix2[][MAXCOLS], int cols2,
              float product[][MAXCOLS]);

int main(void)
  {
    float  matrix1[MAXROWS][MAXCOLS],
           matrix2[MAXROWS][MAXCOLS],
           product[MAXROWS][MAXCOLS];
    int    rows1, cols1, rows2, cols2;
```

```c
/* get the actual dimensions of the matrices */

do
  {
    printf("dimensions of matrix1?\n");
    scanf("%d %d", &rows1, &cols1);
    printf("dimensions of matrix2?\n");
    scanf("%d %d", &rows2, &cols2);

    if (cols1 != rows2)
        printf("columns in matrix1 must "
                "equal rows in matrix2\n");
    else if (rows1 > MAXROWS || cols1 > MAXCOLS)
        printf("matrix1 is too big\n");
    else if (rows2 > MAXROWS || cols2 > MAXCOLS)
        printf("matrix2 is too big\n");
    else
        break;
  }
while(1);

/* read the matrices */

printf("enter row-wise the elements of matrix1\n");
readm(matrix1, rows1, cols1);

printf("enter row-wise the elements of matrix2\n");
readm(matrix2, rows2, cols2);

/* compute the product matrix */

multiply(matrix1, rows1, cols1,
         matrix2, cols2, product);

/* print results */

printf("product matrix:\n");
writem(product, rows1, cols2);

return 0;

}
```

```c
void readm(float matrix[][MAXCOLS],
           int rows, int cols)
  {
    int i, j;

    for (i = 0; i < rows; i++)
        for (j = 0; j < cols; j++)
            scanf("%f", &matrix[i][j]);
  }

void multiply(float matrix1[][MAXCOLS],
              int rows1, int cols1,
              float matrix2[][MAXCOLS], int cols2,
              float product[][MAXCOLS])
  {
    int i, j, k;

    for (i = 0; i < rows1; i++)
        for (j = 0; j < cols2; j++)
          {
            product[i][j] = 0;
            for (k = 0; k < cols1; k++)
                product[i][j] +=
                    matrix1[i][k] * matrix2[k][j];
          }
  }

void writem(float matrix[][MAXCOLS],
            int rows, int cols)
  {
    int i, j;

    for (i = 0; i < rows; i++)
      {
        for (j = 0; j < cols; j++)
            printf("%f ", matrix[i][j]);
        printf("\n");;
      }
  }
```

The program first obtains the dimensions of the matrices to be multiplied. It then checks that the number of columns cols1 in matrix1 is equal to the number of rows rows2 in matrix2, for otherwise the product of the two matrices is not defined and a new set of inputs is obtained. The program can handle matrices of up to MAXROWS × MAXCOLS elements, and it is ensured that none of the input matrices exceeds this limit. The two matrices are then read row-wise using the function readm, and the product matrix product is computed using the function multiply. The computation of product is a direct implementation of the definition of the product of two matrices. Finally, the function `writem` prints out `product`. Note that we have omitted row lengths in the declaration of matrices in the parameter list of these functions, but it is necessary to specify column lengths in these declarations.

An important observation with regard to this program is in order. We did not know *a priori* the size of the input matrices. We therefore allocated arrays sufficiently large to cover a wide range of values. Functions manipulating these arrays were then provided with the actual number of rows and columns in use, thus avoiding the processing of unused entries. This approach has the disadvantage that you may end up allocating arrays that are either too small for the problem on hand, or too large, thus wasting memory. In Chapter 7, we will study dynamic creation of arrays of exact sizes.

Example 5

Write a program for sorting a list of integers in descending order using the bubble sort algorithm.

Sorting a list of items is the process of arranging these items in descending or ascending order. The *bubble sort* algorithm for sorting a list of items in descending order consists of the following steps:

1. Compare the first item with the second. If the second is larger, switch the order of the items.
2. Compare the third item with the second, then the fourth with the third, and so on, until the last item in the list has been compared with its predecessor. At each comparison, switch the order of the items if the item being compared is larger than its predecessor. The effect of this step is that the larger items "sink" toward the left of the list, and the smallest item "bubbles up" to the rightmost (last) position on the list.
3. Repeatedly perform the steps (1) and (2), leaving the last item out of the scan every time as it is already in its proper position. The list is sorted when no interchange takes place during a scan.

For example, the following scans are performed to sort the list (0, 5, 3, 2, 1, 4, 6) in descending order:

Scan #	Rearranged List	Interchanges
1	5, 3, 2, 1, 4, 6, 0	(0,5), (0,3), (0,2), (0,1), (0,4), (0,6)
2	5, 3, 2, 4, 6, 1, 0	(1,4), (1,6)
3	5, 3, 4, 6, 2, 1, 0	(2,4), (2,6)
4	5, 4, 6, 3, 2, 1, 0	(3,4), (3,6)
5	5, 6, 4, 3, 2, 1, 0	(4,6)
6	6, 5, 4, 3, 2, 1, 0	(6,5)

The following program implements the bubble sort algorithm:

```c
#include <stdio.h>
#define  MAXSIZE   100

int readl(int arr[], int length);
void writel(int arr[], int last);
void bsort(int arr[], int last);

int main(void)
  {
    int  list[MAXSIZE], total_elements;

    total_elements = readl(list, MAXSIZE);
    bsort(list, total_elements);
    writel(list, total_elements);
    return 0;
  }

int readl(int arr[], int length)
  {
    int  i;

    for (i = 0; i < length &&
                scanf("%d", &arr[i]) != EOF; i++)
        ;
    return i;
  }

void bsort(int arr[], int last)
  {
    int  i, not_done;

    do
      {
        not_done = 0;

        /* scan and interchange as needed */

        for (i = 1; i < last; i++)
            if (arr[i-1] < arr[i])
              {
                int t;

                t = arr[i];
                arr[i] = arr[i-1];
                arr[i-1] = t;
                not_done++;
              }
```

```
        /* do not scan the last data item in the next iteration */

        last--;
      }
    while (not_done);
  }

void writel(int arr[], int last)
  {
    int  i;

    for (i = 0; i < last; i++)
        printf("%d\n", arr[i]);
  }
```

The function readl reads the input list into the array list and returns a count of the number of items in the list in total_elements. The function bsort repeatedly performs the scan-interchange step outlined above until no interchange takes place, which is signaled by the variable not_done remaining *false* at the end of the do-while loop. The number of items compared in each scan is controlled by the variable last which is reduced by 1 after each loop iteration. The function writel prints the sorted list at the end.

How would you change the preceding program if the items were required to be sorted in ascending order?

Example 6
Write a program that uses the binary search to look up the price in an item-price database, given an item number.

Searching a database for a specified item and retrieving associated information about the item is a frequently encountered problem. The *binary search* is an efficient algorithm for searching large data sets, if the data to be searched has been sorted. The basic idea of the binary search is to repeatedly reduce the search space by dividing it into two halves and determining the half to which the desired item belongs, until the item is found. The binary search algorithm is given in Figure 6.4.

To illustrate the binary search algorithm, assume that the data to be searched is the list X consisting of (20, 19, 17, 16, 12, 11, 10, 5, 4, 1) sorted in descending order. If the item to be located is the number 11, the following sequence of scans takes place.

Scan #	first	last	mid	Test
1	1	10	5	X(5) > 11
2	6	10	8	X(8) < 11
3	6	7	6	X(6) = 11

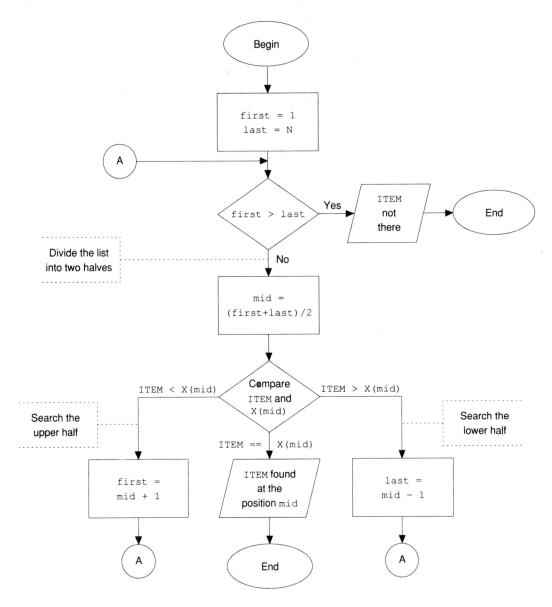

Figure 6.4. Binary search for ITEM in the list X(1), X(2), ..., X(N) sorted in descending order

The search succeeds when the item is found at position 6. However, if the item to be located were the number 18, the following scans would take place:

Scan #	first	last	mid	Test
1	1	10	5	X(5) < 18
2	1	4	2	X(2) > 18
3	3	4	3	X(3) < 18
4	3	2		first > last

The search fails at the fourth iteration when *first* becomes greater than *last*.

The following program first builds an item-price database, and then uses the binary search to look up the price of an item, given its item number:

```c
#include <stdio.h>
#define   ITEMS        1000
#define   NOT_FOUND    -1

void bld_database(int item[],
                  float price[], int total_items);
int  bsearch(int value, int arr[], int length);

int main(void)
   {
     int    item[ITEMS], item_no, index;
     float  price[ITEMS];

     /* build the item-price database */

     bld_database(item, price, ITEMS);

     /* get item_no of the item whose price is to be found */

     scanf("%d", &item_no);

     /* binary search */

     index = bsearch(item_no, item, ITEMS);

     /* output */

     if (index == NOT_FOUND)
         printf("item %d is not in the database\n",
                 item_no);
     else
         printf("price of item %d = %f\n",
                 item_no, price[index]);

     return 0;
   }

void bld_database(int item[],
                  float price[], int total_items)
   {
     int i;

     for (i = 0; i < total_items; i++)
         scanf("%d %f", &item[i], &price[i]);
   }
```

```
int bsearch(int value, int arr[], int length)
  {
    int first = 0, last = length-1, mid;

    while (first <= last)
      {
        mid = (first + last) / 2;

        if (value == arr[mid])      /* search succeeds */
            return mid;
        else if (value > arr[mid])/* search lower half */
            last = mid - 1;
        else                        /* search upper half */
            first = mid + 1;
      }

    return NOT_FOUND;
  }
```

The function `bld_database` builds the item-price data base by reading from input *<item number, price>* pairs and storing them in the arrays `item` and `price` respectively. It is assumed that the input data is sorted on item number in descending order. The `item_no` of the item, whose price is to be looked up, is then read from the input. The function `bsearch` then makes a binary search in the `item` array for the `item_no`. If the search succeeds, `bsearch` returns the position at which the item was found, and is used as the index into the `price` array to fetch the desired price information.

How would you change the preceding program if the items were sorted in ascending order?

Exercises 6

1. Find the number of elements in each of the following arrays:

    a. `float f[4][8][2];`   *b.* `double d[2][5][4][3];`

    c. `char s1[] = "ibm";`   *d.* `char s2[] = {'i','b','m'};`

    e. `char s3[5] = "ibm";`

2. Write appropriate type declarations to create the following:

    a. An array to record the heights of 25 students in a class.

    b. A two-dimensional array to classify students by sex and by one of five occupations that the students intend to take up after the completion of their studies.

    c. A three-dimensional array to classify students by age (15 years to 25 years), years of study (10 to 15 years), and one of 10 major subjects of study.

3. Analyze the output of the following programs:

a. ```
#include <stdio.h>

int n[10] = {1, 1};

int main(void)
  {
    int   i;

    for (i = 2; i < 10; i++)
          n[i] = n[i-1] + n[i-2];

    for (i = 0; i < 10; i++) printf("%d\n", n[i]);

    return 0;
  }
```

*b.* ```
#include <stdio.h>

int  n[10] = {1};

int main(void)
  {
    int   i, j;

    for (i = 0; i < 10; i++)
        for (j = 0; j < i; j++)
            n[i] += n[j];

    for (i = 0; i < 10; i++) printf("%d\n", n[i]);

    return 0;
  }
```

c. ```
#include <stdio.h>

char s[] = "radar";

int main(void)
  {
    int   i, j, c;

    for (j = 0; s[j] != '\0'; j++) ;

    for (i = 0, j--; i < j; i++, j--)
        c = s[i], s[i] = s[j], s[j] = c;

    printf("%s\n", s);
    return 0;
  }
```
```

d.
```c
#include <stdio.h>

int   n1[4][3] = { {1}, {0,1}, {0,0,1} };
int   n2[4][3] = {0,1,1,1,0,1,1,1,0,1,1,1};

int main(void)
    {
       int   i, j, c = 0;

       for (i = 0; i < 4; i++)
           for (j = 0; j < 3; j++)
               if (n1[i][j] && n2[i][j]) c++;

       printf("%d\n", c);
       return 0;
    }
```

e.
```c
#include <stdio.h>

int main(void)
    {
       int   n[10][10], i, j, u=0, d=0, l=0;

       for (i = 0; i < 10; i++)
           for (j = 0; j < 10; j++)
               n[i][j] = i + j;

       for (i = 0; i < 10; i++)
           for (j = 0; j < 10; j++)
               {
                  if (i > j)  u += n[i][j];
                  if (i == j) d += n[i][j];
                  if (i < j)  l += n[i][j];
               }

       printf("%d %d %d\n", u, d, l);
       return 0;
    }
```

4. Write a program that computes for a linear array A.

    a. $A_1^{1/2} + A_2^{1/2} + \ldots + A_n^{1/2}$

    b. $(1 - A_1)(1 - A_2) \ldots (1 - A_n)$

5. U and V are linear arrays each with n elements. Write a program to compute

$$\frac{(u_1^2 + u_2^2 + \ldots + u_n^2)^{1/2} \cdot (v_1^2 + v_2^2 + \ldots + v_n^2)^{1/2}}{(u_1 v_1 + u_2 v_2 + \ldots + u_n v_n)^{1/2}}$$

by using a function that calculates the inner product

$a_1 b_1 + a_2 b_2 + \ldots + a_n b_n.$

of two linear arrays A and B.

6. A common problem in statistics is that of generating the *frequency distribution* of the given data. Assuming that the data consists of 500 positive integers in the range 1 to

25, write a program that prints the number of times each of the integers occurs in the input.

Modify this program so that it prints the number of integers that are in the range 1 to 100, 101 to 200, 201 to 300, and so on, assuming that the integers are in the range 1 to 1000.

7. The prime numbers in the range 2 through n can efficiently be found using the following *sieve of Eratosthenes:*.

   i. Make a list of all consecutive integers 2 through n.

   ii. Cross out all multiples of 2, as they cannot be primes.

   iii. Find the next integer remaining in the list beyond the one whose multiples were just crossed out, and cross out its multiples, as they cannot be primes.

   iv. Repeat step (iii) until an integer is reached that has not been crossed out and whose square is greater than n. This termination condition depends on the fact that if i and j are the two factors in a product then both i and j cannot exceed the square root of the product.

   v. All the numbers remaining in the list are the primes from 2 through n.

   Write a program that implements this algorithm and finds all the primes less than 1000.

8. A problem with the bubble sort algorithm given in Example 5 of Section 6.3 is that, although smaller values move toward their proper positions rapidly, larger values move slowly in the other direction. The *Shell sort* algorithm attempts to improve this situation. A series of compare-interchange scans are made as in the bubble sort, but the items compared on each scan are not consecutive. Instead, there is a fixed gap between the items that are compared. If the gap is g, then item x_i is compared with item x_{i+g} and exchanged if necessary. When no more interchanges can be made using a given gap, the gap is cut in half and the compare-interchange scan continues. The initial gap is taken to be $n/2$, where n is the number of items in the list. For example, to sort the list $(0, 5, 3, 2, 1, 4, 6)$ in descending order, the following sequence of scans and gaps is used:

Scan #	Gap	Rearranged List	Interchanges
1	3	1, 5, 6, 2, 0, 4, 3	(0,1), (3,6)
2	3	1, 5, 6, 2, 0, 4, 3	none
3	1	6, 5, 1, 4, 3, 2, 0	(1,6), (2,4), (0,3)
4	1	6, 5, 3, 4, 1, 2, 0	(1,3)
5	1	6, 5, 3, 4, 1, 2, 0	none
6	0	6, 5, 4, 3, 2, 1, 0	(3,4), (1,2)
7	0	6, 5, 4, 3, 2, 1, 0	none

Write a program to sort a list of items using the Shell sort algorithm.

9. The *insertion sort* algorithm begins with the first item x_1, then inserts x_2 into this one-item list in the correct position to form a sorted two-item list, then inserts x_3 into this two-item list in the correct position to form a sorted three-item list, and so on. For example, to sort the list $(0, 5, 3, 2, 1, 4, 6)$ in descending order, the steps are as follows:

0
5   0   (shift 0 to the right one position)
5   **3**   0   (shift 0 again)
5   3   **2**   0   (shift 0 again)
5   3   2   **1**   0   (shift 0 again)
5   **4**   3   2   1   0   (shift 3 through 0 to the right)
6   5   4   3   2   1   0   (shift 5 through 0 to the right)

The element inserted at each step has been indicated in the bold print.

Write a program to sort a list of items using the insertion sort algorithm.

10. The *exchange* algorithm for sorting a list of items $x_1, x_2, \ldots, x_n$ in descending order consists of the following steps:

    i. Locate the largest item in the list x_1 through x_n; exchange it with x_1.

    ii. Locate the largest item in the list x_2 through x_n; exchange it with x_2.

    iii. Locate the largest item in the list x_3 through x_n; exchange it with x_3.

    iv. Continue this process for a total of $n - 1$ steps.

    Write a program that sorts a list of items using the exchange sort algorithm.

11. The binary search algorithm given in Example 6 of Section 6.3 requires that the items to be searched be presorted in some order. The *linear search* algorithm does not require items to be kept sorted. The search is performed by examining each item for the desired value until a match is found or all items are exhausted. Replace the binary search component of the program in Example 6 with the linear search.

12. Write a recursive version of the `bsearch` function given in Example 6 of Section 6.3.

13. The *first difference D1* of a sequence *D* of *N* elements is obtained by subtracting each element, except the last, from the next element in the array, that is,

    $$D1(I) = D(I + 1) - D(I), \qquad I \le N - 1$$

    The *second difference D2* is defined as the first difference of *D1*, and so on. For example, if

    D: 1, 2, 4, 7, 11, 16, 22

    then

    D1:   1, 2, 3, 4, 5, 6
    D2:   1, 1, 1, 1, 1
    D3:   0, 0, 0, 0

    Write a program that reads a sequence and finds its first, second, and third differences.

14. Each row of *Pascal's triangle* begins and ends with 1's and each number in the interior is the sum of the numbers on either side of it in the row above. Write a program to compute and print the first 10 rows of Pascal's triangle. Printing need not be in the following symmetric triangle form:

```
            1
         1     2     1
      1     3     3     1
   1     4     6     4     1
```

15. A *square* matrix, that is, one having the same number of rows and columns, is called a *diagonal* matrix if its only nonzero elements are on the diagonal. It is called *upper triangular* if all elements below the diagonal are 0, and *lower triangular* if all elements above the diagonal are 0. Write a program that determines if a given square matrix is one of these matrices.

16. Write the following matrix manipulation functions:

    i. `void scalar_multiply(int matrix[ROWS][COLS]), int k);`

    Multiplies each element of `matrix` by the scalar `k`.

    ii. `void transpose(int matrix1[ROWS][COLS]),`
    `             int matrix2[COLS][ROWS]);`

    Creates `matrix2`, the transpose of `matrix1`, by writing the rows of `matrix1` as columns.

    iii. `void add(int matrix1[ROWS][COLS]),`
    `          int matrix2[ROWS][COLS],`
    `          int sum[ROWS][COLS]);`

    Creates `sum` by adding the corresponding elements of `matrix1` and `matrix2`.

    Use these functions to verify the correctness of the equation

    $$X^T = mY + nZ,$$

    where X^T is the transpose of X, $m = 2$, $n = 3$, and

    $$X = \begin{bmatrix} 1 & 0 & 0 \\ 0 & 0 & 1 \end{bmatrix}, \quad Y = \begin{bmatrix} -1 & 3 \\ 6 & -6 \\ -3 & -1 \end{bmatrix}, \quad Z = \begin{bmatrix} 1 & -2 \\ -4 & 4 \\ 2 & 1 \end{bmatrix}.$$

17. Rent-It-All rents time on ten of its machines. Each time a customer uses a machine, a time card is filled in. Write a program to help the company bill its customers. The bill should include the following information:

    i. customer number;

    ii. machine number, total hours, and total costs for each machine used by the customer;

    iii. total cost for the customer.

    Rates on the machines are different for different customers and for different time periods during the day. Therefore, the initial input is 100 lines of data, each line specifying a price code (00-99) and the cost per hour for the price code. This input is followed by customer data, with one line of data corresponding to each time card. Time cards are sorted by customer number and contain the following information:

    i. customer number

    ii. machine number (0-9)

    iii. price code (00-99)

    iv. hours

18. Innovations Unlimited has created three prototypes of a product VZOOM in its research laboratory. The number of transistors, capacitors, and resistors used in each of the prototypes is as follows:

Prototype	Transistors	Capacitors	Resistors
1	20	155	250
2	50	125	150
3	35	180	140

1000 transistors cost \$12.50, 1000 capacitors \$5.00, and 1000 resistors \$2.50. Write a program that determines which prototype has the least component cost, using a function similar to `multiply` given in Example 4 of Section 6.3.

19. Miniaturization Unlimited sells five types of memory chips through its retail outlets in 10 cities. The weekly sales of the company are stored in a $5 \times 10 \times 7$ array *sale* such that *sale(m,c,d)* denotes the sale of the mth memory chip in the cth city on the dth day of the week. Write a program that computes the total weekly sales of each type of memory chip, the total weekly sales in each city, and the average daily sales of the company.

20. A *magic square* is an $n \times n$ matrix in which each of the integers 1, 2, 3, . . ., n^2 appears exactly once and the sums of every row, column, and diagonal are equal. In fact, these sums will always be $n(n^2 + 1)/2$. Here is a magic square for $n = 3$:

2	9	4
7	5	3
6	1	8

No magic square exists for even values of n. An algorithm for creating a magic square for any odd integer n is as follows:

Place 1 in the middle of the bottom row. After an integer k has been placed, the next integer $k + 1$ is placed by moving diagonally downward to the left, that is, by moving down one row and to the left one column, unless one of the following occurs:

i. If a move takes you below the bottom row in the jth column, move to the top of the jth column and put the integer there.

ii. If a move takes you outside to the left of the square in the ith row, move to the rightmost column and put the integer in the ith row there.

iii. If a move takes you to an already filled square, or if you move out of the square at the lower left-hand corner, place the integer immediately above k.

Write a program to construct a magic square for any odd integer n.

7 Pointers

We shall examine in this chapter *pointers*, the most sophisticated feature of C. Pointers are used in almost every C program, partly because they at times provide the only way to express a computation, and partly because they lead to more efficient and compact code. In particular, pointers enable us to achieve parameter passing by reference, deal concisely and effectively with arrays, represent complex data structures, and work with dynamically allocated memory.

7.1 BASICS OF POINTERS

Memory, as indicated in Section 1.1.1, can be visualized as an ordered sequence of consecutively numbered storage locations. A data item is stored in memory in one or more adjacent storage locations depending upon its type. The address of a data item is the address of its first storage location. This address can be stored in another data item and manipulated in a program. The address of a data item is called a *pointer* to the data item, and a variable that holds an address is called a pointer variable. Thus, if `ip` is a pointer variable that contains the address of `i`, an `int`, this situation can be depicted as shown below:

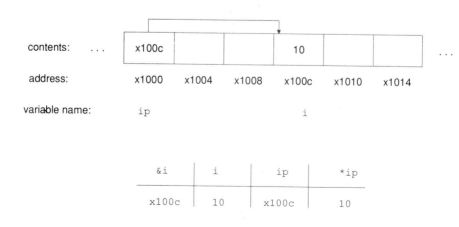

&i	i	ip	*ip
x100c	10	x100c	10

7.1.1 Address and Dereferencing Operators

C provides two unary operators, & and *, for manipulating data using pointers. The operator &, when applied to a variable, yields its address (pointer to the variable), and the operator *, when applied to an address (pointer), fetches the value at that address. These operators can be remembered as "the address of" and "the value at the address" respectively. For example, if the integer variable i has been allocated the storage location numbered x100c and contains the integer value 10, then the address of i, indicated as &i, is 0x100c, and the value at the address &i, indicated as *(&i), is 10. Accessing an object through a pointer is called dereferencing, and the operator * is referred to as the *dereferencing* or *indirection* operator. The operator & is referred to as the *address* operator.

The & operator can only be applied to an lvalue, and constructs like

```
&10                    &'C'                    & (x+3)
```

that involve the addresses of constants and expressions are not valid. If the type of the operand is *T* then the type of the result is "pointer to *T*". For example, if i is an int, then &i is of type "pointer to int".

The * operator can only be applied to a pointer. If the operand is "pointer to *T*", then the type of the result is *T*. For example, if ip is a pointer to an integer, then the type of *ip is int.

The expression *ip, where ip is a pointer to integer i, can occur in any expression in any context where i can. Thus,

```
j = *ip + 10;
```

is equivalent to

```
j = i + 10;
```

and assigns 10 more than i to j;

```
k = ++(*ip);
```

is equivalent to

```
k = ++i;
```

and increments the value of i and assigns the incremented value to k;

```
x = sqrt((double) *ip);
```

is equivalent to

```
x = sqrt((double) i);
```

and casts i to double before it is passed to sqrt, and assigns the result to x; and

```
printf("%d\n", *ip);
```

is equivalent to

```
printf("%d\n", i);
```

and prints the current value of i.

7.1.2 Pointer Type Declaration

For each type of object that can be declared in C, a corresponding type of pointer can be declared. To indicate that a variable contains a pointer to a specified type of object, rather than the object itself, an asterisk is included before the name of the object in the type declaration. Thus,

*type *identifier;*

declares the *identifier* to be of type "pointer to *type*". Note that the declaration allocates space for the named pointer variable, but not for what it points to.

For example, to declare cp to be a pointer to an object of type char, ip a pointer to an object of type int, and dp a pointer to an object of type double, we write

```
char    *cp;
int     *ip;
double *dp;
```

The preceding pointer declarations may appear to you somewhat obscure. C's philosophy is that the declaration of a variable should follow the form of use. Thus, when we declare

```
int     *ip;
```

we are stating that the appearance of *ip in a program statement will have an int value. But, since the name ip has been prefixed with the dereferencing operator, ip must be a pointer to an int object.

7.1.3 Pointer Assignment

A pointer value may be assigned to another pointer of the same type. For example, in the program fragment

```
int i = 1, j, *ip;
ip  = &i;
j   = *ip;
*ip = 0;
```

the first assignment statement assigns the address of variable i to ip, the second assigns the value at address ip, that is, 1 to j, and finally the third assigns 0 to i since *ip is the same as i.

Note that the two statements

```
ip = &i;
j  = *ip;
```

are equivalent to the single assignment

```
j   = *(&i);
```

or to the assignment

```
j   = i;
```

That is, the address operator & is the inverse of the dereferencing operator *.

Pointers and integers are not interchangeable. An exception to this rule is the constant zero that can be assigned to a pointer of any type. By convention, a pointer value of 0 is known as the NULL pointer. The standard header file <stdio.h> contains the definition of NULL.

7.1.4 Pointer Initialization

The declaration of a pointer variable may be accompanied by an initializer. The form of an initialization of a pointer variable is

type **identifier* = *initializer*;

The initializer must either evaluate to an address of previously defined data of appropriate type or it can be the NULL pointer. For example, the declaration

```
#include <stdio.h>
float *fp = NULL;
```

initializes fp to NULL; the declarations

```
short s;
short *sp = &s;
```

initialize sp to the address of s; and the declarations

```
char   c[10];
char   *cp = &c[4];
```

initialize cp to the address of the fifth element of the array c.

The following is a simple program that illustrates declaration, initialization, assignment, and dereferencing of pointers:

```
#include <stdio.h>

int main(void)
  {
    int i, j = 1;
    int *jp1, *jp2 = &j;  /* jp2 points to j */

    jp1 = jp2;            /* jp1 also points to j */
    i = *jp1;             /* i gets the value of j */
    *jp2 = *jp1 + i;      /* i is added to j */

    printf("i = %d, j = %d, *jp1 = %d, *jp2 = %d\n",
           i, j, *jp1, *jp2);
    return 0;
  }
```

This program prints:

```
i = 1, j = 2, *jp1 = 2, *jp2 = 2
```

7.1.5 Pointer Arithmetic

Arithmetic can be performed on pointers. However, in pointer arithmetic, a pointer is a valid operand only for the addition (+) and subtraction (−) operators. The semantics of arithmetic operations on pointers are as follows:

1. An integral value n may be added to a pointer p. Assuming that the object that p points to lies within an array of such objects, the result is a pointer to the object that lies n objects after the one p points to. For example, as depicted below, if p points to the object $object_k$, then p+1 points to the object $object_{k+1}$, and p+(-1), that is, p-1 points to the object $object_{k-1}$.

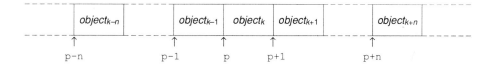

The value of $p + n$ is the storage location $p + n$ * `sizeof(*p)`, where `sizeof` is an operator that yields the size in bytes of its operand.

2. An integral value n may be subtracted from a pointer p. Assuming that the object that p points to lies within an array of such objects, the result is a pointer to the object that lies n objects before the one p points to. For example, if p points to the object $object_k$, then p-1 points to the object $object_{k-1}$, and p-(-1), that is, p+1 points to the object $object_{k+1}$. The value of $p − n$ is the storage location $p − n$ * `sizeof(*p)`.

3. Two pointers of the same type may be subtracted. When a pointer p1 is subtracted from another pointer p2 of the same type, the result is a signed integral value n such that p1 + n is p2, that is, subtracting one pointer from the other yields the number of objects that can fit in between the two pointers. For example, as depicted below, if p1 points to $object_k$, and p2 to $object_{k+n}$, then the result of p2 − p1 is n.

The result of the subtraction of two pointers is undefined if the pointers do not point to objects within the same array. However, if the pointer p points to the last member of the array, and the value of $p − q$ is n, then the expression (p+1) − q is well-defined and its value is $n + 1$. The type of the result of subtracting two pointers is implementation-dependent, and is defined in the standard header <stddef.h> as `ptrdiff_t`.

The preceding rules of pointer arithmetic apply regardless of how the arithmetic operation is written. Thus, applying the increment operator ++ to a pointer p has the effect of incrementing p to point to the object next to the object that p is currently pointing to. Similarly, applying the decrement operator -- to a pointer p has the effect of decrementing p to point to the previous object.

7.1.6 Precedence of Address and Dereferencing Operators

The unary address & and dereferencing * operators have equal precedence, which is the same as that of the other unary operators, and they associate from right to left. You have to be careful when you mix * with ++ or -- in a pointer expression. Thus, if cp is a pointer to char, then

```
*++cp
```

is interpreted as

```
*(++cp)
```

and it first increments cp and then fetches the character it points to, but the expression

```
*cp++
```

is interpreted as

```
*(cp++)
```

and it first fetches the character cp points to and then increments cp. Is this confusing? It is not if you remember that

```
c   = *(cp++);
```

is equivalent to

```
c  = *cp;
cp = cp + 1;
```

in the same way that

```
j   = (i++);
```

is equivalent to

```
j  = i;
i  = i + 1;
```

Pointer expressions involving the dereferencing operator * and the increment and decrement operators ++ and -- are so commonly used in C programs that they qualify to be called *C idioms*. The meanings of these idioms are summarized below:

c = *++cp	or c = *(++cp)	increments the pointer cp, and then assigns the value pointed to by cp to c.
c = *cp++	or c = *(cp++)	assigns the value pointed to by cp to c, and then increments the pointer cp.

`c = ++*cp` or `c = ++(*cp)`	increments the value pointed to by `cp`, and then assigns the new value to `c`; `cp` remains unchanged.
`c = (*cp)++`	fetches the value pointed to by `cp`, assigns it to `c`, and then increments the value pointed to by `cp`; `cp` remains unchanged.
`c = *--cp` or `c = *(--cp)`	decrements the pointer `cp`, and then assigns the value pointed to by `cp` to `c`.
`c = *cp--` or `c = *(cp--)`	assigns the value pointed to by `cp` to `c`, and then decrements the pointer `cp`.
`c = --*cp` or `c = --(*cp)`	decrements the value pointed to by `cp`, and then assigns the new value to `c`; `cp` remains unchanged.
`c = (*cp)--`	fetches the value pointed to by `cp`, assigns it to `c`, and then decrements the value pointed to by `cp`; `cp` remains unchanged.

7.1.7 Pointer Comparison

The relational comparisons `==` and `!=` are permitted between pointers of the same type, between a pointer of type `void *` and any other pointer, and between any pointer and the `NULL` pointer. Pointer operands are considered equal only if they point to the same object or if they are both `NULL`.

The relational comparisons `<`, `<=`, `>`, and `>=` are permitted between pointers of the same type, and the result depends on the relative location of the two objects pointed to. However, the result is portable only if the objects pointed to lie within the same array, or at least are aligned as if they did, in which case "greater than" means having a higher index in the array. The pointer to the first element beyond the end of an array is well represented to permit relational comparisons with a pointer located within an array.

For example, given that

```
int a[10], *ap;
```

the expression

```
ap == &a[9];
```

is true if `ap` is pointing to the last element of the array `a`, and the expression

```
ap < &a[10];
```

is true as long as `ap` is pointing to one of the elements of `a`.

Recall that `NULL` is defined to be 0 in `<stdio.h>`. Since 0 also represents false in a Boolean test, an expression involving comparison of a pointer with `NULL` may be abbreviated. Hence, the statement

```
if (ip != NULL) j += *ip;
```

can equivalently be written as

```
if (ip) j += *ip;
```

Similarly, the statement

```
if (ip == NULL) printf("null pointer, eh?\n");
```

can equivalently be written as

```
if (!ip) printf("null pointer, eh?\n");
```

The following function that determines the sum of elements of an integer array `arr` illustrates pointer arithmetic and comparison. The pointer `ap` is initialized to point to the first element `arr[0]`. The value of the element pointed to by `ap` is added to the accumulator `sum` and `ap` is incremented to point to the next element as long as `ap` is pointing to an element within the array. Note that `arr[length]` is the first element beyond the end of the array.

```
int asum(int arr[], int length)
  {
    int sum = 0, *ap = &arr[0];

    while (ap < &arr[length])
        /* add *ap to sum and then increment ap */
        sum += *ap++;

    return sum;
  }
```

7.1.8 Pointer Conversion

A pointer of one type can be converted to a pointer of another type by using an explicit cast. The cast $(T\ *)$ converts its operand into a pointer to an object of type T. For example, a `double` pointer `dp` can be converted into an `int` pointer `ip` by writing

```
ip = (int *) dp;
```

and back to a `double` pointer by writing

```
dp = (double *) ip;
```

The conversion of a pointer to P into a pointer to Q and back is guaranteed to work correctly only if Q requires less or equally strict storage alignment when compared to P. Thus, on an implementation that requires `int` objects to have an address that is a multiple of 4 bytes and `double` objects to have an address that is a multiple of 8 bytes, `dp` may be converted into `ip` and recovered as shown in the preceding example without loss of information. On the other hand, if Q has a more stringent alignment requirement than P and a pointer to P is converted to a pointer to Q, then an addressing exception may occur when the resulting pointer is dereferenced. For example, given that `cp` is a character pointer, the statements

```
ip = (int *) cp;
i  = *ip;
```

will cause an addressing exception if `cp` was pointing to an odd address.

Sometimes, we need *generic pointers* to define functions whose formal parameters can accept pointers of any type. In such situations, the type `void *` is used as the proper type for a generic pointer. Any pointer may be converted to type `void *` and back without loss of information. An explicit cast for such conversion may be added for clarity, but is not necessary. Here is a prototype of a function that uses a generic pointer in its definition:

```
void free(void *);
```

and here is an example of a call to this function:

```
free(cp);
```

7.2 FUNCTIONS AND POINTERS

A function can take a pointer to any data type as argument and can return a pointer to any data type. Consider, for example, the function definition:

```
double *maxp(double *xp, double *yp)
  {
     return *xp >= *yp ? xp : yp;
  }
```

This function definition specifies that the function `maxp` returns a pointer to a `double` object, and expects two arguments, both of which are pointers to `double` objects. The function dereferences the two argument pointers to get the values of the corresponding variables, and returns the pointer to the variable that has the larger of the two values. Thus, given that

```
double u = 1, v = 2, *mp;
```

the statement

```
mp = maxp(&u, &v);
```

makes `mp` point to `v`.

7.2.1 Call by Reference

We stated in Section 5.3 that parameters are passed by value in C. In a call by value, values of the arguments are used to initialize parameters of the called function, but the addresses of the arguments are not provided to the called function. Therefore, any change in the value of a parameter in the called function is not reflected in the variable supplied as argument in the calling function. In contrast, in a call by reference, addresses of the arguments are supplied to the called function and changes to the parameter values in the called function cause changes in the values of the arguments. The principal application of call by reference is when a function produces more than one value and provides these values to the caller.

Call by reference can be effected by passing pointers to the variables as arguments to the function. These pointers can then be used by the called function to access the argument variables and change them. Thus, given that the function `exchange` is defined as

```
void exchange(int *ip, int *jp)
    {
      int t;

      t = *ip, *ip = *jp, *jp = t;
    }
```

and that the values of the integer variables i and j are 1 and 2, they become 2 and 1 respectively after the function call

```
exchange(&i, &j);
```

Compare this definition of `exchange` with the one given in Section 5.3.

When a pointer is passed as an argument to a function, the pointer itself is copied but the object pointed to is not copied. Hence, any change made to the pointer parameter by the called function does not affect the pointer supplied as argument to the function, which is consistent with the call by value parameter passing. However, using the pointer supplied as the argument, the called function can access and modify the object pointed to by the pointer in the calling function. The following example further illustrates this point:

```
#include <stdio.h>

void change(int *ip)
    {
      ++(*ip);     /* increment what ip is pointing to */
      ip = NULL;   /* set ip to NULL */
    }

int main(void)
    {
      int i = 0, *ip, *pi;

      ip = pi = &i;

      change(ip);
      printf("new value of i = %d\n", i);
      if (ip == pi) printf("no change in ip\n");

      return 0;
    }
```

The output of this program is:

```
new value of i = 1
no change in ip
```

The operator & can be applied to a parameter. However, the address of a parameter is not the address of the argument, but the address of the copy of the argument. Thus, the function exchange written as

```
void exchange (int i, int j)
  {
    int t;

    t = *(&i),  *(&i) = *(&j),  *(&j) = t;  /* wrong */
  }
```

does not produce the intended effect of exchanging the values of the two arguments to the function.

7.2.2 Illustrative Example

We now give an example to further illustrate how pointers can be used to realize the effect of parameter passing by reference.

Example

Rewrite, without using external variables, the program for transforming rectangular coordinates to polar coordinates, given in Example 2 of Section 5.6.

External variables were used in the program given in Section 5.6 to allow the function polar to communicate two values to main. Instead of external variables, pointers can be used to communicate these values as shown in the following program:

```
#include <math.h>
#include <stdio.h>
#define  PI            3.1415927

void polar(float x, float y,
           float *pr,  float *ptheta);

int main(void)
  {
    float   x, y;
    float   r, theta;

    scanf("%f %f", &x, &y);

    /* provide addresses of r and theta to polar */
    polar(x, y, &r, &theta);

    printf("%f %f\n", r, theta);
    return 0;
  }
```

```
void polar(float x, float y,
           float *pr,  float *ptheta)
   {
      if (x == 0 && y == 0)   /* origin */
         *pr = *ptheta = 0;
      else
         {
            *pr = sqrt(x*x + y*y);
            *ptheta = atan2(y,x);
         }
   }
```

7.3 ARRAYS AND POINTERS

In C, there is a close correspondence between arrays and pointers that results not only in notational convenience but also in code that uses less memory and runs faster. Any operation that can be achieved by array subscripting can also be done with pointers.

C treats a variable of type "array of T" as "pointer to T", whose value is the address of the first element of the array. Thus, given that

```
char c[MAX];
```

the array name c is a synonym for the pointer to the first element of the array, that is, the value of c is the same as &c[0]. Hence, if cp is a character pointer, the two assignments

```
cp = c;
```

and

```
cp = &c[0];
```

are equivalent.

Array subscripting has also been defined in terms of pointer arithmetic. Thus, the expression

```
c[i]
```

is defined to be the same as

```
*(c+i)
```

Applying the operator & to both, it follows that

```
&c[i]
```

and

```
c+i
```

are also equivalent.

This equivalence means that the pointers may also be subscripted. Thus,

```
cp[i]
```

is equivalent to

```
*(cp+i)
```

These equivalences are summarized in the following table:

char *cp, c[MAX]; int i;	
Array Notation	**Pointer Notation**
&c[0]	c
c[i]	*(c+i)
&c[i]	c+i
cp[i]	*(cp+i)

For example, given that

```
char c[5] = {'a', 'b', 'c', 'd', 'e'};
char *cp;
```

and

```
cp = c;
```

we have

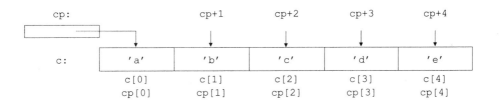

and

c[0]	is	'a',	and so are	*cp	and	cp[0].
c[1]	is	'b',	and so are	*(cp+1)	and	cp[1].
c[2]	is	'c',	and so are	*(cp+2)	and	cp[2].
c[3]	is	'd',	and so are	*(cp+3)	and	cp[3].
c[4]	is	'e',	and so are	*(cp+4)	and	cp[4].

Although array names and pointers have strong similarities, array names are not variables. Thus, if a is an array name and ap a pointer, then the expressions like

```
a = ap;
```

and

```
a++;
```

are illegal. One way of viewing array names is that they are constant pointers whose values may not be changed.

7.3.1 Arrays as Function Arguments

An array name, as we have seen in Section 6.2.2, can be passed as argument to a function. When an array name is specified as argument, it is actually the address of the first element of the array that is passed to the called function. Hence, a formal parameter declared to be of type "array of T" is treated as if it were declared to be of type "pointer to T". Thus, the declaration for x in

```
void array_cuberoot(double x[], int length);
```

can equivalently be written as

```
void array_cuberoot(double *x, int length);
```

The following is an example of a function that finds the value of the largest element in an integer array:

```
int max(int a[], int length)
  {
    int i, maxv;

    for (i = 1, maxv = a[0]; i < length; i++)
        if (a[i] > maxv)   maxv = a[i];
    return maxv;
  }
```

Using pointers, this function can equivalently be written as

```
int max(int *a, int length)
  {
    int i, maxv;

    for (i = 1, maxv = *a; i < length; i++)
        if (*(a+i) > maxv)   maxv = *(a+i);
    return maxv;
  }
```

Since pointers can be subscripted, the preceding function can also be written as

```
int max(int *a, int length)
  {
    int i, maxv;

    for (i = 1, maxv = a[0]; i < length; i++)
        if (a[i] > maxv)   maxv = a[i];
    return maxv;
  }
```

Yet another way to write this function is

```
int max(int *a, int length)
  {
    int maxv, *end = a + length;

    for (maxv = *a; a < end; a++)
        if (*a > maxv)   maxv = *a;
    return maxv;
  }
```

In this version, end is initialized to point to the first element beyond the end of the array, and the pointer variable a is repeatedly incremented to step through all the elements of the array.

With any of the preceding function definitions and the declaration

```
int inp[5] = {10, 6, 4, 2, 8};
```

the function call

```
printf("%d\n", max(inp, 5));
```

causes 10 to be printed.

You may also provide a pointer to an element other than the first element of an array as an argument. To pass a pointer to the $(i+1)$th element of the array c to the function f, we write

```
f(&c[i]);
```

or

```
f(c+i);
```

In the declaration of f, the parameter declaration can read as

```
void f(char a[]);
```

or

```
void f(char *a);
```

The fact that the argument refers to an element in the middle of an array is of no consequence to f. What is given to f is just a pointer, and f can do what it likes with it. Thus, given any of the preceding definitions of the function max and the array inp, the function call

```
printf("%d\n", max(&inp[2], 3));
```

or

```
printf("%d\n", max(inp+2, 3));
```

causes 8 to be printed, whereas the function call

```
printf("%d\n", max(&inp[2], 2));
```

or

```
printf("%d\n", max(inp+2, 2));
```

causes 4 to be printed.

It should now be clear why the changes in a parameter array in the called function are reflected in the array passed as argument. Since the called function is provided the address of the argument array, it is an element of the argument array that is accessed when an element of the parameter array is accessed in the called function. Thus, the function definition

```
#include <math.h>

void array_cuberoot(double x[], int length)
  {
    int i;
```

```
    for (i = 0; i < length; i++)
        x[i] = pow(x[i], 1.0/3.0);
}
```

is equivalent to

```
#include <math.h>

void array_cuberoot(double *x, int length)
    {
        int i;

        for (i = 0; i < length; i++)
            *(x+i) = pow(*(x+i), 1.0/3.0);
    }
```

and when it is called as

```
double y[5] = {0.1, 0.2, 0.3, 0.4, 0.5};
array_cuberoot(y, 5);
```

x is bound to the address of the first element of y and `array_cuberoot` converts the value of every element of the argument array to the cube root of the current value.

7.3.2 Illustrative Examples

We now give some example programs to further illustrate the relationship between arrays and pointers.

Example 1
Rewrite, using pointers, the program of Example 1 in Section 6.3 that cyclically permutes the values of an integer array.

The desired program is as follows.

```
#include <stdio.h>
#define  LAST  10

int main(void)
    {
        float  array[LAST], temp;
        int    i;

        /* read array */
        for (i = 0; i < LAST; i++)
            scanf("%f", array+i);
```

```
    /*  permute  array  */
    temp = *array;
    for  (i = 1;  i < LAST;  i++)
        *(array+i-1)  =  *(array+i);
    *(array+LAST-1)  =  temp;

    /*  output  the  permuted  array  */
    for  (i = 0;  i < LAST;  i++)
        printf("%f\n",  *(array+i));

    return 0;
}
```

In this version, the $(i+1)$th element of `array` is referenced as `*(array+i)`, and `array+i` is the address of this element.

Example 2

Rewrite, using pointers, the program of Example 5 in Section 6.3 for sorting a list of integers in descending order.

The desired program is as follows.

```
#include <stdio.h>
#define  MAXSIZE  100

int readl(int *arr, int length);
void writel(int *arr, int last);
void bsort(int *arr, int last);

int main(void)
    {
    int   list[MAXSIZE], total_elements;

    total_elements = readl(list, MAXSIZE);
    bsort(list, total_elements);
    writel(list, total_elements);
    return 0;
    }

int readl(int *arr, int length)
    {
    int   i;

    for (i = 0;  i < length
                && scanf("%d", arr+i)  != EOF; i++)
        ;
    return i;
    }
```

```
void bsort(int *arr, int last)
  {
    int   i, not_done;

    do
      {
        not_done = 0;

        /* scan and interchange as needed */

        for (i = 1; i < last; i++)

            if (*(arr+i-1) < *(arr+i) )
              {
                int t;

                t = *(arr+i);
                *(arr+i) = *(arr+i-1);
                *(arr+i-1) = t;
                not_done++;
              }

        /* do not scan the last data item in the next iteration */

        last--;
      }
    while (not_done);
  }

void writel(int *arr, int last)
  {
    int   *end = arr + last;

    while (arr < end) printf("%d\n", *arr++);
  }
```

7.4 STRINGS AND POINTERS

String manipulation is often a large part of any programming task. C does not have a built-in string data type, but uses null-terminated arrays of characters to represent strings. To create a *string variable*, you must allocate sufficient space for the number of characters in the string and the null character ' \0'. The null character helps find the end of a string. For example, you can define a string variable capable of storing the word "r2d2" as follows:

```
char robot[5];
```

This variable, as we discussed in Section 6.1.3, can be initialized at the time of its definition as

```
char robot[5] = {'r', '2', 'd', '2', '\0'};
```

or simply as

```
char robot[5] = "r2d2";
```

in which case the compiler automatically provides the terminating null character. The following figure shows the effect of such an initialization:

robot: | 'r' | '2' | 'd' | '2' | '\0' |

Since the string variable robot is an array of characters, the name robot is a pointer to the first character of the string and can be used to access and manipulate the characters of the string.

A *string constant*, syntactically, is a sequence of characters enclosed in double quotation marks. The storage required for a string constant is one character more than the number of characters enclosed within the quotation marks, since the compiler automatically places the null character at the end. The type of a string constant is an "array of char." However, when a string constant appears anywhere (except as an initializer of a character array or an argument to the sizeof operator), the characters making up the string together with the null character are stored in consecutive memory locations, and the string constant becomes a pointer to the location where the first character of the string has been stored. For example, given the declaration for a character pointer

```
char *probot;
```

after the assignment

```
probot = "r2d2";
```

the pointer variable probot contains the address of the first memory location where the string "r2d2" has been stored, as shown in the following:

probot: | → | 'r' | '2' | 'd' | '2' | '\0' |

The characters of the string can then be accessed using this pointer.

Before giving examples of how strings can be manipulated using pointers, we must emphasize the difference between a character array initialized to a string constant and a character pointer initialized to a string constant. The name of a character array, such as robot, always refers to the same storage, although the individual characters within the array may be changed by new assignments. On the other hand, a character pointer, such as probot, may be reassigned to point to new memory locations, but if it is pointing to a string constant and you try to modify the contents of the locations accessible through this pointer, the result is undefined.

To illustrate string handling, we write a function strlen that computes the length of a given string, and returns the number of characters that precede the terminating null character '\0'. This function can be written using arrays as

```
int strlen(char str[])
  {
    int i = 0;

    while (str[i] != '\0') i++;
    return i;
  }
```

Here is a pointer version of the same function:

```
int strlen(char *str)
  {
    char *first = str;

    while (*str != '\0') str++;
    return str - first;
  }
```

In this version, the desired length is determined as the difference in value between a pointer to the terminating null character and a pointer to the first character of the string. The character pointer `str` is initialized to point to the first character of the source string at the time of function call. This pointer value is also saved in another pointer variable `first`. We then check in a loop that `str` is not pointing to the terminating null character, and if not, `str` is advanced by one character. The length of the string is then determined by subtracting from `first` the last value of `str`.

Since the loop termination condition in the preceding function merely tests whether the expression is nonzero, the function can be written more succinctly as

```
int strlen(char *str)
  {
    char *first = str;

    while (*str) str++;
    return str - first;
  }
```

As another example of a string handling function, consider the following function `strcpy` that copies a string into another string:

```
void strcpy(char *to, char *from)
  {
    while(*to = *from) to++, from++;
  }
```

The character pointers `to` and `from` are initialized to the destination and source strings respectively at the time of function call. These pointers are then advanced one character at a time, and at each pointer position, one character is copied from the `from` string to the `to` string. The copy loop terminates when the character `'\0'` terminating the `from` string has been copied into the `to` string.

The preceding function can be further abbreviated to

```
void strcpy(char *to, char *from)
   {
      while(*to++ = *from++);
   }
```

Due to the relative precedence of `*` and `++`, the value of `*from++` is the character that `from` pointed to before `from` was incremented; `from` is incremented only after this character has been fetched. For the same reason, this character is stored in the old `to` position before `to` is incremented, and is also the value used to control the loop termination. Thus, the complete `from` string, including `'\0'`, is copied into the `to` string.

Finally, here is a function `strcat` that concatenates the string `addend` to the end of the string `str` :

```
void strcat(char *str, char *addend)
   {
      strcpy(str+strlen(str), addend);
   }
```

Note that `str+strlen(str)` points to the position in `str` that contains the terminating `'\0'`, and `strcpy` copies `addend` into `str` starting at this position.

7.4.1 Library Functions for Processing Strings

Although C does not have built-in string data type, it provides a rich set of library functions for processing strings. The standard header file `<string.h>` contains the prototypes for these functions. We now discuss the most frequently used of these functions.

In the following discussion, `size_t` is an unsigned integral type defined in the standard header file `<stddef.h>`. String parameters that are not modified by the function are declared to be of type `const char *`. The type qualifier `const` will be discussed in Chapter 12.

```
size_t strlen(const char *s);
```

computes the length of the string *s*, and returns the number of characters that precede `'\0'`.

```
char *strcpy(char *s1, const char *s2);
```

copies the string *s2* to *s1* (including `'\0'`), and returns *s1*.

```
char *strncpy(char *s1, const char *s2, size_t  n);
```

copies at most the first *n* characters of the string *s2* to *s1* (stopping after `'\0'` has been copied and padding the necessary number of `'\0'` at the end, if *s2* has fewer than *n* characters), and returns *s1*.

```
char *strcat(char *s1, const char *s2);
```

concatenates the string *s2* to the end of *s1*, placing `'\0'` at the end of the concatenated string, and returns *s1*.

```
char *strncat(char *s1, const char *s2, size_t  n);
```

concatenates at most the first *n* characters of the string *s2* to the end of *s1* (stopping before a ' \0' has been appended), places ' \0' at the end of the concatenated string, and returns *s1*.

```
int strcmp(const char *s1, const char *s2);
```

compares the string *s1* to *s2*, and returns a negative value if *s1* is lexicographically less than *s2*, zero if *s1* is equal to *s2*, and a positive value if *s1* is lexicographically greater than *s2*.

```
int strncmp(const char *s1, const char *s2, size_t  n);
```

compares at most the first *n* characters of the string *s1* to *s2* (stopping after a ' \0' has been compared), and returns a negative value if *s1* is lexicographically less than *s2*, zero if *s1* is equal to *s2*, and a positive value if *s1* is lexicographically greater than *s2*.

```
int *strchr(const char *s, int c);
```

locates the first occurrence of *c* (converted to a char) in the string *s*, and returns a pointer to the located character if the search succeeds and NULL otherwise.

```
int *strrchr(const char *s, int c);
```

locates the last occurrence of *c* (converted to a char) in the string *s*, and returns a pointer to the located character if the search succeeds and NULL otherwise.

The following table illustrates string handling functions:

char s1[MAX], s2[MAX];	
Statement	Result
`printf("%d", strlen("cord"));`	4
`printf("%s", strcpy(s1, "string"));`	string
`printf("%s", strncpy(s2, "endomorph", 4));`	endo
`printf("%s", strcat(s1, s2));`	stringendo
`printf("%d", strcmp(s1, s2));`	1
`printf("%d", strncmp(s1+6, s2, 4));`	0
`printf("%s", strchr(s1, 'n'));`	ngendo
`printf("%s", strrchr(s1, 'n'));`	ndo

7.4.2 Illustrative Examples

We now give some example programs to further illustrate string manipulations using pointers.

Example 1
Write a function that extracts a substring of specified length from a given string by locating the last occurrence of the starting character of the substring.

The prototype of the desired function is of the form

```
char *subrstr(char *str, char c, int n, char *result);
```

and it extracts from the string `str` at most n characters, starting from the last occurrence of the character c. If the remaining characters in the string are less than the specified length, the function returns the largest possible substring. The extracted substring is null-terminated and returned in the character array `result`, assumed to be large enough to hold the extracted string. The function returns `NULL` if c does not occur in `str`.

The desired function is as follows:

```
#include <stdio.h>
#include <string.h>

char *subrstr(char *str, char c, int n, char *result)
  {
    char *cp;

    if (cp = strrchr(str, c))
      {
        /* cp points to the last occurrence of c in str   */
        /* copy at most n characters from str to result */
        strncpy(result, cp, n);

        /* null terminate result */
        *(result + n) = '\0';

        return result;
      }
    else
        return NULL;
  }
```

Given that

```
char substr[80];
```

the function call

```
printf("%s\n",
       subrstr("doctor dolittle", 'd', 2, substr));
```

prints

```
do
```

and the function call

```
printf("%s\n",
       subrstr("doctor dolittle", 'd', 10, substr));
```

prints

Example 2

Write a function that locates the first occurrence of a character string inside another string.

The desired function is as follows:

```
#include <stdio.h>
#include <string.h>

char *strloc(char *str, char *pattern)
    {
      char *cp;

      for (cp = str; cp = strchr(cp, *pattern); cp++)
          if (!strncmp(cp, pattern, strlen(pattern)))
              return cp;
      return NULL;
    }
```

This function returns a pointer to the starting position of the pattern string in the given string, and NULL if the pattern string is not found.

The function strchr locates the position of the first character of the pattern string in the given string, and strncmp checks if the following characters match those in the pattern string. If the comparison succeeds, this position is returned as the value of strloc; otherwise, the search is repeated in the remainder of the string.

Thus, the function call

```
printf("%s\n",
          strloc("ad majorem Dei gloriam", "or"));
```

prints

```
orem Dei gloriam
```

and the function call

```
printf("%s\n",
          strloc("ad majorem Dei gloriam", "ori"));
```

prints

```
oriam
```

Example 3

Write a function that determines if a given string is a palindrome.

A *palindrome* is a word or phrase that reads the same backward as forward. Blanks, punctuation marks and capitalizations do not count in determining palindromes. Here are some well-known palindromes:

Radar
Too hot to hoot

Madam! I'm Adam.
A Man, A Plan, A Canal — Panama
Doc, note, I dissent! A fast never prevents a fatness; I diet on cod.

The desired function is as follows:

```
#include <string.h>
#define  MAXSIZE    80

void transform(char *rawstr, char *stdstr);
int test(char *stdstr);

int palindrome(char *rawstr)
  {
    char stdstr[MAXSIZE];

    transform(rawstr, stdstr);
    return test(stdstr);
  }

void transform(char *rawstr, char *stdstr)
  {
    for( ; *rawstr; rawstr++)
        if(*rawstr >= 'a' && *rawstr <= 'z')
            /*  convert to uppercase */
            *stdstr++ = *rawstr - 'a' + 'A';
        else if((*rawstr >= 'A' && *rawstr <= 'Z') ||
                (*rawstr >= '0' && *rawstr <= '9'))
                    *stdstr++ = *rawstr;
  }

int test(char *str)
  {
    /* pointer to the first character */
    char *left = str;
    /* pointer to the last character */
    char *right = str + strlen(str) - 1;

    for ( ; left < right; left++, right--)
        if (*left != *right)
            return 0;

    return 1;
  }
```

The function transform converts the given string into a standard form by converting lowercase letters into uppercase letters and by removing all characters other than letters and numerals from the string. The function test then checks whether the transformed string is a palindrome by simultaneously traversing it forward and backward and checking at every position that the characters match.

7.5   MULTI-DIMENSIONAL ARRAYS AND POINTERS

A multi-dimensional array in C is really a one-dimensional array, whose elements are themselves arrays, and is stored such that the last subscript varies most rapidly. The name of the multi-dimensional array is, therefore, a pointer to the first array. Thus, the declaration

```
int matrix[3][5];
```

specifies that the array `matrix` consists of three elements, each of which is an array of five integer elements, and that the name `matrix` is a pointer to the first row of the matrix.

Instead of using subscripts, an element in a multi-dimensional array can be referenced using an equivalent pointer expression. For example, the element `matrix[i][j]` can be referenced using the pointer expression

```
*(*(matrix+i) + j)
```

since

matrix	is a pointer to the first row;
matrix+i	is a pointer to the ith row;
*(matrix+i)	is the ith row which is converted into a pointer to the first element in the ith row;
*(matrix+i) + j	is a pointer to the jth element in the ith row; and
((matrix+i) + j)	is matrix[i][j], the jth element in the ith row.

We now illustrate how a multi-dimensional array can be processed using pointers by writing a function `colsum` that determines the sum of a given column of the matrix declared as

```
int matrix[MAXROWS][MAXCOLS];
```

Since, as mentioned in Section 7.1.5, pointer arithmetic works correctly with pointers of any type, a two-dimensional array can be traversed by initializing a pointer to the first row of the array and then incrementing the pointer each time we need to get to the next row. Let `rptr` be the pointer to the rows of `matrix`. We can declare and initialize this pointer to the first row of `matrix` as

```
int (*rptr)[MAXCOLS] = matrix;
```

This declaration specifies that `rptr` is a pointer to an array of `MAXCOLS` integers. The parentheses around `*rptr` are necessary because the dereferencing operator `*` has lower precedence than the indexing operator `[]`, and without the parentheses, the declaration

```
int *rptr[MAXCOLS];
```

specifies `rptr` to be an array of `MAXCOLS` elements, each a pointer to an integer. Having declared `rptr` to be a pointer to a row of `matrix`, `(*rptr)[j]` refers to the $(j + 1)$th element of this row.

The function `colsum` is as follows:

```
int colsum(int (*matrix)[MAXCOLS],
           int rows, int column)
{
   int (*rptr)[MAXCOLS] = matrix;
   int i, sum;

   for (i = 0, sum = 0; i < rows; i++)
       sum += (*rptr++)[column];
   return sum;
}
```

Note that the parameter declaration

```
int (*matrix)[MAXCOLS]
```

specifies that `matrix` is a pointer to an array of MAXCOLS integer elements. This declaration is equivalent to

```
int matrix[][MAXCOLS]
```

Given that

```
int m[][MAXCOLS] =
   {
     {1, 2, 3},
     {4, 5, 6}
   }
```

the function call

```
colsum(m, 2, 0)
```

produces 5 as the sum of the first column.

We now write another function `rowsum` that finds the sum of the elements of a given row of `matrix`. As discussed at the beginning of this section, `*(matrix+i)` is a pointer to the first element in row `i` of `matrix`. Thus, if `cptr` points to elements of `matrix` in row `i`, it can be initialized to point to the first element of row `i` by a declaration of the form

```
int *cptr = *(matrix+i);
```

The function `rowsum` is as follows:

```
int rowsum(int (*matrix)[MAXCOLS],
           int columns, int row)
{
   int *cptr = *(matrix+row);
   int j, sum;

   for (j = 0, sum = 0; j < columns; j++)
       sum += *cptr++;
   return sum;
}
```

With the same `m` as defined above, the function call

```
rowsum(m, 3, 1)
```

produces 15 as the sum of the second row.

7.5.1 Illustrative Example

We now give an example program to further illustrate the processing of multi-dimensional arrays using pointers.

Example

Rewrite, using pointers, the program given in Example 2 of Section 6.3 that calculates the average score of each student, the average of each test, and the class average over all tests.

The desired program is as follows:

```c
#include <stdio.h>
#define   TESTS      4
#define   STUDENTS   10

int score[TESTS+1][STUDENTS+1] =
    {
        {0, 0, 0, 0, 0, 0, 0, 0, 0, 0, 0},
        {0, 4, 3, 4, 2, 1, 0, 3, 4, 1, 0},
        {0, 4, 4, 3, 3, 2, 1, 2, 3, 1, 2},
        {0, 4, 3, 4, 3, 2, 2, 2, 3, 0, 1},
        {0, 4, 3, 4, 4, 1, 3, 3, 3, 1, 2}
    };

int main(void)
  {
    int  i, j;

    for (i = 1; i <= TESTS; i++)

        for (j = 1; j <= STUDENTS; j++)
          {
            /* total for a test */
            *(*(score+i) + 0) += *(*(score+i) + j);
            /* total for a student */
            *(*(score+0) + j) += *(*(score+i) + j);
            /* total for the class */
            *(*(score+0) + 0) += *(*(score+i) + j);
          }

    for (j = 1; j <= STUDENTS; j++)
        printf("student %d: average score = %f\n",
            j, (float)(*(*(score+0)+j))/TESTS);
```

```
for (i = 1; i <= TESTS; i++)
    printf("test %d: average score = %f\n",
        i, (float)(*(*(score+i)+0))/STUDENTS);

printf("class average = %f\n",
    (float)(*(*(score+0)+0))/(STUDENTS*TESTS));

return 0;
}
```

In the above program, we have shown explicit addition of zero in some of the pointer expressions for clarity; this addition, however, is unnecessary and not written in practice.

Compare this program to that given in Section 6.3. The pointer version is more complex and difficult to understand, but some compilers generate more efficient code for the pointer version.

7.6 POINTER ARRAYS

An array, as we have seen in Chapter 6, is an ordered collection of data items, each of the same type, and the type of an array is the type of its data items. When the data items are of pointer type, we have what is known as a *pointer array* or an *array of pointers*. For example, the declaration

```
char *day[7];
```

defines day to be an array consisting of seven character pointers; it is not a pointer to an array of seven characters, since the indexing operator [] has precedence over the dereferencing operator *. The declaration would have been written as

```
char (*day)[7];
```

if day were to be a pointer to an array of seven characters.

The elements of a pointer array, like that of any other array, can be assigned values by following the array definition with a list of comma-separated initializers enclosed in braces, as in

```
char *day[7]   =
    {
    "monday", "tuesday", "wednesday",
    "thursday", "friday", "saturday", "sunday"
    };
```

or through assignment statements as in

```
char *day[7];

day[0] = "monday";
day[1] = "tuesday";
day[2] = "wednesday";
day[3] = "thursday";
day[4] = "friday";
day[5] = "saturday";
day[6] = "sunday";
```

In both the cases, the necessary storage is allocated for the string constants, and pointers to them are stored in day. The following figure depicts the result:

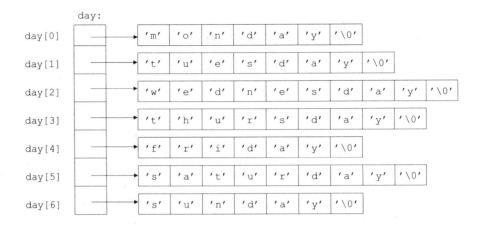

Note that the arrays that store the day names are of different lengths, depending upon the number of characters in the name.

Given the pointer array day, the following function converts a day number into a pointer to that day's name:

```
char *dayname(int n)
    {
        return n >= 0 && n <= 6 ? day[n] : NULL;
    }
```

Instead of a pointer array, we could have used a two-dimensional character array to store the day names. However, such an array will have to make provision for the largest possible name. In general, fixed-length arrays could result in a substantial waste of storage, if there is large variance in the storage required for each name.

A major application of pointer arrays is in specifying command-line arguments to main, which we shall study now.

7.6.1 Command-Line Arguments

All C programs, as we mentioned in Section 2.1, define a function main that designates the entry point of the program and is invoked by the environment in which the program is executed. In the programs considered so far in the text, main did not take any arguments. However, main can be defined with formal parameters so that the program may accept command-line arguments, that is, arguments that are specified when the program is executed. Thus, one could compute the factorial of a desired number by executing the program factorial as

```
factorial 5
```

instead of invoking it as

```
factorial
```

and then reading 5 within the program.

The function `main` is then defined as having two parameters, customarily called `argc` and `argv`, and appears as

```
int main(int argc, char *argv[])
   {
       . . .
   }
```

The parameter `argc` (for argument count) is the count of the number of command-line arguments, and the parameter `argv` (for argument vector) is a pointer to a one-dimensional array of pointers to character strings representing arguments. By convention, `argv[0]` points to a string which is the name of the program, `argv[i]`, where i = 1, 2, . . ., argc-1, points to the ith argument, and `argv[argc]` is `NULL`. The argument count `argc` is at least one, since the first argument is the name of the program itself.

For example, if the command line for a program `printargs` is

```
printargs vox populi vox Dei
```

then, when the function `main` is called, `argc` will be 5 and `argv` a null-terminated array of pointers to strings as shown below:

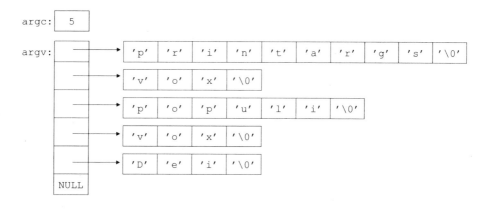

The following is the code for `printargs`, which simply echoes its command-line arguments:

```
#include <stdio.h>

int main(int argc, char *argv[])
   {
      int  i;

      for (i = 1; i < argc; i++)
          printf("%s ", argv[i]);

      printf("\n");
      return 0;
   }
```

Whitespaces are used to delimit the command-line arguments. If an argument contains whitespaces, it must be placed within quotation marks. Thus, if `printargs` is invoked as

```
printargs "vox populi" "vox Dei"
```

then `argc` will be 3 and `argv` an array of three pointers pointing to the strings `"printargs"`, `"vox populi"`, and `"vox Dei"` respectively.

The command-line arguments are always stored as character strings. For example, the command-line arguments 35 and 56 as in

```
lcm 35 56
```

will be stored as character strings `"35"` and `"56"` respectively, and `argv[1]` and `argv[2]` will contain pointers to them. If the integer values of these arguments are of interest, the strings must be converted into numbers by the program. The standard C library provides several functions for number conversions including `atoi` that converts a given string to `int` and `atof` that converts a given string to `double`. The header file `<stdlib.h>` contains the prototypes for these functions.

7.6.2 Pointers to Pointers

A pointer provides the address of the data item pointed to by it. The data item pointed to by a pointer can be an address of another data item. Thus, a given pointer can be a pointer to a pointer to an object. Accessing this object from the given pointer then requires two levels of indirection. First, the given pointer is dereferenced to get the pointer to the given object, and then this later pointer is dereferenced to get to the object.

Consider, for example, the declarations

```
int i = 1;
int *p;
```

that declare two objects: `i`, an integer, and `p`, a pointer to an integer. We may apply the address operator `&` to both `i` and `p` as in

```
p = &i;      /* make p point to i */
q = &p;      /* make q point to p */
```

These statements imply that `q` is a pointer to the pointer `p`, which in turn points to the integer `i`. The relationship between `i`, `p`, and `q` is pictorially depicted below:

To handle such situations, the notation

```
**q
```

which means "apply the dereferencing operator to q twice" can be used, and the variable q declared as

```
int **q;
```

In order to fetch the value of i, starting from q, we go through two levels of indirection. The value of *q is the content of p which is the address of i, and the value of **q is *(&i) which is 1. Thus, each of the expressions

```
i + 1
*p + 1
**q + 1
```

has the value 2.

There is no limit on the number of levels of indirection, and a declaration such as

```
int ***p;
```

means

***p	is an integer,
**p	is a pointer to an integer,
*p	is a pointer to a pointer to an integer, and
p	is a pointer to a pointer to a pointer to an integer.

In the following definition of main

```
int main(int argc, char *argv[])
```

argv is really a pointer to a pointer, since C passes an array argument by passing the pointer to the first element of the array. Thus, the declaration

```
char *argv[]
```

can be replaced by an equivalent declaration

```
char **argv
```

The following is the program printargs, rewritten treating argv as a pointer to a pointer:

```
#include <stdio.h>

int main(int argc, char **argv)
  {
    while (--argc) printf("%s ", *++argv);
    printf("\n");

    return 0;
  }
```

In the printf statement, argv is incremented before the string pointed to by argv is fetched to avoid printing the name of the program.

If the command line for a program printargs is

```
printargs vox populi vox Dei
```

then `argc` and `argv` will be as shown below:

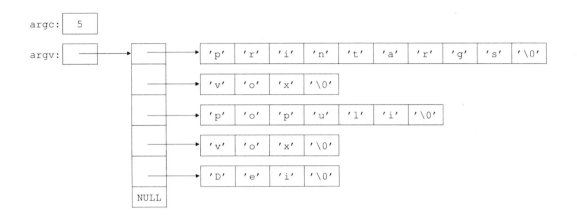

7.6.3 Illustrative Examples

We now give some example programs to further illustrate pointer arrays.

Example 1
Write a program that converts a given day of the year into date and month.

The desired program is as follows:

```
#include <stdio.h>
#include <stdlib.h>
#include <limits.h>   /* defines INT_MAX */
#define   MONTHS   12

char *mname[] =
  {
    "january", "february", "march", "april",
    "may", "june", "july", "august", "september",
    "october", "november", "december"
  };

int leap[] =
  {
    31, 29, 31, 30, 31, 30, 31,
    31, 30, 31, 30, 31, INT_MAX
  };
int regular[] =
  {
    31, 28, 31, 30, 31, 30, 31,
    31, 30, 31, 30, 31, INT_MAX
  };
int *days[] = {leap, regular};
```

```
    void datemonth(int day, int year,
                   int *pdate, int *pmonth)
      {
        int  normal, *pday;

        /* is it a normal or a leap year? */
        normal = ((year%4) || !(year%100)) && (year%400);

        /* get the appropriate element of days array */
        pday = days[normal];

        /* find the month in which this day falls */
        while (day > *pday) day -= *pday++;

        *pdate = day;
        *pmonth = pday - days[normal];
      }

char *name(int month)
  {
    return mname[month];
  }

int main(int argc, char *argv[])
  {
    int  day, year, date, month;

    if (argc != 3)
      {
        printf("usage: %s <day> <year>\n", argv[0]);
        return 1;
      }

    day = atoi(argv[1]);
    year = atoi(argv[2]);

    datemonth(day, year, &date, &month);

    if (date > 0 && month < MONTHS)
      {
        printf("%d %s\n", date, name(month));
        return 0;
      }
    else
      {
        printf("an out-of-range day\n");
        return 1;
      }
  }
```

The `main` function obtains the values of `day` and `year` as command-line arguments, and uses the standard library function `atoi` (see Appendix A) to convert the string representation of these values into integers. If the correct number of command-line arguments is not provided, `main` prints the names of the arguments it is expecting. Thus, if this program, kept in `day.c`, is compiled as

```
cc -o day day.c
```

on a UNIX machine, or as

```
cl day.c
```

on an IBM PC using the Microsoft C Compiler, and then executed as

```
day
```

it will print

```
usage: day <day> <year>
```

It is a good feature to incorporate in all the programs you write.

The function `datemonth` determines the date and month in which the given day of the year falls. It uses a pointer array `days` of two elements. As shown below, the first element points to an integer array `leap`, whose elements contain the number of days in the months of a leap year. The second element points to another integer array `regular`, whose elements contain the number of days in the months of a nonleap year.

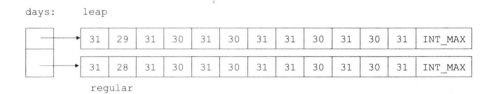

The function `monthdate` first determines whether the given year is a regular or a leap year, and sets `pday` to point to the first element of the array `leap` if it is a leap year and `normal` turns out to be 0; otherwise, it sets `pday` to point to the first element of the array `regular`. The function then steps through the selected array by incrementing `pday` to determine the month in which the given `day` falls. The last dummy entry guarantees that we will not go out of bounds. This technique avoids the need for bounds checking inside the search loop, and is often used when searching an array for a value that may not be present.

The function `name` is straightforward. The pointer array `mname` stores the names of months as shown below:

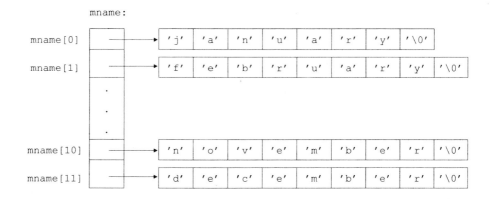

The function `name` uses the given `month` to index into `mname` and returns a pointer to the corresponding name string.

Example 2

Write a program that converts a given nonnegative decimal integer into its equivalent binary, octal, or hexadecimal representation depending upon the options specified in the command line.

We follow the convention used in the UNIX systems to specify the options by preceding an argument with a minus sign, and use -b, -o, and -x to specify binary, octal, and hexadecimal conversions respectively. Thus, the command

```
convert -x 20
```

specifies that the decimal 20 is to be converted into its equivalent hexadecimal form. More than one option can be specified in one command line as in

```
convert -b -x 20
```

to mean that the decimal 20 is to be converted into its binary as well as hexadecimal form. Options can also be combined as in

```
convert -bx 20
```

The desired program is as follows:

```c
#include <stdio.h>
#include <stdlib.h>
#include <string.h>
#define  MAXLEN  80

char *convert(int number, int base, char *string);
char *strrev(char *string);
```

```c
int main(int argc, char **argv)
  {
    int  binary = 0, octal = 0, hex = 0, i;
    char c, *cp, *name, str[MAXLEN];

    name = *argv++, argc--;

    for (; argc > 0 && **argv == '-';
           argc--, argv++)
      {
        cp = *argv;
        while (c = *++cp)
            switch (c)
                {
                  case 'b':
                      binary = 1;
                      break;
                  case 'o':
                      octal = 1;
                      break;
                  case 'x':
                      hex = 1;
                      break;
                  default:
                      printf("%s: illegal option "
                             "%c\n", name, c);
                      argc = 0;
                      break;
                }
      }

    if (argc != 1)
      {
        printf("usage: %s -box <integer>\n", name);
        return 1;
      }

    i = atoi(*argv);

    if (binary)
        printf("binary: %s\n", convert(i, 2, str));
    else if (octal)
        printf("octal: %s\n", convert(i, 8, str));
    else /* hexadecimal */
        printf("hex: %s\n", convert(i, 16, str));

    return 0;
  }
```

```
char *convert(int num, int base, char *str)
  {
    char *sp = str;
    int digit;

    do
      {
        digit = num % base;
        *sp++ = digit < 10 ?
                digit + '0' : digit - 10 + 'a';
        num /= base;
      }
    while(num);

    *sp = '\0'; /*  null terminate str */

    return strrev(str);
  }

char *strrev(char *str)  /*  reverse str in place */
  {
    char *left = str,
         *right = str + strlen(str) - 1, temp;

    for ( ; left < right; left++, right--)
        temp = *left, *left = *right, *right = temp;

    return str;
  }
```

The program begins by saving the name of the program in `name` and incrementing `argv` to point to the first optional argument. The outer loop is executed once for each optional argument. Thus, at the end of the outer loop, `argc` should be 1 and `argv` pointing to the string representation of the decimal integer number to be converted.

The function `convert` creates the equivalent representation of the given number `num` in the character array `str` and returns a pointer to it. The conversion depends on the value of `base`, which is 2 for binary, 8 for octal, and 16 for hexadecimal conversions. To find the base-b equivalent of a decimal integer number, the number is divided repeatedly by b until a quotient of zero results. The successive remainders are the digits from right to left of the base-b representation. In the `do-while` loop, the remainder d resulting from dividing `num` by `base` is converted into the corresponding character by adding the value of the character 0 to it, if d is between 0 and 9. If d is between 10 and 15 for the hexadecimal conversion, it is converted into the corresponding hexadecimal digit by adding `'a'` -10 to it. Thus, at the end of the `do-while` loop, the string representing the desired equivalent representation is generated in `str` in the reverse order, and the function `strrev` is called to put it back in the right order.

The function `strrev` initializes `left` to point to the first character of the string and initializes `right` to point to the character preceding `'\0'`. The characters in these two positions are exchanged, `left` is incremented to point to the next character, and `right` is decremented to point to the previous character. When `left` and `right` start pointing to the same character position, or `left` goes beyond `right`, the string has been reversed in place.

7.7 POINTERS TO FUNCTIONS

In C, a function itself is not a variable, but it is possible to define a pointer to a function. A pointer to a function can best be thought of as the address of the code executed when the function is called.

While declaring a pointer to a function, the pointed-to function's type together with the type of its parameters is specified. For example, the declaration

```
int (*fp)(int i, int j);
```

declares `fp` to be a variable of type "pointer to a function that takes two integer arguments and returns an integer as its value." The identifiers `i` and `j` are written for descriptive purposes only. The preceding declaration can, therefore, also be written as

```
int (*fp)(int, int);
```

The parentheses around `*fp` are used to distinguish this declaration from that of a function, called `fp`, that returns a pointer to an integer. Keep in mind that:

`int i(void);`	declares `i` to be a function with no parameters that returns an `int`.
`int *pi(void);`	declares `pi` to be a function with no parameters that returns a pointer to an `int`.
`int (*ip)(void);`	declares `ip` to be a pointer variable that can be assigned to point to a function that returns an integer value and takes no arguments.

In order to make a pointer point to a specific function, we assign to it the function name without the following parentheses and the parameter declarations. For example, given that

```
int (*fp)(int, int), gcd(int, int);
```

the function pointer `fp` can be made to point to the function `gcd` with the assignment

```
fp = gcd;
```

To call the function pointed to by such a pointer, we simply dereference it like any other pointer, and include within a set of parentheses the arguments to be passed to the function. For example, after the previous assignment, the expression

```
(*fp)(42,56)
```

calls the function `gcd` pointed to by `fp`, passing 42 and 56 as arguments to it. The parentheses around `fp` are necessary to ensure that the dereferencing operator is applied before the function call is made. If the function being called takes no arguments, an empty argument list is provided. Thus, given that

```
void (*gp)(void), initialize(void);
gp = initialize;
```

the statement

```
(*gp)();
```

calls `initialize`.

The result returned by a function called by dereferencing a function pointer is equivalent to a direct call to that function. Thus, given that `fp` is pointing to the function `gcd` that finds the greatest common divisor of its arguments, the statement

```
i = (*fp)(42,56);
```

is equivalent to

```
i = gcd(42,56);
```

and assigns the value of `gcd(42,56)`, that is 14, to `i`.

A useful application of pointers to functions is in passing them as arguments to other functions. Consider, for example, the following function definition:

```
#include <stdio.h>
#include <math.h>

void table(double (*fp)(double),
           int init, int end, int incr)
  {
    int theta;

    for (theta = init; theta <= end; theta += incr)
        printf("%d %f\n",
               theta, (*fp)(theta/180.0*PI));
  }
```

The first parameter of `table` declared as

```
double (*fp)(double)
```

specifies that it is a pointer to a function that takes a `double` argument and returns a `double` value. The function `table` makes a table of values for the function passed to it as argument. For example, given that

```
double sin(double theta);
double cos(double theta);
```

the function calls

```
table(sin, 0, 180, 10);
table(cos, 90, 180, 5);
```

cause a table of sine values, followed by a table of cosine values, to be printed. The sine table is printed for $\theta = 0°$ through $180°$ in increments of $10°$, whereas the cosine table is printed for $\theta = 90°$ through $180°$ in increments of $5°$.

7.7.1 Illustrative Example

We now give an example program to further illustrate the concept of pointers to functions.

Example

Rewrite the program given in Example 6 of Section 6.3 that determines the price of a given item from an item-price database, without assuming that the item-price database is necessarily maintained in decreasing order of the item number.

Given an item number, we determine its price by using a binary search if the database is indeed sorted; otherwise, we do a linear search. A linear search is performed by examining each item for the desired value until a match is found or all items are exhausted.

The desired program is as follows:

```c
#include <stdio.h>
#include <limits.h> /* defines INT_MAX */
#define   ITEMS      1000
#define   NOT_FOUND  -1

int  bld_database(int *item, float *price,
                  int total_items);
int  bsearch(int value, int *arr, int max_items);
int  lsearch(int value, int *arr, int max_items);
void find_price(int (*search)(int, int *, int),
                int item_no, int *item,
                float *price, int total_items);

int main(void)
  {
    int    item[ITEMS], item_no, sorted;
    float  price[ITEMS];

    /* build the item-price database */

    sorted = bld_database(item, price, ITEMS);

    /* get item_no of the item whose price is to be found */

    scanf("%d", &item_no);

    /* print price */

    find_price(sorted ? bsearch : lsearch,
               item_no, item, price, ITEMS);
    return 0;
  }
```

```
int bld_database(int *item, float *price,
                 int total_items)
  {
    int i, last = INT_MAX, sorted = 1;

    for (i = 0; i < total_items; i++)
      {
        scanf("%d %f", item+i, price+i);
        if (last < *(item+i)) sorted = 0;
        last = *(item+i);
      }

    return sorted;
  }

void find_price(int (*search)(int, int *, int),
                int item_no, int *item,
                float *price, int total_items)
  {
    int index;

    index = (*search)(item_no, item, total_items);

    if (index == NOT_FOUND)
        printf("item %d is not in the database\n",
                item_no);
    else
        printf("price of item %d = %f\n",
                item_no, price[index]);
  }

/* binary search */
int bsearch(int val, int *arr, int length)
  {
    int first = 0, last = length-1, mid;

    while ( first <= last)
      {
        mid = (first + last) / 2;

        if (val == *(arr+mid))      /*search succeeds*/
            return mid;
        else if (val > *(arr+mid))/*search lower half*/
            last = mid - 1;
        else                        /*search upper half*/
            first = mid + 1;
      }

    return NOT_FOUND;
  }
```

```
/* linear search */
int lsearch(int val, int *arr, int length)
   {
     int i;

     for (i = 0; i < length; i++)
         if (*(arr+i) == val) return i;

     return NOT_FOUND;
   }
```

In this version, the function `bld_database` keeps track of the last item read to determine if the input data is indeed sorted in decreasing order of the item number. The function `find_price` now has an additional parameter `search` declared as

```
int (*search)(int, int *, int)
```

meaning that `search` can be assigned a pointer to a function that returns an `int` value, and takes three arguments: an `int`, a pointer to an `int`, and another `int`. The `main` function passes the pointer to either `bsearch` or `lsearch` to `find_price`, depending upon the value of `sorted` returned by `bld_database`, to specify the function that `find_price` should use. Within `find_price`, when `search` is dereferenced as

```
(*search)(item_no, item, total_items)
```

the appropriate search function is called. Note that one can now modify the search strategy by simply passing a pointer to another search function, without having to modify `find_price`.

7.8 DYNAMIC MEMORY MANAGEMENT

In many programs, the number of objects to be processed by the program and their sizes are not known *a priori*. One way to handle such situations is to make provision for the maximum number of objects expected and assume each to be of the maximum expected size. This is the approach taken in the example programs given in Section 6.3. This approach, however, may waste considerable memory and may even cause the size of the executable program to exceed the permissible size. Another disadvantage of this approach is that any guess eventually goes wrong and the program is presented with objects bigger and more in number than expected.

C provides a collection of dynamic memory management functions that enable storage to be allocated as needed and released when no longer required. Before describing these functions, we first introduce the `sizeof` operator that is often used in calls to these functions.

7.8.1 `sizeof` Operator

The `sizeof` operator is a unary operator that is used to obtain the size of a type or data object. It takes as its operand a parenthesized type name or an expression, and has the following forms:

```
sizeof (typename)
sizeof expression
```

The result of the `sizeof` operator is of type `size_t`, which is an unsigned integral type defined in the standard header file `<stddef.h>`.

The `sizeof` operator, when applied to a *typename*, yields the size in bytes of an object of the type named. For example, on an IBM PC, `sizeof(char)` is 1, `sizeof(int)` is 2, and `sizeof(long)` is 4.

The `sizeof` operator, when applied to an *expression*, analyzes the expression at compile time to determine its type, and then yields the same result as if it had been applied to the type of the expression. For example, if

```
short s, *sp;
```

then

`sizeof(s)`	is the same as	`sizeof(short)`
`sizeof(sp)`	is the same as	`sizeof(short *)`
`sizeof(*sp)`	is the same as	`sizeof(short)`

If the operand to `sizeof` is an *n*-element array of type *T*, the result of `sizeof` is *n* times the result of `sizeof` applied to the type *T*. Thus, if

```
int a[10];
```

then

```
sizeof(a);
```

is 20 on an IBM PC. Since a string constant is a null-terminated array of characters, `sizeof` applied to a string constant yields the number of characters in the string constant including the trailing `'\0'`. For example,

```
sizeof("computer")
```

is 9.

The `sizeof` operator does not cause any of the usual type conversions in determining the type of the expression. For example, when applied to an array name, `sizeof` does not cause the array name to be converted to a pointer. However, if the expression contains operators that do perform usual type conversions, those conversions are taken into account in determining its type. For example, if

```
char c;
```

then	`sizeof(c)`	is the same as	`sizeof(char),`
but	`sizeof(c+0)`	is the same as	`sizeof(int).`

because the type of the expression `c+0`, after the usual type conversion, is `int`.

When `sizeof` is applied to an expression, the expression is compiled to determine its type; it is, however, not compiled into executable code, with the result that any side effects that are to be produced by the execution of the expression do not occur. Thus, on IBM PC, the expression

```
int i, j;
i = 1;
j = sizeof(--i);
```

assigns 2 to j, but `i` remains 1 after the assignment.

7.8.2 Dynamic Memory Management Functions

The four dynamic memory management functions are `malloc`, `calloc`, `realloc`, and `free`. The functions `malloc` and `calloc` are used to obtain storage for an object, the function `realloc` for changing the size of the storage allocated to an object, and the function `free` for releasing the storage. The allocation of storage by calling `malloc`, `calloc`, and `realloc` yields a pointer to the beginning of the storage allocated and is suitably aligned, so that it may be assigned to a pointer to any type of object. The order and contiguity of the storage allocated by successive calls to these functions is not specified.

The prototypes for the functions `malloc`, `calloc`, `realloc`, and `free` are included in the header file `<stdlib.h>`. The functions `malloc`, `calloc`, and `realloc` return the generic pointer `void *` that can safely be converted to a pointer of any type.

```
void *malloc(size_t   size);
```

The function `malloc` allocates storage for an object whose size is specified by *size*. It returns a pointer to the allocated storage and `NULL` if it is not possible to allocate the storage requested. The allocated storage is not initialized in any way.

For example, if

```
float *fp, fa[10];
```

then

```
fp = (float *) malloc(sizeof(fa));
```

allocates the storage to hold an array of 10 floating-point elements and assigns the pointer to this storage to `fp`. Note that the generic pointer returned by `malloc` has been coerced into `float *` before it is assigned to `fp`.

```
void *calloc(size_t   nobj, size_t   size);
```

The function `calloc` allocates the storage for an array of *nobj* objects, each of size *size*. It returns a pointer to the allocated storage and `NULL` if it is not possible to allocate the storage requested. The allocated storage is initialized to zeros.

For example, if

```
double *dp, da[10];
```

then

```
dp = (double *) calloc(10, sizeof(double));
```

allocates the storage to hold an array of 10 `double` values and assigns the pointer to this storage to `dp`.

```
void *realloc(void *p, size_t  size);
```

The function `realloc` changes the size of the object pointed to by *p* to *size*. It returns a pointer to the new storage and NULL if it is not possible to resize the object, in which case the object (**p*) remains unchanged. The new size may be larger or smaller than the original size. If the new size is larger, the original contents are preserved and the remaining space is uninitialized; if smaller, the contents are unchanged up to the new size.

For example, if

```
char *cp;
cp = (char *) malloc(sizeof("computer"));
strcpy(cp, "computer");
```

then `cp` points to an array of 9 characters containing the null-terminated string `computer`. The function call

```
cp = (char *) realloc(cp, sizeof("compute"));
```

discards the trailing `'\0'` and makes `cp` point to an array of 8 characters containing the characters in `computer`, whereas the call

```
cp = (char *) realloc(cp, sizeof("computerization"));
```

makes `cp` point to an array of 16 characters, the first 9 of which contain the null-terminated string `computer` and the remaining 7 are uninitialized.

The function `realloc` behaves like `malloc` for the specified size if *p* is a NULL pointer.

```
void free(void *p);
```

The function `free` deallocates the storage pointed to by *p*, where *p* is a pointer to the storage previously allocated by `malloc`, `calloc`, or `realloc`. If *p* is a null pointer, `free` does nothing. For example, the storage allocated through calling `malloc`, `calloc`, and `realloc` in the preceding examples can be deallocated by

```
free(fp);
free(dp);
free(cp);
```

The behavior of the functions `realloc` and `free` is undefined, if *p* does not match a pointer earlier returned by a call to `malloc`, `calloc`, or `realloc`, or if the storage has been deallocated by a call to `realloc` or `free`.

7.8.3 Illustrative Examples

We now give some example programs to illustrate the use of dynamic memory management.

Example 1
Write a program that allocates enough storage to hold a given string, copies the string into this storage, and then increases the storage to append an additional character at the end of the string.

The desired program is as follows:

```c
#include <stdio.h>
#include <string.h>
#include <stdlib.h>
#define  STRING  "quis custodiet ipsos custodes"

int main(void)
  {
    char *cp;

    cp = (char *) malloc(sizeof(STRING));
    if (!cp)
      {
        printf("no memory\n");
        return 1;
      }

    strcpy(cp, STRING);

    cp = (char *) realloc(cp, sizeof(STRING) + 1);
    if (!cp)
      {
        printf("no memory\n");
        return 1;
      }

    printf("%s\n", strcat(cp, "?"));

    free(cp);

    return 0;
  }
```

Example 2
Rewrite the matrix multiplication program given in Example 4 of Section 6.3, using the dynamic memory management functions to allocate the exact amount of storage needed for the matrices.

The desired program is as follows:

```c
#include <stdio.h>
#include <stdlib.h>
```

```
float *alloc(char *name, int rows, int cols);
void  readm(float *matrix, int rows, int cols);
void  writem(float *matrix, int rows, int cols);
void  multiply(float *matrix1, int rows1, int cols1,
               float *matrix2, int cols2,
               float *product);

int main(void)
  {
    float   *matrix1, *matrix2, *product;
    int     rows1, cols1, rows2, cols2;

    for(;;)
      {
        /*  get the actual dimensions of the matrices  */

        printf("dimensions of matrix1?\n");
        scanf("%d %d", &rows1, &cols1);
        printf("dimensions of matrix2?\n");
        scanf("%d %d", &rows2, &cols2);

        if (cols1 != rows2)
          {
            printf("columns in matrix1 must "
                   "equal rows in matrix2\n");
            continue;
          }

        /*  allocate space for matrices  */
        matrix1 = matrix2 = product = NULL;

        if ((matrix1 =
              alloc("matrix1", rows1, cols1)) &&
            (matrix2 =
              alloc("matrix2", rows2, cols2)) &&
            (product =
              alloc("product", rows1, cols2)))
                  break;
        else
            free(matrix1), free(matrix2),
            free(product);
      }

    /*  read the matrices  */

    printf("enter row-wise "
           "the elements of matrix1\n");
    readm(matrix1, rows1, cols1);

    printf("enter row-wise "
           "the elements of matrix2\n");
    readm(matrix2, rows2, cols2);
```

```
    /* compute the product matrix */

    multiply(matrix1, rows1, cols1,
             matrix2, cols2, product);

    /* print results */

    printf("product matrix:\n");
    writem(product, rows1, cols2);

    free(matrix1), free(matrix2), free(product);

    return 0;

}

float *alloc(char *name, int rows, int cols)
    {
    float *matrix;

    matrix =
        (float *)calloc(rows, cols * sizeof(float));
    if (!matrix)
        printf("%s is too big\n", name);

    return matrix;
    }

void readm(float *matrix, int rows, int cols)
    {
    float *last = matrix + rows * cols;

    while (matrix < last)
        scanf("%f", matrix++);
    }

void multiply(float *matrix1, int rows1, int cols1,
              float *matrix2, int cols2,
              float *product)
    {
    int i, j, k;

    for (i = 0; i < rows1; i++)
        for (j = 0; j < cols2; j++)
          {
            for (k = 0, *product = 0; k < cols1; k++)
                /* p[i,j] += m1[i,k] * m2[k,j] */
                *product += matrix1[i * cols1 + k] *
                            matrix2[k * cols2 + j];
            product++;
          }
    }
```

```
void writem(float *matrix, int rows, int cols)
  {
    int i;
    for (i = 1; i <= rows*cols; i++)
      {
        printf("%f ", *matrix++);
        if (i % cols == 0) /* end of a row */
            printf("\n");;
      }
  }
```

This version of the matrix multiplication program relies on the fact that a multi-dimensional array in C is really a one-dimensional array, each of whose elements is an array. Multi-dimensional arrays are stored in such a way that the last subscript varies most rapidly. For example, the elements of a matrix declared as

```
float  m[3][2];
```

are stored as

```
m[0][0], m[0][1], m[1][0], m[1][1], m[2][0], m[2][1]
```

Therefore, the elements of a matrix of type T can be visited in row order by simply setting a pointer of type T to point to the first element of the matrix and then successively incrementing it. Similarly, if a matrix m has MAXCOLS columns, then its element m[i][j] can be accessed as

```
m[i * MAXCOLS + j]
```

With this background, the preceding program should be easy to follow. The matrices matrix1, matrix2, and product have been defined to be pointers to float. Having obtained the exact dimensions of these matrices from the user, to allocate storage for, say matrix1, the program calls the function calloc to allocate rows1 number of objects, each of which is of size cols1 * sizeof(float). If the matrices are too big to fit in available storage, any allocated storage is freed and the user is requested to provide new dimensions.

The function readm is provided the address of the first element of the matrix to be read. It starts with the first element and reads the rest of the elements in row order by successively incrementing the pointer provided to it. The function printm is similar. It also visits the matrix elements in row order and prints them, but it additionally checks for the end of a row and prints a new line after a complete row has been printed.

The function multiply computes the elements of the product matrix in row order. To compute the element product[i][j], it needs access to elements matrix1[i][k] and matrix2[k][j]. These elements are accessed as

```
matrix1[i * cols1 + k]
```

and

```
matrix2[k * cols2 + j]
```

respectively, where `cols1` and `cols2` are the number of columns in `matrix1` and `matrix2` respectively.

7.9 ILLUSTRATIVE EXAMPLES

We now give two example programs to tie together the concepts introduced in this chapter.

Example 1
Write a program for evaluating integer expressions specified in the postfix form.

In the *postfix* form, also called the *reverse Polish* notation, each operator follows its operands, and parentheses are not needed. Thus, an *infix* expression like

1 + (2 * 3)

is written in the postfix form as

1 2 3 * +

We assume that the integer expressions use only four binary operators: +, −, *, and /, and that the terms of these expressions are separated by whitespaces. Each expression is specified on a separate line.

Expressions in the postfix form can be conveniently evaluated using a stack. A stack is an abstract data object that can be manipulated by adding elements to its top and removing elements from its top; it satisfies the property that the last element *pushed* onto the stack is the first element removed from the stack. In evaluating an expression using a stack, the expression is scanned from left to right. If the next term of the expression is an operand, it is pushed onto the stack; if it is an operator, an appropriate number of operands (two for binary operators) are *popped* from the top of the stack, the operator is applied to them, and the result is pushed back onto the stack. At the end of the successful evaluation of an expression, there is only one item left on the stack, which is the value of the expression. Thus, in the evaluation of the expression

1 2 3 * +

first the operands 1, 2, and 3 are pushed onto the stack. On seeing *, 3 and 2 are popped from the top, they are multiplied, and the result 6 is pushed back onto the stack. Finally, on encountering +, 6 and 1 are popped, they are added, and 7 is pushed back onto the stack, which is the value of the expression.

The desired program is as follows, and consists of five files:

1. `global.h`: macro definitions and external declarations.
2. `main.c`: `main` and functions to evaluate and print the result of an expression.
3. `io.c`: functions to read and parse expressions.
4. `stack.c`: functions to manipulate the stack.
5. `err.c`: functions to print error messages.

```
/******************** global.h ********************/

#include <stdio.h>

/* error codes */

#define  STACKFULL    1
#define  STACKEMPTY   2
#define  LONGEXP      3
#define  ILLFORMEXP   4
#define  ILLEGALOP    5
#define  ZERODIVIDE   6

/* status codes */

#define  NOMORE       0
#define  OK           1
#define  ERR          2
#define  OPERATOR     1
#define  OPERAND      2

/* i/o functions */

int   readexp(void);
void  printexp(void);
int   next(int *operator, int *operand);

/* stack functions */

void clearstack(void), push(int), printstack(void);
int  pop(void), stacksize(void);

/* error function */

void perror(void);

/* global variable */

extern int error;

/******************** main.c ********************/

#include "global.h"

static void evalterm(int operator);
static void evalexp(void);
static void result(void);
```

```c
int main(void)
  {
    int status;

    /* read expressions one at a time and evaluate them */
    while((status = readexp()) != NOMORE)
      {
        clearstack();          /* initialize stack */

        if (status == ERR)/* error in reading the expression */
            error = LONGEXP;
        else                   /* evaluate the expression */
            evalexp();

        result();              /* print result */
      }

    return 0;
  }

static void evalexp(void)
  {
    int what, operator, operand;

    error = 0;

    /* obtain terms of the expression one at a time
       and do appropriate stack operations */
    while((what = next(&operator, &operand)) != NOMORE)
      {
        if (what == OPERAND)
            push(operand);
        else /* OPERATOR */
            evalterm(operator);
        if (error) return;
      }
  }

static void evalterm(int operator)
  {
    int operand1, operand2;

    operand2 = pop();
    if (error) return;
    operand1 = pop();
    if (error) return;
```

```
        switch (operator)
          {
            case '+':
                push(operand1 + operand2);
                break;
            case '*':
                push(operand1 * operand2);
                break;
            case '-':
                push(operand1 - operand2);
                break;
            case '/':
                if (operand2 != 0)
                    push(operand1 / operand2);
                else
                    error = ZERODIVIDE;
                break;
            default:
                error = ILLEGALOP;
                break;
          }
    }

  static void result(void)
    {
        /* only the result should have been left on the stack */
        if (stacksize() > 1 && !error) error = ILLFORMEXP;

        if (error)
          {
            perror();        /* print error message */
            printexp();      /* print expression */
            printstack();    /* print stack contents */
          }
        else
            printf("%d\n", pop()); /* print result */
    }

/********************   io.c   ********************/

#include "global.h"

#define  BUFSIZE   80

void skip(void);

char buf[BUFSIZ];
int bp;  /* position in buf while parsing an expression */
         /* set to 0 in readexp after reading an expression */
```

```
int readexp(void)
  {
    int c, i;

    for(i = 0; i < BUFSIZE ; i++)
      {
        if (c = getchar(), c != EOF && c != '\n')
            buf[i] = c;
        else  /* reached the end of the expression */
           {
             buf[i] = '\0'; /* null terminate the expression */
             bp = 0;/*set bp to the start of the expression */
             return c == EOF ? NOMORE : OK;
           }
      }

    /* expression cannot fit in buf */

    buf[BUFSIZE-1] = '\0';/*null terminate whatever is in buf*/

    /* discard the rest of the expression */
    while(c = getchar(), c != EOF && c != '\n');

    return ERR;
  }

void printexp(void)
  {
    printf("expression: %s\n", buf);
  }

int next(int *operator, int *operand)
  {
    /* skip over whitespaces */
    while(buf[bp] == ' ' || buf[bp] == '\t') bp++;

    if (buf[bp] == '\0')
        return NOMORE;
    else if (buf[bp] >= '0' && buf[bp] <= '9')
      {
        /* determine the integer value of the operand */
        for(*operand = 0;
            buf[bp] >= '0' && buf[bp] <= '9'; bp++)
              *operand = 10 * (*operand) +
                             (buf[bp] - '0');
        return OPERAND;
      }
    else
```

```
      {
         *operator = buf[bp++];
         return OPERATOR;
      }
   }

/******************    stack.c    *******************/

#include "global.h"
#define   STACKSIZE   80

int   stack[STACKSIZE];
int   *sp = stack;   /* pointer to the current top of the stack */

static int stackfull(void), stackempty(void);

void clearstack(void)
   {
      sp = stack;
   }

void push(int n)
   {
      error = 0;

      if (stackfull())
          error = STACKFULL;
      else
          /* put n on the stack and increment sp */
          *sp++ = n;
   }

int pop(void)
   {
      error = 0;

      if (stackempty())
        {
          error = STACKEMPTY;
          return 0;
        }
      else
          /* decrement sp and return what it is pointing to */
          return *--sp;
   }
```

```c
int stacksize(void)
  {
    return sp - stack;
  }

void printstack(void)
  {
    int i = stacksize();

    printf("stack: ");
    while (i) printf("%d ", stack[--i]);
    printf("\n");
  }

static int stackfull(void)
  {
    return sp >= stack + STACKSIZE ? 1 : 0;
  }

static int stackempty(void)
  {
    return sp == stack ? 1 : 0;
  }

/********************   err.c   ********************/

#include "global.h"

int error = 0;

static char *errmsgs[] =
  {
    "not an error",
    "no space on stack",
    "nothing to pop from stack",
    "too long an expression",
    "ill-formed expression",
    "illegal operator",
    "division by zero"
  };

void perror(void)
  {
    printf("%s\n", errmsgs[error]);
  }
```

The function `readexp` reads an expression into the buffer `buf`. The function `next` parses this expression and returns either an operand or an operator until the expression is exhausted. The string representation of the operand is converted into its integer form before it is returned to the calling function.

The stack has been implemented as an integer array. Observe how the correspondence between arrays and pointers allows stack manipulation functions to be written very succinctly. In studying these functions, bear in mind that the pointer to the top of the stack, sp, points to the position where the next operand pushed onto the stack will be added, and not the position of the operand currently on top. Observe further that since the internal representation of the stack is unavailable to any function outside the file stack.c, its representation can be changed without a change being required in other source files.

An interesting aspect of this program is the way it handles errors. Instead of sprinkling error messages all over the program, the global variable error is set to the appropriate error code whenever an error occurs. Error messages are kept in the pointer array, errmsgs, and by calling the function perror that uses error to index into the errmsgs array, a message describing the last error is printed.

Example 2

Generalize the bubble sort program given in Example 2 of Section 7.3.2 so that it can sort input in descending order either numerically or lexicographically.

In a numerical sort, the relative ordering of data items depends on their numerical values. In a lexicographical sort, data items are compared character by character and the relative ordering of characters in the first position where the two data items differ determines their relative ordering. For example, 10 precedes 9 in a numerical sort in descending order, whereas 9 precedes 10 in a lexicographical sort.

We assume that, by default, the input is to be sorted numerically and that the lexicographical sort is indicated by the command line option -l. A line of input contains only one data item and the data items are integer quantities for a numerical sort.

The generalized sorting program is as follows, and consists of four files:

1. global.h: macros and external declarations.
2. main.c: main and functions for comparing the two given strings lexicographically and numerically.
3. io.c: functions for reading input data and printing sorted output.
4. bsort.c: the generalized bubble sort function.

```
/******************** global.h ********************/

#include <stdio.h>
#include <stdlib.h>
#include <string.h>
#define  MAXLINES  1000
#define  MAXLEN    80

int  getdata(char **data, int maxlines);
void printdata(char **data, int lines);
void bsort(char **data, int last,
          int (*compare)(char *, char *));
int  lexcmp(char *string1, char *string2);
int  intcmp(char *string1, char *string2);
```

```c
/********************   main.c   ********************/

#include "global.h"

char *data[MAXLINES]; /* pointer array to hold data lines */

int main(int argc, char **argv)
  {
    int  numeric = 1; /* numerical sort by default */
    int  lines;       /* the number of data lines in input */

    if (argc > 1)/* -l option specified? */
        if (lexcmp(*(argv+1), "-l") == 0)
            numeric = 0;
        else
          {
            printf("usage: %s [-l]\n", *argv);
            return 1;
          }

    /* read data */
    lines = getdata(data, MAXLINES);

    if (lines > 0)
      {
        /* sort data and print result */
        bsort(data, lines, numeric ? intcmp : lexcmp);
        printdata(data, lines);
        return 0;
      }
    else if (lines == 0)
      {
        printf("no data\n");
        return 1;
      }
    else
      {
        printf("too much data\n");
        return 1;
      }
  }

/* returns -1 if s1 < s2, 0 if s1 = s2, and 1 if s1 > s2 */

int intcmp(char *s1, char *s2)
  {
    int i = atoi(s1), j = atoi(s2);

    return i > j ? 1 : i < j ? -1 : 0;
  }
```

```
/* returns < 0 if s1 < s2, 0 if s1 = s2, and > 0 if s1 > s2 */

int lexcmp(char *s1, char *s2)
   {
      for ( ; *s1 == *s2; s1++, s2++)
          if (*s1 == '\0') return 0;

      return *s1 - *s2;
   }

/********************  io.c  ********************/

#include "global.h"

/*
 *   reads a data line into buf, discarding what cannot fit in buf.
 *   returns 0 on end-of-file and 1 + line-length otherwise.
 */

static int readline(char *buf, int maxlen)
   {
      int c, len = 0;
      char *bufp = buf;

      while (c = getchar(), c != '\n' && c != EOF)
          if (len++ < maxlen && c != '\n' && c != EOF)
             *bufp++ = c;

      *bufp = '\0';   /* null terminate each line */

      return c == EOF && !len ? 0 : bufp - buf + 1;
   }
/*
 * saves input in a pointer array data,
 * with each element of the array pointing to a data line.
 * returns the number of data lines in input and -1 if
 * the input is too large.
 */

int getdata(char **data, int maxlines)
   {
      int lines = 0, len;
      char buf[MAXLEN+1];

      /* first read a dataline into buf to determine its size, and
         then get the necessary storage */
      while (len = readline(buf, MAXLEN))
        {
          if (lines++ >= maxlines ||
             !(*data = (char *) malloc(len)))
                return -1;
```

```
      /* copy contents of buf into storage just allocated */
        strcpy(*data++, buf);
      }
   return lines;
 }

/*
 * print sorted data
 */

void printdata(char **data, int lines)
  {
    int i;

    for (i = 0; i < lines; i++)
        printf("%s\n", *data++);
  }

/******************** bsort.c ********************/

void bsort(char **data, int last,
           int (*compare)(char *, char *))
  {
    int  i, not_done;

    do
      {
        not_done = 0;

        /* scan and interchange as needed */

        for (i = 1; i < last; i++)

            if ((*compare)(data[i-1], data[i]) < 0)
              {
                char *p;

                /* out-of-order data; interchange pointers */
                p = data[i-1];
                data[i-1] = data[i];
                data[i] = p;

                not_done++;

              }

        /* do not scan the last data item in the next iteration */

        last--;

      } while (not_done);
  }
```

The function `bsort`, defined as

```
void bsort(char **data, int last,
           int (*compare)(char *, char *));
```

now takes an additional argument `compare` which is a pointer to the function that is used for comparing two data items in the scan and interchange loop. The file `main.c` defines two functions, `intcmp` and `lexcmp`, that perform numerical and lexicographical comparisons of two strings respectively. Depending upon the command line argument, `main` supplies a pointer to one of these two functions when calling `bsort` as follows:

```
bsort(data, lines, numeric ? intcmp : lexcmp);
```

The input data is maintained in a pointer array `data`. Each element of this array points to a data line. The function `getdata` calls `readline` to read one line of the input, and then invokes `malloc` to allocate the exact amount of storage required for this line. This dynamic allocation can result in considerable saving in storage, if there is large variance in the length of input lines. The use of the pointer array also simplifies the exchange step in `bsort`. The two data lines that are not in order are interchanged by simply exchanging the pointers and not the data lines themselves, as shown below:

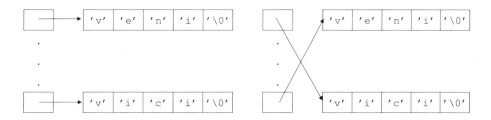

Exercises 7

1. Given that
    ```
    char c, *p, s[10];
    ```
    what, if anything, is wrong with the following expressions?

    a. `c = s`   *b.* `c = *s`

    c. `*s = c`   *d.* `p = s`

    e. `s = p`   *f.* `p = c`

    g. `p = &c`   *h.* `p = s[0]`

    i. `c = p`   *j.* `c = *p`

    k. `c = &p`   *l.* `++s`

2. Hand-simulate the execution of the following programs:

```
a. #include <stdio.h>
   char c[] = "hacker";

   int main(void)
     {
       char *cp;
       int i;

       for (cp = &c[5]; cp >= &c[0]; )
           printf("%c", *cp--);
       printf("\n");

       for (cp = c+5, i = 0; cp-i >= c; )
           printf("%c", *(--cp - i++));
       printf("\n");

       for (cp = &c[5], i = 0; i <= 5; i++)
           printf("%c", cp[-i]);
       printf("\n");

       for (cp = c+5; cp >= c; cp--)
           printf("%c", c[cp-c]);
       printf("\n");

       return 0;
     }
b. #include <stdio.h>
   char *w[] = {"wee", "willie", "winkie"};
   char **wp = w;

   int main(void)
     {
       printf("%s ", *(wp+2));
       printf("%s ", *++wp);
       printf("%s ", *wp++ + 3);
       printf("%s ", wp[-2]);
       printf("%c ", *(wp[-1]+2));
       printf("\n");
       return 0;
     }
c. #include <stdio.h>
   float f[]   = {0, 1, 2, 3};
   float *fp[] = {f+3, f+2, f+1, f};
   float **fpp = fp+3;

   int main(void)
     {
       printf("%f %f %f\n", *f, **fp, **fpp);
       printf("%d %d %d\n", *fp-f, fpp-fp, *fpp-f);
       printf("%f\n", **fpp--);
       printf("%f\n", **(--fpp - 1));
       printf("%f\n", **fpp++);
       printf("%d %d %d\n", *fp-f, fpp-fp, *fpp-f);
       return 0;
     }
```

3. Write a function that converts a given string to its floating-point equivalent.

4. Write a function that appends a string to a given string. In the resultant string, any lowercase character in the original string needs to be converted into uppercase, and any uppercase character in the addend into lowercase.

5. Write a function that replaces the first occurrence of a given substring in a source string by the specified substitution string.

6. Write a program that copies its input to output, except that it removes trailing blanks and tabs from the end of lines and prints only one line from each group of adjacent identical lines.

7. A common mistake in typing is that the same word is typed more than once. Write a program that finds such double words and the line numbers on which they occur in input. A sentence may span more than one line, and there may be more than one sentence on one line.

8. Write a program that prints only those lines in its input that contain its argument.

9. Write a program that prints the user-specified last n lines of its input. If n is more than the number of lines in the input, all the lines should be printed. If n is not specified, a default number of lines, say 10, should be printed.

10. The binary search function `bsearch`, given in Section 7.7, assumes that the data to be searched is arranged in descending order. Generalize `bsearch` so that it can search data arranged either in descending or ascending order by accepting an additional argument which is a pointer to the appropriate comparison function. Use this function in the program given in Section 7.7.

11. A *concordance* is an alphabetical list of all the words in a text along with the number of occurrences of each word. Write a program that makes a concordance from an input text.

12. The encoding and decoding of messages is called *cryptography*, the original message being referred to as the *plain text* and the encoded message as the *cipher text*. The *substitution* method of encoding replaces each letter of the plain text by its substitute, but retains the order of the characters in the message. Here is a substitution cipher:

    letter: A B C D E F G H I J K L M N O P Q R S T U V W X Y Z
    substitute: Q W E R T Y U I O P A S D F G H J K L Z X C V B N M

and an example of a plain text and its cipher text:

    plain text: PURPLE CHEESE ON GREEN MOON
    cipher text: HXKHST EITTLT GF UKTTF DGGF

Write a program that takes as input either a plain text or a cipher text and encodes or decodes it using the above substitution cipher.

13. The *Morse code* is a standard encoding scheme used in telegraphy that employs substitutions similar to the scheme described in the previous example. The substitutions used in this case are shown below:

```
A  . -          K  - -          U  - . - -
B  - . . .      L  - .          V  - - . .
C  - . - .      M  - - -         W  . - - - -
D  - . .        N  . - - .       X  . . - - -
E  .            O  - - . -       Y  . . . - -
F  . . - .      P  . - .         Z  . . . . -
G  - - .        Q  . . .         1  . . . . .
H  . . . .      R  -             2  - . . . .
I  . .          S  . . -         3  - - . . .
J  . - - -      T  . . . -       4  - - - . .
```

```
5   - . -        7   . - -        9   - - - - .
6   . - . .      8   - . . -      0   - - - - -
```

Write a program that accepts as input a message in plain text or in Morse code and encodes or decodes it using the preceding substitutions.

14. The transposition method of encoding scrambles the characters of a message according to some rule. One such method is to write the plain text in a matrix row-wise and then read the matrix column-wise to obtain the cipher text. For example, the cipher text of the message

$$\begin{bmatrix} O & P & E & R & A & T \\ I & O & N & & D & E \\ S & E & R & T & & S \\ H & I & E & L & D & \end{bmatrix}$$

is

OISHPOEIENRER TLAD DTES

The cipher text now depends on the size of the matrix that is used for the transposition. For example, using a 2×12 matrix, the cipher text of the same message is

OSPEERRTA TSIHOINE LDDE

The two dimensions of the matrix can be thought of as the *key* that is necessary to decode the cipher text. Write a program that accepts the key in the command line, and uses it to encode or decode the given input text.

15. For large values of n, its factorial may not fit in a single integer. For example,

25! = 15,511,210,043,330,985,984,000,000.

One way to compute the factorial of such a number is to use an array to store the answer and partial results, using one element of the array per digit. Thus, you would store 12! = 479,001,600 as

			8	7	6	5	4	3	2	1	0
			4	7	9	0	0	1	6	0	0

To find 13!, multiply each element of the array by 13, taking care to move the carries, to get

		9	8	7	6	5	4	3	2	1	0
		6	2	2	7	0	2	0	8	0	0

Write a program to compute factorials of large numbers using this scheme.

16. You have been called upon to write a matchmaking program for a dating bureau. The bureau's questionnaire has fifteen statements, and applicants indicate their degree of agreement on a scale of 1 to 5. Responses of the applicants have been recorded such that each data line contains an applicant's name (up to 25 characters), sex (F or M), and the responses to the questionnaire (15 integers). Your program should match each person with the three most compatible persons of the opposite sex.

The measure of compatibility of two persons is the cosine of the angle between their response vectors; the larger the cosine, the more compatible the couple. The cosine of the angle between the vectors $(x_1, x_2, \ldots, x_n)$ and $(y_1, y_2, \ldots, y_n)$ is given by $u_1v_1 + u_2v_2 + \ldots + u_nv_n$, where

$$u_i = x_i / (x_1^2 + x_2^2 + \ldots + x_n^2)^{\frac{1}{2}}$$

$$\text{and } v_i = y_i / (y_1^2 + y_2^2 + \ldots + y_n^2)^{\frac{1}{2}}.$$

17. The program of the previous problem has a feature that would not be acceptable to a real dating service. If one person is particularly compatible, he or she will receive the names of three matches, but may be listed as a good match on many people's list. The whole thing could get out of hand with almost everybody trying to date a few highly compatible persons. Redo the previous problem so that no one person is listed for more than five other people. Print all the matches a person is involved in, not just the three optimal matches as before. Now another problem arises — some applicants may not find any match. Print a polite apology to them.

18. Write a program that allows two users to play *tic-tac-toe*. The program should ask for moves alternately from player X and player O. The program displays the game positions as

```
1 2 3
4 5 6
7 8 9
```

The players enter their moves by providing the position number. After each move, the program displays the changed board. A sample board configuration is

```
X X O
O X 6
7 X O
```

Enhance the preceding program so that the computer may optionally be one of the two players.

19. The game of *Life* takes place on a two-dimensional array of cells, each of which may contain an organism. Let $occ(i)$ be the number of cells adjacent to cell i that are occupied by an organism. The configuration of a new generation of organisms is obtained from the previous generation by applying the following rules:

   i. An organism in cell i survives to the next generation if $2 \leq occ(i) \leq 3$; otherwise, it dies.

   ii. An organism is born in an empty cell i if $2 \leq occ(i) \leq 3$; otherwise, it remains empty.

   Write a program that reads an initial configuration of occupied cells and prints a series of generations. Note that the program must maintain two copies of the configuration, since all changes occur simultaneously.

20. A traveling salesman must stop in five cities, $C_1, C_2, \cdots, C_5$. The distance d_{ij} between each pair of cities C_i and C_j is given in a 5×5 matrix. Write a program that finds for the salesman a route from C_i to C_j that passes through all the three other cities and requires the least total distance among all such routes.

✚ 8 Structures and Unions

In Chapter 6 we introduced arrays that provide the facility for grouping related data items of the same type into a single object. However, at times we need to group related data items of different types. An example is the inventory record of a stock item that groups together its item number, price, quantity currently in stock, economic order quantity, and reorder level. In order to handle such situations, C provides a facility, called *structures*, that allows a fixed number of data items, possibly of different types, to be treated as a single object.

Often it is useful to have a single structure that has several variants. Such a structure ordinarily has one or more components that are common to all variants. In addition, each variant has several other components with names and data types that are unique to that variant. For example, a stock item may be imported or domestic, and some common and some different information may have to be included in the inventory record for the two types. For such situations, C provides a facility, called *unions*, that allows a number of different types of grouped data items to be referred to using the same name.

We introduce in this chapter the techniques for defining and using structures and unions.

8.1 BASICS OF STRUCTURES

A *structure* is a collection of logically related data items grouped together under a single name, called a *structure tag*. The data items that make up a structure are called its *members*, *components*, or *fields*, and can be of different types. The general format for defining a structure is

```
struct tag
    {
        variable declarations
    };
```

where `struct` is a key word that introduces a structure definition, *tag* is the name of the structure, and *variable declarations* is the set of type declarations for the member data items that make up the structure.

For example, the structure for the inventory record of a stock item may be defined as

```
struct item
  {
    int itemno;
    float price;
    float quantity;
    float eoq;
    int reorderlevel;
  };
```

All the members of a structure can be of the same type, as in the following definition of the structure date:

```
struct date
  {
    int day, month, year;
  };
```

The name of a member variable in a structure can be the same as its tag since they can be differentiated by context. Similarly, the name of a member variable or a structure tag can be the same as that of some non-member variable, and two member variables in different structures can have the same name. Thus, given the preceding definitions of the structures item and date, the following are permissible:

```
int itemno;   /* no conflict with itemno in the structure item */
struct day    /* no conflict with day in the structure date */
  {
    int day; /* no conflict with the tag day */
    int year;/* no conflict with year in the structure date */
  };
```

8.1.1 Structure Variables

A structure definition defines a new type, and variables of this type can be declared by including a list of variable names between the right brace and the terminating semicolon in the structure definition. For example, the declaration

```
struct date
  {
    int day, month, year;
  } order_date, arrival_date;
```

declares order_date and arrival_date to be variables of type struct date.

The structure tag can be thought of as the name of the type introduced by the structure definition, and variables can also be declared to be of a particular structure type by a declaration of the form:

```
struct tag variable-list;
```

For example, the declarations

```
struct item m68020;
struct item intel386;
```

or the single declaration

```
struct item m68020, intel386;
```

declares m68020 and intel386 to be variables of type struct item.

The structure tag may be omitted if all the variables of a particular structure type have been declared when the structure is defined. Thus, the declaration

```
struct
   {
     float  r, theta;
   } polar1, polar2;
```

declares polar1 and polar2 to be structure variables of the same type whose member variables are the two floating-point variables, r and theta. However, in such a case, we cannot subsequently declare another variable polar3 whose type is the same as that of polar1 and polar2.

Each occurrence of a structure definition introduces a new structure type that is neither the same nor equivalent to any other type. Thus, given that

```
struct { char c; int i; } u;
struct { char c; int i; } v;
struct s1 { char c; int i; } w;
struct s2 { char c; int i; } x;
struct s2 y;
```

the types of u, v, w, and x are all different, but the types of x and y are the same.

Note that a structure definition does not allocate any storage; it merely describes a template or the shape of the structure. Storage is allocated only when a variable of the corresponding type is declared.

8.1.2 Structure Initialization

A variable of a particular structure type can be initialized by following its definition with an initializer for the corresponding structure type. If a structure type T has n member variables of types $T_1, T_2, ..., T_n$ and I_i is an initializer for the type T_i, then $\{I_1, I_2, ..., I_n\}$ is an initializer for the type T.

Thus, the declaration

```
struct date
   {
     int day, month, year;
   } independence = {15, 8, 1947};
```

initializes the member variables day, month, and year of the structure variable independence to 15, 8, and 1947 respectively, and the declaration

```
struct date republic = {26, 1, 1950};
```

initializes the member variables `day`, `month`, and `year` of the structure variable `republic` to 26, 1, and 1950 respectively.

If there are fewer initializers than there are member variables in the structure, the remaining member variables are initialized to zero. Thus, the initialization

```
struct date newyear = {1, 1};
```

is the same as

```
struct date newyear = {1, 1, 0};
```

It is an error to provide more initializers than the number of member variables.

8.1.3 Accessing Structure Members

C provides a special operator, the *structure member* or *dot* operator, to access the individual members of a structure variable by a construction of the form

structure-variable . member-name

Thus, the statements

```
struct date man_on_moon;
man_on_moon.day = 20;
man_on_moon.month = 7;
man_on_moon.year = 1969;
```

set the values of the member variables `day`, `month`, and `year` within the variable `man_on_moon` to 20, 7, and 1969 respectively, and the statement

```
struct date today;
    ...
if (today.day == 25 && today.month == 12)
    printf("merry christmas");
```

tests the values of `day` and `month` to check if they are 25 and 12 respectively, and if so, prints `merry christmas`.

The dot operator has the same precedence as that of the function call operator `()`, the array subscript operator `[]`, and the arrow operator `->` (to be discussed shortly), but higher than that of any other C operator, and is left-associative.

8.1.4 Structure Assignment

A structure variable may be assigned to another structure variable of the same type. Thus, given that

```
struct date american, revolution = {4, 7, 1776};
```

the assignment

```
american = revolution;
```

assigns 4 to `american.day`, 7 to `american.month`, and 1776 to american. `year`.

The following program summarizes the definition, initialization, assignment, and access of structures:

```
#include <stdio.h>

/* define a structure type struct launchdate */
/* declare satellite to be a variable of this type */
struct launchdate {int day, month, year;} satellite;

int main(void)
  {
    /* declare sputnik2 to be of type struct launchdate
       and initialize it */
    struct launchdate sputnik2 = {3, 11, 1957};

    /* assign sputnik2 to satellite */
    satellite = sputnik2;

    /* access members of satellite */
    printf("Laika went orbiting on %d-%d-%d\n",
        satellite.month, satellite.day, satellite.year);

    return 0;
  }
```

8.1.5 Size of a Structure

The size of a structure can be determined using the `sizeof` operator discussed in Section 7.8.1. For example, given the declaration

```
struct porous
  {
    char c;
    long l;
  };
```

the statement

```
i = sizeof(porous);
```

assigns to `i` the size of the structure `porous` in bytes.

The size of a structure need not be the same as the sum of the sizes of its members; there may be holes in structures due to the alignment requirements for different objects. For example, on most machines, the size of `porous` is likely to be 8, rather than 5.

8.1.6 Nested Structures

Structures can be nested. For example, the structures item and date may be embedded inside another structure that records the ordering date and the quantity of an item to be purchased as in

```
struct order
   {
     struct item purchaseitem;
     struct date orderdate;
     float quantity;
   };
```

Note that the member variable quantity in the structure order does not conflict with the member variable quantity in the structure item embedded in it.

Another example of a nested structure is the definition of the following structure that contains two occurrences of the structure date:

```
struct project
   {
     int number;
     struct date start;
     struct date finish;
     float budget;
   };
```

There is no limit on the depth of nesting. For example, we can have

```
struct projects
   {
     struct date as_of;
     float revenue;
     struct project starbase;
     struct project hal;
   };
```

However, a structure cannot be nested within itself. Thus, the following is illegal:

```
struct company
   {
     struct projects government;
     struct projects industrial;
     struct company  parent;      /* illegal */
   };
```

Variables of a nested structure type can be defined as usual by either including them in the structure definition between the right brace and the terminating semicolon or by separate declarations. They may also be initialized at the time of declaration. Thus, we can have

```
struct stockindex
  {
    float high, low, close;
    struct date weekending;
  } dowjones =
    {2520.79, 2381.19, 2520.79, {19, 10, 1990}};
```

The inner pair of braces is optional and certainly not necessary when all the initializers are present. Thus, we can have

```
struct stockindex sp500 =
    {312.48, 296.41, 312.48, 19, 10, 1990};
```

Here is a somewhat more involved example:

```
struct projects space =
  {
    {31, 12, 2000},      /* as_of */
    1000,                /* revenue */
    {                    /* starbase */
        007,                 /* number */
        {1, 6, 1999},        /* start */
        {1, 6, 2001},        /* finish */
        100                  /* budget */
    },
    {013, {1, 1, 1999}, {1, 1, 2001}, 500} /* hal */
  };
```

A particular member inside a nested structure can be accessed by repeatedly applying the dot operator. Thus, the statement

```
space.hal.budget = 200;
```

resets the budget variable in the hal structure within space from 500 to 200; the statement

```
printf("%d", space.starbase.start.year);
```

prints 1999; and the statement

```
struct date newdate = {31, 12, 2001};
space.hal.finish = newdate;
```

resets the completion date for the hal project to December 31, 2001.

8.1.7 Pointers to Structures

A pointer to a structure identifies its address in memory, and is created in the same way that a pointer to a simple data type such as int or char is created. For example, the declaration

```
struct date carnival, *mardigras;
```

declares `carnival` to be a variable of type `struct date`, and the variable `mardigras` to be a pointer to a `struct date` variable. The address operator `&` is applied to a structure variable to obtain its address. Thus, the assignment

```
mardigras = &carnival;
```

makes `mardigras` point to `carnival`.

The pointer variable `mardigras` can now be used to access the member variables of `carnival` using the dot operator as

```
(*mardigras).day
(*mardigras).month
(*mardigras).year
```

The parentheses are necessary because the precedence of the dot operator (`.`) is higher than that of the dereferencing operator (`*`). In the absence of the parentheses, the preceding expressions are interpreted as

```
*(mardigras.day)
*(mardigras.month)
*(mardigras.year)
```

which is an error since none of the member variables of the structure `date` is a pointer.

Pointers are so commonly used with structures that C provides a special operator `->`, called the *structure pointer* or *arrow* operator, for accessing members of a structure variable pointed to by a pointer. The general form for the use of the operator `->` is

pointer-name->member-name

Thus, the preceding expressions for accessing member variables of the structure pointed to by `mardigras`, written using the dot operator, can equivalently be written using the arrow operator as

```
mardigras->day
mardigras->month
mardigras->year
```

The arrow operator obviously is not only more convenient, but also more suggestive of the intended operation.

It is permissible to take addresses of the member variables of a structure variable; that is, it is possible for a pointer to point into the middle of a structure. For example, the statement

```
float *sales = &space.revenue;
```

defines `sales` to be a floating-point pointer and initializes it to point to the member variable `revenue` within the structure variable `space`. The pointer expression `&space.revenue` is interpreted as `&(space.revenue)` since the precedence of the dot operator is higher than that of the address operator. Similarly, the statement

```
int *year = &space.as_of.year;
```

makes `year` point to the integer member variable `year` within `as_of` within `space`, and the statement

```
struct date *completion = &space.starbase.finish;
```

makes `completion` point to the structure member `finish` within `starbase` within `space`. Therefore, the statement

```
printf("year = %d   sales = %f", *year, *sales);
```

prints

```
year = 2000   sales = 1000.000000
```

whereas the statement

```
printf("starbase completion day = %d", completion->day);
```

prints

```
starbase completion day = 1
```

The arrow operator has the same precedence as the dot operator, and is left-associative.

Pointers to structures improve execution speed; the larger the structure, the greater is the gain because transferring pointers from one part of the program to another is usually faster than copying all the individual components of a large structure. A major use of pointers to structures, as we shall see in the next section, is in the interaction of structures with functions. Pointers to structures also enable us to create sophisticated data structures such as linked lists and trees, which will be discussed in Section 8.4.

The following program summarizes various aspects of nested structures and pointers to structures:

```
#include <stdio.h>

struct job
  {
    float rate;   /* wage rate */
    float hrs;    /* hours worked */
  };

struct person
  {
    int ssn;
    struct job regular;
    struct job moonlighting;
  };

int main(void)
  {
    /* hardy's ssn = 123456789,
       regular rate = 25, moonlighting rate = 20 */
    struct person hardy = {123456789, {25}, {20}};

    /* pointer to hardy's moonlighting job structure */
    struct job *avantgarde = &hardy.moonlighting;
```

```
    /* access members */
    scanf("%f", &hardy.regular.hrs);
    scanf("%f", &avantgarde->hrs);
    printf("earnings of %d = %f\n", hardy.ssn,
            hardy.regular.hrs * hardy.regular.rate +
            avantgarde->hrs * avantgarde->rate);

    return 0;
}
```

We could not have omitted the inner braces in the initialization of `hardy` in

```
    struct person hardy = {123456789, {25}, {20}};
```

since the initializers for `hardy.regular.hrs` and `hardy.moonlighting.hrs` have not been specified.

8.2 STRUCTURES AND FUNCTIONS

A structure type definition may be local to a function or it may be external to any function. Structures may be passed as function arguments and functions may return structures. We now discuss these features.

8.2.1 Scope of a Structure Type Definition

The scoping rules for a structure type definition are identical to those discussed for variable names in Chapter 5. A structure may be defined within a function or outside of any function; in the former case, it is called the *local*, and in the latter, the *external* structure definition. An external structure definition with a structure tag allows subsequent definition of external and local variables of that structure type, whereas a local structure definition permits only local variables of that structure type to be defined within the same block. The following program fragment illustrates these scoping rules:

```
/* external structure definition */
struct rate {float fromdollar, todollar;};
/* external structure variable */
struct rate yen = {.007868, 127.10};

void germany(void)
  {
    struct rate mark = {.6760, 1.4793};/* legal */
    struct date
        {int day, month, yr;} /* local structure definition */
    struct date on =
        {21, 11, 90}; /* local structure variable */

    printf("dollar = %f mark\n",
            mark.fromdollar);            /* legal */
    printf("on %d-%d-%d\n",
            on.month, on.day, on.yr); /* legal */
  }
```

```
void japan(void)
  {
     struct date today;  /* illegal: the definition of
                              date unavailable */

     printf("dollar = %f yen\n", yen.fromdollar);/* legal */
  }
```

Structure definitions are usually collected in a header file. This file is then included in those modules that need these structure definitions.

8.2.2 Structures as Function Arguments

C provides three methods of passing structures to a function. The first method involves supplying structure members as the arguments in a function call. These arguments are then treated as separate non-structure values, unless they themselves are structures.

To illustrate this method of passing structures, we write a function that determines if a point lies within a given circle by computing the distance of the point from the center of the circle and comparing this distance with the radius of the circle. The point is represented by its coordinates and the circle by its radius and the coordinates of its center:

```
struct point
  {
     float x, y;
  };

struct circle
  {
     float r;              /* radius */
     struct point o;       /* center */
  };
```

Recalling that the distance between two points (x_c, y_c) and (x_p, y_p) is given by $((x_c - x_p)^2 + ((y_c - y_p)^2)^{1/2}$, we can write the desired function as

```
float sqr(float x)
  {
     return x * x;
  }

int contains(float cr, float cx, float cy,
             float px, float py)
  {
     return sqr(cx - px) + sqr(cy - py)
            > sqr(cr) ? 0 : 1;
  }
```

The first three arguments correspond to the radius and the two coordinates of the center of the circle, and the last two correspond to the two coordinates of the point. Thus, given that

```
struct circle c = {2, {1, 1}};
struct point  p = {2, 2};
```

the function `contains` can be called as

```
contains(c.r, c.o.x, c.o.y, p.x, p.y)
```

and it will return 1 (true), since the distance of the point (2,2) from the center of the circle (1,1) is less than 2, the radius of the circle.

The disadvantage of this method is that the relationship between the member variables encapsulated in a structure is lost in the called function. This method should only be used if a few structure members need to be passed to the called function.

The second method involves passing the complete structure to a function by simply providing the name of the structure variable as the argument in the function call. The corresponding parameter in the called function must be of the same structure type. Thus, using this method, the function `contains` can be written as

```
int contains(struct circle c, struct point p)
 {
   return sqr(c.o.x - p.x) + sqr(c.o.y - p.y)
          > sqr(c.r) ? 0 : 1;
 }
```

and called simply as

```
contains(c, p)
```

Unlike array names, structure names are not pointers and are passed by value. Thus, when a structure name is provided as argument, the entire structure is copied to the called function, and changes to member variables of the structure argument in the called function are not reflected in the corresponding structure variable in the calling function.

The third method involves passing pointers to the structure variables as the function arguments. Using this method, the function `contains` can be written as

```
int contains(struct circle *c, struct point *p)
 {
   return sqr(c->o.x - p->x)+sqr(c->o.y - p->y)
          > sqr(c->r) ? 0 : 1;
 }
```

and called as

```
contains(&c, &p)
```

The arrow operator has been used inside `contains` to access member variables, since `c` and `p` are now pointers to structures. Note that when a called function is provided with the address of a structure variable supplied as argument, any change in the called function to the member variables accessed using this address will be reflected in the structure variable in the calling function.

This method becomes particularly attractive when large structures have to be passed as function arguments because it avoids copying overhead. Another reason for using this method is that some older compilers do not allow structure variables to be passed as function arguments.

8.2.3 Structures as Function Values

Structures may be returned as function values. Reconsider, for example, the problem of converting rectangular coordinates of a point into polar coordinates discussed in Example 2 of Section 5.6. We need a function

```
struct polar convert(struct rectangular rec);
```

that takes as argument a structure of the type

```
struct rectangular
    {
      float x, y;
    };
```

giving the rectangular coordinates of a point, and returns a structure of the type

```
struct polar
    {
      float r, theta;
    };
```

giving the polar coordinates of the point. Recalling that the polar coordinates (r,θ) corresponding to the rectangular coordinates (x,y) of points other than the origin are given by

$$r = (x^2 + y^2)^{1/2}, \qquad \tan \theta = y/x, \quad -\pi < \theta \leq \pi,$$

this function can be written as

```
#include <math.h>

struct polar convert(struct rectangular rec)
    {
      struct polar pol;

      if (rec.x == 0 && rec.y == 0)   /* origin */
          pol.r = pol.theta = 0;
      else
        {
          pol.r = sqrt(rec.x * rec.x + rec.y * rec.y);
          pol.theta = atan2(rec.y, rec.x);
        }

      return pol;
    }
```

Given this function, the program fragment

```
struct rectangular r = {2, 1};
struct polar p;

p = convert(r);
printf("%f %f", p.r, p.theta);
```

prints

```
2.236068 0.463648
```

Instead of returning a structure, a function may also return a pointer to the structure. Thus, the function `convert` can also be written as

```
#include <math.h>
#include <stdlib.h>

struct polar *convert(struct rectangular rec)
  {
     struct polar *polp;

     polp = (struct polar *)malloc(sizeof(struct polar));
     if polp
       {
          if (rec.x == 0 && rec.y == 0)
             polp->r = polp->theta = 0;
          else
             {
                polp->r = sqrt(rec.x*rec.x + rec.y*rec.y);
                polp->theta = atan2(rec.y, rec.x);
             }
       }
     return polp;
  }
```

and used as

```
struct rectangular r = {2, 1};
struct polar *pp;
if (pp = convert(r)) printf("%f %f", pp->r, pp->theta);
```

The storage allocated by calling `malloc`, unlike the storage allocated to the automatic variables, is not automatically released when the function containing the call to `malloc` exits. Hence, when `convert` returns, the storage allocated to the automatic pointer variable `polp` in `convert` is released, but the storage allocated to the structure that `polp` points to is not released. Since `convert` returns the pointer to this storage, this pointer can be used in the calling function to access the member variables of this structure.

Note that it is incorrect to write the preceding function as

```
struct polar *convert(struct rectangular rec)
  {
     struct polar pol;
     ...
     return &pol;
  }
```

since this function returns a pointer to an automatic variable, and once the function exits, the values accessed using this pointer are meaningless.

8.2.4 Illustrative Example

We now give an example program to further illustrate the relationship between structures and functions.

Example
Write a set of functions to perform input, output, relational comparison, and arithmetic operations on complex numbers, and use these functions to determine if three given numbers form a Pythagorean triplet.

We shall represent a complex number $z = x + iy$ by a pair of real numbers, the first being the real part x and the second the real coefficient y of i in the imaginary part iy. The file `complex.c` implements the abstract data object *complex*, and the `main` function in `main.c` uses the functions defined in `complex.c` to determine if the given three numbers form a Pythagorean triplet.

Recall that the arithmetic operations on two complex numbers $z_1 = (x_1, y_1)$ and $z_2 = (x_2, y_2)$ are defined as follows:

$$z_1 + z_2 = (x_1 + x_2, y_1 + y_2)$$
$$z_1 - z_2 = (x_1 - x_2, y_1 - y_2)$$
$$z_1 \times z_2 = (x_1 \times x_2 - y_1 \times y_2, x_1 \times y_2 + x_2 \times y_1)$$
$$z_1/z_2 = (x_1 \times x_2 + y_1 \times y_2, x_2 \times y_1 - x_1 \times y_2)/(x_2^2 + y_2^2)$$

Only equality and inequality comparisons are defined on two complex numbers. Two complex numbers are equal if and only if the real and imaginary parts of one are equal to the corresponding real and imaginary parts of the other number. Finally, three numbers form a Pythagorean triplet if the sum of the squares of two numbers equals the square of the third number.

The desired program is as follows:

```
/********************   global.h   *******************/

#include <stdio.h>

struct complex
   {
      float x, y;
   };

struct complex
     add(struct complex u, struct complex v);
struct complex
     subtract(struct complex u, struct complex v);
struct complex
     multiply(struct complex u, struct complex v);
struct complex
     divide(struct complex u, struct complex v);
```

```c
int equal(struct complex u, struct complex v);
void readc(struct complex *u);
void writec(struct complex *u);

/******************** complex.c ********************/

#include "global.h"

struct complex add(struct complex u,
                   struct complex v)
  {
    struct complex z;

    z.x = u.x + v.x;
    z.y = u.y + v.y;
    return z;
  }

struct complex subtract(struct complex u,
                        struct complex v)
  {
    struct complex z;

    z.x = u.x - v.x;
    z.y = u.y - v.y;
    return z;
  }

struct complex multiply(struct complex u,
                        struct complex v)
  {
    struct complex z;

    z.x = u.x * v.x - u.y * v.y;
    z.y = u.x * v.y + u.y * v.x;
    return z;
  }

struct complex divide(struct complex u,
                      struct complex v)
  {
    v.x /= v.x * v.x + v.y * v.y;
    v.y /= - (v.x * v.x + v.y * v.y);
    return multiply(u, v);
  }

int equal(struct complex u, struct complex v)
  {
    return u.x == v.x && u.y == v.y;
  }
```

```c
void readc(struct complex *u)
  {
    scanf("%f %f", &u->x, &u->y);
  }

void writec(struct complex *u)
  {
    printf("(%f, %f)", u->x, u->y);
  }

/******************** main.c ********************/

#include "global.h"
int triplet(struct complex z1,
          struct complex z2, struct complex z3)
  {
    return
      equal(add(multiply(z1,z1), multiply(z2,z2)),
            multiply(z3,z3));
  }

int main(void)
  {
    struct complex z1, z2, z3;
    int p;

    readc(&z1);
    readc(&z2);
    readc(&z3);

    p = triplet(z1,z2,z3) ||
        triplet(z2,z3,z1) || triplet(z3,z1,z2);

    printf("%s\n", p ? "yes" : "no");
    return 0;
  }
```

8.3 STRUCTURES AND ARRAYS

Arrays and structures can be freely intermixed to create arrays of structures, structures containing arrays, or arrays of structures that themselves contain arrays.

8.3.1 Arrays of Structures

Arrays of structures are commonly used when a large number of similar records are required to be processed together. For example, if there were 1000 items used in a motor, this data can be organized in an array of structures as

```
struct item motor[1000];
```

This statement declares `motor` to be an array containing 1000 elements of the type `struct item`.

Arrays of structures can be initialized in a manner similar to the initialization of multidimensional arrays as in

```
struct date birthdays[3] =
   {
      {14, 3, 1879},   /* Einstein */
      {0, 10}          /* Gandhi */
   };
```

or equivalently as

```
struct date birthdays[3] =
   {
      {14, 3, 1879},
      {0, 10, 0},
      {0, 0, 0}
   };
```

The inner pair of braces is optional and can be omitted when all the initializers are present, as in

```
struct date atombomb[2] =
   {
      6, 8, 1945,      /* hiroshima */
      9, 8, 1945       /* nagasaki */
   };
```

A particular member variable inside an array of structures can be accessed using the array subscript and dot operators. Thus, the statement

```
birthdays[1].day = 2;
```

assigns 2 to the member variable `day` in the second structure element of the array `birthdays`, and the statement

```
birthdays[2] = birthdays[0];
```

assigns the value of the first structure element to the third structure element of the array `birthdays`.

Pointers can also be used to access structure elements and member variables thereof. Thus, the statement

```
struct date *bday = &birthdays[1];
```

defines `bday` to be a pointer to a variable of type `struct date` and initializes it to point to the second structure element of `birthdays`. The preceding two assignments can then be written as

```
bday->day = 2;

*(bday + 1) = *(bday - 1);
```

8.3.2 Structures Containing Arrays

A structure may contain arrays as members. This feature is frequently used when a string needs to be included in a structure. For example, the structure `date` can be expanded to also include the names of the day of the week and the month as

```
struct ndate
   {
      int day;
      char weekday[10];
      int month;
      char monthname[10];
      int year;
   };
```

A structure variable of the type `ndate` can now be declared as

```
struct ndate newcentury;
```

and initialized at the same time as

```
struct ndate newcentury =
     {1, {'m','o','n','d','a','y','\0'}, 1,
        {'j','a','n','u','a','r','y','\0'}, 2001};
```

or equivalently as

```
struct ndate newcentury =
     {1, "monday", 1, "january", 2001};
```

An element of an array contained in a structure can be accessed using the dot and array subscript operators. Thus, the statement

```
printf("%c", newcentury.monthname[2]);
```

prints

```
n
```

Pointers can also be used to access elements of the array embedded in a structure. Thus, the statements

```
int i;
for (i = 0; newcentury.weekday[i]; i++)
    ;
printf("%d", i);
```

or the statements

```
char *cp = newcentury.weekday;
while (*cp) cp++;
printf("%d", cp - newcentury.weekday);
```

print the number of characters in the name of the day of the week.

When a structure containing an array is passed as an argument to a function, the member array is passed by value, even when it is the only member variable. Thus, given that

```
struct time
  {
    int val[3];
  } noon = {12, 0, 0};
```

and

```
void advance(struct time tm)
  {
    int i;

    for (i = 0; i < 3; i++) tm.val[i] += 5;
  }
```

the statements

```
advance(noon);
for (i = 0; i < 3; i++) printf("%d ", noon.val[i]);
```

print

```
12  0  0
```

since the structure variable `noon` is passed by value and changes to the array member variable `val` inside `advance` are not reflected in the argument `noon`.

8.3.3 Arrays of Structures Containing Arrays

A natural corollary of the discussion so far is that we can define arrays of structures that contain arrays as member variables. Thus, we can have

```
struct student
  {
    char name[10];
    float  height;
    int  grades[4];
  } students[3] =
      {
        { "sleepy",  9,  {1, 0, 0, 1} },
        { "happy",   7,  {4, 3, 4, 4} },
        { "dopey",   8,  {2, 2, 1, 1} }
      };
```

Elements of the member arrays can be accessed as before using the array subscript and dot operators. Thus, the statement

```
printf("%s %d", students[1].name, students[1].grades[1]);
```

prints

```
happy 3
```

Pointers can also be used to access the elements of the member arrays. Thus, the preceding `printf` can also be written as

```
struct student *sp = &students[1];
printf("%s %d", sp->name, sp->grades[1]);
```

or as

```
printf("%s %d", sp->name, *(sp->grades + 1));
```

8.3.4 Illustrative Examples

We now give some example programs to further illustrate the relationship
between structures and arrays.

Example 1
*Rewrite, using structures, the program given in Example 6 of Section 6.3 that deter-
mines the price of a given item from an item-price database.*

To illustrate arrays of structures containing arrays, we assume that associated with each item are five prices (presumably quoted by five different suppliers), and the minimum of these prices for the given item needs to be retrieved.
We keep the item number and the associated prices of an item in a structure
and organize the database as an array of these structures.
   The desired program is as follows:

```
#include <stdio.h>
#define   ITEMS    1000
#define   PRICES   5

struct iteminfo
   {
     int    item;
     float price[PRICES];
   };

void bld_database(struct iteminfo *db,
                  int items, float prices);
struct iteminfo *bsearch(int val,
                  struct iteminfo *db, int length);
float min_price(struct iteminfo *ip, int prices);

int main(void)
   {
     struct iteminfo database[ITEMS], *ip;
     int    item_no;

     /* build the item-price database */
     bld_database(database, ITEMS, PRICES);
```

```
      /* get item_no of the item whose price is to be found */
      scanf("%d", &item_no);

      /* binary search */
      ip = bsearch(item_no, database, ITEMS);

      /* output */
      if (ip)
         printf("price of %d = %f\n",
                   item_no, min_price(ip, PRICES));
      else
         printf("%d not in the database", item_no);

      return 0;
   }

void bld_database(struct iteminfo *database,
                    int items, float prices)
   {
      int i, j;

      for (i = 0; i < items; i++)
        {
          scanf("%d", &database[i].item);
          for (j = 0; j < prices; j++)
              scanf("%f", &database[i].price[j]);
        }
   }

struct iteminfo *bsearch(int val,
      struct iteminfo *database, int len)
   {
      int first = 0, last = len-1, mid;

      while (first <= last)
        {
          mid = (first + last) / 2;

          if (val == database[mid].item)
              /* search succeeds */
              return &database[mid];
          else if (val > database[mid].item)
              /* search lower half */
              last = mid - 1;
          else
              /* search upper half */
              first = mid + 1;
        }
      return NULL;
   }
```

```
float min_price(struct iteminfo *ip, int prices)
  {
    float min = ip->price[0];
    int j;

    for (j = 1; j < prices; j++)
        if (min > ip->price[j])  min = ip->price[j];
    return min;
  }
```

Instead of returning the array subscript at which the given item_no is found, this version of bsearch returns a pointer to the structure containing the desired item number and the associated prices. The price array in this structure is then scanned to determine the minimum price.

Example 2
Write a program to plot the curve $y = x^2$ for $-1 < x < 1$.

To print a two-dimensional picture on a character-oriented ordinary printer, we conceptually lay a grid over the picture and let each grid square correspond to a character position on the printed page. A suitable symbol is then printed for each grid square. The print grid may be represented by a character matrix, initially filled with blanks. Non-blank symbols are then stored in those matrix elements that correspond to dark spots in the picture.

A point (X, Y) in the picture plane can be converted into the matrix subscripts (I, J) by the conversion formulas:

$$I = (X - XMIN) * WIDTH / (XMAX - XMIN)$$
$$J = (Y - YMIN) * HEIGHT / (YMAX - YMIN)$$

where the matrix dimensions are WIDTH × HEIGHT, the left and right boundaries of the picture are XMIN and XMAX, and the bottom and top boundaries are YMIN and YMAX.

The desired program is as follows:

```
#include <stdio.h>
#include <stdlib.h>
#define   HEIGHT   15
#define   WIDTH    25
#define   XMIN     -1
#define   XMAX     1
#define   XINCR    0.05
#define   YMIN     0
#define   YMAX     1
#define   SYMBOL   '+'

struct point
  {
    float x, y;
  };
```

```
struct grid
  {
    char *matrix;
    int  ht, wid;
  };

struct plotdata
  {
    struct grid frame;
    struct { float min, max; } x, y;
    char symbol;
  };

char *create(struct grid *frame);
void paint(struct plotdata *p, struct point pt);
void print(struct grid *frame);

int main(void)
  {
    struct plotdata plot =
      {
        NULL, HEIGHT, WIDTH,
        XMIN, XMAX, YMIN, YMAX,
        SYMBOL
      };
    struct point pt;

    /* create and initialize the matrix */
    if (!create(&plot.frame)) return 1;

    /* form the desired picture in this matrix */
    for (pt.x = XMIN; pt.x <= XMAX; pt.x += XINCR)
      {
        pt.y = pt.x * pt.x;
        paint(&plot, pt);
      }

    /* print it */
    print(&plot.frame);

    return 0;
  }

char *create(struct grid *frame)
  {
    int i;

    frame->matrix = (char *)
        calloc(frame->ht, frame->wid * sizeof(char));

    if (frame->matrix)  /* initialize */
        for (i = 0; i < frame->ht * frame->wid; i++)
            frame->matrix[i] = ' ';
```

```
        return frame->matrix;
    }

void paint(struct plotdata *p, struct point pt)
    {
    int i, j;

    /* normalize */
    pt.x = (pt.x - p->x.min) * p->frame.wid
            / (p->x.max - p->x.min);
    pt.y = (pt.y - p->y.min) * p->frame.ht
            / (p->y.max - p->y.min);

    i = (int)(pt.x + 0.5); /* round off */
    j = (int)(pt.y + 0.5); /* round off */

    if (i >= 0 && i < p->frame.wid &&
        j >= 0 && j < p->frame.ht)
        /* matrix[i][j] = symbol */
        p->frame.matrix[j * p->frame.wid + i]
            = p->symbol;
    }

void print(struct grid *frame)
    {
    int i, j;

    /* print from top to bottom */
    for (j = frame->ht - 1; j >= 0; j--)
        {
        for (i = 0; i < frame->wid; i++)
                printf("%c", /* print matrix[i][j] */
                    frame->matrix[j * frame->wid + i]);
        printf("\n");
        }
    }
```

The function create allocates space for matrix and fills it with blank characters. The function paint transforms the coordinates of a point in the picture plane into array subscripts and puts the desired SYMBOL into the corresponding array element. The main program repeatedly calls paint, passing it the various points in the picture plane. Finally, a call to print results in the curve being printed. The for loop steps backward from ht-1 to 0 as the high values of j correspond to points at the top of picture and must be printed first to get the picture right side up.

Note that matrix and the other information required for forming the curve in the memory have been encapsulated in one structure variable. When main calls paint, it passes a pointer to this structure variable to avoid copying and to ensure that the changes made to `matrix` by `paint` persist after returning from it. The point in the picture plane, on the other hand, is passed by value to `paint`. This allows the parameter `pt` to be used as a local variable inside `paint`.

As in the matrix multiplication program presented in Section 7.8.3, this program also dynamically obtains the storage required for `matrix` by calling `calloc` to allocate `frame->ht` number of objects, each of which is of size `frame->wid * sizeof(char)`. It also exploits the fact that the elements of a two-dimensional matrix are stored in row order and accesses the matrix element `matrix[i][j]` as `matrix[j * frame->wid + i]`.

8.4 STRUCTURES CONTAINING POINTERS

A structure can contain pointers as member variables. For example, the structure definition

```
struct location
  {
    char *name;
    char *addr;
  };
```

defines a structure `location` that contains two character pointers, `name` and `addr`, as member variables. Variables of type `struct location` can now be defined and manipulated as in:

```
struct location att =
    {"bell labs", "murray hill, new jersey"};
struct location ibm;

ibm.name = "almaden research center";
ibm.addr = "san jose, california";
printf("%s", att.name);
```

8.4.1 Self-Referential Structures

We mentioned in Section 8.1.6 that a structure may not be nested within itself. However, structures may contain pointers to structures of their own type. For example,

```
struct company
  {
    struct projects government;
    struct projects industrial;
    struct company *parent;      /* legal */
  };
```

is a legal structure declaration, since `parent` in this example is a pointer to the `company` structure, and not an embedded occurrence of the `company` structure.

list pointer :

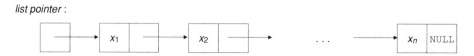

Figure 8.1. A singly linked list

Structures that contain pointers to structures of their own type provide a basis for several useful data structures. We discuss two of these: linked lists and trees.

Linked Lists

A *list* is a sequence of zero or more elements of a given type. Lists arise routinely in applications such as information retrieval, programming language translation, and simulation. Arrays can be used to implement lists but have the disadvantage that the insertion or deletion of elements in the middle of a list requires shifting of elements to make room for the new elements or to close up gaps created by deleted elements. An array implementation may also waste space because the maximum space is used irrespective of the number of elements actually in the list. On the other hand, the maximum size, if underestimated, may cause runtime error.

In the linked implementation of a list, pointers are used to link successive list elements. A *singly linked list* is made up of nodes, each node consisting of an element of the list and a pointer to the next node on the list. If the list is x_1, x_2, ..., x_n, the node containing x_i has a pointer to the node containing x_{i+1}, for $i = 1$, $2, ..., n$-1. The node containing x_n has a NULL pointer to indicate the end of the list. The first element of the list x_1 is sometimes referred to as the *head* of the list, and the last element x_n as the *tail* of the list. There is also a *list pointer*, pointing to the head of the list. Figure 8.1 depicts a linked list of this form.

The advantage of linked lists is that the list elements can be inserted and deleted by adjusting the pointers without shifting other elements, and storage for a new element can be allocated dynamically and freed when an element is deleted.

We now write some functions to illustrate operations on linked lists. The structure for a node of a linked list can be defined as

```
struct node
   {
      int data;
      struct node *next;
   };
```

and a function that allocates storage for a node, initializes it, and returns a pointer to it as

```
struct node *mknode(int data)
   {
      struct node *np;
```

```
        np = (struct node *) malloc(sizeof(struct node));
        if (np)
          {
            np->data = data;
            np->next = NULL;
          }
        return np;
    }
```

A node created by calling `mknode` is not yet inserted into the linked list. The following function inserts the node into the list in such a way that all preceding nodes on the list have larger data values:

```
struct node *insert(struct node **list, int data)
  {
    struct node *np;

    if (np = mknode(data))
      {
        struct node *curr = *list, *prev = NULL;

        /* locate the position of this node in the list */
        for ( ; curr && data < curr->data;
               curr = curr->next) prev = curr;

        /* let this node point to the node next in the list */
        np->next = curr;

        /* let the previous node in the list point to this node */
        if (prev)
            prev->next = np;
        else
            *list = np;   /* this node is the first in the list */
      }
    return np;
  }
```

This function takes as one of its arguments a pointer to the list pointer, since the list pointer may be updated if the new node becomes the head node. Note that the new node has been inserted in the list by simply adjusting the pointers. Figure 8.2 depicts the insertion process.

The following function prints the data values of all the elements in the list:

```
void print(struct node *list)
  {
    for ( ; list; list = list->next)
        printf("%d ", list->data);
    printf("\n");
  }
```

Here is an insertion-sort function that uses the preceding functions to sort and print in descending order the numbers in its input:

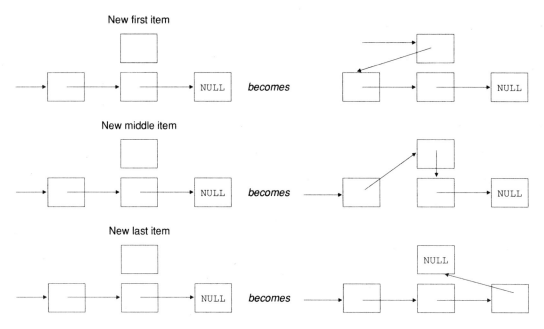

Figure 8.2.   Insertion of a node into a singly linked list

```
void sort(void)
  {
     struct node *list = NULL;
     int i;

     while (scanf("%d", &i) != EOF &&
            insert(&list, i)) /* build list */
               ;
     print(list);
  }
```

We encourage you to write a function that deletes a specified node from the list.

Trees

A tree imposes a hierarchical structure on a collection of items. Organization and genealogical charts are familiar examples of trees. Trees also arise in many computer science applications, such as the organization of information in a database system and the representation of the syntactic structure of source programs in compilers. Trees are also used in the representation of sets, in decision making, and in computer games.

A tree *T* is defined recursively as a finite set of zero or more nodes such that if there is a nonzero number of nodes then (i) there is a specially designated

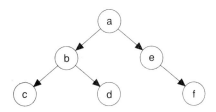

Figure 8.3. A binary tree

node n called the *root*; (ii) the remaining nodes are partitioned into $m \geq 0$ disjoint sets $T_1, T_2, \ldots, T_m$, where each of these sets is a tree. $T_1, T_2, \ldots, T_m$ are called the *subtrees* of n and their roots the *children* of n. A tree with zero nodes is called an *empty* tree.

A *binary tree* is a special kind of tree in which each node has at most two children: the *left* and the *right* child. Figure 8.3 depicts a binary tree.

There are several ways in which the nodes of a tree can be systematically traversed. The three most important traversal orderings are called *preorder*, *inorder*, and *postorder*. For a binary tree T, these orderings can be defined recursively as follows:

If T consists of a single node, then that node by itself is the preorder, inorder, and postorder traversal of T; otherwise

    i. the preorder traversal of T is the root n of T, followed by the preorder traversal of nodes in the left subtree of n, and then the preorder traversal of nodes in the right subtree of n;

    ii. the inorder traversal of T is the inorder traversal of nodes in the left subtree of root n of T, followed by the root n, and then the inorder traversal of nodes in the right subtree of n, and

    iii. the postorder traversal of T is the postorder traversal of nodes in the left subtree of root n of T, followed by the postorder traversal of nodes in the right subtree of n, and then the root n.

Thus, the preorder traversal of the binary tree given in Figure 8.3 is (a, b, c, d, e, f), the inorder traversal is (c, b, d, a, e, f), and the postorder traversal is (c, d, b, f, e, a).

We now write some functions for manipulating binary trees. The structure for a node of a binary tree can be defined as

```
struct node
    {
        char data;
        struct node *lchild;
        struct node *rchild;
    };
```

The following function reads the data for a binary tree specified in preorder and builds the tree, where a ' – ' in input signifies an empty subtree:

```
struct node *mktree(void)
  {
    int c;
    struct node *np;

    c = getchar();
    if (c != '-')
      {
        np = (struct node *)malloc(sizeof(struct node));
        np->data = c;
        np->lchild = mktree(); /* build left subtree */
        np->rchild = mktree(); /* build right subtree */
        return np;
      }
    else
        return NULL;
  }
```

We have omitted the check for the value returned by `malloc` for clarity; you should rewrite the preceding function to include this check.

The following function traverses a binary tree in postorder:

```
void postorder(struct node *parent)
  {
    if (parent)
      {
        postorder(parent->lchild);/* traverse left subtree */
        postorder(parent->rchild);/* traverse right subtree */
        printf("%c", parent->data);
      }
  }
```

The following function uses the preceding functions to read a binary tree specified in preorder and prints it in postorder:

```
void transform(void)
  {
    struct node *root;

    root = mktree();
    postorder(root);
  }
```

8.4.2 Illustrative Examples

We now give some example programs to further illustrate the use of self-referential structures.

Example 1
Rewrite the expression evaluation program given in Example 1 of Section 7.9 using a linked list representation for the stack.

In the linked list representation of a stack, new elements are pushed onto the stack by allocating storage for them and appending them to the front of the list. Elements are popped from the stack by deleting them from the front of the list and freeing the storage. The following figure depicts a linked-list representation of a stack:

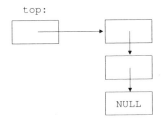

In the program given in Section 7.9, the stack was implemented as an abstract data object. If the interface of the externally visible stack functions is not changed, we can simply replace the file `stack.c` with another version without having to make any change in other source files. Here is the new `stack.c` that uses a linked-list representation for implementing the stack:

```
/********************    stack.c    ********************/

#include "global.h"
#include <stdlib.h>

static void removenode(void);

struct node
   {
     int val;             /* data value */
     struct node *prev;/* pointer to the previous stack node */
   };


struct node *top = NULL;/*pointer to the top stack element */

void clearstack(void)
   {
     while (top)   /* remove all nodes starting from top */
         removenode();
   }

void push(int n)
   {
     struct node *np;

     error = 0;
```

```c
      np = (struct node *)malloc(sizeof(struct node));
      if (np)
        {
          np->val = n;/* fill data value in the new node */
          np->prev = top;/* it points to the current top node */
          top = np;    /* reset top to point to the new node */
        }
      else
          error = STACKFULL;
    }

int pop(void)
  {
    int val;

    error = 0;

    if (top)
      {
        val = top->val;/*fetch data value from the top node */
        removenode();   /* remove the top node */
        return val;
      }
    else
      {
        error = STACKEMPTY;
        return 0;
      }
  }

int stacksize(void)
  {
    struct node *np;
    int size = 0;

    for (np = top; np; np = np->prev) size++;
    return size;
  }

void printstack(void)
  {
    struct node *np;

    printf("stack:");
    for (np = top; np; np = np->prev)
        printf("%d ", np->val);
    printf("\n");
  }
```

```
static void removenode(void)
  {
    struct node *np;

    np = top;          /*save a pointer to the current top node*/
    top = top->prev;/*reset top to point to the previous node*/
    free(np);          /*delete what used to be the top node*/
  }
```

The pointer variable top always points to the head of the list. The function clearstack starts from the top and removes one by one the elements on the stack and frees storage allocated to them. The function push obtains a new node, fills the data value in it, makes this node point to the node currently at the top of the stack, and then sets top to point to this node. The function pop takes reverse actions: it resets top to point to the previous node and frees the storage allocated to the old top of the stack node. Both stacksize and printstack traverse the list starting from the top to the end, the difference being that the former increments a counter every time a node is traversed while the latter prints the data value associated with the node.

Example 2
Rewrite the program given in Example 6 of Section 6.3 so that the item-price database is maintained as a binary tree and the price of a given item is determined by searching this tree.

If the input data for building the item-price data is not sorted, then one option is to maintain the database as an unordered list and use a linear search for finding the desired item. This option was considered in the example program given in Section 7.7.1. Another alternative is to build a binary search tree as the data is being read, and this option is the one considered in this example. The tree is built in such a way that the left subtree of any node contains only item numbers greater than the item number of the node, and the right subtree contains only item numbers that are smaller.

To determine the price of a given item, we start at the root and compare its item number with the given item number. If the two match, the corresponding price is the result of the query. If the given item number is greater, the left subtree is searched; otherwise, the right subtree is searched. This search procedure is applied recursively. If there are no more nodes in the required direction, the given item is not in the database.

The desired program is as follows:

```
#include <stdio.h>
#include <stdlib.h>
#define  ITEMS   1000

struct iteminfo
  {
    int    item;
    float price;
  };
```

```
struct node
  {
    struct iteminfo itemrec;
    struct node *lchild;
    struct node *rchild;
  };

struct node *bld_database(int items);
struct node *addtree(struct node *p,
                     int item, float price);
struct node *mknode(int item, float price);
struct iteminfo *search(int val, struct node *db);

int main(void)
  {
    struct node *database;
    struct iteminfo *ip;
    int     item_no;

    /* build the item-price database */
    if (!(database = bld_database(ITEMS)))
      {
        printf("too big a database\n");
        return 1;
      }

    /* get item_no of the item whose price is to be found */
    scanf("%d", &item_no);

    /* search */
    ip = search(item_no, database);

    /* output */
    if (ip)
        printf("price of item %d = %f\n",
               item_no, ip->price);
    else
        printf("item %d is not in the database\n",
               item_no);

    return 0;
  }

struct node *bld_database(int items)
  {
    struct node *database = NULL;
    int item, i;
    float price;
```

```
        for (i = 0; i < items; i++)
          {
            scanf("%d %f", &item, &price);
            database = addtree(database, item, price);
            if (!database) return NULL;
          }
        return database;
    }

struct node *addtree(struct node *np,
                     int item, float price)
    {
      if (!np)
          np = mknode(item, price);
      else if (item > np->itemrec.item)
          np->lchild = addtree(np->lchild, item, price);
      else
          np->rchild = addtree(np->rchild, item, price);
      return np;
    }

struct node *mknode(int item, float price)
    {
      struct node *np;

      np = (struct node *) malloc(sizeof(struct node));
      if (np)
        {
          np->itemrec.item = item;
          np->itemrec.price = price;
          np->lchild = np->rchild = NULL;
        }
      return np;
    }

struct iteminfo *search(int val, struct node *db)
    {
      struct iteminfo *ip;

      if (!db)
            /* item not in the database */
            ip = NULL;
      else if (val == db->itemrec.item)
            /* found the item's record */
            ip = &db->itemrec;
      else if (val > db->itemrec.item)
            /* search the left subtree */
            ip = search(val, db->lchild);
      else
            /* search the right subtree */
            ip = search(val, db->rchild);
```

```
        return ip;
    }
```

8.5 UNIONS

The *union* is a construct that allows different types of data items to share the same block of memory. The compiler automatically allocates sufficient space to hold the largest data item in the union. However, it is the programmer's responsibility to keep track of what is currently stored in the union.

The syntax for defining and accessing a union is similar to that for structures, except that the keyword `union` is used in place of `struct`. For example, the statement

```
union chameleon
    {
        double d;
        int i;
        char *cp;
    } data;
```

defines a variable `data` that can hold either a `double`, an `int`, or a pointer to `char`. When `data` needs to be accessed as a `double`, it is accessed as

```
data.d
```

when it needs to be accessed as an `int`, it is accessed as

```
data.i
```

and when it needs to be accessed as a pointer to `char`, it is accessed as

```
data.cp
```

Although a union contains sufficient storage for the largest type, it may contain only one value at a time; it is incorrect to store something as one type and then extract as another. Thus, the following statements

```
data.d = 1.0;
printf("%s", data.cp);
```

produce anomalous results.

To keep track of what is currently stored in `data`, another variable `dtype` may be defined. Whenever a value is assigned to `data`, the variable `dtype` is also set to indicate its type. Later in the program, `dtype` may be tested to determine the type of the value in `data`. Thus, following the definitions

```
#define   DOUBLE   1
#define   INT      2
#define   CP       3
int dtype;
```

the statements

```
data.cp = "anolis";
dtype = CP;
```

place a pointer to the string "anolis" (a genus of lizards capable of changing their colors) in data. The following statement can then be used to print data.

```
switch (dtype)
  {
    case DOUBLE:
        printf("%f", data.d);
        break;
    case INT:
        printf("%d", data.i);
        break;
    case CP:
        printf("%s", data.cp);
        break;
    default:
        printf ("unknown type of data");
  }
```

Union variables may be initialized, albeit in a restricted way — a union variable may only be initialized with a value of the type of its first member.

Unions may occur within arrays and structures and vice versa. Consider, for example, the following definition of the structure item:

```
struct item
  {
    int itemno;
    struct
      {
        int stype;
        union
          {
            struct
              {
                char *streetaddr;
                char *city;
                char *state;
              } domestic;
            struct
              {
                char *country;
                char *completeaddr;
              } foreign;
          } addr;
        float price;
      } suppliers[MAXSUPPLIERS];
  } items[MAXITEMS];
```

The above definition stores information about the items in an array. Associated with each item is a list of supplier and price pairs. Suppliers can be domestic or foreign, and addresses of these two categories of suppliers are stored in different forms. Therefore, a union type has been used for addresses. The variable stype is used to keep track of the type of the supplier. Note that by using a union, we have been able to create arrays that contain different types of elements.

The method of accessing a member of a union in a structure or that of a structure in a union is identical to the method of accessing a member of a structure in a structure. For example, the following program fragment prints the names of the countries of all the foreign suppliers:

```
for (i = 0; i < MAXITEMS; i++)
    for (s = 0; s < MAXSUPPLIERS; s++)
        if (stype == FOREIGN)
            printf("%s\n",
                items[i].suppliers[s].addr.foreign.country);
```

As in the case of structures, unions may not contain instances of themselves, although they may contain pointers to instances of themselves.

8.5.1 Illustrative Examples

We now give an example program to further illustrate the definition and use of a union.

Example

Rewrite the expression evaluation program given in Example 1 of Section 7.9 using a union to get the next term in the input expression.

The prototype of the function `next`, given in Section 7.9, is of the form

```
int  next(int *operator, int *operand);
```

and it returns one of the three values: (i) NOMORE to indicate that there are no more terms in the expression, (ii) OPERATOR to indicate that the next term is an operator, and (iii) OPERAND to indicate that the next term is an operand. If the next term is an operator or operand, its value is also returned using one of the two pointers provided as arguments.

We change the prototype of `next` to

```
void  next(struct token *newterm);
```

where `token` is defined as

```
struct token
    {
    int type;   /* one of NOMORE, OPERATOR, or OPERAND */
    union
        {
        int operator;
        char operand;
        } value;
    };
```

Only one of `operator` or `operand` in the union `value` is used, depending on the `type` of the token.

Besides the above changes in the `global.h`, we redefine the functions `next` in the file `io.c` and `evalexp` that calls `next` in the file `main.c`; no other change is required in the rest of the program. We only provide the code for `evalexp` and `next`.

```
/*********************   main.c    *********************/

static void evalexp(void)
  {
    struct token newterm;

    error = 0;

    /* obtain terms of the expression one at a time
       and do appropriate stack operations */
    while(next(&newterm), newterm.type != NOMORE)
      {
        if (newterm.type == OPERAND)
            push(newterm.value.operand);
        else /* OPERATOR */
            evalop(newterm.value.operator);
        if (error) return;
      }
  }

/*********************   io.c    *********************/

void next(struct token *newterm)
  {
    /* skip over whitespaces */
    while(buf[bp] == ' ' || buf[bp] == '\t') bp++;

    if (buf[bp] == '\0')
        newterm->type = NOMORE;
    else if (buf[bp] >= '0' && buf[bp] <= '9')
      {
        newterm->type = OPERAND;
        /* determine the integer value of the operand */
        for (newterm->value.operand = 0;
            buf[bp] >= '0' && buf[bp] <= '9'; bp++)
            newterm->value.operand =
                10 * (newterm->value.operand)
                + (buf[bp] - '0');
      }
    else
      {
        newterm->type = OPERATOR;
        newterm->value.operator = buf[bp++];
      }
  }
```

This example reaffirms the value of well-structured programs in modifying and maintaining them.

Exercises 8

1. Hand-simulate the execution of the following program:

```c
#include <stdio.h>

struct currency
    {
    int value;
    char *name;
    struct currency *next;
    } coins[] = { {1, "penny", coins+1},
                  {5, "nickel", coins+2},
                  {10, "dime", coins} };

int main(void)
    {
    struct currency *cp = coins;
    int i;

    for (i = 0; i < 3; i++)
        printf("%d %c\n",
            coins[i].value, coins[i].name[0]);

    printf("%d  ", ++cp->value);
    printf("%d  ", (++cp)->value);
    printf("%c  ", *cp->name);
    printf("%c  ", *cp->name++);
    printf("%c  ", *(cp->name)--);
    printf("%c  ", *cp++->name);
    printf("%c  ", cp->next->name[4]);
    printf("%d\n", --cp->next->value);

    cp = coins;
    do
        printf("%d %s\n", cp->value, cp->name);
    while ((cp = cp->next) != coins);

    return 0;
    }
```

2. Define a structure for the following employee record:
   a. name (last, first, middle)
   b. date of birth (year, month, day)
   c. marital status
      i. married => date of marriage, name of the spouse
      ii. widowed => date of marriage

        iii. divorced => date of marriage, date of divorce

        iv. single

   d. children (name and date of birth) : maximum 5

   e. annual salary

3. Define a structure to represent time in hours (0-23), minutes (0-59), and seconds (0-59), and then write a function that accepts as an argument a time represented by this structure and updates it by 1 second.

4. Write a function that takes as its arguments two time structures specified in the previous problem and returns a time structure that represents the elapsed time between the two times.

5. Write a function that determines tomorrow's date, given today's date.

6. Write a function that determines the number of days elapsed from the turn of the century for any date passed as structure, and then use it in a program to determine the difference between two given dates.

7. *Clock patience* is a solitaire game played with a standard deck of 52 cards. The cards are dealt into 12 piles of 4 each in a clocklike pattern, with the remaining 4 cards placed in the middle. A move consists of taking the top card from a pile and placing it under the pile where it belongs (Jack = 11, Queen = 12, King at center), and this pile provides the card for the next move. The game terminates when the four Kings have been placed on the center pile, and is considered successful if all the other cards are correctly placed. Write a program to simulate clock patience, using a pseudo-random number generator to deal the cards.

8. Write an interactive coordinate geometry program that enables the user to write simple commands to draw figures of various shapes to which the user may give names. For example, the user may write

    p = point 0 0

    q = point 1 2

    l = line p q

9. Write a program to draw a picture of the path taken by Joe caught in an unruly mob. Plot Joe's new position every time he moves, assuming that every time he goes 2 feet in a straight line but in a random direction. To generate a random direction, multiply 2π with a random value between 0 and 1.

10. Write a program that makes a list of the chemical elements and then makes the data available on demand. The program first builds the list by prompting the technician by atomic number to enter the element's full name, symbol, and atomic weight. It then prompts the chemist to enter an element's symbol and prints the rest of the information for this element.

11. Write a function that removes the first node in a linked list with a given value.

12. Write a function that merges two sorted lists into one.

13. Write a function that takes a pointer to a linked list and reverses the order of the nodes by simply altering the pointers. If the original list were (5, 3, 7, 1), the function should transform it into (1, 7, 3, 5).

14. A *doubly linked list* is a list in which each element contains a pointer to the previous element as well as to the next element in the list. There is also a pointer `head` to the leftmost element in the list, and a pointer `tail` to the rightmost element. Both `head->prev` and `tail->next` are set to `NULL`. Write functions that perform the following operations on a doubly linked list:

i. Create, destroy, and print the list.

ii. Search the list to return a pointer to the first/last element with a certain specified value.

iii. Insert an element before/after a specified element.

iv. Delete a specified element.

15. Write functions that read, add, subtract, multiply, and evaluate polynomials of the form

$$a_n x^n + a_{n-1} x^{n-1} + \ldots + a_2 x^2 + a_1 x + a_0.$$

Such polynomials can be represented by a linked list in which each node has three fields: coefficient a_i, exponent i, and a pointer to the next node. For evaluating a polynomial, use Horner's method:

$$a_n x^n + a_{n-1} x^{n-1} + \ldots + a_1 x + a_0 = (((a_n x + a_{n-1})x + a_{n-2})x + \cdots + a_1)x + a_0.$$

16. Implement an abstract data object *queue* by defining functions to create and destroy the queue, add an element to the queue, delete an element from the queue, count the length of the queue, and print the queue. A queue is an ordered list in which all additions are made at the end and all deletions from the front.

    Use this abstract data object to write a simulation program to investigate the average length of the input queue of a computer system. Jobs arrive in the queue at a mean rate of λ and are serviced at a mean rate of μ. If events occur at a mean rate of r, then the time t between any two consecutive events is a random variable

    $$t = ln(x)/r,$$

    where x is uniformly distributed between 0 and 1.

17. Algebraic expressions may be represented by binary trees. Each node of the tree contains an operator (+, -, *, or /) and pointers to two subexpressions. For example, the tree corresponding to the expression (a - b) / (c + d) is

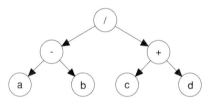

    Write a function that reads an expression and constructs a binary tree corresponding to the expression.

18. The *level-order* listing of the nodes of a tree first lists the root, then all the nodes of depth 1, then all the nodes of depth 2, and so on. Nodes at the same depth are listed from left to right. Write a program to list the nodes of a tree in level order.

19. One of eight given coins is counterfeit and has a weight different from others. Write a program that determines which coin it is and whether it is heavier or lighter than the rest by doing a minimum number of comparisons on an equal-arm balance.

20. Write a function that creates a family tree. Each person is represented by a structure that contains the person's name and pointers to parents, spouse, and children. Use this tree in a program that determines whether two persons are cousins.

■ 9 Operations on Bits

C was originally designed to be a systems programming language. Systems programs frequently require the capability to manipulate individual bits of a word. C provides four operators, called *bitwise logical operators*, for masking operations on bits, and two operators, called the *bitwise shift operators*, for shifting bits in a word. In addition, C allows you to partition a word into groups of bits, called *bit-fields*, and assign names to them. We study in this chapter these features of the C language.

9.1 BITWISE LOGICAL OPERATORS

The four bitwise logical operators are: *bitwise AND* (&), *bitwise inclusive OR* (|), *bitwise exclusive OR* (^), and *bitwise complement* (~). Except bitwise complement, which is unary, all others are binary operators.

Bitwise logical operators can only be applied to integral operands. When evaluating expressions containing these operators, the automatic unary and binary conversions, discussed in Section 2.9.1, are first performed on the operands. The type of the result is that of the converted operands.

The result of applying these operators to signed operands is implementation-dependent, as different implementations may use different representations for signed integers. Hence, for portability, these operators should only be used on unsigned operands.

All the three binary bitwise logical operators are both commutative and associative. They can also be used, like other binary operators, to form compound assignment operators &=, |=, and ^=.

9.1.1 Bitwise AND Operator

The bitwise AND operator & has the formation

intvalue & *intvalue*

When it is applied to two integral operands, the binary representations of the converted values of the operands are compared bit by bit. If *b1* and *b2* represent corresponding bits of the two operands, then the result of *b1* & *b2* is as shown in the following truth table:

b1	b2	b1 & b2
1	1	1
1	0	0
0	1	0
0	0	0

For example, given that

```
unsigned int e1 = 0xd, e2 = 0x7;
```

and that an integer is represented in 16 bits in the machine being used, the expression e1 & e2 has the value 0x5 as shown below:

Expression	Binary Representation	Value
e1	0000 0000 0000 1101	0xd
e2	0000 0000 0000 0111	0x7
e1 & e2	0000 0000 0000 0101	0x5

The logical AND operator && and the bitwise AND operator & are quite different. The result of applying && is always 0 or 1, but that of & depends upon the values of the operands. For example, whereas the value of the expression 0xd && 0x7 is 1, the value of 0xd & 0x7 is 0x5. Only in the special case when the values of the operands are restricted to be 0 or 1 is the result of applying & and && the same. Moreover, in the case of &&, the second operand is not evaluated if the first operand is 0, but both operands are evaluated in the case of &.

The bitwise AND operator is often used to turn some specified bits off, that is, to set them to 0. For example, the statement

```
e1 &= e2;
```

as shown in the preceding example, turns off all but the low-order three bits of e1. Those three bits remain unchanged.

9.1.2 Bitwise Inclusive OR Operator

The bitwise inclusive OR operator |, frequently referred to simply as the bitwise OR operator, has the formation

intvalue | *intvalue*

As in the case of the bitwise AND operator, when the bitwise OR operator is applied to two integral operands, the binary representations of the converted values of the operands are compared bit by bit. If *b1* and *b2* represent corresponding bits of the two operands, then the result of *b1* | *b2* is as shown in the following truth table:

b1	b2	b1 | b2
1	1	1
1	0	1
0	1	1
0	0	0

Thus, given that `unsigned int e1` and `e2` are `0xd` and `0x7` respectively, the expression `e1 | e2` has the value `0xf` as shown below:

Expression	Binary Representation	Value
e1	0000 0000 0000 1101	0xd
e2	0000 0000 0000 0111	0x7
e1 | e2	0000 0000 0000 1111	0xf

The logical OR operator `||` and the bitwise OR operator `|` are also quite different. The result of applying `|` depends upon the values of the operands, but that of `||` is always `0` or `1`. Only in the special case when the values of the operands are restricted to be `0` or `1` is the result of `|` and `||` the same. Further, in the case of `||`, the second operand is not evaluated if the first operand is `1`, but both operands are evaluated in the case of `|`.

The bitwise OR operator is frequently used to turn some specified bits on, that is, to set them to `1`. For example, the statement

```
e1 |= e2;
```

as shown in the preceding example, ensures that the three rightmost bits of `e1` are turned on.

9.1.3 Bitwise Exclusive OR Operator

The bitwise exclusive OR operator `^`, frequently referred to as the *XOR* operator, has the formation

intvalue `^` *intvalue*

In the case of the bitwise exclusive OR operator also, the binary representations of the converted values of the two integral operands are compared bit by bit. If *b1* and *b2* represent corresponding bits of the two operands, then the result of *b1* `^` *b2* is as shown in the following truth table:

b1	b2	b1 ^ b2
1	1	0
1	0	1
0	1	1
0	0	0

Thus, given that `unsigned int e1` and `e2` are `0xd` and `0x7` respectively, the expression `e1 ^ e2` has the value `0xa` as shown below:

Expression	Binary Representation	Value
e1	0000 0000 0000 1101	0xd
e2	0000 0000 0000 0111	0x7
e1 ^ e2	0000 0000 0000 1010	0xa

The exclusive OR operator has the property that any value XORed with itself produces 0 as the result. Thus, we have

Expression	Binary Representation	Value
e1	0000 0000 0000 1101	0xd
e1	0000 0000 0000 1101	0xd
e1 ^ e1	0000 0000 0000 0000	0x0

This property is often used by assembly language programmers to set a value to 0 or to compare two values to determine if they are equal.

Another useful property of this operator is that if the result of XORing a value with another value is again XORed with the second value, the result is the first value. Thus, we have

Expression	Binary Representation	Value
e1	0000 0000 0000 1101	0xd
e2	0000 0000 0000 0111	0x7
e1 ^ e2	0000 0000 0000 1010	0xa
e2	0000 0000 0000 0111	0x7
(e1 ^ e2) ^ e2	0000 0000 0000 1101	0xd

That is, `(e1 ^ e2) ^ e2` is equal to `e1`. This property is frequently used in designing bit-manipulation ciphers in cryptography. We will consider one such cipher later in the chapter.

The bitwise exclusive OR operator can also be used to interchange two values without using a temporary variable. Thus, the statement

```
e1 ^= e2, e2 ^= e1, e1 ^= e2;
```

swaps the values of `e1` and `e2`, as shown below:

Expression	Binary Representation	Value
e1	0000 0000 0000 1101	0xd
e2	0000 0000 0000 0111	0x7
e1 ^= e2	0000 0000 0000 1010	0xa
e2 ^= e1	0000 0000 0000 1101	0xd
e1 ^= e2	0000 0000 0000 0111	0x7

9.1.4 Bitwise Complement Operator

The bitwise complement operator has the formation

$\sim$ *intvalue*

and yields the 1's complement of the converted integral operand; that is, it converts each 1-bit into a 0-bit and vice versa. Thus, if *b* represents a bit of the operand, then the result of $\sim b$ is as shown in the following truth table:

b	$\sim b$
1	0
0	1

Thus, assuming 16-bit integers and that `unsigned int e1` is `0xd`, the expression `~e1` has the value `0xfff2` as shown below:

Expression	Binary Representation	Value
e1	0000 0000 0000 1101	0xd
~e1	1111 1111 1111 0010	0xfff2

The bitwise complement operator should not be confused with the arithmetic unary minus (–) or the logical negation (!). For example, if e is defined to be an `int` and set equal to 0, then –e results in 0 and !e in 1, but $\sim$ e yields –1 on a 2's complement machine.

The bitwise complement operator is useful in writing portable code as it avoids inclusion of machine-dependent information in the program. For example, the statement

```
e &=   ~0xff;
```

sets the last 8 bits of e to 0, independent of word length.

9.1.5 Precedence and Associativity

The order of precedence of the bitwise logical operators is bitwise complement, bitwise AND, bitwise exclusive OR, and then bitwise inclusive OR. Except for the bitwise complement that associates from right to left, all others associate from left to right. Thus, the expression

```
01 |  ~   01 ^ 01 & 01
```

is interpreted as

```
01 | ( ( ~   01) ^ (01 & 01) )
```

The position of these operators in the precedence hierarchy is given in Appendix B. Note that the precedence of the binary bitwise logical operators is lower than the equality operator `==` and the inequality operator `!=`. Thus, parentheses are necessary in expressions such as

```
(i & 01) == 0
```

or

```
(i ^ 01) != 0
```

Omitting these parentheses is a common error found in many programs.

9.2 BITWISE SHIFT OPERATORS

C provides two bitwise shift operators, *bitwise left shift* (<<) and *bitwise right shift* (>>), for shifting bits left or right by an integral number of positions in integral data. Both of these operators are binary, and the left operand is the integral data whose bits are to be shifted, and the right operand, called the *shift count*, specifies the number of positions by which bits need shifting. The shift count must be nonnegative and less than the number of bits required to represent data of the type of the left operand.

Automatic unary conversions are performed on both the operands. However, the type of the result is that of the promoted left operand; the right operand does not promote the result.

The result of applying these operators to signed operands is implementation-dependent. For portability, therefore, these operators should only be used on unsigned operands.

These operators can also be used, like other binary operators, to form compound assignment operators >>= and <<=.

9.2.1 Left Shift Operator

The left shift operator shifts bits to the left, and has the formation

intvalue << *intvalue*

As bits are shifted toward high-order positions, 0 bits enter the low-order positions. Bits shifted out through the high-order position are lost. For example, given

```
unsigned int i = 5;
```

and 16-bit integers, that is,

i is binary 00000000 00000101,

then

i << 1   is   binary 00000000 00001010,   or   decimal 10,

and

i << 15   is   binary 10000000 00000000,   or   decimal 32768.

In the second example, the 1 originally in the third bit position has dropped off. Another left shift by one position will drop off the 1 in the sixteenth bit position, and the value of the expression will become zero.

9.2.2 Right Shift Operator

The right shift operator shifts bits to the right, and has the formation

> *intvalue* >> *intvalue*

As bits are shifted toward low-order positions, 0 bits enter the high-order positions, if the data is `unsigned`. If the data is signed and the sign bit is 0, then 0 bits also enter the high-order positions. However, if the sign bit is 1, the bits entering high-order positions are implementation-dependent. On some machines 1s, and on others 0s, are shifted in. The former type of operation is known as the *arithmetic right shift*, and the latter type the *logical right shift*. For example, given

```
unsigned int i = 40960;
```

and 16-bit integers, that is,

> `i` is 10100000 00000000,

then

> `i >> 1`   is   binary 01010000 00000000,   or   decimal 20480,

and

> `i >> 15`   is   binary 00000000 00000001,   or   decimal 1.

In the second example, the 1 originally in the fourteenth bit position has dropped off. Another right shift will drop off the 1 in the first bit position, and `i` will become zero.

9.2.3 Multiplication and Division

The left shift of a value by one position has the effect of multiplying the value by two, unless an overflow occurs due to a 1 falling off from the high-order position. Similarly, the right shift of a value by one position has the effect of dividing the value by two, provided the value is nonnegative. Here are some examples, assuming 16-bit integers:

`unsigned int i`	`i` as each statement executes	
	Binary Representation	Decimal Value
`i`	00000000 00000011	3
`i << 1`	00000000 00000110	6
`i << 4`	00000000 01100000	96
`i << 9`	11000000 00000000	49152
`i << 1`	10000000 00000000	32768
`i >> 1`	01000000 00000000	16384
`i >> 9`	00000000 00100000	32
`i >> 4`	00000000 00000010	2
`i >> 1`	00000000 00000001	1
`i >> 1`	00000000 00000000	0

The operation i << 1, when the value of i is 49152, results in an overflow and does not have the effect of multiplication by 2. However, the operation i >> 1, when the value of i is 1, has the right effect of integer division.

9.2.4 Precedence and Associativity

Left and right shift operators have equal precedence and they associate from left to right. Thus, the expression

```
1 << 1 >> 2
```

is interpreted as

```
(1 << 1) >> 2.
```

The relative precedence of the shift operators with respect to other operators is given in Appendix B. The precedence of the shift operators is lower than that of any arithmetic operator, but higher than that of any bitwise logical operator except the unary bitwise complement operator. Thus, the expression

```
1 << 2 - 1
```

is interpreted as

```
1 << (2 - 1)
```

and the expression

```
01 | ~ 01 << 1
```

is interpreted as

```
01 | ( ( ~ 01) << 1).
```

9.3   BIT-FIELDS

Information can be *packed* by representing several data items within a single machine word using non-overlapping adjacent groups of bits, particularly when the values that the data items can assume are small. Such packing becomes necessary when storage is at a premium or some hardware-defined data structures have to be matched exactly in the program. For example, in the PC-DOS operating system, the list of equipment installed is encoded in the AX register in the following format:

bit 0:	1 if diskettes present
bit 1:	not used
bits 2,3:	system board RAM, 11 => 64K
bits 4,5:	video mode, 01 => 40-column color,
	10 => 80-column color, 11 => monochrome
bits 6,7:	number of disk drives
bit 8:	DMA chip, 0 => installed

bits 9,10,11:   number of RS-232 ports
bit 12:   1 => game adapter installed
bit 13:   1 => serial printer (PC *jr* only)
bit 14,15:   number of printers

When the information has been packed within a word, the desired data items can be accessed by extracting the corresponding bits using the bit-manipulation operators. For example, if the unsigned integer `ax` contains the above encoding of the equipment list, then the statement

```
if (((ax >> 4) &  ~ ( ~ 0 << 2)) == 03)
    printf("monochrome\n");
```

determines if the video mode is monochrome.

C provides a more convenient method for defining and accessing fields within a word than the use of the bit-manipulation operators. This method uses a special syntax in the structure definition to define bit-fields and assign names to them. A *bit-field* is a set of adjacent bits within an implementation-dependent storage unit, called a "word." The syntax for defining a bit-field is

type field-name : *bit-length;*

where *bit-length* is the number of bits assigned to the bit-field variable *field-name* of the type *type*. Bit-fields can only be of type `int`; for portability, they should explicitly be specified to be `signed` or `unsigned`. Thus, the variable `ax`, containing the encoding of the equipment list, can be defined using bit-fields as

```
struct
  {
    unsigned diskette       : 1;
    unsigned unused         : 1;
    unsigned sysboard_ram    : 2;
    unsigned video          : 2;
    unsigned disks          : 2;
    unsigned dma_chip        : 1;
    unsigned rs232_ports     : 3;
    unsigned game_adapter    : 1;
    unsigned serial_printer : 1;
    unsigned printers       : 2;
  } ax;
```

A bit-field with no name may be included in a structure. An unnamed bit-field is useful for padding to conform to externally imposed data formats. Thus, instead of the bit-field declaration

```
unsigned unused          : 1;
```

we can write

```
unsigned                 : 1;
```

An unnamed bit-field of zero width forces alignment at the next word boundary.

A structure that contains bit-fields may also include non-bit-field members. Thus, we may have

```
struct node
  {
    char *name;
    unsigned keyword_flag : 1;
    unsigned extern_flag  : 1;
    unsigned static_flag  : 1;
    char *value;
  } table[MAXSYMBOLS];
```

Non-bit-field members are aligned in an implementation-dependent manner appropriate to their types.

Individual bit-fields are accessed as any other structure members. Thus, we can write

```
if (ax.video == 03) printf("monochrome\n");
```

Bit-fields behave like small integers and may participate in arithmetic expressions just like other integers. We can, therefore, write:

```
devices = ax.disks + ax.rs232_ports + ax.printers;
```

or

```
for (i = 0; i < MAXSYMBOLS; i++)
    table[i].keyword_flag =
        table[i].extern_flag =
            table[i].static_flag = 0;
```

A bit-field cannot be dimensioned; that is, an array of bit-fields, such as

```
flag : 1[5];
```

cannot be formed. Moreover, the address operator & cannot be applied to a bit-field object, and hence we cannot define a variable of type "pointer to bit-field."

The major problem with bit-fields is that almost everything about them is implementation-dependent. Compilers may impose constraints on the maximum size of a bit-field, and most of them do not support bit-fields larger than the natural word size of the target computer. An implementation may allocate any addressable storage unit large enough to hold a bit-field. If enough space remains, a bit-field that immediately follows this bit-field in the structure is packed into adjacent bits of the same unit; otherwise, whether a bit-field that does not fit is put into the next unit or overlaps adjacent units is implementation-dependent. Within a unit, bit-fields are packed left to right on some computers and right to left on others. The alignment of the addressable storage unit is also implementation-dependent. The use of bit-fields is, therefore, likely to be nonportable, and should be restricted to situations in which memory is scarce or the externally defined data structures must be matched exactly.

9.4 ILLUSTRATIVE EXAMPLES

We now give some example programs to further illustrate the concepts introduced in this chapter.

Example 1
Write a function that rotates bits in an integer to the right by a specified number of bit positions.

The desired function is as follows:

```
/*
 *   determine  the  number  of  bits  in  an  integer
 */
int  intlen(void)
  {
    unsigned int  intnum =  ~ 0, bitcnt = 1;

    while (intnum <<= 1) bitcnt++;
    return bitcnt;
  }


/*
 *   extract at most nbits bits to the left of and including the bit
 *   at position pos and return them right-adjusted
 */
int  getbits(int  word,  int  pos,  int  nbits)
  {
    int  intbits = intlen();

    if (pos >= intbits) /* return the word unchanged */
        return word;
    if (pos + nbits >= intbits)
        nbits = intbits) - pos;/* bits to the left of pos */
    if (nbits == intbits) /* pos = 0 and nbits ≥ intlen */
        return word;
    word >>= pos; /* right adjust */
    word &=  ~(~0 << nbits);/* clear off other bits */
    return word;
  }
```

```
/*
 *   rotate word to the right by nbits bit positions
 */
int rrotate(int word, int nbits)
  {
    int rbits;

    if (nbits %= intlen())
      {
        /* get nbits rightmost bits */
        rbits = getbits(word, 0, nbits);
        /* shift to right by nbits positions */
        word >>= nbits;
        /* clear the propagated sign bits */
        word &=  ~ (unsigned) 0 >> nbits;
        /* put back the saved bits */
        word |= rbits << (intlen() - nbits);
      }
    return word;
  }
```

The function `intlen` determines the size of an integer in number of bits. It initializes an unsigned integer variable `intnum` to all ones, and then counts how many left shifts are performed until `intnum` becomes all zeros. We could have alternatively determined the number of bits in an integer by multiplying `sizeof(int)` with the symbolic constant `CHAR_BIT` defined in the standard header `<limits.h>`.

The function `getbits` extracts a maximum of `nbits` bits to the left of and including the bit at position `pos`, and returns them right-adjusted. The expression

```
~ ( ~ 0 << nbits)
```

in `rrotate` creates a mask that has all ones in the rightmost `nbits` positions and zeros everywhere else.

The function `rrotate` makes use of the above two functions in rotating the integer `word` to the right by `nbits` bit positions. If `nbits` is the same as the size of an integer, `word` remains the same as before. If `nbits` exceeds the size of an integer, `nbits` is reset to the remainder of `nbits` divided by the size of an integer, since a rotation by as many positions as the number of bits in integer leaves the integer unchanged. The function `rrotate` simply extracts the rightmost `nbits` bits of `word` into `rbits`, shifts bits in `word` to the right by `nbits` bit positions, clears propagated bits, if any, due to this right shift, and puts back the bits saved in `rbits` in the leftmost `nbits` positions of `word`. Note that the expression

```
~ (unsigned) 0 >> nbits
```

creates a mask that has all zeros in the leftmost `nbits` positions and ones everywhere else.

Example 2

Write a program that takes as input either a plain text or a cipher text and encodes or decodes it using a bit manipulation cipher.

Bit manipulation ciphers encode the plain text by manipulating the bits that compose the characters of the text. A simple, although not very secure, bit manipulation cipher creates the cipher text by using the bitwise complement operator to invert every bit of the plain text. The plain text can be recovered from the cipher text by reapplying the bitwise complement operator to the cipher text.

A better encoding method is to take the exclusive OR of the plain text with a key. If the text is larger than the key, the key is cycled until the whole text has been encoded. The plain text can be recovered from the cipher text by taking the exclusive OR of the cipher text with same key, since the exclusive OR has the property that it yields the original byte when a byte is exclusive-ORed twice with some other byte.

The program to encode or decode a text by exclusive-ORing it with a key is as follows:

```c
#include <stdio.h>
#include <string.h>
#define  KEY "snuffle-upagus"

unsigned char key[] = KEY;

int main(void)
  {
    int c, i = 0, keylen = strlen(KEY);

    while ((c = getchar()) != EOF)
        putchar(c ^ key[i++ % keylen]);
    return 0;
  }
```

Example 3

Write functions to compress an ASCII text and to recover the original text from the compressed text.

Compression squeezes a given amount of information so that it requires less storage. We consider a bit compression technique in which eight characters are compressed into seven bytes, resulting in a 12.5% saving in storage. This technique exploits the fact that no ASCII letter or punctuation mark uses the eighth bit of a byte. Therefore, the eighth bit of each of the seven bytes can be used to store the eighth character.

For example, the word ziggurat is represented in eight bytes as

byte 0   0111 1010
byte 1   0110 1001

byte 2   0110 0111
byte 3   0110 0111
byte 4   0111 0101
byte 5   0111 0010
byte 6   0110 0001
byte 7   0111 0100

The seven significant bits of byte 0 can be distributed into the seven unused positions of bytes 1 through 7. The seven remaining bytes then appear as

byte 1   1110 1001
byte 2   1110 0111
byte 3   1110 0111
byte 4   1111 0101
byte 5   0111 0010
byte 6   1110 0001
byte 7   0111 0100

The following function reads ASCII text from the standard input and writes the compressed text to the standard output:

```c
#include <stdio.h>
#define  DUMMY  '\xff'

void compress(void)
  {
    int c, i;
    unsigned char first, rest;

    while ((c = getchar()) != EOF)
      {
        first = (unsigned char) c;

        first <<= 1;   /* shift out the unused 8th bit */

        for (i = 0; i < 7; i++)
          {
            if ((c = getchar()) != EOF)
                /* turn off the 8th bit */
                rest = (unsigned char) c & '\x7f';
            else
                rest = DUMMY;

            /* piggyback one bit of first */
            rest |= (first << i) & '\x80';

            putchar(rest);
          }
      }
  }
```

The number of characters in the input may not be an even multiple of 8. Dummy bytes are inserted at the end to cover any such deficiency.

The following function takes as input a compressed text created using the compress function, and decompresses it to recover the original text:

```c
#include <stdio.h>
#define  DUMMY  '\xff'

void decompress(void)
   {
      int c, i;
      unsigned char byte[8];

      for (;;)
         {
           for (i = 1, byte[0] = 0; i < 8; i++)
              {
                 if ((c = getchar()) == EOF) return;
                 /* turn off the 8th bit */
                 byte[i] = (unsigned char) c & '\x7f';
                 /* assemble the first character */
                 byte[0] |= ((unsigned char) c & '\x80') >> i;
              }
           for (i = 0; i < 8; i++) /* output 8 characters */
              if (byte[i] != DUMMY) putchar(byte[i]);
         }
   }
```

Example 4

Write a program that computes the transitive closure of a given directed graph.

A *directed graph G* consists of a set of nodes and a set of arcs. An *arc* is an ordered pair of nodes (i, j); i is called the *tail* and j the *head* of the arc. A *path* from node i_1 to i_n is a sequence of nodes $i_1, i_2, \ldots, i_n$, such that $(i_1,i_2), (i_2,i_3), \ldots, (i_{n-1},i_n)$ are arcs in G. In many applications, we are interested in determining whether there exists a path from node i to node j. The *transitive closure $\hat{G}$* of G is a directed graph such that $\hat{G}$ has an arc from node i to node j, if and only if there is a path from i to j in G.

A directed graph can be represented by an *adjacency matrix A* such that the element $a_{ij} = 1$ if there is an arc from i to j, and 0 otherwise. Given an initial $v \times v$ adjacency matrix, its transitive closure can be obtained, using the *Warshall* algorithm, as

For $k = 1$ to v do
    For $i = 1$ to v do
        For $j = 1$ to v do
            $a_{ij} = a_{ij} \mid (a_{ik} \,\&\, a_{kj})$.

The following program computes the transitive closure of a given directed graph using the Warshall algorithm:

```c
#include <stdio.h>
#define N        5              /* assume 32-bit integers */
#define INTSIZE (1 << N)        /* 32 */
#define MAXNODE 250             /* highest node number */
#define MAXROW   MAXNODE + 1 /* rows in the adjacency matrix */
#define MAXCOL   (MAXNODE >> N) + 1 /* columns */

/*
 *  returns true if the bit at position p in the integer i is 1
 */
int bitset(unsigned int num, int pos)
  {
    return num >> pos & 1;
  }


void warshall(unsigned int matrix[MAXROW][MAXCOL],
              int nodes)
  {
    int i, j, k;

    for (k = 0; k <= nodes; k++)
        for (i = 0; i <= nodes; i++)
            if (bitset(matrix[i][k >> N], k % INTSIZE))
                for (j = 0; j <= nodes >> N; j++)
                    matrix[i][j] |= matrix[k][j];
  }

int input(unsigned int matrix[MAXROW][MAXCOL])
  {
    int tail, head, maxnode = -1, greater;

    while (scanf("%d %d", &tail, &head) != EOF)
      {
        if (tail >= MAXROW || head >= MAXROW) continue;
        matrix[tail][head >> N] |= 1 << head % INTSIZE;
        greater = tail > head ? tail : head;
        if (greater > maxnode) maxnode = greater;
      }
    return maxnode;   /* the highest node number in input */
  }

void output(unsigned int matrix[MAXROW][MAXCOL],
          int nodes)
  {
    int i, j;
```

```
        for (i = 0; i <= nodes; i++)
            for (j = 0; j <= nodes; j++)
                if (bitset(matrix[i][j >> N], j % INTSIZE))
                    printf("% %d\n", i, j);
    }

int main(void)
    {
        unsigned int matrix[MAXROW][MAXCOL];
        int nodes;

        nodes = input(matrix);
        warshall(matrix, nodes);
        output(matrix, nodes);
        return 0;
    }
```

The adjacency matrix is represented in memory by the two-dimensional array matrix. We assume that the node numbers are nonnegative, including 0. Therefore, the number of rows in matrix is one more than the highest expected node number MAXNODE. Instead of allocating one full word to represent an element of the adjacency matrix, we pack information in one word for as many elements as the size of the word in bits, since each element can assume only a 0 or 1 value. Therefore, the size of each row of matrix in words is one more than MAXNODE divided by the size of the word in number of bits.

The input graph is specified as a set of arcs. Each arc is specified as a pair of node numbers, the first being the tail and the second the head. The function input reads data for one arc at a time and sets the corresponding bit in matrix to 1. The function warshall computes the transitive closure of the adjacency matrix. Finally, the function output examines bits of matrix and outputs the corresponding arc if the bit is 1.

Example 5
Define a concise data structure to store the current date and time, and use it in a function that prints this information.

The desired data structure and function, using bit-fields, are as follows:

```
#include <stdio.h>
#define  BASE    1900

char *monthname[] =
    {
      "Jan", "Feb", "Mar", "Apr", "May", "Jun",
      "Jul", "Aug", "Sep", "Oct", "Nov", "Dec"
    };
```

```
char *dayname[] =
  {
    "Mon", "Tue", "Wed", "Thu", "Fri", "Sat", "Sun"
  };

struct dt
  {
    unsigned day       : 5;   /* 1 - 31 */
    unsigned month     : 4;   /* 0 - 11 (0 => january) */
    unsigned year      : 8;   /* 1900 - 2099 */
    unsigned weekday   : 3;   /* 0 - 6 (0 => monday) */
    unsigned hour      : 4;   /* 1 - 12 */
    unsigned minute    : 6;   /* 0 - 59 */
    unsigned am        : 1;   /* 1 => a.m. 0 => p.m. */
  } now = {1, 0, 0, 0, 12, 0, 1};

void date(struct dt t)
  {
    printf("%s %s %d %d:%d %s %d\n", dayname[t.weekday],
        monthname[t.month], t.day, t.hour, t.minute,
        t.am ? "AM" : "PM", t.year+BASE);
  };
```

Given the above initialization of the variable now, the function call date(now) prints

```
Mon Jan 1 12:0 AM 1900
```

Exercises 9

1. Determine the mask that reproduces the second and fourth bits and sets all other bits to zero when

   a. ANDed with an integer variable;

   b. inclusively ORed with an integer variable.

2. Determine the mask and operation that complement the values of the second and fourth bits of an integer variable, leaving all other bits unchanged.

3. Determine the value of each of the following expressions:

   a. 3 | 2 & 1   *b.* 3 | 2 & ~ 1

   c. 3 ^ 2 & 1   *d.* 3 ^ 2 & ~ 1

   e. ~ 1 | 1   *f.* ! 1 | 1

4. Determine the value of each of the following expressions:

   a. 1 << 3 >> 2 << 2 >> 3

   b. 1 << 2 >> 3 << 3 >> 2

   c. 6 - 5 >> 4 - 3 << 2 - 1

   d. (6 - 5 >> 4) - (3 << 2 - 1)

> e. `1 << 2 << 3 >> 1 + 5 / 4 >> 3 % 2 + (int) 1.5 * 2`
>
> f. `( 1 << 2 << ( 3 >> 1 ) + 5`
> `    / ( 4 >> 3 % 2 ) + (int) 1.5 ) * 2`
>
> g. `- 2 * - 3 / 4 % 5 << 1 - - 6 + 8 >> 1`
>
> h. `- ( 2 * ( - 3 / (double) ( 4 % ( 5 << 1 ) ) ) )`
> `    - ( - 6 + ( 8 >> 1 ) )`

5. Write a program that determines whether the right shift on your computer is an arithmetic or a logical one.

6. Write a program that determines whether the bit-fields are packed left to right or right to left on your computer.

7. Write a program that prints the binary representation of an integer using shift operators.

8. Write a program that prints a 32-bit integer as eight hexadecimal digits using bit-fields.

9. Write a function that, starting from position p, inverts n bits of an integer to the left or the right of p according to whether n is positive or negative.

10. Write a function that, starting from position p, sets n bits of an integer to a bit pattern specified right-justified in another integer. The bits are to be set to the left or the right of p according as n is positive or negative.

11. Write a function that searches, starting from the leftmost position of an integer, for an n-bit-long pattern, specified right-justified in another integer, and returns the starting position of the bit pattern.

12. Redo the problem of finding all primes less than 1000 using the *sieve of Eratosthenes* discussed in Exercise 8 of Chapter 6, but now use the 32 bits of a word to represent 32 adjacent numbers.

13. A manufacturing process requires monitoring the temperature of 3000 points. The temperature of a point can be in the range -400° F to +400° F. Three temperatures have been packed in one 32-bit word, with 9 bits being used to represent a temperature value and 1 bit to indicate its sign. Write a function that prints the points having minimum and maximum temperatures.

14. In binary coded decimal codes, four bits are used to represent a decimal digit. Thus, a 4-digit decimal number can be represented in a 16-bit word. Write functions to convert the binary coded decimal representation of a decimal number into its binary representation, and vice versa.

15. Write a program that compresses a text file by duplicating a specified 8-bit mask for every group of eight characters and deleting the characters corresponding to a 0 bit in the mask. For example, if the mask and text were

```
10110101
```

and

```
Never trust to general impressions, my boy,
1011010110110101101101011011010110110101101
but concentrate yourself upon details.
0101101101011011010110110101101101101101
```

respectively, then the compressed text would be

```
Nve rut ogeerlimreson, ybo,
u cncnrae orslfuondeals
```

10 File Processing

In all the C programs considered so far, we have assumed that the input data was read from standard input, normally the terminal, and the output was displayed on standard output, also the terminal. These programs are adequate if the volume of data involved is not large. However, many applications, particularly business-related applications, require that a large amount of data be read, processed, and saved for later use. Programs may require simultaneous access to more than one kind of data and may produce more than one form of output. The preparation of the payroll of a large company is an example of such an application. Not only is the pay data of a large number of employees processed to print the paychecks, but many results of the current month's processing, such as taxes withheld so far, are saved for future payroll processing. The data in such cases is stored on an auxiliary storage device, usually a magnetic tape or disk, discussed in Chapter 1.

Information stored on auxiliary devices is arranged in the form of *files*, and each line of data in the file is called a *record*. A record is a collection of related data items. Examples of a record are all data items related to an employee, all data items related to the inventory of a material in a store, or all responses of a person to some survey questionnaire. The corresponding collection of records will constitute an employee file, an inventory file, or a survey file, respectively.

C does not provide language constructs for input/output operations. However, ANSI C has defined a rich *standard I/O library*, a set of functions designed to provide a standard I/O system for C programs. We shall discuss in this chapter the functions available in the I/O library and their use in writing applications involving file processing.

10.1 OVERVIEW

The standard library supports a simple model of input and output based on the concept of a *stream*. Input and output, whether to or from a physical device such as a terminal, or to or from a file resident on a storage device such as a disk, are mapped into streams of characters, so that the programmer does not have to be concerned about the diverse properties of various types of I/O devices. A stream can be a text stream or a binary stream.

A *text stream* is a sequence of characters composed into lines, each line consisting of zero or more characters and a terminating newline character. ANSI C requires implementations to allow for at least 254 characters in a line. The characters in a text stream need not have one-to-one correspondence with the characters in its external representation; transparent to the user of the stream, characters may be added, altered, or deleted on input and output to conform to different conventions for representing text in the host environment (such as mapping '\n' to carriage return and linefeed). A *binary stream*, on the other hand, is a sequence of unprocessed bytes. The newline character has no special significance in binary streams. Binary streams can be used to record internal data, since any C data value may be mapped into an array of characters.

A stream can be *unbuffered*, *fully buffered*, or *line buffered*. Characters are transmitted to and from the external representation of the stream immediately if it is unbuffered, as a block when a buffer is filled if it is fully buffered, and as a block when a newline character is encountered or the buffer is filled if it is line buffered.

A stream is associated with a file or device by *opening* it. A file may also be created when it is opened. A structure of type FILE, declared in <stdio.h>, is associated with every open stream and contains the information necessary for controlling the stream, such as the *file position indicator, error indicator, end-of-file indicator* and pointer to the associated buffer. When a file is opened, a pointer to this structure, referred to as the *file pointer*, is returned to be used in subsequent file operations. A stream may be disassociated with the corresponding file or device by *closing* it. Before an output stream is disassociated, it is flushed automatically; i.e., any unwritten buffer contents are transferred to the external representation of the stream.

When a C program is started, three text streams are opened automatically: *standard input* for reading input, *standard out* for writing output, and *standard error* for writing diagnostic output. The corresponding file pointers are called stdin, stdout, and stderr, and are declared in <stdio.h>. Normally, stdin is connected to the terminal keyboard and stdout and stderr to the terminal screen, but they may be redirected to other files. The separation of error messages from normal output allows, for example, the standard output to be redirected to a file while the errors are displayed on the screen.

The specific functions provided in the standard library to implement this I/O model have been classified into the following groups:

i. *File access.* This group includes functions to open a file (fopen), close a file (fclose), flush out the buffer associated with a file (fflush), and change the file associated with a stream (freopen). Also included in this group are functions to allow the users to explicitly control the file buffering strategy (setvbuf and setbuf).

ii. *Operations on files.* This group includes functions to remove (remove) and rename (rename) a file. Functions to create a temporary binary file (tmpfile) and generate a unique file name (tmpnam) are also included in this group.

iii. *Formatted input/output.* This group includes functions to read (fscanf, scanf, and sscanf) and write (fprintf, printf, sprintf, vfprintf, vprintf, and vsprintf) formatted data.

iv. *Character input/output.* This group includes functions to read a character from an input stream (fgetc, getc, and getchar) and push back a character to an input stream (ungetc), and also functions for reading strings (fgets and gets). The corresponding output functions (fputc, putc, putchar, fputs, and puts) are also included in this group.

v. *Direct input/output*. This group includes functions to read (fread) and write (fwrite) a certain number of data items of specified size.

vi. *File positioning*. This group includes functions to set the file position to some specified value to allow access to a specific portion of the file (fseek), interrogate the current file position (ftell), and reset the file position to the beginning of the file (rewind). An object type fpos_t, capable of recording all the necessary information to specify every position within a file, is defined in <stdio.h>. Functions to record the current file position in a variable of type fpos_t (fgetpos) and to set the file position to a value of type fpos_t (fsetpos) are also included in this group of functions.

vii. *Error handling*. This group includes functions to test whether EOF returned by a function indicates an end-of-file or an error (feof and ferror), clear end-of-file and error indicators (clearerr), and map the error number errno to an error message (perror). The macro EOF is defined in <stdio.h>. The macro errno is defined in <errno.h> and is set to an appropriate error number by many library functions to facilitate error diagnosis.

Before discussing the details of these library functions, we show you two examples of file processing. The copy function first opens an input file infile and an output file outfile. Then it reads one character at a time from the input file and writes it to the output file. After all the characters from the input file have been copied, it closes both the files. Here is the code for the function:

```
#include <stdio.h>

void copy(char *infile, char *outfile)
  {
    FILE *ifp;      /* file pointer for the input file */
    FILE *ofp;      /* file pointer for the output file */
    int c;          /* character read */

    /* open infile for reading */
    ifp = fopen(infile, "r");

    /* open outfile for writing */
    ofp = fopen(outfile, "w");

    /* copy */
    while ((c = fgetc(ifp)) != EOF)  /* read a character */
        fputc(c, ofp);               /* write a character */

    /* close the files */
    fclose(ifp);
    fclose(ofp);
  }
```

The second function, randcopy, also copies characters from an input file to an output file. However, instead of copying characters sequentially to the output file and creating a replica of the input file, randcopy reads characters to be written to the output file under the control of another file, idxfile. Every line of the idxfile contains two numbers. The first number indicates the start position in the input file from which the next sequence of characters must be read. The second number specifies the number of characters to be read. For example, if the input file contains

```
antiestablishmentarianism
```

and the idxfile contains

```
17 3
4  2
```

randcopy creates an output file containing

```
aries
```

The following is the code for randcopy:

```c
#include <stdio.h>
#define   MAX   80

void randcopy(char *infile,
              char *idxfile, char *outfile)
  {
    FILE *ifp; /* file pointer for the input file */
    FILE *xfp; /* file pointer for the index file */
    FILE *ofp; /* file pointer for the output file */
    long pos;   /* start position in the input file for next read */
    int nbytes;/* number of bytes to be read */
    char buf[MAX];/* buffer to hold the characters read */

    /* open the files */
    ifp = fopen(infile, "r");
    xfp = fopen(idxfile, "r");
    ofp = fopen(outfile, "w");

    /* create the output file */
    while (fscanf(xfp, "%ld %d", &pos, &nbytes) != EOF)
      {
        /* seek to the correct position in the input file */
        fseek(ifp, pos, SEEK_SET);

        /* read nbytes characters into buf */
        fread(buf, sizeof(char), nbytes, ifp);

        /* write the characters read to the output file */
        fwrite(buf, sizeof(char), nbytes, ofp);
      }
```

```
/* close the files */
fclose(ifp); fclose(xfp); fclose(ofp);
}
```

We now describe the functions provided in the standard I/O library. In these functions, the arguments or return values that represent the length of a string are declared to be of type `size_t` and the unmodifiable string arguments to be of type `const char *`. Unless mentioned otherwise, the macros used in this description are defined in `<stdio.h>`.

10.2 FILE ACCESS

The file access functions provide facilities for opening and closing a file, flushing out the file buffer, changing the file associated with a stream, and controlling the file buffering strategy.

10.2.1 `fopen`, `fclose`, `fflush`, `freopen`

```
FILE *fopen(const char *fname, const char *mode);
int   fclose(FILE *fp);
int   fflush(FILE *fp);
FILE *freopen(const char *fname,
              const char *mode, FILE *fp);
```

The function `fopen` opens the file named *fname* in the manner indicated by the argument *mode*. A successful `fopen` returns a pointer of type `FILE *`, which is used to identify the file in subsequent I/O operations; otherwise, a `NULL` value is returned. At most `FOPEN_MAX` files can be opened simultaneously. A file name can have at most `FILENAME_MAX` characters. Permitted values for *mode* include:

`"r"`	Open an existing text file for reading, starting at the beginning of the file.
`"w"`	Create a new text file, or truncate an existing one, for writing.
`"a"`	Create a new text file for writing, or write at the end of an existing one.

An additional plus in the *mode* string (`"r+"`, `"w+"`, and `"a+"`) indicates that the file has been opened for update, that is, it may be used for both input and output. However, an input operation, unless it encounters end-of-file, may not be followed by an output operation, nor an output operation by an input operation, without an intervening call to `fflush`, `fseek`, `rewind`, or `fsetpos`. A b may also be included in *mode* (`"rb"`, `"wb"`, `"ab"`, `"rb+"`, `"wb+"`, and `"ab+"`) to indicate operation on a binary file. The modes `"rb+"`, `"wb+"`, and `"ab+"` can also be written as `"r+b"`, `"w+b"`, and `"a+b"` respectively. For example, the first `fopen` in

```
FILE *fp1, *fp2;
fp1 = fopen("payroll", "w");
fp2 = fopen("inventory", "ab+");
```

opens the text file named `payroll` for writing. If `payroll` already exists, its contents are truncated; otherwise, an empty file is created for storing payroll records. The second `fopen` opens the binary file `inventory` for both reading and writing. If `inventory` already exists and a write is issued after opening it, the new inventory record will be written after the last record in the file. A new file with the name `inventory` is created if it does not already exist. Henceforth, the file pointers `fp1` and `fp2` are used to refer to these files in the program.

The function `fclose` discards any unread buffered input, flushes any unwritten buffered output, frees any automatically allocated buffer, and closes the file identified by the file pointer *fp*. It returns 0 when successful, and EOF otherwise. For example, the call

```
fclose(fp1)
```

closes the `employee` file opened earlier. Any operation on the `employee` file using the file pointer `fp1` will now result in an error.

The function `fflush` flushes any buffered but unwritten output to the file identified by the file pointer *fp*, without closing the file. It returns 0 when successful, and EOF otherwise. For example, the call

```
fflush(stderr)
```

causes any buffered error messages to be written out. When debugging a program, a `fflush` is sometimes put after every write to the standard error to ensure that no error message is lost if the program terminates abnormally. Some transaction processing systems also require that all outputs of a transaction be written to disk before the transaction is committed.

The function `freopen` first closes the file associated with the file pointer *fp* as if by a call to `fclose`. It then opens the file named *fname* in the manner indicated by *mode* as if by a call to `fopen`, except that this file is now associated with *fp* rather than a new value of type `FILE *`. It returns *fp* when successful, and NULL otherwise. Permitted values for *mode* are the same as discussed with `fopen`. `freopen` is primarily used to reassociate one of the standard input/output files `stdin`, `stdout`, and `stderr` with another file. For example, the call

```
freopen("errfile", "a", stderr)
```

causes the standard error output to be redirected to the file `errfile`.

10.2.2 `setvbuf, setbuf`

```
int  setvbuf(FILE *fp, char *buf, int mode, size_t sz);
void setbuf(FILE *fp, char *buf);
```

The function `setvbuf` is used to control buffering when the default strategy is unsatisfactory. The file pointer *fp* identifies the stream whose buffering is being controlled. The character array *buf*, if not NULL, is used in place of the automatically-generated buffer, when buffering is requested. The size of the buffer is specified by *sz*, and the type of buffering by *mode* which can be:

```
_IOFBF    The stream is fully buffered.
_IOLBF    The stream is line buffered.
_IONBF    The stream is not buffered.
```

A call to `setvbuf` must occur only after the file has been opened, but before any data has been read or written. It returns 0 when successful, and a nonzero value otherwise.

The function `setbuf` is a special form of `setvbuf`. The call

```
setbuf(fp,  buf)
```

is equivalent to

```
buf == NULL ? (void) setvbuf(fp, NULL, _IONBF, 0) :
              (void) setvbuf(fp, buf, _IOFBF, BUFSIZ)
```

10.3 OPERATIONS ON FILES

The operations on files functions provide facilities to remove and rename files, create temporary binary files, and generate unique file names.

10.3.1 `remove, rename`

```
int remove(const char *fname);
int rename(const char *oldname, const char *newname);
```

The function `remove` deletes the file named *fname*. Any subsequent `fopen` call to read this file fails, unless it is created anew. The function `rename` changes the name of a file from *oldname* to *newname*. Both functions return 0 when successful, and a nonzero value otherwise.

10.3.2 `tmpfile, tmpnam`

```
FILE *tmpfile(void)
char *tmpnam(char *s)
```

The function `tmpfile` creates a temporary binary file for update using the `fopen` mode `"wb+"`, and returns a file pointer to it. A null pointer is returned if the file could not be created. A temporary file can only be used during the current program's execution and is automatically removed when closed or when the program terminates normally. If the program terminates abnormally, the result is implementation-dependent. Temporary files are useful for storing the intermediate results of a computation.

The function `tmpnam` creates a new file name that does not conflict with that of any of the existing files, stores it in an internal static character array, and returns a pointer to it. If the argument *s* is not NULL, *s* must be an array of not less than L_tmpnam characters, and `tmpnam` also copies the newly created file name into *s*. At most TMP_MAX successive calls to `tmpnam` are guaranteed to generate unique names in a program. Note that `tmpnam` does not create a file; it only creates a name. A new file then can be created with that name using fopen. The file so created is not automatically removed when the program ter-minates. If tmpnam does not succeed, it returns a null pointer.

10.4 FORMATTED INPUT/OUTPUT

The formatted input/output functions allow input and output of formatted data. We introduced preliminary ideas related to scanf and printf in Section 2.8. We now discuss in detail these and other formatted input/output func-tions.

10.4.1 fscanf, scanf, sscanf

```
int fscanf(FILE *fp, const char *format, arg1, arg2, ...);
int scanf(const char *format, arg1, arg2, ...);
int sscanf(char *s, const char *format, arg1, arg2, ...);
```

The function fscanf reads characters from the stream *fp*, converts them according to the control string *format*, and assigns converted values to objects pointed to by the remaining arguments *arg1*, *arg2*, ... This function returns the number of objects that have received conversion results, or EOF if an input fail-ure occurs before any conversion. Remember that each argument *argi* must be a *pointer* to the variable where the result of input is to be stored — if you want the result to be stored in i, you must specify &i as the argument.

The function scanf is equivalent to fscanf, except that the characters are read from the standard input stdin.

The function sscanf is equivalent to fscanf, except that the characters are read from the string *s*. A read beyond the end of *s* is treated analogously to reading beyond the end-of-file.

The *control string* can be viewed as a picture of the expected form of input, with the formatted input function performing a matching operation between the control string and the input stream. The control string can contain:

i. *Whitespace characters.* Any sequence of consecutive whitespace charac-ters in the control string matches any sequence of consecutive whitespace characters in the input stream.

ii. *Conversion specifications.* A conversion specification begins with the character %, and is followed in order by an optional *assignment sup-pression character*, an optional *maximum field width specification*, an optional *size modifier*, and a required *conversion control character*. Con-version specifications usually result in assignment of values to the variables pointed to by the corresponding arguments.

iii. *Ordinary characters.* Any character other than a whitespace or % must match the next input character.

We now discuss the various components of a *conversion specification*.

The *conversion control character* determines the number of input characters read and their interpretation. The conversion control characters d, f, e, and c, and their effects have already been discussed in Section 2.8.2. The rest are described below:

i	An integer is expected in the input. The corresponding argument must be of type `int *`. The input integer may be in decimal, octal, or hexadecimal notation.
o	An octal integer (with or without a leading 0) is expected in the input. The corresponding argument must be of type `int *`.
x	A hexadecimal integer (with or without leading `0x`) is expected in the input. The corresponding argument must be of type `int *`.
u	A decimal integer is expected in the input. The corresponding argument must be of type `unsigned int *`.
g	Its effect is identical to that of `f` and `e`.
s	A character string is expected in the input. The corresponding argument must be a pointer to the first element of an array of characters large enough to hold the string and the terminating null character that gets added automatically.
p	A pointer value, written by the `%p` conversion in `fprintf`, is converted and assigned to the variable pointed to by the corresponding argument, which must be of type `void **`.
n	The number of characters read from the input so far by this call to `fscanf` is written into the variable pointed to by the corresponding argument, which must be of type `int *`. No input is read and the assignment count returned is not incremented.
%	A single character `%` is expected in the input. No conversion or assignment is made.
[...]	The longest string consisting of characters from the set between brackets is read into the corresponding argument, which must be a character array large enough to hold the string and an automatically appended terminating null character. If and only if the circumflex `^` immediately follows the initial `[`, it serves as a negation flag. In other words, the longest string of characters not from the set between brackets is then read.

The conversion control characters e, g, and x may be capitalized without changing their effects.

The *assignment suppression character* `*` is used for skipping over the input. It causes input characters to be read and processed in the usual way for the corresponding conversion control character, but no assignment is made and no pointer argument is consumed.

The *maximum field width specification*, specified as a decimal integer, limits the maximum number of characters read as the result of a conversion specification.

A *size modifier* (h, l, or L), when it precedes certain conversion control characters, alters the interpretation of the corresponding arguments as follows:

h (or l)	preceding d, i, n, o, or x implies that the corresponding argument is a pointer to `short` (or `long`) `int`, rather than a pointer to `int`.
h (or l)	preceding u implies that the corresponding argument is a pointer to `unsigned short` (or `long`) `int`, rather than a pointer to `unsigned int`.

1 (or L)   preceding e, f, or g implies that the corresponding argument is a pointer to double (or long double), rather than a pointer to float.

We now describe the execution of the fscanf function. If a failure occurs at any stage during the execution of fscanf, the function returns immediately with a nonzero value. A failure can be *input failure* due to the unavailability of input characters, or *matching failure* due to inappropriate input. The control string is scanned from left to right and the following actions take place:

- A whitespace in the control string is matched by reading input up to the first non-whitespace character which remains unread, or until no more characters can be read. Thus, a sequence of whitespaces in the control string matches the largest sequence of whitespaces (possibly of length zero) in the input stream.
- An ordinary character in the control string is matched with the next character of the input stream. If the input character is different, the character remains unread, and fscanf fails. fscanf also fails if there are no more characters in the stream.
- A conversion specification is processed in the following steps:

  i. Input whitespaces are skipped, unless the specification contains the conversion control character c, n, or [.
  ii. An item is read from the input stream as per the conversion control character in the specification (observing the maximum field width specification, if any), unless the specification contains the conversion control character n. The first character after the input item remains unread. fscanf fails if the length of the input item read is zero, or if some error prevents input from the stream.
  iii. Except in the case of the conversion control character %, the input item (or the count of input characters in the case of the conversion control character n) is converted to a type appropriate to the conversion control character in the specification. Unless assignment suppression is indicated, the result of conversion is placed in the object pointed to by the first argument following the control string that has not already received a conversion result. If this object does not have an appropriate type, or if the result of conversion cannot be represented in the space provided, the behavior is undefined.

The function fscanf returns EOF if an input failure occurs before any conversion; otherwise, it returns the number of objects that have received conversion results, which can be less than the number of arguments following the control string, or even zero, if an early conflict occurs between an input character and the control string.

Here are some examples:

The call to fscanf in

```
int i;  float f;
fscanf(stdin, "%i%f", &i, &f);
```

with the input

```
-123.456
```

assigns -123 to i and .456 to f because the decimal point terminates the integer data item being read. On the other hand, the call to fscanf in

```
int i;   float f;   short s;
fscanf(stdin, "%3i%4f%5hd", &i, &f, &s);
```

with the same input first assigns -12 to i because only 3 characters are read due to the maximum field width specification. It then assigns 3.45 to f because the maximum field width has been specified to be 4. Finally, it assigns 6 to s because the space terminates the input item although the maximum field width is 5. Note the use of the size modifier h to assign the converted value to a short variable.

The call to scanf in

```
int n;   double d;   float f;
n = scanf("%3lf %25g%50*d foo %%", &d, &f);
```

with the input

```
-12345   6789foo        %
```

processes %3lf by first reading three characters from the input and assigning -12.0 to d (the maximum field width specification limits the number of characters read and the size modifier l assigns the converted value to a double variable). It then matches the whitespace in the control string by reading up to the first non-white character, which is 3 and remains unread. Next, it processes %25g by assigning 345.0 to f (the space terminates the input item). It then processes %50*d by first skipping the two whitespace characters in the input and then reading 6789, but no assignment is made due to the assignment suppression character * (the character f in the input terminates the integer data item being read). Next, it matches the next space in the control string but no character is read because the next input character is f. Then it matches the next three ordinary characters foo in the control string with foo in the input and discards them. It now matches the next space in the control string with six spaces in the input and discards them. Next, it processes %% by reading % from the input and discarding it. Finally, it assigns 2, the number of arguments successfully read, to n.

The call to scanf in

```
char s1[10], s2[10], s3[10], c;
scanf("%s%c%1s%s", s1, &c, s2, s3);
```

with the input

```
a       bcd
```

assigns a\0 to s1, ⃥ (space) to c, b\0 to s2, and cd\0 to s3, because the specification %c does not cause whitespaces to be skipped, but %1s skips whitespaces before the input item is read. Note that the call

```
scanf("%s %c%1s%s", s1, &c, s2, s3);
```

with the same input would have assigned a\0 to s1, b to c, c\0 to s2, and d\0 to s3, because the space in the control string would have matched all the spaces between a and b in the input.

The call to `sscanf` in

```
char s1[10], s2[10], s3[10], *s = "213431^2";
sscanf(s, "%[012]%[^012]%[0^12]", s1, s2, s3);
```

reads from string s. It assigns $21\backslash 0$ to s1 because `%[012]` matches the largest string consisting of characters $0, 1$, or 2. Next, it assigns $343\backslash 0$ to s2 because `%[^012]` matches the largest string consisting of characters other than $0, 1$, or 2, as ^ immediately follows [. Finally, it assigns $1^2\backslash 0$ to s3 because `%[0^12]` matches the largest string consisting of characters $0, ^, 1$, or 2, as ^ does not immediately follow [.

The execution of the program fragment

```
int n;  float q1, q2;  char u1[16], u2[16];
while ((n = scanf("%f %15s = %f %15s",
                   &q1, u1, &q2, u2)) != EOF)
    scanf("%*[^\n]");
```

with the input

```
1 pole = 11/2 yards
one gram = 0.035 ounces
1 gallon equals 3.79 litres
1electron = 1/1837 proton
```

is equivalent to the following assignments:

```
n = 4; q1 = 1; strcpy(u1,"pole");
       q2 = 11; strcpy(u2,"/2");
n = 0; /* o fails to match %f */
n = 2; q1 = 1; strcpy(u1,"gallon");/* e fails to match =  */
n = 0; /* 1e fails to match %f */
n = EOF;
```

10.4.2 `fprintf`, `printf`, `sprintf`, `vfprintf`, `vprintf`, `vsprintf`

```
int fprintf(FILE *fp, const char *format, arg1, arg2, ...);
int printf(const char *format, arg1, arg2, ...);
int sprintf(char *s, const char *format, arg1, arg2, ...);
int vfprintf(FILE *file, const char *format, va_list arg);
int vprintf(const char *format, va_list arg);
int vsprintf(char *s, const char *format, va_list arg);
```

The function `fprintf` converts *arg1, arg2, . . .* according to the control string *format*, writes them to the stream *fp*, and returns the number of characters written. A negative value is returned in the event of an output error.

The function `printf` is equivalent to `fprintf`, except that the output is written to the standard output `stdout`.

The function `sprintf` is equivalent to `fprintf`, except that the output is written to the array *s*. A null character is automatically written at the end of the output, but the return count does not include this terminating null character. It is the programmer's responsibility to ensure that *s* is large enough to hold the output.

The last three functions, vfprintf, vprintf and vsprintf, are equivalent to fprintf, printf, and sprintf respectively, except that the arguments *arg1, arg2, . . .* are specified in a variable argument list *arg*. These functions are useful for defining functions that take a variable number of arguments and write formatted output. The variable argument facility is discussed in Chapter 12.

The *control string* is the text to be copied verbatim to the output stream, except that it may also contain *conversion specifications* that cause successive arguments to be converted, resulting in output characters not explicitly contained in the string.

A *conversion specification* begins with the character %, and is followed in order by zero or more *flag characters*, an optional *minimum field width specification*, an optional *precision specification*, an optional *size modifier*, and a required *conversion control character*. We now discuss the various components of a conversion specification.

The *conversion control character* controls the conversion operation. The conversion control characters d, i, f, e, c, and s and their effects have already been discussed in Section 2.8.1. The rest are described below:

u, o, x	The integer argument is converted to unsigned decimal, unsigned octal, or unsigned hexadecimal notation respectively. A number in the octal notation is printed without the leading 0, and in the hexadecimal notation without the leading 0x.
g	The float or double argument is converted into style f or e, depending on the value converted; style e is used only if the resulting exponent is less than –4 or greater than or equal to the precision (the number of significant digits to be printed), which by default is 6. Trailing zeros are removed from the fractional part; a decimal point appears only if it is followed by a digit.
p	The argument, a pointer to void, is converted to an implementation-dependent sequence of printable characters.
n	The number of characters written to the output stream so far by this call to fprintf is written into the argument, which must be of type int *.
%	A single character % is written to the output stream. No argument is consumed.

The conversion control characters e, g, and x may be capitalized. The E conversion produces numbers with E instead of e introducing the exponent, the G conversion produces numbers in style E, and the X conversion produces hexadecimal numbers using the letters ABCDEF instead of abcdef.

The *flag characters* modify the meaning of the conversion specification as follows:

–	The result of conversion is left-justified within the field width, rather than right-justified.
+	The result of a signed conversion always begins with a sign; normally, a sign is printed only if the value is negative.

ƀ (*space*)   If the first character of a signed conversion is not a sign, a space is prefixed to the result.

0   For numeric conversions, leading zeros, rather than spaces, are used for padding to the field width.

The result is converted to an "alternate" output form. For o conversion, the precision is increased to force the first digit of the result to be a 0. For x conversion, a nonzero result is prefixed with 0x. For e, f, and g conversions, the output always has a decimal point character even when no digit follows the decimal; for g, trailing zeros are not removed from the result.

The *minimum field width*, specified as a decimal integer, causes the converted argument to be written to the output stream in a field of the specified size, and wider if necessary. If the converted value has fewer characters than the minimum field width, the field is padded on the left (or right, if the – flag is present) to make up the field width. The padding character is a space, unless modified by the 0 flag.

The *precision* is specified as a period (.) followed by an optional decimal integer, which is treated as 0 if omitted. The precision determines, for conversion control characters,

d,i,o,u,x   the minimum number of digits to be written (leading zeros are added, if necessary). With 0 precision, a zero value results in no characters in output.

e,f   the number of digits to be written after the decimal point (the value is rounded). With 0 precision, the decimal point is not written to output.

g   the maximum number of significant digits to be written (leading zeros do not count). If precision has been specified to be 0, it is taken as 1.

s   the maximum number of characters to be written from a string.

A minimum field width or precision may be specified by an asterisk (*), instead of an integer, in which case their values are computed by converting arguments. The arguments must be of type int and are consumed.

A *size modifier* (h, l, or L), when it precedes certain conversion control characters, alters the interpretation of the corresponding argument as follows:

h (or l)   preceding d, i, o, or x implies that the conversion applies to a short (or long) int argument.

h (or l)   preceding u implies that the conversion applies to an unsigned short (or long) int argument.

h (or l)   preceding n implies that the conversion applies to a pointer to a short (or long) int argument.

L   preceding e, f, or g implies that the conversion applies to a long double argument.

Here are some examples:
The statement

```
printf("%g %G %G %g\n",
        999999.0, 1000000.0, .0001, .00001);
```

prints

```
999999 1E+06 0.0001 1e-05
```

because the g (or G) conversion uses the style e (or E) only if the resulting exponent is greater than or equal to precision (6 by default) or less than –4.

The statement

```
printf("%g %g %g %g %g\n",
       2/2.0, 2/3.0, 2/4.0, 4/3.0, 0);
```

prints

```
1 0.666667 0.5 1.33333 0
```

because the g conversion removes trailing blanks from the fractional part, removes the decimal point if not followed by a digit, and prints, by default, at most six digits (leading zeros do not count) of the rounded value.

The statement

```
printf("{%d} {%.2d} {%.0d} {%.d}\n", 0, 0, 0, 0);
```

prints

```
{0} {00} {} {}
```

because the precision specifies for d conversions the minimum number of digits to be printed, but no digits are printed when the precision has been specified to be 0 or omitted and the value to be printed is zero.

The statement

```
printf("{%d} {%3d} {%-3d} {%03d} {%3.2d} {%3.0d}\n",
       0, 0, 0, 0, 0, 0);
```

prints

```
{0} {  0} {0  } {000} { 00} {   }
```

because the minimum field width specifies the minimum size in which the value must be printed. The – flag causes the value to be left-justified within the field and the 0 flag makes zero the padding character.

The statements

```
char *s = "snare";
printf("{%4s}    {%-4s}    {%.4s}    {%-.4s}\n",
       s, s, s, s);
printf("{%6s}    {%-6s}    {%.6s}    {%-.6s}\n",
       s, s, s, s);
printf("{%6.4s}    {%-6.4s}    {%4.6s}    {%-4.6s}\n",
       s, s, s, s);
```

print

```
{snare}    {snare}    {snar}    {snar}
{ snare}   {snare }   {snare}   {snare}
{  snar}   {snar  }   {snare}   {snare}
```

because the precision specifies for s conversions the maximum number of characters to be printed from the string, the minimum field width specifies the minimum size in which the string must be printed, and the – flag causes the string to be left-justified.

The statements

```
printf("{%4.0f} %.1f %.2f %.5f\n",
        1/3.0, 1/3.0, 1/3.0, 1/3.0, 1/3.0);
printf("{%4.0e} %.1e %.2e %.5e\n",
        1/3.0, 1/3.0, 1/3.0, 1/3.0, 1/3.0);
printf("{%4.0g} %.1g %.2g %.5g\n",
        1/3.0, 1/3.0, 1/3.0, 1/3.0, 1/3.0);
```

print

```
{   0} 0.3 0.33 0.33333
{3e-01} 3.3e-01 3.33e-01 3.33333e-01
{ 0.3} 0.3 0.33 0.33333
```

because the precision specifies the number of digits to be printed after the decimal point for f and e conversions, but the maximum number of significant digits to be printed (not counting the leading zeros) for g conversions. With 0 precision, the decimal point is not printed for f and e conversions, but the precision is taken as 1 for g conversions.

The statements

```
float f;
for (f = 1; f >= -1; f--)
    printf("% E  %+e  %E\n", f, f, f);
```

print

```
 1.000000E+00   +1.000000e+00   1.000000E+00
 0.000000E+00   +0.000000e+00   0.000000E+00
-1.000000E+00   -1.000000e+00  -1.000000E+00
```

because the space flag causes a space and the + flag a + to be prefixed before a positive value.

The statements

```
long lg;
for (lg = 0;  lg <= 10; lg += 10)
    printf("0%lo %#lo 0X%lX %#lX\n", lg, lg, lg, lg);
```

print

```
  00 0 0X0 0
  012 012 0XA 0XA
```

because the # flag forces the first digit to be 0 for o conversions and a nonzero result to be prefixed with 0X for X conversions. The size modifier l has been used to specify that the corresponding arguments are long integers. This example also illustrates that the effect of the # flag is not the same as prefixing the conversion specification with ordinary characters 0 or 0X inside the control string.

The statement

```
printf("%f %.0f %#.0f %g %#g\n",
       1.0, 1.0, 1.0, 1.0, 1.0);
```

prints

```
1.000000 1 1. 1 1.00000
```

because the # flag forces the decimal point to be printed for f and g conversions even when no digit follows the decimal, and forces trailing zeros to be retained for g conversions.

The statement

```
printf("%06.1f %0*.*f\n", -1.55, 6, 0, -1.55);
```

prints

```
-001.6 -00002
```

because the 0 flag alters the padding character to zero, the asterisks for the minimum field width and precision specifications cause their values to be computed by converting arguments, making the second specification %06.0f, and 0 precision for the f conversion causes the rounded value of the next argument to be printed without a decimal point.

Finally, the statements

```
int nchars;
printf("%%n has been added by ANSI C\n%n", &nchars);
```

print

```
%n has been added by ANSI C
```

and sets nchars to 28, because the % conversion causes % to be printed and the n conversion causes the number of characters printed so far to be assigned to the next argument. Note that the argument corresponding to the %n specification must be a pointer to an integer.

10.5 CHARACTER INPUT/OUTPUT

The character input/output functions provide facilities for reading and writing characters and strings of characters.

10.5.1 fgetc, getc, getchar, ungetc

```
int fgetc(FILE *fp);
int getc(FILE *fp);
int getchar(void);
int ungetc(int c, FILE *fp);
```

The function fgetc reads as unsigned char a character from the stream *fp* and returns it as a value of type int. Successive calls to fgetc return successive characters from the specified stream, until an error occurs or the end-of-file is reached, in which case `fgetc` returns `EOF`.

The function `getc` behaves like `fgetc`, except that it is usually implemented as a macro for efficiency. When implemented as a macro, its argument may be evaluated more than once, and hence should not have side effects.

The function `getchar` is identical to `getc` with argument `stdin`.

The function `ungetc` pushes the character specified by c (converted to an `unsigned char`) back to the stream *fp*. The same character will be returned by a subsequent read from that stream. A pushed-back character is not actually written to the stream but is only placed in the buffer associated with the stream. A file positioning operation (`fseek`, `fsetpos`, or `rewind`) discards the pushed-back character. Only one character of pushback is guaranteed; more than one call to `ungetc` on the same stream without an intervening read or file positioning operation on that stream may cause `ungetc` to fail. `EOF` may not be pushed back. When successful, `ungetc` returns the character pushed back, and `EOF` otherwise. `ungetc` is useful for implementing input scanning operations like `scanf`. A program can peek ahead at the next input character by reading it, and push it back if not found suitable.

Note that the value returned by these functions is that of type `int`, and not `char`. The reason for it has to do with detecting the end of input. When the end of input is reached, these functions return `EOF`, the conventional value for which is -1. Since C does not require that a `char` be able to hold a signed quantity, these functions are made to return an `int`. For the same reason, if the value returned by any of these functions is to be assigned to some variable, then this variable should be declared to be of type `int`.

10.5.2 `fgets`, `gets`

```
char *fgets(char *s, int n, FILE *fp);
char *gets(char *s);
```

The function `fgets` reads characters from the stream *fp* into the character array *s* until a newline character is read (which is retained), or end-of-file is reached, or *n*-1 characters have been read. It then appends a terminating null character after the last character read, and returns *s*. If end-of-file occurs before reading any character or an error occurs during input, `fgets` returns `NULL`.

The function `gets` reads characters from the standard input `stdin` into the character array *s* until a newline character is read or end-of-file is reached. It is the programmer's responsibility to ensure that *s* is large enough to accommodate the largest line in input. Unlike `fgets`, `gets` discards the newline character, but, like `fgets`, appends a terminating null character after the last character and returns *s*. If an error occurs during input, or if no characters are read, a `NULL` is returned.

You should use `gets` with utmost discretion. Since array bounds are not checked in C, if there is a line in input larger than *s*, `gets` will go beyond *s* and corrupt your program.

10.5.3 `fputc, putc, putchar`

```
int fputc(int c, FILE *fp);
int putc(int c, FILE *fp);
int putchar(int c);
```

The function `fputc` writes the character specified by c (converted to an unsigned `char`) to the stream fp, and also returns this character as a value of type `int`. Successive calls to `fputc` write successive given characters to the specified stream, unless an error occurs, in which case `fputc` returns `EOF`.

The function `putc` behaves like `fputc`, except that it is usually implemented as a macro for efficiency. When implemented as a macro, its argument may be evaluated more than once, and hence the argument should not have side effects.

The function `putchar` is identical to `putc` with argument `stdout`.

10.5.4 `fputs, puts`

```
int fputs(const char *s, FILE *fp);
int puts(const char *s);
```

The function `fputs` writes to the stream fp all but the terminating null character of string s. It returns `EOF` if an error occurs during output; otherwise, it returns a nonnegative value.

The function `puts` is identical to `fputs`, except that it writes to the standard output `stdout` and appends a newline character immediately after the characters written from s irrespective of whether or not s already contains the newline character.

10.6 DIRECT INPUT/OUTPUT

Direct input/output functions provide facilities to read and write a certain number of data items of specified size.

10.6.1 `fread, fwrite`

```
size_t fread(void *s, size_t sz, size_t n, FILE *fp);
size_t fwrite(const void *s, size_t sz,
              size_t n, FILE *fp);
```

The function `fread` reads into array s up to n data·items of size sz from the binary stream fp, and returns the number of items read. The return value may be less than n if a read error or end-of-file is encountered. The file position indicator is advanced by the number of characters successfully read. For example, assuming 4-byte integers, the statement

```
rchar = fread(buf, sizeof(int), 20, input);
```

reads 80 characters from `input` into the array `buf` and assigns 80 to `rchar`, unless an error or end-of-file occurs.

The function `fwrite` writes *n* items, each of size *sz*, from the array *s* into the stream *fp*, and returns the number of items written, which may be less than *n* if an output error occurs. The file position indicator is advanced by the number of characters successfully written. For example, the statement

```
wchar = fwrite(buf, sizeof(char), 80, output);
```

writes 80 characters from the array `buf` to `output`, advances the file position indicator for `output` by 80 bytes, and assigns 80 to `wchar`, unless an error or end-of-file occurs.

10.7 FILE POSITIONING

A file may be accessed *sequentially* or *randomly*. In a sequential access, all the preceding data is accessed before accessing a specific portion of a file. Random access permits direct access to a specific portion of a file. The file positioning functions provide facilities for realizing random access.

10.7.1 `fseek, ftell, rewind`

```
int    fseek(FILE *fp, long offset, int whence);
long   ftell(FILE *fp);
void   rewind(FILE *fp);
```

The function `fseek` sets the file position indicator associated with the stream *fp* to a value that is *offset* bytes from the beginning, the current position, or the end of the corresponding file, according as *whence* is SEEK_SET, SEEK_CUR or SEEK_END respectively. The function returns 0 when successful, and a nonzero value otherwise. Here are some examples of calls to `fseek` and their effect on the file position indicator:

```
fseek(fp, 0L, SEEK_SET)    /* sets to the beginning of the file */
fseek(fp, 0L, SEEK_END)    /* sets to the end of the file */
fseek(fp, n, SEEK_SET)     /* sets to the nth byte in the file */
fseek(fp, n, SEEK_CUR)     /* sets ahead by n bytes */
fseek(fp, -n, SEEK_CUR)    /* sets back by n bytes */
fseek(fp, -n, SEEK_END)    /* sets to the nth byte
                              before the end of the file */
```

The function `ftell` returns the current value of the file position indicator associated with the stream *fp*. On failure, `ftell` returns -1L.

The function `rewind` resets the current value of the file position indicator associated with the stream *fp* to the beginning of the file. The call

```
rewind(fp);
```

has the same effect as

```
(void) fseek(fp, 0L, SEEK_SET);
```

The use of `rewind` allows a program to read through a file more than once without having to close and open the file.

10.7.2 `fgetpos`, `fsetpos`

```
int fgetpos(FILE *fp, fpos_t *pos);
int fsetpos(FILE *fp, fpos_t *pos);
```

The function `fgetpos` stores the current value of the file position indicator associated with the stream *fp* in the object pointed to by *pos*.

The function `fsetpos` sets the file position indicator associated with the stream *fp* to the value stored in the object pointed to by *pos*.

Both functions return 0 when successful, and nonzero values otherwise.

10.8 ERROR HANDLING

The error handling functions provide facilities to test whether EOF returned by a function indicates an end-of-file or an error, to clear the end-of-file and error indicators, and to map the error number `errno` to an error message.

10.8.1 `feof`, `ferror`, `clearerr`, `perror`

```
int  feof(FILE *fp);
int  ferror(FILE *fp);
void clearerr(FILE *fp);
void perror(const char *s);
```

The function `feof` returns a nonzero value if the end-of-file indicator is set for the stream *fp*, and 0 otherwise. A call to `feof` does not reset the end-of-file indicator.

The function `ferror` returns a nonzero value if the error indicator is set for the stream *fp*, and 0 otherwise. Once an error has occurred for a file, repeated calls to `ferror` continue to return nonzero values unless the error indication is reset by calling `clearerr` or closing the file.

The function `clearerr` clears the end-of-file and error indicators for the stream *fp*.

The function `perror` writes to the standard error output `stderr` the string *s* followed by a colon and a space and then an implementation-defined error message corresponding to the integer in `errno`, terminated by a newline character.

10.9 ILLUSTRATIVE EXAMPLES

We now give some example programs to illustrate the file processing facilities in C.

Example 1

Mega Micros pays commission c to its salespersons as a multiple f of sales s in excess of quota q, that is,

$$c = f(s - q).$$

If quota is not met, no commission is paid. Write a program to print the sales commission report.

The report is to be printed in the following form:

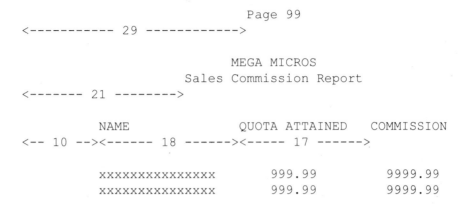

```
                                   Page 99
<----------- 29 ------------>


                         MEGA MICROS
                  Sales Commission Report
<------- 21 -------->


          NAME              QUOTA ATTAINED   COMMISSION
<-- 10 --><------ 18 ------><----- 17 ------>


        xxxxxxxxxxxxxxx         999.99         9999.99
        xxxxxxxxxxxxxxx         999.99         9999.99
```

The report headers are printed on every page, and each page contains information for 25 salespersons. The input data is available in the following form:

Columns	Contents
1-15	Name
16-19	Multiplier
20-26	Quota
27-33	Actual Sales

This example exhibits an alternate way of specifying input and output formats. Although not as convenient as using the layout sheets illustrated in Figures 1.3 and 1.4, these forms are helpful if the layout sheets are not available.

The desired program is as follows:

```c
#include <stdio.h>
#define   MAXLINES   25
#define   SPACE      " "

int process(char *progname, FILE *inp, FILE *out);
void pagehdr(FILE *out, int pageno);

int main(int argc, char *argv[])
  {
    int status;
    FILE *inp = stdin;  /* default input */
    FILE *out = stdout; /* default output */
```

```
    if (argc != 3 && argc != 1)
      {
        fprintf(stderr,
          "Usage: %s [<input> <output>]\n", argv[0]);
        return 1;
      }
    else if (argc == 3)
      {
        if ((inp = fopen(argv[1], "r")) == NULL)
          {
            fprintf(stderr,"%s: couldn't open %s\n",
                          argv[0],argv[1]);
            return 1;
          }
        if ((out = fopen(argv[2], "w")) == NULL)
          {
            fprintf(stderr,"%s: couldn't open %s\n",
                          argv[0],argv[2]);
            fclose(inp);
            return 1;
          }
      }

    status = process(argv[0], inp, out);

    if (argc == 3) { fclose(inp); fclose(out); }

    return status;
  }

int process(char *progname, FILE *inp, FILE *out)
  {
    int pageno = 0, linecnt = 0;
    float multiplier, quota, sales;
    char name[16];

    while (fscanf(inp,"%15s%4f%7f%7f", name,
            &multiplier, &quota, &sales) != EOF)
      {
        if (linecnt++ % MAXLINES == 0)
            pagehdr(out, ++pageno);

        fprintf(out,"%10s%-15s%7s%6.2f%9s%7.2f\n",
            SPACE, name, SPACE,
            (sales / quota) * 100, SPACE,
            sales > quota ?
            multiplier * (sales - quota) : 0);
      }
```

```
      if (ferror(inp))
        {
          fprintf(stderr, "%s: error in reading input\n",
                              progname);
          return 1;
        }
      else
          return 0;
    }

void pagehdr(FILE *out, int pageno)
    {
      fprintf(out,"\f%29sPage %2d\n\n\n", SPACE, pageno);
      fprintf(out,"%27sMEGA MICROS\n", SPACE);
      fprintf(out,"%21sSales Commission Report\n\n\n",
                    SPACE);
      fprintf(out,"%10sNAME%14sQUOTA ATTAINED"
                  "%3sCOMMISSION\n\n",
                    SPACE, SPACE, SPACE);
    }
```

The program accepts the names of input and output files as command line arguments and opens them in read and write mode respectively. The value returned by fopen is checked for possible errors and the program execution is terminated if an error is found. If both input and output file names are not specified, they are assumed to be standard input and output respectively.

The function process prints one line of output for each data line. It uses two counters: pageno keeps track of the current page number and linecnt counts the number of data lines printed. When the maximum permissible data lines MAXLINES have been printed on a page, the page counter is incremented and the report headers are printed on a new page by the function pagehdr.

At the end of the while loop, it is checked whether the loop was exited due to end of input or because of some input error. The error messages have been written to stderr to keep them separate from output, and the name of the program is included in the message to identify the source of error when the program is used with other programs.

We will not check the values returned by input/output functions in future programs in order to keep them concise and emphasize the major points being illustrated, but robust production-quality programs must always include extensive error checking.

Example 2
Write a program that compares two text files and prints the lines where they first differ.

The desired program is as follows:

```c
#include <stdio.h>
#include <string.h>
#define  MAXLINE 256
#define  MAXNAME 15

void compare(char *fn1, FILE *fp1,
             char *fn2, FILE *fp2, FILE *out);

int main(int argc, char *argv[])
  {
    FILE *fp1, *fp2;

    if (argc < 3)
      {
        fprintf(stderr,
          "Usage: %s <file1> <file2>\n", argv[0]);
        return 1;
      }

    fp1 = fopen(argv[1], "r");   /* open file1 */
    fp2 = fopen(argv[2], "r");   /* open file2 */

    compare(argv[1], fp1, argv[2], fp2, stdout);

    fclose(fp1); fclose(fp2);
    return 0;
  }

void compare(char *fn1, FILE *fp1,
             char *fn2, FILE *fp2, FILE *out)
  {
    char line1[MAXLINE], line2[MAXLINE];
    char *pline1 = line1, *pline2 = line2;
    int lineno;

    for (lineno = 1; ; lineno++)
      {
        pline1 = fgets(line1, MAXLINE, fp1);
        pline2 = fgets(line2, MAXLINE, fp2);

        if (!pline1 && !pline2)
          {
            fprintf(out,"%s and %s are identical\n",
                        fn1, fn2);
            return;
          }
```

```
      else if (pline1 && !pline2)
        {
          fprintf(out,"Files differ at line %d\n",
                          lineno);
          fprintf(out,"%*s: %s",
                          MAXNAME, fn1, line1);
          fprintf(out,"%s exhausted\n", fn2);
          return;
        }
      else if (!pline1 && pline2)
        {
          fprintf(out,"Files differ at line %d\n",
                          lineno);
          fprintf(out,"%s exhausted\n", fn1);
          fprintf(out,"%*s: %s",
                          MAXNAME, fn2, line2);
          return;
        }
      else if (strcmp(line1, line2) != 0)
        {
          fprintf(out,"Files differ at line %d\n",
                          lineno);
          fprintf(out,"%*s: %s",
                          MAXNAME, fn1, line1);
          fprintf(out,"%*s: %s",
                          MAXNAME, fn2, line2);
          return;
        }
    }
}
```

The program reads one line each from two files until a differing line is found or one of the files is exhausted, in which case the line read from the other file is the first differing line. If both the files are exhausted simultaneously and no differing line has been found, the two files are identical.

The use of `*` in the minimum field width specification in the `fprintf` statements causes the minimum field width to be determined by the argument `MAXNAME` and avoids embedding integer constants in the control string. We could not have written the conversion specification as

```
%MAXNAMEs
```

since the preprocessor does not reach inside strings.

We have used the function `fgets` for reading lines. Therefore, if there are lines in the files that are longer than `MAXLINE`, the line count will not be correct, although the program will correctly detect the first differing lines. An alternative solution is to read files one character at a time, keeping track of line boundaries. Rewrite the `compare` function using this approach.

Example 3
Write a program to append a file to another file.

The desired program is as follows:

```c
#include <stdio.h>

void append(char *destination, char *addendum);

int main(int argc, char *argv[])
  {
    char *tfile;

    if (argc != 3)
      {
        fprintf(stderr,
          "Usage: %s <file-1> <file-2>\n", argv[0]);
        return 1;
      }

    /* obtain a unique name for a temporary file */
    tfile = tmpnam(NULL);

    /* create and copy the first file to the temporary file */
    append(tfile, argv[1]);
    /* append the second file to the temporary file */
    append(tfile, argv[2]);

    /* remove the first file */
    remove(argv[1]);
    /* rename the temporary file as the first file */
    rename(tfile, argv[1]);

    return 0;
  }

void append(char *fn1, char *fn2)
  {
    FILE *fp1, *fp2;
    int c;

    /* open the first file in the append mode */
    fp1 = fopen(fn1, "a");
    /* open the second file in the read mode */
    fp2 = fopen(fn2, "r");

    /* append */
    while ((c = getc(fp2)) != EOF)  putc(c, fp1);

    fclose(fp1); fclose(fp2);
  }
```

We create a temporary file, copy the first file into it, and then append the second file to the temporary file. The first file is now removed and the temporary file is renamed as the first file. Note that tmpnam does not create the temporary file but only generates a unique file name; the file is created when fopen is called the first time with this name in the append mode.

The advantage of this approach over directly appending the second file to the first is that the processing may be aborted without clobbering the first file if an error occurs during the append. Add error checks in the preceding program to provide this feature.

Example 4
Write a program that extracts the specified lines from a text file.

To efficiently extract the requested lines, which may be specified in any order, we first build an index for the file. This index is created in a temporary file by making one pass over the input file and contains the starting position of every line. Now, given a line number, its starting position can be determined by a look-up in the index file, and the requested line can be directly accessed without accessing any of the preceding lines. The desired program is as follows:

```c
#include <stdio.h>
#define  MAXLINE  256

void mkidx(FILE *inpf, FILE *idxf);
void mkout(FILE *inpf, FILE *outf, FILE *idxf);

int main(int argc, char *argv[])
  {
    FILE *inpf, *outf, *idxf;

    if (argc != 3)
      {
        fprintf(stderr,
          "Usage: %s <infile> <outfile>\n", argv[0]);
        return 1;
      }

    inpf = fopen(argv[1], "r"); /* input file */
    outf = fopen(argv[2], "w"); /* output file */
    idxf = tmpfile();           /* index file */

    mkidx(inpf, idxf);          /* make indices */
    mkout(inpf, outf, idxf);    /* create output file */

    fclose(inpf); fclose(outf);
    return 0;
  }
```

```c
void mkidx(FILE *inpf, FILE *idxf)
  {
    long lines = 0, pos = 0;
    int c;

    /* leave slot for the total number of lines */
    fseek(idxf, (long)sizeof(long), SEEK_SET);
    /* write index of the first line */
    fwrite((char *)&pos, sizeof(long), 1, idxf);

    for (++pos; (c = getc(inpf)) != EOF; ++pos)
        if (c == '\n')
          {
            lines++;
            /* write index of the next line */
            fwrite((char *)&pos,sizeof(long),1,idxf);
          }

    /* fill in total lines in the slot left empty at the beginning
       of the file */
    rewind(idxf);
    fwrite((char *)&lines, sizeof(long), 1, idxf);
  }

void mkout(FILE *inpf, FILE *outf, FILE *idxf)
  {
    long totlines, lineno, spos, epos;
    char buf[MAXLINE];

    rewind(idxf);
    /* determine the total number of lines */
    fread((char *)&totlines, sizeof(long), 1, idxf);

    while (scanf("%ld", &lineno) != EOF)
      {
        if (lineno <= 0 || lineno > totlines)
            continue;

        /* seek to the index for this line */
        fseek(idxf, lineno*sizeof(long), SEEK_SET);
        /* determine the start of this line */
        fread((char *)&spos, sizeof(long), 1, idxf);
        /* determine the start of the next line */
        fread((char *)&epos, sizeof(long), 1, idxf);

        /* seek to the start of the line in the input file */
        fseek(inpf, spos, SEEK_SET);
        /* read the line */
        fread((char *)buf, 1, epos-spos, inpf);
        /* write it out */
        fwrite((char *)buf, 1, epos-spos, outf);
      }
  }
```

The index file can be viewed as an array of `long` integers. We store in the first entry the total number of lines in the input file to ensure that the requested line is not out of bounds. The function `mkidx` initially leaves this entry blank by moving forward the file position indicator by the size of `long`. After the index entries have been created for all the lines, `mkidx` rewinds the index file and writes the total of the number of lines in this entry.

The function `mkout` uses the index file created by the function `mkidx` to extract the desired lines. Given a line number, `mkout` seeks to the entry in the index file where the starting position of the line is stored and reads the starting position. This read automatically advances the file position indicator in the index file to the entry where the starting position of the next line is stored. A read of this position gives the number of characters in the requested line. `mkout` now seeks to the starting position of the requested line in the input file, reads it into an internal buffer (how would you modify the program to handle lines that may be longer than `MAXLINE`?), and writes it to the output file.

Instead of making a separate pass over the input file to create index entries, the index file can be created on the fly. If a line does not already have an index entry when it is requested for the first time, we can create index entries corresponding to the part of the input file preceding this line. How would you incorporate this feature in the preceding program?

We used a temporary file for storing indices to illustrate the handling of temporary files. In many applications, particularly database systems, indices are created in permanent files and maintained along with the data files.

Example 5
Write functions to save a linked list in a file and reconstruct it.

The nodes of the linked list have the following structure:

```
struct node
  {
    char *info;
    struct node *next;
  };
```

`info` points to a character array that contains data for the node as a null-terminated string. The following function accepts the head of the linked list and the file pointer to the output file opened in the write mode as arguments, traverses nodes of the list, and writes data strings including the terminating null character to the output file:

```
void savelist(struct node *lp, FILE *fp)
  {
    for ( ; lp; lp = lp ->next)
        fwrite(lp->info, strlen(lp->info)+1, 1, fp);
  }
```

The following function takes as its argument the file pointer to the file opened in the read mode in which the data for the linked list has been saved, reconstructs the list, and returns the head of the list as its value:

```
struct node *mklist(FILE *fp)
  {
    struct node *head = NULL, *lp, *np;
    fpos_t pos;
    int len;

    for (fgetpos(fp, &pos); getc(fp) != EOF;
         fgetpos(fp, &pos))
      {
        /* determine the length of the data string */
        for (len = 1; getc(fp); len++)
            ;

        /* reset file position indicator to beginning of string */
        fsetpos(fp, &pos);

        /* create new node */
        np = (struct node *)malloc(sizeof(struct node));
        np->info = (char *)malloc(len);
        fread(np->info, sizeof(char), len, fp);
        np->next = NULL;

        /* link it */
        if (!head)
            head = lp = np;
        else
          {
            lp->next = np;
            lp = np;
          }
      }
    return head;
  }
```

For each node, the function first records in `pos` the position in the file at which the data string for the node begins. It then determines the length of the string by reading one character at a time from the file till the terminating null character has been found. The file position indicator is advanced in this process, and hence it is reset to the beginning of the data string using the value saved in `pos`. Memory space is then allocated for the node and the array to store the data string, and the data string is read from the file into this array. Finally, the node is attached to the linked list built so far.

Note that `mklist` makes two passes over every data string — once to determine its length and then to read it. How would you avoid this inefficiency without placing arbitrary restrictions on the length of the string? Also add suitable error checks in `mklist`. Finally, how would you write `mklist` using `ftell` and `fseek`, instead of `fgetpos` and `fsetpos`?

Exercises 10

1. Given the declarations

   ```
   int n; long l1; float f1, f2; double d1, d2;
   char c1, c2, s1[20], s2[20], s3[20], s4[20];
   ```

   and the data line

   ```
   -12e3-4.567 12^3  %%a
   ```

   what values are assigned by each of the following statements:

   a. ```
   n = scanf("%lE %20lf%g %[1^2] %ld% %[% b] %*[^\n]",
             &d1, &d2, &f1, s1, &l1, s2);
   ```

   *b.* ```
   n = scanf("%2lg %*[^3] %20f %[^ ]%1s "
             "%s%c %c %%%s %*[^\n]",
             &d1, &f1, s1, s2, s3, &c1, &c2, s4);
   ```

   c. ```
   n = scanf("%f %e 12^3 %% %% %c %*[^\n]",
             &f1, &f2, &c1);
   ```

2. Given

   ```
   double x = 5.5;
   char *s1 = "%%risky%%", *s2 = "%*disaster*%";
   ```

   what is printed by each of the following statements:

   a. `printf(s1); printf("%s", s1);`

   b. `printf(s2); printf("%s", s2);`

   c. `printf("%u %o %x\n", -1, -1, -1);`

   d. `printf("%-5%%.4d/%.2d/%.2d%5%\n", 2000, 1, 1);`

   e. ```
   printf("|%-*s %-.*s %-*.*s|\n",
          5, s1, 5, s1, 5, 5, s1);
   ```

   f. ```
   printf("|%d % d %+d %6d %.3d %06d "
          "%#d %#6d %#6.3d %#-6d|\n",
          -1, -1, -1, -1, -1, -1, -1, -1, -1, -1);
   ```

   *g.* ```
   printf("|%o %6o %.3o %06o %#o %#6o %#6.3o %#-6o|\n",
          7, 7, 7, 7, 7, 7, 7, 7);
   ```

   h. ```
   printf("|%X %6x %.3x %06x %#x %#6x %#6.3x %#-6X|\n",
          11, 11, 11, 11, 11, 11, 11, 11);
   ```

   *i.* `printf("|% f %+f %.3f %.0f %#.0f|\n", x, x, x, x, x);`

   *j.* `printf("|% e %+e %.3e %.0e %#.0e|\n", x, x, x, x, x);`

   *k.* ```
   printf("|% g %+g %.0g %#g %#.3g %#.0g|\n",
          x, x, x, x, x, x);
   ```

3. Write a program that draws a square and its diagonals using asterisks.

4. Write a program that prints your name in large letters composed of asterisks.

5. Write a program that reads a file containing a C program and writes it to another file stripping out all comments.

6. Write a program that prints itself.

7. Write a program to generate personalized junk mail. The program works with a text file containing the letter in which the location of the recipient's *name* is indicated by the string *name*. The program obtains the name from the user and then makes a

copy of the letter into another file with the user-specified name inserted where indicated.

8. Write a program to produce a report that shows the status of user accounts in the following format:

```
                    ZAP   REPORT
                    dd/mm/yy


    USER NAME       USER-ID     LIMIT       USED
    ---------       -------     -------     --------


      AMAR          10001       2000        1200.57
      AKBAR         10002       3000        2850.89  ***
      ANTHONY       10003       2500        2501.02  ###
```

where the three asterisks (***) indicate that the user has already used 90% or more of the resources allocated, and the three sharps (###) indicate that the user has exceeded the quota and will be zapped within a week. The first data line has the date in the form *yymmdd*, and the rest have the data recorded in the following format:

Columns	Contents
1-8	Name
9-10	Blank
11-15	ID
16-19	Resource Limit
20-23	Blank
24-30	Resources Used

9. Write a simple *text formatter* to format raw text into pages of specified size, say 55 lines of 60 characters each. The text in each line should be adjusted both on left and right margins by including the maximum possible words in a line and adding extra blanks between the words. Two slashes (//) at the start of a sentence in the raw text mark the beginning of a new paragraph. The formatter should also print the title of the text and a page number at the top of each page.

10. Two files contain records sorted on the same key. Write a program to merge these files to produce a file also sorted on the same key.

11. An employee data file is kept sorted on employee name and contains, besides other information, the name of the department in which the employee works. Write a program that prints the names of the employees in each department by creating a temporary file for each department containing names of the employees in that department, and then printing the files.

12. The previous problem would be more frequently tackled by first sorting the employee file on department name, and then printing the sorted file. Sorting programs that we considered in Chapter 6 are appropriate when data is sufficiently small to fit in the main memory, and are often referred to as *internal* sort programs. To sort a large amount of data, *external* sort programs are used. A simple but often used procedure for external sorting divides the file into small subfiles, and each subfile is sorted separately using an internal sort method. The sorted subfiles are then merged into one sorted file by repeatedly merging them in a balanced manner. If there are four subfiles F1, F2, F3, and F4, first F1 is merged with F2, and F3 with F4,

and then their output is merged. Write an external sort function, and use it for solving the previous problem.

13. Student grades in the C course are determined by the scores in five programming assignments, a midterm, and a final examination. Write a program that creates, corrects, and adds to a file of student scores. The file should have one record for each student. Each record should be of fixed length and should have fields for student ID, student name, and scores in programs and examinations. Initially, records will have values only in student ID and name fields, and the remaining fields will be blank. Scores will be added to the appropriate fields when the scores of all students become available after a program or an exam has been graded. Sometimes, corrections may have to be made after the original score has been recorded.

14. In a batch-oriented inventory control system, transactions for the day are collected in a transaction file, and the master inventory file is then updated using this transaction file at the end of the day. There are four types of transactions: addition of a new item, deletion of an item, withdrawal (possibly more than one) for an item, and deposit (possibly more than one) for an item. The updated master is created on a new file, saving the old master for inventory analysis. This form of update is referred to as "update by copying" as opposed to "in-place updating" considered in the previous problem. Write the update program.

15. In an on-line banking system, active customer accounts are maintained in a file using the account number as the key. To speed up accesses, an index file is also maintained that stores for each account number in ascending order the location of the corresponding record in the accounts file. Write a program for the following banking transactions: opening of a new account, balance enquiry, deposit to an account, withdrawal from an account, and closing of an account. Your program should first do a binary search in the index file to fetch the record for a given account from the accounts file.

11 The Preprocessor

The C preprocessor can conceptually be thought of as a program that processes the source text of a C program before the compiler. It can be an independent program or its functionality may be embedded in the compiler. It has three major functions: *macro replacement, conditional inclusion,* and *file inclusion*. Macro replacement is the replacement of one string by another, conditional inclusion is the selective inclusion and exclusion of portions of source text on the basis of a computed condition, and file inclusion is the insertion of the text of a file into the current file.

Actions of the preprocessor are controlled by special directives placed in the source file. A preprocessor directive begins with the character # on a fresh line, and is terminated by the newline character unless continued on the next line by placing a backslash at the end of the line. Whitespaces may precede or follow the directive-introducing character #.

11.1 MACRO REPLACEMENT

We introduced in Section 2.10 the `#define` directive for defining *simple macros* that can be used to specify symbolic constants and isolate implementation-dependent restrictions. The general form for a simple macro definition is

    #define macro-name sequence-of-tokens

and it associates with the *macro-name* whatever *sequence-of-tokens* appears from the first blank after the *macro-name* to the end of the line. These tokens constitute the *body* of the macro. Previously defined macros can be used in the definition of a macro. The preprocessor replaces every occurrence of a simple macro in the program text by a copy of the body of the macro, except that the macro names are not recognized within comments or string constants. Some examples of simple macro definitions are

```
/* mass of an electron at rest in grams */
#define  ELECTRON   9.107e-28
/* mass of a proton at rest in grams */
#define  PROTON     1837 * ELECTRON
/* number of bits in an integer */
#define  BITSININT  32
```

The #define directive can also be used for defining *parameterized macros*. The general form for defining a parameterized macro is

#define *macro-name* (*param1, param2, . . .*) *sequence-of-tokens*

The *macro-name* is followed by a comma-separated list of formal parameters enclosed within a pair of parentheses. The sequence of tokens following the formal parameters to the end of line define the macro body. If a macro body needs to be continued onto the next line, the line to be continued is ended with a backslash (\) character. Note that the left parenthesis must immediately follow the *macro-name* without any intervening whitespace; otherwise, the definition is considered to define a simple macro that takes no arguments and has the *sequence-of-tokens* beginning with a left parenthesis. However, blank spaces following the commas that separate formal parameters are permitted.

Parameterized macros are primarily used to define functions that expand into in-line code. Some examples of parameterized macro definitions are

```
#define ABS(N)     ((N) >= 0 ? (N) : -(N))
#define READ(I)    scanf("%d", &I)
#define CONVERT(I) \
     printf("decimal %d = octal %o, hex %x\n", I, I, I)
```

A macro can be defined to have zero parameters as in

```
#define  getchar()  getc(stdin)
```

which is useful for simulating functions that take no arguments.

The preprocessor performs two levels of replacement on parameterized macros: first the formal parameters in the body of the macro are replaced by the actual arguments, and then the resulting macro body is substituted for the macro call. Thus, the preprocessor will replace the following statements

```
x = ABS(x);
READ(n);
CONVERT(n);
c = getchar();
```

by

```
x = ((x) >= 0 ? (x) : -(x));
scanf("%d", &n);
printf("decimal %d = octal %o, hex %x\n", n, n, n);
c = getc(stdin);
```

It is permissible to include newline characters in the whitespaces around the macro name and the argument list in a macro call as in

```
#define TWINS(A,B) printf("%s %s\n", A, B)

TWINS ("Tweedledee",
       "Tweedledum"
       );
```

which is replaced by

```
printf("%s %s\n", "Tweedledee", "Tweedledum");
```

Arguments in a macro call can be any token sequence, including commas, provided that the sequence is bracketed within a pair of parentheses as in

```
#define DEBUG(FORMAT,ARGS) printf(FORMAT, ARGS)

DEBUG("%s = %f\n", ("x", 0));
```

which is replaced by

```
printf("%s = %f\n", "x", 0);
```

The following is a function that uses some of the preceding macro definitions to read a decimal number and print its octal and hexadecimal equivalents:

```
void d2ox(void)
   {
      int n;

      READ(n);
      if (n < 0) DEBUG("negative input n = %d", n);
      CONVERT(ABS(n));
   }
```

Here is the function `transform` used in the palindrome detection program in Section 7.4.2, rewritten using several parameterized macros:

```
#define islower(c)   ((c) >= 'a' && (c) <= 'z' ? 1 : 0)
#define isupper(c)   ((c) >= 'A' && (c) <= 'Z' ? 1 : 0)
#define isdigit(c)   ((c) >= '0' && (c) <= '9' ? 1 : 0)
#define toupper(c)   ((c) - 'a' + 'A')

void transform(char *rawstr, char *stdstr)
   {
      for ( ; *rawstr; rawstr++)
        if (islower(*rawstr))
           *stdstr++ = toupper(*rawstr);
        else if (isupper(*rawstr) || isdigit(*rawstr))
           *stdstr++ = *rawstr;
   }
```

Good use of parameterized macros improves the readability of the program. Although defined and used in a manner similar to functions, they have the advantage that a macro call is expanded in-line and hence avoids the function-call overhead. Another advantage of using a macro definition is that the same macro can be used with arguments of different types. Thus, the macro ABS can be used to determine the absolute value of any numeric type, whereas if the function ABS were defined as

```
int ABS(int N) { return N >= 0 ? N : -N; }
```

it could only be used for integer arguments.

Parameterized macros are quite valuable, and experienced programmers invariably end up creating their own set of macros that they use repeatedly. However, as we will see shortly, the use of parameterized macros is fraught with pitfalls. But let us first study some additional facilities for defining macros and a few more details of the macro replacement process.

11.1.1 The # Operator

If a macro parameter appears inside a string in the body of a macro, the parameter is not replaced by the corresponding argument at the time of macro expansion. Thus, if you define a macro as

```
#define PRINT(V,F) printf("V = %F", V)
```

and call it as

```
PRINT(i,d);
```

the call will expand into

```
printf("V = %F", i);
```

ANSI C introduced a new preprocessing operator #, called the *stringizing* operator, which in conjunction with string concatenation provides a facility to overcome this difficulty. If a parameter follows the character # in the definition of a parameterized macro, both # and the parameter are replaced during macro expansion by the corresponding actual argument enclosed within double quotes. For example, given the macro definition

```
#define PRINT(V,F) printf(#V  " = "  #F, V)
```

the macro call

```
PRINT(i,%d);
```

expands into

```
printf("i"  " = "  "%d", i);
```

which after string concatenations becomes

```
printf("i = %d", i);
```

A \ character is automatically inserted before each " or \ character that appears inside, or surrounding, a character constant or string literal in the argument. For example, given the macro definition

```
#define PRINT(s) printf("%s\n", #s)
```

the macro call

```
PRINT(use \ ("backslash") not /);
```

expands into

```
printf("%s\n", "use \\ (\"backslash\") not /");
```

11.1.2 The ## Operator

ANSI C introduced another preprocessing operator ##, called the *token pasting* operator, to build a new token by macro replacement. The ## operator is recog-

nized within both forms of macro definitions, and concatenates the two preprocessing tokens surrounding it into one composite token during a macro expansion. For example, given the macro definition

```
#define processor(n) intel ## n
```

the macro call

```
processor(386)
```

expands into

```
intel386
```

11.1.3 Rescanning of Macro Expressions

The preprocessor replaces every occurrence of a *simple macro* in the program
text by a copy of the body of the macro. The body of a macro may itself contain
other macros. After a macro call has been expanded, the result of the macro
expansion is rescanned and the names of macros are recognized within the
expansion for further replacement. The rescanning resumes at the beginning of
the expansion and is performed from left to right. Thus, the macro call

```
mass = PROTON;
```

is expanded into

```
mass = 1837 * ELECTRON;
```

which is rescanned and expanded into

```
mass = 1837 * 9.107e-28;
```

At the time a #define directive is processed, the macro replacement is not
performed in any part, not even in the body of the macro. It is only after the
body has been expanded for some particular macro call that the macro names
are recognized within the body and replacements made. For example, given
the macro definitions

```
#define  SIZE     BLOCKS << 32
#define  BLOCKS   250
```

the declaration

```
int diskmap[SIZE];
```

expands as follows:

```
int diskmap[BLOCKS << 32];
int diskmap[250 << 32];
```

To process a *parameterized macro* call, all of its arguments are first identified.
The identifiers naming the parameters in the macro body are then replaced by
the token sequences supplied as the arguments. Unless the parameter in the
body is preceded by one of # or ##, or followed by ##, the argument tokens are
examined for macro calls, and expanded as necessary, just before insertion.
Thus, given the macro definition

```
#define  RATIO(X,Y)  ((X)/(Y))
```

the macro call

```
x = RATIO(PROTON,ELECTRON);
```

expands into

```
x = ((1837 * 9.107e-28)/(9.107e-28));
```

After all the parameters in the macro body have been substituted, the resulting replacement text is repeatedly rescanned from left to right for more macro names to expand until no new macro names are found. Thus, given the macro definitions

```
#define  PLUS(X,Y)  ADD(X,Y)
#define  ADD(X,Y)   ((X) + (Y))
```

the macro call

```
x = PLUS(PROTON, ELECTRON);
```

expands into

```
x = ADD(1837 * 9.107e-28, 9.107e-28);
```

which when rescanned results in

```
x = ((1837 * 9.107e-28) + (9.107e-28));
```

If the name of the macro being expanded is found within the replacement text, it is not expanded. Further, because the macro expansion is nested, it is possible for several macros to be in the process of being expanded. However, none of these is a candidate for further expansion in the inner levels of this process. This prevents infinite recursion during preprocessing and allows redefinition of existing functions as macros as in

```
#define sqrt(x)  ( (x) > 0 ? sqrt(x) : 0 )
```

We now give an example that illustrates some subtle aspects of the macro replacement process. Given the definitions

```
#define paste(x,y)  join(x,y)
#define join(x,y)   x ## y
#define dolittle    "Who"
#define do          "Dr. " do
```

the macro call

```
join(do,little)
```

results in the following replacements:

```
do ## little/* ## prevents the expansion of the argument do */
dolittle     /* token pasting during the rescan of
                the replacement text */
"Who"        /* the result of another rescan */
```

However, the macro call

```
paste(do,little)
```

results in the following replacements:

```
/* do is expanded before it replaces the parameter x */
join("Dr. " do, little)
"Dr. " do ## little
"Dr. " dolittle
"Dr. " "Who"
"Dr. Who"
```

Note that do after being expanded into "Dr. " do is not expanded any further.

11.1.4 Scope of Macro Definitions

A macro definition, independent of the block structure, lasts until the end of the program unit. A directive of the form

```
#undef identifier
```

causes the *identifier* to be no longer defined as a macro name. This directive is ignored if the *identifier* is not currently defined as a macro name.

Note that, as stated in Chapter 10, some library functions (for example, getchar and putchar) may actually be macros. The #undef directive is usually used to ensure access to a real function as in

```
#undef putchar
putchar(c++);
```

11.1.5 Macro Redefinitions

A macro may be redefined, provided that it has been previously undefined. For example, the following program fragment

```
#define  MODULUS       (1 << 32)
#define  srand(seed)   number = seed % MODULUS
#undef   MODULUS
#define  MODULUS       (1 << 16)
srand(1);
```

results in

```
number = 1 % (1 << 16);
```

However, it is an error to redefine a macro that has not been undefined, unless it is a *benign* redefinition in which the number and spelling of parameters, if any, and the sequence of tokens specifying the macro body are identical. All whitespace separations are taken to be equivalent in determining if a redefinition is benign. Some common macro definitions, such as NULL and EOF, are contained in more than one header file. The benign redefinition rule allows such header files to be included in the same program, but avoids bugs resulting from inadvertently using the same macro name in different header files to refer to different entities.

11.1.6 Pitfalls

We now discuss some common errors that an unwary programmer is liable to make when using parameterized macros.

Precedence Errors in Macro Expansions

Macros operate by textual substitution, which can lead to errors. Consider, for example, the macro definition

```
#define CUBE(X) X * X * X
```

to compute the cube of the argument. However, the statement

```
j = CUBE (i+1);
```

expands into

```
j = i+1 * i+1 * i+1;
```

and assigns $3i+1$ to j. Placing parentheses around each parameter in the macro body, as in

```
#define CUBE(X) (X) * (X) * (X)
```

is also not adequate, since the statement

```
j = k/CUBE(i+1);
```

expands into

```
j = k/(i+1) * (i+1) * (i+1);
```

which is interpreted as

```
j = (k/(i+1)) * (i+1) * (i+1);
```

To prevent such errors, each parameter appearing in the macro body and the macro body, if it is syntactically an expression, should be parenthesized. Thus, a correct definition of CUBE would be

```
#define CUBE(X) ((X) * (X) * (X))
```

Side Effects in Macro Arguments

A macro argument may contain a side effect. If the macro body contains more than one instance of the corresponding parameter, then the side effect may occur more than once. Consider, for example, the macro definition

```
#define  MIN(A,B)  ((A) < (B) ? (A) : (B))
```

and the statement

```
z[k++] = MIN(x[i++],y[j++]);
```

The intent is to assign the minimum of the ith element of the array x and the jth element of the array y to the kth element of the array z, and then increment i, j, and k. However, after the macro call expansion, the assignment statement becomes

```
z[k++] = ((x[i++]) < (y[j++]) ? (x[i++]) : (y[j++]));
```

and either i or j will be incremented twice.

Interaction with Control Structure

When a macro is used inside a control structure, it may interact with the control structure. Consider, for example, the macro definition

```
#define TRACE(v)  if (verbose) printf(#v " = %f\n", v)
```

and the program fragment

```
if (x == 0) TRACE(x);
else printf("ratio = %f\n", y/x);
```

The intent is to compute and print the ratio of y to x only if x is nonzero, and to trace x if it is zero, which in turn prints the value of x only in the verbose mode. However, the expansion of TRACE yields

```
if (x == 0) if (verbose) printf("x = %f\n", x);
else printf("ratio = %f\n", y/x);
```

which results in a null action when x is nonzero, and computes y/x when x is zero and the verbose mode is off.

The intended effect can be realized by defining TRACE as

```
#define TRACE(v)  verbose ? printf(#v " = %f\n", v) :
```

The expansion of TRACE now yields

```
if (x == 0) verbose ? printf("x = %f\n", x) : ;
else printf("ratio = %f\n", y/x);
```

Name Conflicts

When the body of a macro includes a compound statement, its local variables may conflict with the variable names passed as arguments. For example, given the macro definition

```
#define EXCHANGE(type,i,j)  {type t = i; i = j; j = t;}
```

the call

```
EXCHANGE(float,s,t)
```

expands into

```
{float t = s; s = t; t = t;}
```

which does not result in the expected exchange. Some naming convention must be followed for the local variables defined in a macro body to avoid such conflicts.

11.2 CONDITIONAL INCLUSION

Conditional inclusion allows selective inclusion of lines of source text on the basis of a computed condition. Conditional inclusion is performed using the preprocessor directives:

`#if`   `#ifdef`   `#ifndef`   `#elif`   `#else`   `#endif`

A directive of the form

`#if` *constant-expression*

checks whether the *constant-expression* evaluates to nonzero (true) or 0 (false). A directive of the form

`#ifdef` *identifier*

is equivalent in meaning to

`#if 1`

when *identifier* has been defined, and to

`#if 0`

when *identifier* has not been defined, or has been undefined with a `#undef` directive. The `#ifndef` directive has just the opposite sense, and a directive of the form

`#ifndef` *identifier*

is equivalent in meaning to

`#if 0`

when *identifier* has been defined, and to

`#if 1`

when *identifier* has not been defined, or has been undefined with a `#undef` directive. An *identifier* can be defined by writing

`#define` *identifier*

The constant expression that controls conditional inclusion must be an integral expression, not containing a `sizeof` operator, a cast, or an enumeration constant. It may, however, contain unary expressions of the form

`defined` *identifier*

or

`defined` (*identifier*)

that evaluate to 1 if the *identifier* is currently defined as a macro name, and 0 if it is not. The directive

`#ifdef` *identifier*   is equivalent to   `#if defined` (*identifier*)

and the directive

> #ifndef *identifier*   is equivalent to   #if !defined(*identifier*) .

However, the `defined` form is more flexible because it can be used in expressions as in

```
#if defined(SystemV) && DEBUG
```

The `#else` directive indicates alternatives when the previous `#if`, `#ifdef`, or `#ifndef` test fails.

The `#endif` directive ends the conditional text. There must be a matching `#endif` for every `#if`, `#ifdef`, or `#ifndef` directive.

The `#elif` directive allows a nested conditional of the form

```
#if expr1
    group-of-lines-1
#else
    #if expr2
        group-of-lines-2
    #else
        group-of-lines-3
    #endif
#endif
```

to be written in a more convenient form by combining `#else` and `#if` directives

```
#if expr1
    group-of-lines-1
#elif expr2
    group-of-lines-2
#else
    group-of-lines-3
#endif
```

and avoids multiple `#endif` directives.

Each directive's condition is evaluated in order. If the condition evaluates to false (zero), the associated group of lines is skipped. Only the first group of lines whose control condition evaluates to true (nonzero) is included. If none of the conditions evaluate to true, the group of lines associated with `#else` is included; lacking a `#else`, all the lines until `#endif` are skipped.

Conditional inclusion is frequently used in developing programs that run under different environments. For example, INTSIZE may be defined as

```
#if HOST == IBMPC
    #define INTSIZE 16
#elif HOST == HONEYWELL6000
    #define INTSIZE 36
#else
    #define INTSIZE 32
#endif
```

The preprocessor can then select an appropriate value for INTSIZE, depending upon the defined value of HOST.

Conditional inclusion is also used to control debugging. You may write in your program

```
#ifdef DEBUG
    if (!(i % FREQUENCY)) printf("iteration: %d\n", i);
#endif
```

and then turn debugging on and off simply by defining and undefining DEBUG. Rather than using #ifdef, you could have also used an if statement

```
if (debug)
    if (!(i % FREQUENCY)) printf("iteration: %d\n", i);
```

But this alternative can be quite inefficient, particularly when the debugging statement is inside a tight loop, since the truth value of debug will be checked at run time in every loop iteration. If the program contains many such statements, the size of the executable program may also increase considerably. With the conditional inclusion, the preprocessor eliminates the debugging statements when the debugging mode is off, and there is no storage or run-time penalty.

Instead of embedding #ifdef DEBUG directives all over the code when you require many debugging statements in a program, you may define a PRINT macro as

```
#ifndef DEBUG
    #define PRINT(arg)
#else
    #define PRINT(arg) printf arg
#endif
```

and then write

```
PRINT(("iteration: %d\n", i));
PRINT(("x = %f, y = %f\n", x, y));
```

which expand into

```
printf ("iteration: %d\n", i);
printf ("x = %f, y = %f\n", x, y);
```

or null statements depending on whether DEBUG has been defined or not. Note the use of two pairs of parentheses when calling PRINT.

You may also control levels of debugging with more output at each level as in

```
#if defined(DEBUG)
    #if DEBUG >= 5
        printf("iteration: %d\n", i);
        #if DEBUG >= 10
            printf("x = %f, y = %f\n", x, y);
        #endif
    #else
        if (!(i % FREQUENCY))
            printf("iteration: %d\n", i);
    #endif
#endif
```

Another important use of conditional inclusion is in commenting out a group of source lines containing comments:

```
#if 0
    printf("iteration: %d\n", i);        /* comment out */
    printf("x = %f, y = %f\n", x, y); /* after debugging */
#endif
```

You cannot comment out these lines by enclosing them within a pair of /* and */, since comments are not allowed to be nested.

Many compilers allow you to define or undefine a macro on the command line used to compile the program. For example, on an IBM PC equipped with the Microsoft C compiler, the command

```
cl /DDEBUG=10 /DVERBOSE myprog.c
```

defines the macro DEBUG to have a value 10 and causes the macro VERBOSE to be defined, whereas the command

```
cl /UDEBUG /UVERBOSE myprog.c
```

undefines them. The equivalent commands on the UNIX operating system are:

```
cc -DDEBUG=10 -DVERBOSE myprog.c
cc -UDEBUG -DVERBOSE myprog.c
```

This facility avoids the need for editing the source file every time a change has to be made to a macro value.

11.3 FILE INCLUSION

We discussed in Section 5.8 that a large program is developed by grouping logically related functions into separate files. Symbolic constants and data types common to more than one file and the external declarations for the shared variables are then collected in one or more files, called *header* files, and included in files that need them using the #include directive. This approach ensures that all the source files will be supplied with the same definitions and variable declarations. You may also collect useful macro definitions that may be required in different programs in one or more files, and then include them in your programs as needed.

The #include directive has the following two forms:

```
#include <filename>
#include "filename"
```

In either form, the #include directive instructs the preprocessor to replace the line containing the #include directive by the contents of the file named *filename*. The two forms differ in the order in which the search is made for the desired file.

A directive of the first form searches a sequence of implementation-defined places according to implementation-dependent search rules. For example, on UNIX systems, the named file is searched for in the directory /usr/include.

With a directive of the second form, the search takes place in two steps. First, the named file is searched for in an implementation-dependent manner.

On UNIX systems, the rule is to search for the file in the same directory in which the file containing the #include directive was found. If this search is not supported, or if the search fails, the directive is reprocessed as if it read

```
#include  <filename>
```

with the identical *filename* from the original directive.

The general practice is to use the form "*filename*" to include the user files and the form <*filename*> to include the standard library files.

Besides the above two forms, a new form

```
#include  token-sequence
```

is allowed by ANSI C if the *token-sequence* is a macro name that evaluates to one of these forms, and it is then treated as previously described. Here is an example:

```
#ifdef STDC
    #define  IO  <stdio.h>
#else
    #define  IO  "myio.h"
#endif
#include IO
```

Nesting of #include directives is permitted — an included file may itself contain #include directives, up to an implementation-defined nesting limit.

11.4 ADDITIONAL FACILITIES

11.4.1 Line Directive

A preprocessor directive of the form

```
#line  linenumber  filename
```

makes the compiler believe that the line number of the next source line is *linenumber*, which must be a decimal integer constant, and the name of the source file is *filename*, which must be a string literal. The file name can be omitted, in which case the remembered name does not change.

A directive of the form

```
#line  token-sequence
```

is also permitted if the *token-sequence* is a macro name that evaluates to either a line number followed by a file name or simply a line number.

The line control facility is useful to provide better error diagnostics when writing preprocessors that generate C programs.

11.4.2 Error Directive

A directive of the form

```
#error  token-sequence
```

causes the implementation to produce a diagnostic message containing the specified *token-sequence*. The following example demonstrates the use of the `#error` directive:

```
#if !defined(ADD) && !defined(MUL)
    #error "operator not specified"
#endif
```

If it is found during the compilation of the program that both `ADD` and `MUL` have not been defined, a compile-time error occurs and the error message is printed.

11.4.3 Pragma Directive

A directive of the form

```
#pragma token-sequence
```

causes the implementation to behave in an implementation-dependent manner. An unrecognized pragma is ignored.

11.4.4 Null Directive

A directive of the form

```
#
```

is a "do-nothing" directive. The preprocessor takes no action except to eliminate the line.

11.4.5 Predefined Macro Names

An ANSI C preprocessor defines five special macro names. These names begin and end with two underscore characters and expand to produce the following information:

`__LINE__`	a decimal constant giving the line number of the current source line.
`__FILE__`	a string literal giving the name of the current source file.
`__DATE__`	a string literal of the form `"Mmm dd yyyy"` giving the date of compilation.
`__TIME__`	a string literal of the form `"hh:mm:ss"` giving the time of compilation.
`__STDC__`	the constant 1, indicating an implementation conforming to the ANSI standard.

11.5 ILLUSTRATIVE EXAMPLES

We now give some example programs to further illustrate the preprocessor features.

Example 1

The number of combinations c of m things taken n at a time is given by

$$c = \frac{m!}{n! \, (m-n)!}$$

For large values, the factorial can be approximated by Stirling's formula:

$$k! = e^{-k} k^k \sqrt{2\pi k}$$

Write a program that reads m and n and prints c.

The desired program is as follows.

```
#include <math.h>
#include <stdio.h>
#define  PI              3.14159265

#define  get(n1,n2)      scanf("%d %d", &n1, &n2)
#define  print(str,val)  printf("%s = %g\n", str, val)

#define  factorial(k)    (exp(- (k)) * \
                          pow((k), (k)) * \
                          sqrt(2 * PI * (k)))
int main(void)
  {
    int     m, n;
    double  c;

    get(m, n);

    c = factorial(m) /
        (factorial(n) * factorial(m - n));

    print("combinations", c);

    return 0;
  }
```

The number of combinations determined by the program may have a non-zero fractional part as we are using an approximate formula for calculating the factorials. We could have rounded this number and printed the result as a whole number, but we have chosen to print the number of combinations as a floating-point number since the range of values that may be represented as a floating-point number is larger. For example, for $m = 100$ and $n = 80$, the program prints

```
combinations = 5.38333e+20
```

Carefully examine the definition of the parameterized macro `factorial` in this program. All the parentheses used in the definition are necessary.

Example 2

Write a program to generate suites of addition and multiplication problems.

The desired program is as follows:

```c
#include <stdio.h>
#define MAXPROBS 10   /* number of problems */
#define MAXTERMS 5    /* maximum terms in a problem */
#define LARGEST  10   /* largest value of a term */
#define SMALLEST 0    /* smallest value of a term */
#define MAXOPS   2    /* '+' and '*' */
#define SEED      781 /* for the random number generator */

#if defined ADD
    #undef MUL
    #undef MIX
    char  operator  = '+';
#elif defined MUL
    #undef ADD
    #undef MIX
    char  operator  = '*';
#else
    #define MIX
    #undef ADD
    #undef MUL
    char  operator;
#endif

char opcode[MAXOPS] = {'+', '*'};

int  rand(void); /* random number generator */
void srand(int); /* initializes the random number generator */
void probgen(int terms); /* problem generator */

int main(void)
  {
    int i, terms;

    srand(SEED);

    for (i=0; i < MAXPROBS; i++)
      {
        #ifdef MIX
            operator = opcode[rand() % MAXOPS];
        #endif
        terms = (rand() % (MAXTERMS-1) ) + 2;
        probgen(terms);
      }
    return 0;
  }
```

```
void probgen(int terms)
  {
    int i, spread = LARGEST - SMALLEST + 1;

    for (i=0; i < terms; i++)
      {
        printf("%2d", SMALLEST + rand() % spread);
        printf(" %c ", i < terms-1 ? operator : '=');
      }
    printf("\n");
  }
```

See Section 5.8.3 for the code of the `srand` and `rand` functions. The problems in a suite can be addition problems, multiplication problems, or a mix of them. The user specifies the types of problems to include in a suite by defining one of ADD, MUL, or MIX. Different problem suites can be generated by changing SEED and other constants.

Example 3

Write a macro to generate C functions for determining the absolute value of a numeric data item of a desired type.

We define a parameterized macro ABS that takes two arguments: a function name and a type. Such macros are sometimes referred to as *generic* functions, since they yield ordinary C functions when instantiated with function names and appropriate data types. Here is the definition of ABS:

```
#define ABS(FNAME, TYPE) \
              \
          TYPE FNAME(TYPE x) \
            { \
              return x >= 0 ? x : -x; \
            }
```

The macro call

```
ABS(iabs,int)
```

generates the function

```
int iabs(int x) { return x >= 0 ? x : -x; }
```

whereas the macro call

```
ABS(dabs,double)
```

generates the function

```
double dabs(double x) { return x >= 0 ? x : -x; }
```

Exercises 11

1. Given the macro definitions

```
#define   i       0
#define   a(j)    a((j) + (i))
#define   b(i)    i
#define   c       a
#undef    i
#define   i       1
#define   d       d(i)
#define   e(j)    j(i)
```

determine the result of each of the following macro calls:

a. `a(2)`   *b.* `a(a(2))`

c. `a(a(d))`   *d.* `b(b(c)(2))`

e. `c(i-d)`   *f.* `e(b)`

g. `e(c)`   *h.* `e(d)`

i. `e(e)`

2. Given the macro definitions

```
#define str(s)    quote(s)
#define print(n)  printf("i" # n " = %d", i ## n)
#define quote(s)  # s
#define name(n)   bsd ## n
```

determine the result of each of the following macro calls:

a. `print(1);`

b. `printf("%s", quote(cmp("x", "x ", '\3')));`

c. `#include str(name(4.3));`

d. `#include quote(name(4.3));`

3. Define a macro that expands into a `for` statement to iterate over the loop body for a minimum to a maximum value of the loop variable.

4. Define a macro that determines whether a given character is a special character.

5. Define a macro that converts a character to uppercase if it is a lowercase letter and leaves it unchanged otherwise.

6. Define a macro that determines the minimum of three values.

7. Define a macro that takes a value, a starting bit position, and the number of bits, and determines the value of those bits.

8. Define a macro that generates a program fragment to subtract from every element of an array a constant value.

9. Define a macro that can be used to generate C functions to exchange values of desired types.

10. Define a macro that can be used to generate C functions to make a binary search in arrays of desired types.

■ 12 Additional Features

We now discuss some additional features of the C language. In particular, we discuss the type definition facility that allows synonyms to be defined for existing data types, the type qualification facility that permits greater control over program optimization, the enumeration type that provides the facility to specify the possible values of a variable by meaningful symbolic names, the facility to define functions that take a variable number of arguments, the storage class specifier `register` that can speed up programs by specifying to the compiler the heavily used variables to be kept in machine registers, trigraph sequences that permit C implementation in character sets that do not have sufficient non-alphabetic characters, and the `goto` statement that can be used to branch around one or more statements.

12.1 TYPE DEFINITIONS

The `typedef` facility allows you to define synonyms for existing data types by writing a declaration of the form:

```
typedef typename declarator;
```

This declaration causes the identifier that appears in the *declarator* to become a synonym for the type *typename*. For example, the declarations

```
typedef float REAL;
typedef unsigned short int BOOL, BOOLEAN;
```

make the identifier REAL a synonym for the type `float`, and the identifiers BOOL and BOOLEAN synonyms for the type `unsigned short int`.

The general rule for defining a synonym for a type is to write out a declaration as if declaring a variable of that type, substitute the synonym in place of the variable name, and precede the declaration with the keyword `typedef`. Thus,

```
typedef long *LPTR;
typedef char STRING[MAX];
typedef int  *FUNC(short, short);
```

define LPTR to be a synonym for the type "pointer to `long`", STRING to be a synonym for the type "character array of MAX elements", and FUNC to be a synonym for the type "function taking two `short` arguments and returning a pointer to `int`".

Once an identifier has been defined to be a synonym for a type, it may appear anywhere a type specifier is allowed. For example, we can now write

```
BOOLEAN debug, flags[SIZE];
LPTR   lp;
STRING s;
FUNC   f;
```

instead of writing

```
unsigned short int debug, flags[SIZE];
long *lp;
char s[MAX];
int  *f(short, short);
```

However, the `typedef` names are not allowed to be mixed with other type specifiers. For example, the following is not permitted:

```
typedef short int smallint; /* smallint becomes a
                                 synonym for short int */
unsigned smallint status;   /* illegal */
```

A typedef declaration does not create a new type; it only defines a synonym for an existing type. For example, after the declaration

```
typedef struct record
    {BOOL valid; REAL value;} ENTRY, ELEMENT;
```

ENTRY, ELEMENT, and `struct record` can be used interchangeably to refer to the same type.

Superficially, a `typedef` declaration resembles the preprocessor `#define` directive. For example, the statements

```
#define BYTE char *
typedef char * BYTE;
```

seem to have the same effect. However, the statement

```
BYTE cp1, cp2;
```

when BYTE is a `typedef` name, declares `cp1` and `cp2` to be of type "pointer to char", whereas it expands into

```
char * cp1, cp2;
```

when BYTE is a macro name, and declares `cp1` to be of type "pointer to `char`" and `cp2` to be of type `char`. The `typedef`s are interpreted by the compiler and provide greater flexibility in assigning names to complex aggregate types. For example, if MATRIX is defined to be a synonym for the type "two-dimensional array containing MAXROW × MAXCOL integer elements" by the `typedef` declaration

```
typedef int MATRIX[MAXROW,MAXCOL];
```

it cannot be equivalently defined with a #define preprocessor directive.

The type definition facility is frequently used to enhance portability by using typedef names for the machine-dependent data types. For example, having defined

```
#ifdef IBMPC
     typedef long SIZE;
#else
     typedef int  SIZE;
#endif
```

the statements such as

```
SIZE offset[MAXFILES];
```

that use SIZE, instead of long or int, remain unchanged when the program moves between an IBM PC and a VAX computer.

This facility also helps in documentation. For example, having defined

```
typedef struct node
  {
    REAL value;
    struct node *next, *prev;
  } LISTNODE, *LISTPTR;
```

the use of LISTNODE and LISTPTR in variable declarations

```
LISTNODE head;
LISTPTR  root;
```

is obviously more informative than

```
struct node head;
struct node *root;
```

Another important use of typedefs is in simplifying complex type declarations. For example, having defined

```
typedef  char  *CP;
typedef  CP    (*FP)(CP, CP);
```

we can declare an integer-valued function that takes as argument a pointer to a function that takes two character pointers as arguments and returns a character pointer as

```
int f(FP);
```

Similarly, we can declare an array of 10 pointers to functions that take two character pointers as arguments and return a character pointer as

```
FP a[10];
```

Write these declarations without using typedefs to appreciate the utility of this facility in such situations.

12.2 TYPE QUALIFIERS

ANSI C introduced two type qualifiers, `const` and `volatile`, to indicate special properties of the objects being declared. Type qualifiers provide greater control over optimization by specifying the assumptions a compiler must make when accessing an object through an lvalue. A type qualifier may be used with any type specifier, or may be used alone, in which case the type specifier `int` is assumed. A type specification may be qualified by both `const` and `volatile` qualifiers.

12.2.1 `const` Type Qualifier

ANSI C introduced `const` objects to allow them to be allocated in the read-only storage and to permit compilers to do extra consistency checking. The `const` qualifier specifies that the object being declared may be initialized, but it cannot be assigned a value thereafter, nor can its value be modified by the operators `++` or `--`. Thus, we have

```
const double PI = 3.14159265;
double E = 2.7182818;
E = PI;                               /* legal */
PI = E;                               /* illegal */
PI++, PI--;                           /* illegal */
```

The declaration of an array, structure, or union object with the `const` qualifier specifies that none of the constituent members can change. Thus, we have

```
const char coldfusion[] = "palladium";
coldfusion[4] = 'e';                  /* illegal */
const struct
  {int atomic_no; float atomic_wt;} Pd = {46, 106.4};
Pd.atomic_no = 78;                    /* illegal */
```

Both pointers to constant data and constant pointers may be declared. Thus, we have

```
const int * ptr_to_const;     /* pointer to constant data */
int * const const_ptr;        /* constant pointer */
```

A pointer to a constant data object is a modifiable pointer, but the object it points to may not be modified. A constant pointer, on the other hand, may not be modified, but the object it points to may be modified. An ordinary pointer may be assigned to a pointer to constant data, but a pointer to constant data may be assigned to an ordinary pointer only by using an explicit cast. When the address operator `&` is applied to a `const` object, the result is a pointer to constant data. Here are some examples illustrating these rules:

```
int ordinary_int, *ordinary_ptr;
*ptr_to_const = ordinary_int;         /* illegal */
*const_ptr = ordinary_int;            /* legal */
const_ptr = ordinary_ptr;             /* illegal */
ptr_to_const = ordinary_ptr;          /* legal */
ordinary_ptr = ptr_to_const;          /* illegal */
ordinary_ptr = (int *) ptr_to_const;  /* legal */
```

Although a pointer to constant data can be assigned to an ordinary pointer, an attempt to modify a `const` object through an ordinary pointer may cause a run-time error because it may have been allocated in the read-only storage. Thus,

```
const int const_int = 0;
ordinary_ptr =
    (int *) ptr_to_const = &const_int;        /* legal, but */
*ordinary_ptr = 10;/*this assignment may cause run-time error */
```

Function parameters may also be declared `const`, which specifies that the referenced objects are not changed through that lvalue in the body of the function. For example, the function declaration

```
char *strcpy(char to[], const char from[]);
```

specifies that the function `strcpy` does not modify the array supplied as the second argument.

12.2.2 `volatile` Type Qualifier

Many optimizing compilers, under certain circumstances, cache the last value accessed from a location and use the cached value the next time that location is read. Using the cached value, rather than accessing memory, makes the code smaller and faster, particularly when the value has been cached in a hardware register.

The type qualifier `volatile`, when applied to the declaration of an object, instructs the compiler that the object should not participate in caching optimizations as its value may be altered in ways which cannot be inferred from a study of the program. This feature is particularly useful when writing programs that deal with memory-mapped I/O or variables shared among multiple processes.

Consider, for example, the following statements

```
while ((device->status & READY) == 0) /* wait */ ;
device->output = data;
```

that may be part of a program to control a hardware device and result in a wait for the `READY` bit to be set in the `status` register of the device before writing data to the `output` register of the device. However, an optimizing compiler may notice that the value of `status` is not changed inside the loop, and arrange to reference memory only once and copy its value into a hardware register to speed up the loop, thus causing the loop never to terminate. By declaring `status` to be a `volatile` object as

```
struct {
    volatile unsigned int status;
    unsigned int output;
} *device;
```

we can force every reference to `status` to be a genuine reference.

Rules for `volatile` are similar to those for `const`. Making an array, structure, or union `volatile` makes every constituent member `volatile`. Pointers to both `volatile` objects and `volatile` pointers may be declared. A pointer to a `volatile` object may be optimized, but the object it points to may not be optimized. On the other hand, a `volatile` pointer may not be optimized, but the object it points to may be optimized. Applying the address operator `&` to a `volatile` object results in a pointer to a `volatile` object. An ordinary pointer may be assigned to a pointer to a `volatile` object, but an explicit cast must be used to assign a pointer to a `volatile` object to an ordinary pointer. Function parameters may also be declared `volatile`. Here are some examples:

```
volatile int volatile_int;
int * ordinary_ptr;
volatile int * ptr_to_volatile;  /*pointer to volatile object*/
int * volatile volatile_ptr;        /*volatile pointer*/
ptr_to_volatile = &volatile_int;            /*legal*/
ptr_to_volatile = ordinary_ptr;             /*legal*/
ordinary_ptr = ptr_to_volatile;             /*illegal*/
ordinary_ptr = (int *) ptr_to_volatile;  /*legal*/
```

Note that `const` and `volatile` are independent concepts, and `volatile` is in no way the opposite of `const` and vice versa. In fact, both `const` and `volatile` may appear in the same declaration. For example, a counter `clock`, which is updated by a clock interrupt routine, can be declared as

```
extern const volatile unsigned long clock;
```

`clock` has been declared to be a `volatile` object because of the asynchronous updates to it, and also a `const` object because it should not be changed by anything other than the clock interrupt routine. An object should be declared `const volatile` if it is a memory-mapped input port or a variable which can be altered by another process but not by this one.

The type qualifiers `const` and `volatile` do not actually define a new type, but serve as modifiers of the variables being declared. For example, the declarations

```
volatile struct dev {unsigned short status, data;} d1;
struct dev d2;
```

declare d1 to be a `volatile` object, but not d2. The `typedef` facility can be used to associate the `const` or `volatile` property with an aggregate type. Thus, the declarations

```
typedef volatile struct
    {unsigned short status, data;} volatiledev;
volatiledev d1, d2;
```

declare both d1 and d2 to be `volatile` objects.

12.3 ENUMERATIONS

Enumeration types provide the facility to specify the possible values of a variable by meaningful symbolic names. The general format for defining an enumeration type is

enum *tag* {ec_0, ec_1, . . ., ec_n};

where *tag* is an identifier that names the enumeration type, and $ec_0, ec_1, \ldots, ec_n$ are identifiers, called *enumeration constants*. For example, the declaration

```
enum wine {champagne, chablis, beaujolais, claret};
```

defines an enumeration type `wine` whose values are `champagne`, `chablis`, `beaujolais`, and `claret`.

An enumeration type is implemented by associating the integer value i with the enumeration constant ec_i. Thus, the value 0 is associated with `champagne`, 1 with `chablis`, 2 with `beaujolais`, and 3 with `claret`. An integer value may explicitly be associated with an enumeration constant by following it with = and a constant expression of integral type. Subsequent enumeration constants without explicit associations are assigned integer values one greater than the value associated with the previous enumeration constant. For example, the declaration

```
enum wine {champagne = 3, chablis,
           beaujolais = 1, claret};
```

results in the value 3 being associated with `champagne`, 4 with `chablis`, 1 with `beaujolais`, and 2 with `claret`.

Any signed integer value may be associated with an enumeration constant. Even the same integer value may be associated with two different enumeration constants. For example, the declaration

```
enum wine {champagne, chablis = 10,
           beaujolais = -1, claret};
```

causes the value 0 to be associated with both `champagne` and `claret`, 10 with `chablis`, and –1 with `beaujolais`.

An enumeration constant must be unique with respect to other enumeration constants and variables within the same name scope. Thus, in the presence of the declaration of `wine`, the declaration

```
enum hue {terracotta, mauve, claret, carnation};
```

is illegal because the identifier `claret` has already been defined to be an enumeration constant of `wine`. Similarly, the variable declaration

```
float *claret;
```

following the declaration of `wine`, is also illegal.

Variables may be declared to be of an enumeration type in the same declaration containing the enumeration type definition, or in subsequent declarations of the form

```
enum tag variablelist;
```

Thus, `bordeaux` and `burgundy` may be declared to be of type `enum wine` and pointer to `enum wine` respectively by writing

```
enum wine
   {
     champagne, chablis, beaujolais, claret
   } bordeaux, *burgundy;
```

or

```
enum wine
   {
     champagne, chablis, beaujolais, claret
   } bordeaux;
```

```
enum wine *burgundy;
```

or

```
enum wine {champagne, chablis, beaujolais, claret};
enum wine bordeaux, *burgundy;
```

The tag may be omitted from the declaration of an enumeration type if all the variables of this type have been declared at the same time. Thus, you may write

```
enum
   {
     champagne, chablis, beaujolais, claret
   } bordeaux, *burgundy;
```

but due to the omission of the enumeration tag, you may not subsequently declare another variable alsace whose type is the same as that of bordeaux or burgundy.

Instead of using enumeration tags, the typedef facility may be used to define enumeration types. Thus, you may write

```
typedef enum {champagne,chablis,beaujolais,claret} wine;
wine bordeaux, *burgundy;
```

A variable of a particular enumeration type can be assigned enumeration constants specified in the definition of the enumeration type. For example, you may write

```
bordeaux = claret;
*burgundy = chablis;
```

You may also compare values as in

```
if (*burgundy == beaujolais) degust();
```

All enumeration types are treated as integer types, and the type of enumeration constants is treated as int. However, you should differentiate between enumeration and integer types as a matter of good programming practice and use casts if they have to be mixed, as shown in the following example:

```
typedef enum
   {
     doc,happy,sneezy,dopey,grumpy,bashful,sleepy
   } dwarf;
```

```
dwarf next(dwarf this)
   {
     return (dwarf) (((int) this + 1) % 7);
   }
```

C does not provide facilities for reading or writing values of enumeration types. They may only be read or written as integer values.

12.4 VARIABLE ARGUMENTS

We often need functions that can take a variable number of arguments. The library functions `printf` and `scanf` are examples of such functions. The parameter list of such functions contains one or more fixed parameters and is terminated with an ellipsis (, ...) to represent the variable part. Here is an example of the declaration of such a function:

```
double min(double oldmin, int nterms, ... );
```

This function may be called, for example, as

```
a = min(0.001, 3, x, y, z);
a = min(a, 6, r, s, t, u, v, w);
```

The standard header file `<stdarg.h>` provides the facility to step through a list of function arguments, whose number and types are unknown to the called function at the time of compilation, by defining a type `va_list` and three macros `va_start`, `va_arg`, and `va_end` that operate on objects of type `va_list`.

Before accessing a variable argument list, the macro `va_start` must be called. It is defined as

```
void va_start(va_list ap, lastparam);
```

The macro `va_start` initializes the variable *ap* for subsequent use by the macros `va_arg` and `va_end`. The second argument to `va_start` is the identifier naming the rightmost fixed parameter in the function definition. Thus, the function `min` will contain

```
va_list ap;
...
va_start(ap, nterms);
```

Having initialized *ap*, the variable arguments can be accessed by using the `va_arg` macro. It is defined as

```
type va_arg(va_list ap, type);
```

The first invocation of the `va_arg` macro after that of the `va_start` macro returns the value of the first variable argument. Subsequently, it returns the value of the remaining arguments in succession. The type of the value returned by `va_arg` is determined by the second argument, which must be a type name that can be converted to such an object simply by appending a `*` to it. If the argument actually supplied is not of specified type, the behavior is undefined. Different types may be specified in successive calls to `va_arg`. Thus, the variable arguments can be extracted in the body of `min` by successively calling `va_arg` as

```
double val;
...
val = va_arg(ap, double);
```

When the variable arguments have been processed, the `va_end` macro should be called before the function is exited. It facilitates a normal return from the function. It is defined as

```
void va_end(va_list ap);
```

The argument list can be retraversed by calling `va_start` again after calling `va_end`.

Here is the complete code for the `min` function:

```
#include <stdarg.h>

double min(double oldmin, int nterms, ... )
  {
    va_list ap;
    double val;
    int i;

    va_start(ap, nterms);
    for(i = 0; i < nterms; i++)
        if ((val = va_arg(ap, double)) < oldmin)
            oldmin = val;
    va_end(ap);
    return oldmin;
  }
```

We stated in Section 10.4 that the library functions `vfprintf`, `vprintf`, and `vsprintf` are useful for defining functions that take a variable number of arguments and write formatted output. These functions are declared as

```
int vfprintf(FILE *file, const char *format, va_list arg);
int vprintf(const char *format, va_list arg);
int vsprintf(char *s, const char *format, va_list arg);
```

We now write a function `err` that takes as arguments (i) the name of the function in which the error was detected, (ii) the format of the error message, which is a control string similar to `fprintf`, and (iii) a variable number of arguments that are converted and written as part of the message as per the conversion specifications contained in the control string. Here is the code for the function:

```
#include <stdio.h>
#include <stdarg.h>

void err(char *name, char *fmt, ... )
  {
    va_list ap;

    va_start(ap, fmt);
    fprintf(stderr, "%s: ", name);
    vfprintf(stderr, fmt, ap);
    fprintf(stderr, "\n");
    va_end(ap);
  }
```

This function when invoked as

```
err("mklist", "too big a node number: %d", node);
```

prints

```
mklist: too big a node number: 32768
```

12.5 `register` STORAGE SPECIFIER

We mentioned in Chapter 1 that the registers are special storage locations with fast access time. Accessing a value stored in a register is much faster than if the value were stored in memory. Where to store a data value is usually not of concern to a higher-level language programmer. Yet, at times, such a decision can have significant impact on the execution time of a program. For example, when a loop is to be executed several times, its execution can be speeded up considerably by keeping the loop counter and the variables used in the loop in machine registers.

C provides a storage class specifier `register` to let the programmer advise the compiler that the specified object is likely to be used heavily and should be kept in a machine register, if possible. A `register` declaration is of the form

```
register datatype identifier;
```

Here are some examples:

```
register short int index;
void print(register int *node);
```

The `register` specifier can only be used for automatic variable or parameter declarations. Depending upon the underlying machine, only a few variables in a function can be kept in registers, and they can only be of certain types. However, excess or disallowed `register` declarations do not cause an error as the compiler treats them simply as `auto` declarations. Many compilers assign variables to registers on a first-come first-serve basis. Objects of type `int` can usually be kept in registers, but not array, structure, or union objects. It is an error to apply the address operator `&` to a variable declared with the `register` specifier.

12.6 ALTERNATIVE REPRESENTATIONS OF CHARACTERS

C derives its character set from the seven-bit ASCII Code Set. However, this set is not a subset of all the commonly used character sets. An internationally agreed-upon standard is ISO 646-1983 which defines an invariant subset of the ASCII Code Set. The following characters in the C character set are absent from the ISO 646-1983 Invariant Code Set:

```
[     ]     {     }     \     |     ^     ~     #
```

ANSI C introduced *trigraph sequences* as an alternate spelling of these characters. A trigraph sequence is two consecutive question mark characters followed by a distinguishing character. All occurrences of the following trigraph sequences are replaced with the corresponding characters:

Trigraph sequence	Replacement character	Trigraph sequence	Replacement character	Trigraph sequence	Replacement character
??(	[	??)	]	??<	{
??>	}	??/	\	??!	|
??'	^	??-	~	??=	#

No other trigraph sequences are defined. The replacement occurs before any other processing. For example, the string

```
"how???/n"
```

after the replacement of the trigraph sequence ??/ becomes

```
"how?\n"
```

A new character escape sequence \? was introduced to allow two adjacent question marks in strings, character constants, comments, or header names. Thus, the string constant

```
"What ???!"
```

should be written as

```
"What ?\??!"
```

to prevent it from being interpreted as

```
"what?|"
```

A dual of the preceding problem arises on some implementations that have an extended set of characters which cannot be represented in the char type. ANSI C has defined an integral type wchar_t in the standard header <stddef.h> for such wide characters. A wide character constant is written with a preceding L, such as L'#'.

12.7 goto STATEMENT

We finally discuss the goto statement that can be used to branch around one or more statements. It is of the form

```
goto label;
```

where *label* is the identifier of the statement to which the branching is to be made and appears in the same function in the form

```
label: statement
```

A label has the syntax of an identifier.

The execution of a goto statement transfers the program control to the statement indicated by the label, and this statement is executed next. For example, here is a program fragment for counting the number of characters in input:

```
for (count=0; ; )
  {
    c = getchar();
    if (c == EOF) goto hop;
    count++
  }
hop: printf("%d\n", count);
```

The `for` loop reads one character at a time and increments `count`. When the end-of-file is reached, the `goto` statement transfers the program control to the statement labeled `hop`, the loop is terminated, and the value of `count` is printed.

You can even set up loops using `goto` statements, as illustrated in the following program fragment for adding integers from 1 to n except those divisible by 5:

```
i = 1;
sum = 0;

back:
    if (i > n) goto done;
    if (i % 5 == 0) goto hop;
    sum += i;
    hop: i++;
goto back;
done: ;
```

Compare the above program fragment with the following structured counterpart for the same problem:

```
for (i = 1, sum = 0; i <= n; i++)
    if (i % 5 != 0)
            sum += i;
```

Obviously, the `goto` version is more complex than its structured counterpart.

The `goto` statement is a carryover from the pre-structured-programming era. The indiscriminate use of `goto` statements results in programs that are difficult to understand, debug, and maintain. Furthermore, when `goto` statements are used, most compilers generate less efficient code compared to the structured constructs. Therefore we strongly advise you against using `goto` statements in your programs — you should be able to write all your programs without having to ever use a `goto` statement.

12.8 ILLUSTRATIVE EXAMPLES

We now give some example programs to further illustrate the concepts introduced in this chapter.

Example 1
Develop a set package by creating a SET data type and functions for the various set operations.

We consider only sets of positive integers. Sets are represented as bit arrays, one bit for each set element. The desired package is as follows:

```
#include <stdio.h>
#define LARGEST      4097 /* largest element of the set */
#define WORDSIZE     32   /* assume 32 bit integer */
#define SIZEINWORDS (LARGEST/WORDSIZE+1)/* bit array size */
#define MAXONLINE    10   /* maximum elements on a print line*/
#define inrange(e)   (e >= 0 && e <= LARGEST)
#define wordpos(e)   (e / WORDSIZE)
#define bitpos(e)    (e % WORDSIZE)
#define bitval(s,e)  ((s[wordpos(e)]>>bitpos(e)) & 01)

typedef unsigned int SET[SIZEINWORDS];
typedef int ELEMENT;
typedef enum {FAILED, SUCCEEDED} STATUS;
typedef enum {FALSE, TRUE} BOOL;

void set_init(SET s)   /* initialize s */
   {
      register int i;

      for (i = 0; i < SIZEINWORDS; i++)  s[i] = 0;
   }

STATUS set_add(SET s, ELEMENT e)   /* add e to s */
   {
      if (!inrange(e)) return FAILED;
      s[wordpos(e)] |= 01 << bitpos(e);
      return SUCCEEDED;
   }

BOOL set_mem(SET s, ELEMENT e)   /* is e in s? */
   {
      return inrange(e) && bitval(s,e) ? TRUE : FALSE;
   }

void set_union(SET s, SET t, SET r)   /* r = s ∪ t */
   {
      register int i;

      for (i = 0; i < SIZEINWORDS; i++)
          r[i] = s[i] | t[i];
   }

void set_print(SET s) /* print members of s */
   {
      register int i, j = 0;
```

```
      printf("{");
      for (i = 0; i <= LARGEST; i++)
         if (set_mem(s,i) == TRUE)
            {
               printf("%s%d", j % MAXONLINE ? ", " :
                                 j != 0 ? ",\n" : "", i);
               j++;
            }
      printf("}");
}
```

We leave it as an exercise for you to write functions for determining if a set is empty, deleting an element from a set, and taking the intersection and difference of two sets.

Example 2
Write a function for printing a list of lists.

Consider a linked list whose elements contain either an integer value or a pointer to a list. The following figure shows such a list:

root:

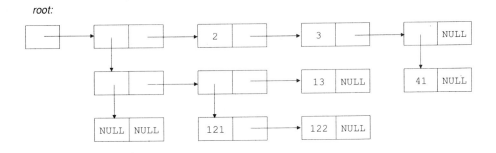

The desired function is as follows:

```
#include <stdio.h>

typedef enum {atom, list} NODETYPE;
typedef struct listnode *NODEPTR;

struct listnode
   {
     NODETYPE type;
     union { int value; NODEPTR first; } data;
     NODEPTR next;
   };
```

```
void printlist(NODEPTR root)
  {
    register NODEPTR p;

    printf("( ");
    for (p = root; p != NULL; p = p->next)
      switch (p->type)
        {
          case list:
              printlist(p->data.first);
              break;
          case atom:
              printf("%d ", p->data.value);
              break;
          default:
              printf("\nfunny node\??!\n");
              return;
        }
    printf(") ");
  }
```

This function will print the list shown in the figure as

((( ) (121 122) 13) 2 3 (41))

A list is represented by enclosing its elements within a pair of parentheses. An empty list is represented as ( ).

We leave it as an exercise for you to write a function that creates such a list.

Example 3

Write a function that copies a specified amount of data from the input port to the output port of a device.

We assume that the device has three registers: an input port, an output port, and a status register. The input port and the status register can be read by a program, but not written; the output port can be written, but not read. Bit 0 of the status register is set to 1 when data arrives at the input port, and is set to 0 when that data is read from the input port. Bit 1 of the status register is set to 1 when the device is ready to accept data from the program. When data is placed at the output port, this bit is set to 0 and the data is written out.

The desired function is as follows:

```
typedef unsigned int DTYPE, STYPE;
#define IPORT ((const volatile DTYPE * const)0xffff0000)
#define OPORT ((volatile DTYPE * const)0xffff0004)
#define STATUS ((const volatile STYPE * const)0xffff0008)
#define IREADY 0x1
#define OREADY 0x2
```

```
void copy(register int n)
  {
    register int i;
    DTYPE temp;

    for (i = 0; i < n; i++)
      {
        while (!(*STATUS & IREADY)) /* wait */ ;
        temp = *IPORT;
        while (!(*STATUS & OREADY)) /* wait */ ;
        *OPORT = temp;
      }
  }
```

Modify the above function so that it waits for the input or output bit to be set to ready as long as the corresponding error bits (bits 2 and 3 respectively of the status register) have not been set. The function should reset the status register and abort the data transfer in that case.

Example 4
Write a function that concatenates multiple strings and returns the address of the concatenated string.

The desired function is as follows:

```
#include <stdio.h>
#include <stdarg.h>
#include <string.h>
#include <stdlib.h>

char *strmcat(int narg, ... )
  {
    va_list argp;
    register int i, size;
    register char *str;

    /* determine the size of the concatenated string */
    va_start(argp, narg);
    for (size = i = 0; i < narg; i++)
        size += strlen(va_arg(argp, char *));
    va_end(argp);

    /* allocate memory for creating the concatenated string */
    str = (char *) calloc(size+1, sizeof(char));
    if (!str)
      {
        fprintf(stderr, "not enough memory\n");
        return NULL;
      }
```

```
            /* create the concatenated string */
            va_start(argp, narg);
            for (i = 0; i < narg; i++)
                strcat(str, va_arg(argp, char *));
            va_end(argp);

            return str;
        }
```

This function when invoked as

```
        strmcat(5, "chloro", "fluoro",
                "carbons ", "destroy ", "ozone");
```

returns the string

```
        "chlorofluorocarbons destroy ozone"
```

Exercises 12

1. Write a function to score five-card poker hands into nothing, one pair, two pairs, three of a kind, straight (in order), flush (all of the same suit), full house (one pair and three of a kind), four of a kind, or straight flush (both straight and flush).

2. Rewrite the linked-list and tree manipulation functions given in Section 8.4 using the `typedef` facility.

3. Write a function that uses the set package developed in Section 12.8 to partition its input into values that appear once and those that appear multiple times.

4. Write a function that prints all the sets of size m having elements with integer values between 0 and n.

5. A company classifies its employees into three categories: regular, hourly, and contract. The personnel record for every employee contains name, sex, date of birth, and years of service. However, the salary information depends on the classification of the employee. Monthly salary is recorded for the regular employees, hourly rate and hours per week for the hourly employees, and the annual value of contract for the contract employees. Write a function that prints the names of the ten highest-paid employees who have worked less than five years for the company.

6. Write `fprintf` in terms of `vfprintf`.

7. Write a function that takes a variable number of arguments of different types and prints their values. The first argument is an array of elements of an enumeration type that indicates the number and types of the following arguments.

A Standard Library

All C compilers have a *standard library*, which is a collection of commonly used C functions for use by other C programs. A major source of nonportability in the earlier versions of C was that the "standard" library was not standard and the functions present in one implementation differed from those in another. ANSI C has standardized the functions that are expected to be found in the standard library. The prototypes for these functions are specified in a standard set of header files. These header files also include a number of macro and type definitions used by the library functions. The following is a list of the standard header files and a brief description of the nature of the information in them:

`<assert.h>`	function to add diagnostics to programs
`<ctype.h>`	character testing and character case mapping functions
`<errno.h>`	error handling functions
`<float.h>`	constants related to floating-point types
`<limits.h>`	sizes of integral types
`<locale.h>`	effect of locale on data types and functions
`<math.h>`	mathematical functions
`<setjmp.h>`	functions for nonlocal goto type of program control
`<signal.h>`	signal processing functions
`<stdarg.h>`	functions for processing variable argument lists
`<stddef.h>`	common symbolic constants and types
`<stdio.h>`	input/output functions
`<stdlib.h>`	miscellaneous utility functions
`<string.h>`	string processing functions
`<time.h>`	time manipulation and time conversion functions

We have already discussed in the text macros, types, and functions declared in the headers `<errno.h>`, `<stdarg.h>`, and `<stdio.h>`. We have also discussed the frequently used macros, types, and functions declared in the headers `<stddef.h>`, `<stdlib.h>`, and `<string.h>`. The headers `<limits.h>` and `<float.h>` define various parameters and limits of the execution environment; `<limits.h>` specifies sizes of integral types, whereas `<float.h>` specifies values of the parameters of the model that describes an implementation's representation of floating-point types. The header `<locale.h>` specifies mechanisms to deal with issues arising out of C becoming an international language, such as alphabet, collation, formatting of numbers and currency amounts, date, and time, in a locale-specific manner. We discuss in this appendix the facilities specified in `<assert.h>`, `<ctype.h>`, `<math.h>`, `<setjmp.h>`, `<signal.h>`, and `<time.h>`, and the rest of the facilities specified in `<stdlib.h>` and `<string.h>`.

A.1 DIAGNOSTICS

The header `<assert.h>` provides a facility to add diagnostics to programs.

```
void assert(int expression);
```

If the *expression* evaluates to 0 when the macro `assert` is executed, it prints on `stderr` a diagnostic message in an implementation-defined format, and then calls `abort` to terminate execution. The diagnostic message includes the text of the argument to `assert`, the source filename, and the source line number; the latter being respectively the values of the predefined preprocessing macros `__FILE__` and `__LINE__`.

If the macro `NDEBUG` is defined at the point in the source file where `<assert.h>` is included, `assert` is ignored.

A.2 CHARACTER HANDLING

The header `<ctype.h>` declares character testing and character case mapping functions. Each of these functions takes an integer argument whose value must be representable as an `unsigned char` or must equal the value of the macro `EOF`.

A.2.1 Character Testing Functions

Character testing functions return true (nonzero) if the argument satisfies the specified condition, and false (zero) otherwise.

```
int islower(int c);
```
returns true if *c* is a lowercase letter.

```
int isupper(int c);
```
returns true if *c* is an uppercase letter.

```
int isalpha(int c);
```
returns true if `islower(c)` or `isupper(c)` is true, that is, if *c* is a lowercase or uppercase letter.

```
int isdigit(int c);
```
returns true if *c* is a decimal digit.

```
int isalnum(int c);
```
returns true if `isalpha(c)` or `isdigit(c)` is true, that is, if *c* is a lowercase or uppercase letter or a decimal digit.

```
int iscntrl(int c);
```
returns true if *c* is a control character, that is, if *c* is one of the characters 0 to 0x1F, or 0x7F, in the seven-bit ASCII Code Set.

```
int isprint(int c);
```
returns true if *c* is a printing character including space, that is, if *c* is one of the characters 0x20 to 0x7E in the seven-bit ASCII Code Set.

```
int isgraph(int c);
```
returns true if *c* is a printing character other than space, that is, if *c* is one of the characters 0x21 to 0x7E in the seven-bit ASCII Code Set.

```
int ispunct(int c);
```
returns true if *c* is a printing character other than space or letter or digit.

```
int isspace(int c);
```
returns true if *c* is a standard whitespace character, that is, space, formfeed, newline, carriage return, horizontal tab, or vertical tab.

```
int isxdigit(int c);
```
returns true if *c* is a hexadecimal digit character.

A.2.2 Character Case Mapping Functions

Character case mapping functions convert the case of a letter.

```
int tolower(int c);
```
returns the corresponding lowercase letter if *c* is an uppercase letter, and *c* otherwise.

```
int toupper(int c);
```
returns the corresponding uppercase letter if *c* is a lowercase letter, and *c* otherwise.

A.3 MATHEMATICS

The header <math.h> declares a rich set of mathematical functions. It also defines a macro HUGE_VAL. For all functions, a *domain error* occurs if an input argument is outside the domain over which the mathematical function is defined. On a domain error, errno is set to EDOM. Similarly, a *range error* occurs if the result of the function cannot be represented as a double value. If the result overflows, the function returns HUGE_VAL and errno is set to ERANGE. If the result underflows, the function returns 0 and errno may be set to ERANGE.

A.3.1 Trigonometric Functions

Angles for trigonometric functions are specified in radians.

```
double acos(double x);
```
returns the arc cosine of *x* in the range $[0, \pi]$ radians.

```
double asin(double x);
```
returns the arc sine of *x* in the range $[-\pi/2, +\pi/2]$ radians.

```
double atan(double x);
```
returns the arc tangent of x in the range $[-\pi/2, +\pi/2]$ radians.

```
double atan2(double x, double y);
```
returns the arc tangent of x/y in the range $[-\pi, +\pi]$ radians.

```
double cos(double x);
```
returns the cosine of x.

```
double sin(double x);
```
returns the sine of x.

```
double tan(double x);
```
returns the tangent of x.

A.3.2 Hyperbolic Functions

```
double cosh(double x);
```
returns the hyperbolic cosine of x.

```
double sinh(double x);
```
returns the hyperbolic sine of x.

```
double tanh(double x);
```
returns the hyperbolic tangent of x.

A.3.3 Exponential and Logarithmic Functions

```
double exp(double x);
```
returns the exponential e^x.

```
double frexp(double x, int *p);
```
expresses x as $mantissa \times 2^{exponent}$, such that *mantissa* is in the interval $[1/2, 1)$, and returns *mantissa* as the function value and *exponent* in $*p$.

```
double ldexp(double x, int n);
```
returns $x \times 2^n$.

```
double log(double x);
```
returns the natural logarithm $ln(x)$.

```
double log10(double x);
```
returns the base 10 logarithm $\log_{10}(x)$.

```
double modf(double x, double *p);
```
splits x into an integer portion returned in $*p$ and a fractional portion returned as the function value.

A.3.4 Power Functions

```
double pow(double x, double y);
```
returns x^y.

```
double sqrt(double x);
```
returns $x^{1/2}$.

A.3.5 Nearest Integer, Absolute Value, and Remainder Functions

```
double ceil(double x);
```
returns the smallest integer not less than x.

```
double fabs(double x);
```
returns the absolute value of x.

```
double floor(double x);
```
returns the largest integer not greater than x.

```
double fmod(double x, double y);
```
returns the floating point remainder of x/y with the same sign as x.

A.4 NON-LOCAL JUMPS

The header `<setjmp.h>` defines a type `jmp_buf`, a macro `setjmp`, and a function `longjmp` that may be used to bypass the normal function call and return mechanism to handle abnormal or exceptional conditions.

```
int setjmp(jmp_buf env);
void longjmp(jmp_buf env, int status);
```

The macro `setjmp` saves its caller's environment in the jump buffer *env*, an object of type `jmp_buf`, and returns 0. The function `longjmp` takes as its arguments a jump buffer *env* in which an environment has been saved by `setjmp` and an integer value *status*, restores the environment, and then the program execution continues as if the corresponding call to `setjmp` had just returned with the value *status*.

ANSI C specifies that *status* cannot be 0; if it is, `setjmp` returns 1. If the environment was not saved earlier in *env* by a call to `setjmp` or if the function containing the invocation of `setjmp` has terminated execution before the call to `longjmp`, the result is undefined.

The following program illustrates the use of `setjmp` and `longjmp`.

```
#include <stdio.h>
#include <setjmp.h>

void set_status(int);
jmp_buf env;
```

```
int main(void)
  {
    int status;

    if ((status = setjmp(env)) != 0) /* setjmp returns 0
                                         the first time */
      {
        printf("return from longjmp with status = %d\n",
                status);
        return 0;
      }
    set_status(1);
    return 0;
  }

void set_status(int status)
  {
    longjmp(env, status); /* jump to main */
  }
```

The call to setjmp in main saves the current environment in buf and returns
0. In set_status, longjmp is called with status set to 0. It restores the
environment as saved in env, causes a jump back to main, and the execution
continues as if setjmp returned with value 1. The message is printed now.

A.5 SIGNAL HANDLING

The header <signal.h> declares macros, functions, and a type for handling
various signals.

A *signal* is a condition that can be reported during program execution. Signals may be generated by the error-detection mechanism of the underlying
hardware or operating system, by actions external to the program, or by the
program itself. Some examples of signals are (i) an erroneous arithmetic operation, such as dividing by 0, (ii) an access outside legal memory limits, such as
an attempt to store a value in an object pointed to by a bad pointer, (iii) an
interrupt from an external source, such as typing "delete" at the terminal, and
(iv) the decision by a program to abort itself on detecting bad input.

The following are the macros defined in <signal.h>, and they specify
the standard set of signals noted against each:

SIGABRT   abnormal termination, such as initiated by the abort function
SIGFPE   erroneous arithmetic operation, such as dividing by zero
SIGILL   invalid function image, such as illegal instruction
SIGINT   interactive attention signal, such as interrupt from the terminal
SIGSEGV   invalid memory access
SIGTERM   termination request

An implementation may define additional signals.

The following are the functions declared in <signal.h>:

```
int raise(int sig);
```
sends the specified signal *sig* to the executing program. It returns zero when successful, and a nonzero value otherwise.

```
void (*signal(int sig, void (*func)(int)))(int);
```
selects, depending upon the value of *func*, one of the three ways in which the receipt of the signal *sig* is handled: if the value of *func* is SIG_IGN, the signal is ignored; if it is SIG_DFL, the implementation-defined default behavior is used; otherwise, the function pointed to by *func*, called the *signal handler*, is used to process the signal. A successful call to signal returns the previous value of *func* for the specified signal; otherwise, SIG_ERR is returned.

When a signal *sig* occurs for which a handler *func* has been specified, the signal is first restored to its implementation-defined default behavior by executing the equivalent of signal(*sig*, SIG_DFL), and then the signal handler is called by executing the equivalent of (*func*)(*sig*). If the signal handler returns, execution resumes from where it was when the signal occurred.

The type defined in <signal.h> is sig_atomic_t. Objects of this type are integral objects that can be accessed as atomic entities, even in the presence of asynchronous interrupts, and should be declared volatile static.

The following program illustrates the use of the signal handling facility:

```
#include <stdio.h>
#include <signal.h>
#define   MAX   5

int cnt = 0, totcnt = 0, interrupts = 0;
void print(void);

int main(void)
  {
    /* catch the interactive attention signal */
    (void) signal(SIGINT, print);

    for ( ; getchar(); cnt++)
       ;
    printf("\ntotal characters read = %d\n", totcnt);

    return 0;
  }

void print(void)
  {
    if (interrupts++ < MAX)
        /* reset to catch the interactive attention signal */
        (void) signal(SIGINT, print);

    printf("\ncharacters read = %d\n", cnt);
    totcnt += cnt;
    cnt = 0;
  }
```

A.6 GENERAL UTILITIES

The header `<stdlib.h>` declares functions for string conversion, pseudo-random sequence generation, memory management, communication with the environment, searching and sorting, and integer arithmetic. We have already discussed the memory management functions `malloc`, `calloc`, `realloc`, and `free` in Section 7.8; the remaining functions are described here.

A.6.1 String Conversion

`double atof(const char *s);`
converts the string *s* to its `double` representation and returns the converted value.

`int atoi(const char *s);`
converts the string *s* to its `int` representation and returns the converted value.

`long int atol(const char *s);`
converts the string *s* to its `long int` representation and returns the converted value.

`double strtod (const char *s, char **endp);`
converts the largest possible initial portion of the string *s* to its double representation, ignoring the leading whitespaces, and stores at *endp* the address of the first character past the converted portion of the string unless *endp* is `NULL`. If no conversion is possible, zero is returned, *endp* (if not `NULL`) is set to the value of *s*, and `errno` is set to `ERANGE`. If the converted value would cause overflow, plus or minus `HUGE_VAL`, depending upon the sign of the converted value, is returned; if the converted value would cause underflow, zero is returned; in either case, `errno` is set to `ERANGE`.

`long int strtol(const char *s, char **endp, int base);`
converts the largest possible initial portion of the string *s* to `long int`, ignoring the leading whitespaces, and stores at *endp* the address of the first character past the converted portion of the string, unless *endp* is `NULL`. If the value of the *base* is zero, the number is a decimal, octal, or hexadecimal constant; the leading o implies octal and the leading ox or OX hexadecimal. If the value of *base* is between 2 and 36, the number consists of a sequence of letters and digits representing an integer in the specified base, optionally preceded by a plus or minus sign. Letters from a through z, or A through Z, are ascribed the values 10 through 35 respectively, only letters with ascribed values less than that of the *base* being permitted. If the value of `base` is 16, the sequence of letters and digits may optionally be preceded by the characters ox or OX. If the conversion is not possible, zero is returned. If the converted value would cause overflow, `LONG_MAX` or `LONG_MIN` is returned depending upon the sign of the converted value, and `errno` is set to `ERANGE`.

```
unsigned long int strtoul(const char *s,
                          char **endp, int base);
```
behaves like strtol, except that the converted value in this case is unsigned
long int, and that if the converted value would cause overflow ULONG_MAX
is returned.

A.6.2 Pseudo-random Sequence Generation

```
int rand(void);
```
generates a pseudo-random integer in the range 0 to RAND_MAX.

```
void srand(unsigned int seed);
```
uses the argument *seed* as the seed for the sequence of pseudo-random numbers to be returned by subsequent calls to rand. If rand is called before any
calls to srand, the default seed value of 1 is used for generating pseudo-
random numbers.

A.6.3 Communication with the Environment

```
void abort(void);
```
causes the abnormal termination of the program, and returns an implementation-defined form of the status "unsuccessful termination" to the host environment by means of the function call raise(SIGABRT).

```
int atexit(void (*func)(void));
```
registers the function *func* to be called at the normal termination of the
program. It returns zero if the registration succeeds, and a nonzero value otherwise.

```
void exit(int status);
```
causes the normal termination of the program. First, all functions registered
with the atexit function are called as many times as they are registered, in the
reverse order of their registration. Next, all output streams are flushed, all open
streams are closed, and all files created by the tmpfile function are removed.
Finally, control returns to the host environment. An implementation-defined
form of the status "successful termination" is returned if the value of *status* is 0
or EXIT_SUCCESS, and an implementation-defined form of the status "unsuccessful termination" is returned if the value of *status* is EXIT_FAILURE. The
status returned is implementation-defined otherwise.

```
char *getenv(const char *name);
```
searches an environment list, provided by the host environment, for a string
that matches *name*, and returns a pointer to the string associated with the
matched list member. If the indicated *name* is not found, a null pointer is
returned.

```
int system(const char *s);
```
passes the string *s* to the host environment for execution by a command processor in an implementation-defined way, and returns an implementation-defined value.

A.6.4 Searching and Sorting

```
void *bsearch(const void *key,
              const void *base, size_t n, size_t size,
              int (* compare)(const void *, const void *));
```
searches in an array of *n* elements for the element that matches the object pointed to by *key*. The first element of this array is pointed to by *base*, and the elements are of size *size*. The pointer *compare* points to a function that is called with two arguments that point respectively to the *key* object and an array element and returns an integer less than, equal to, or greater than zero according as the *key* object is less than, equal to, or greater than the array element. The array elements are assumed to be sorted in ascending order, according to *compare*. The bsearch function returns a pointer to the matched array element, or NULL if no matching element is found. If two array elements compare as equal, the element that is matched is unspecified.

```
void qsort(const void *base, size_t n, size_t size,
           int (* compare)(const void *, const void *));
```
sorts in ascending order, according to *compare*, an array of *n* elements whose first element is pointed to by *base* and the elements are of size *size*. The pointer *compare* is as specified in the description of bsearch. If two array elements compare as equal, their order in the sorted array is not specified.

A.6.5 Integer Arithmetic

```
int abs(int n);
```
computes and returns the absolute value of its int argument *n*.

```
long int labs(long int n);
```
computes and returns the absolute value of its long int argument *n*.

```
div_t div (int num, int denom);
```
computes the quotient and remainder of the division of the numerator *num* by the denominator *denom*, and returns a structure of type div_t containing quotient quot and remainder rem as int members.

```
ldiv_t ldiv(long int num, long int denom);
```
computes the quotient and remainder of the division of the numerator *num* by the denominator *denom*, and returns a structure of type ldiv_t containing quotient quot and remainder rem as long int members.

A.7 STRING PROCESSING

The header <string.h> declares string processing functions. Some of these functions have been discussed in Section 7.4.1; the rest are described below.

```
size_t strspn(const char *s1, const char *s2);
```
locates in the string *s1* the first occurrence of a character that is not included in the string *s2*, and returns the length of the maximum initial segment of *s1* that consists entirely of characters from *s2*.

```
size_t strcpn(const char *s1, const char *s2);
```
locates in the string *s1* the first occurrence of a character that is included in the string *s2*, and returns the length of the maximum initial segment of *s1* that consists entirely of characters not from *s2*.

```
char *strpbrk(const char *s1, const char *s2);
```
locates in the string *s1* the first occurrence of a character that is included in the string *s2*, and returns a pointer to this character. A null pointer is returned if no character from *s2* is found in *s1*.

```
char *strstr(const char *s1, const char *s2);
```
locates in the string *s1* the first occurrence of the sequence of characters (excluding the terminating null character) in the string *s2*, and returns a pointer to the beginning of the first occurrence. A null pointer is returned if *s2* is not found in *s1*.

```
char *strtok(const char *s1, const char *s2);
```
splits, by a sequence of calls, the string *s1* into a sequence of tokens, each of which is delimited by a character from *s2*, and returns a pointer to the first character of a token, and a null pointer when no further token is found. The first call in the call sequence has a non-NULL *s1* as its argument, and locates the first token in *s1* consisting entirely of characters not in *s2*, and terminates the token when located by overwriting the next character in *s1* with the null character. Each subsequent call has NULL as the argument and searches from just past the end of the previous token. The string *s2* may be different from call to call. For example,

```
char *tok, str[ ] = "&&x&&y*|*z";
tok = strtok(str, "&" );   /* tok points to the token "x" */
tok = strtok(NULL, "*" );  /* tok points to the token "&y" */
tok = strtok(NULL, "*|" ); /* tok points to the token "z" */
tok = strtok(NULL, "|" );   /* tok is a null pointer */
```

```
char *strerror(int errnum);
```
maps the error number in *errnum* to an implementation-defined error message string, and returns a pointer to this string.

```
void *memcpy(void *s1, const void *s2, size_t n);
```
copies *n* characters from the object pointed to by *s2* to the object pointed to by *s1*, and returns *s1*. The result is unpredictable if the objects overlap.

```
void *memmove(void *s1, const void *s2, size_t n);
```
copies *n* characters from the object pointed to by *s2* to the object pointed to by *s1*, and returns *s1*. However, unlike memcpy, it works even if the objects overlap.

```
int memcmp(const void *s1, const void *s2, size_t n);
```
compares the first *n* characters of the object pointed to by *s1* with those of the object pointed to by *s2*, and returns a negative value if *s1* is lexicographically less than *s2*, zero if *s1* is equal to *s2*, and a positive value if *s1* is lexicographically greater than *s2*.

```
void *memchr(const void *s, int c, size_t n);
```
locates the first occurrence of *c* (converted to an unsigned char) amongst the first *n* characters of the object pointed to by *s*, and returns a pointer to the located character if the search succeeds and NULL otherwise.

```
void *memset(const void *s, int c, size_t n);
```
copies *c* (converted to an unsigned char) into each of the first *n* characters of the object pointed to by *s*, and returns *s*.

A.8   DATE AND TIME

The header <time.h> declares time manipulation and time conversion functions. Some of these functions deal with *calendar time* that represents the current date and time, some with *local time*, which is the calendar time for some specific time zone, and some with *daylight-saving time*, which temporarily changes the algorithm for determining the local time. The components of calendar time, called the *broken-down time*, can be represented in struct tm defined as

```
struct tm
   {
      int tm_sec;      /* seconds after the minute (0–59) */
      int tm_min;      /* minutes after the hour (0–59) */
      int tm_hour;     /* hours since midnight (0–23) */
      int tm_mday;     /* day of the month (1–31) */
      int tm_mon;      /* months since January (0–11) */
      int tm_year;     /* years since 1900 */
      int tm_wday;     /* days since Sunday (0–6) */
      int tm_yday;     /* days since January 1 (0–365) */
      int tm_isdst;    /* daylight-saving time flag:
                          >0 => daylight-saving time in effect
                           0 => not in effect
                          <0 => information unavailable */
   }
```

The following functions use the types clock_t and time_t, which are arithmetic types capable of representing time.

A.8.1 Time Manipulation

```
clock_t clock(void);
```
returns the processor time used by the program since the beginning of its execution, or −1 (cast to clock_t) if the time used is unavailable. The expression

`clock()`/`CLK_TCK` gives this time in seconds, where `CLK_TCK` is a macro defined in `<time.h>`.

`time_t time(time_t *tp);`
returns the current calendar time, and `-1` (cast to `time_t`) if it is unavailable. The return value is also assigned to `*tp`, if `tp` is not NULL.

`double difftime(time_t time1, time_t time0);`
returns the difference in seconds, *time1 – time0*, between two calendar times, *time1* and *time0*.

`time_t mktime(struct tm *tp);`
converts the broken-down local time specified in `*tp` into a calendar time with the same encoding as that of the values returned by the `time` function. The original values of *tp*->`tm_wday` and *tp*->`tm_yday` are ignored by `mktime`. On successful completion, `mktime` returns the converted value, and adjusts `*tp`, setting appropriately the components `tm_wday` and `tm_yday`; otherwise, `-1` (cast to `time_t`) is returned.

A.8.2 Time Conversion

These functions, except for `strftime`, return values in a broken-down time structure or a character array. The values returned in either of these objects may be overwritten by an execution of any of the other functions.

`char *asctime(const struct tm *tp);`
converts the broken-down time in `*tp` into a string of the form

    Thu June 25 09:05:45 1986\n\0

and returns a pointer to the string.

`struct tm *localtime(const time_t *tp);`
converts the calendar time `*tp` into broken-down local time, and returns a pointer to this structure.

`char *ctime(const time_t *tp);`
converts the calendar time `*tp` into local time in the form of a string. It is equivalent to `asctime(localtime(tp))`.

`struct tm *gmtime(const time_t *tp);`
converts the calendar time `*tp` into Coordinated Universal Time (UTC), represented in a broken-down time structure, and returns a pointer to this structure. If UTC is not available, a null pointer is returned.

`size_t strftime(char *s, size_t maxsize,`
`                const char *format, const struct tm *tp);`
formats date and time information in `*tp` into a string according to *format*, and places the result in the character array pointed to by *s*. The *format* string may contain ordinary characters, which (including the terminating null character)

are copied as is into *s*. It may also contain zero or more conversion specifications, which are replaced in *s* by appropriate characters described below:

%a	abbreviated weekday name
%A	full weekday name
%b	abbreviated month name
%B	full month name
%c	appropriate date and time representation
%d	day of the month (01–31)
%H	hour in 24-hour clock (00–23)
%I	hour in 12-hour clock (01–12)
%j	day of the year (001–366)
%m	month (01–12)
%M	minute (00–59)
%p	equivalent of either AM or PM
%S	second (00–59)
%U	week number of the year with Sunday as the first day of the week (00–53)
%w	weekday with Sunday as 0 (0–6)
%W	week number of the year with Monday as the first day of the week (00–53)
%x	appropriate date representation
%X	appropriate time representation
%y	year without century (00–99)
%Y	year with century
%z	time zone name, if any
%%	%

If the total number of resulting characters including the terminating null character is not more than *maxsize*, strftime returns the number of characters placed into *s* excluding the terminating null character; otherwise, zero is returned and the contents of *s* are indeterminate.

⊞ B Precedence and Associativity of Operators

Symbol	Description	Associativity
()	Function call	Left to right
[]	Array subscript	
.	Structure member	
->	Structure pointer	
+	Unary plus	Right to left
−	Unary minus	
++	Postfix/prefix increment	
−−	Postfix/prefix decrement	
~	Bitwise logical complement	
!	Logical NOT	
*	Indirection (dereferencing)	
&	Address	
sizeof	Size of an object	
(*type*)	Cast to *type*	
*	Multiplication	Left to right
/	Division	
%	Remainder (modulus)	
+	Addition	Left to right
−	Subtraction	
<<	Bitwise left shift	Left to right
>>	Bitwise right shift	
<	Less than	Left to right
<=	Less than or equal to	
>	Greater than	
>=	Greater than or equal to	
==	Equal to	Left to right
!=	Not equal to	
&	Bitwise AND	Left to right

Symbol	Description	Associativity
^	Bitwise exclusive OR	Left to right
|	Bitwise inclusive OR	Left to right
&&	Logical AND	Left to right
||	Logical OR	Left to right
? :	Conditional	Right to left
=	Assignment (simple)	Right to left
*=	Multiplication assignment	
/=	Division assignment	
%=	Remainder assignment	
+=	Addition assignment	
-=	Subtraction assignment	
&=	Bitwise AND assignment	
^=	Bitwise exclusive OR assignment	
|=	Bitwise inclusive OR assignment	
<<=	Left shift assignment	
>>=	Right shift assignment	
,	Comma	Left to right

Operators grouped together between horizontal lines have the same precedence and associativity. Those in higher groups have higher precedence.

Besides the operators given in the table, ANSI C has introduced the operators # and ## for creation of strings and concatenation of tokens. The order of evaluation of these operators is unspecified. The unary plus (+) operator has been introduced by ANSI C for symmetry with the unary minus (–) operator.

C Living with an Old C Compiler

The reference manual contained in Kernighan and Ritchie's 1978 classic book *The C Programming Language* provided the original definition of C. While ANSI C preserves the spirit of the original C, it has incorporated various enhancements to the original C and modern developments in programming languages. Most of the changes, however, are minor. Considering that some of you may still have pre-ANSI-C compilers, we discuss important differences between the original and ANSI C, so that you may be able to write C programs for these compilers as well.

C.1 MOST NOTABLE CHANGE

ANSI C differs from the original C most notably in the way a function is defined and used.

Function Definition

The general form for defining a function in the original C is as follows:

function-type   function-name (parameter-list)
     parameter-declarations

{
     variable-declarations

     function-statements

}

Only the parameter names are specified in the *parameter-list*. Their types are specified in the *parameter-declarations*, following the parameter list. A parameter whose type is not specified is taken to be of type `int`. If a function does not have any parameters, it is indicated by an empty pair of parentheses (), following the function name. The specification of *function-type* is optional, if it is `int`.

Here are some examples of function definitions in ANSI C and their corresponding definitions in the original C:

ANSI C	Original C

```int main(void)```
```{```
  ```...```
```}```
	```main()```
	```{```
	  ```...```
	```}```

```int quotient(int i, int j)```
```{```
  ```...```
```}```
	```int quotient(i, j)```
	```{```
	  ```...```
	```}```

```double chebyshev(int n, float x)```
```{```
  ```...```
```}```
	```double chebyshev(n, x)```
	  ```int n;```
	  ```float x;```
	```{```
	  ```...```
	```}```

```char *cmp(char s[], int n, char *t)```
```{```
  ```...```
```}```
	```char *cmp(s, n, t)```
	  ```char s[], *t;```
	  ```int n;```
	```{```
	  ```...```
	```}```

```void mktree(struct info **parent)```
```{```
  ```...```
```}```
	```mktree(parent)```
	  ```struct info **parent;```
	```{```
	  ```...```
	```}```

In the first example, the return type of `main` has not been specified in the original C version, as it is taken to be `int` by default. Instead of `void`, the empty pair of parentheses following the function name are used to specify that `main` takes no arguments. In the `quotient` example, the types of the parameters i and j have not been specified, and they are taken to be of type `int`. But remember that the omission of type specification is a bad programming practice, and you should avoid it. You should also specify the return type of a function, even if it is `int`, as we have done for `quotient`. The `chebyshev` example shows the type declarations for parameters. Note that each parameter declaration is terminated with a semicolon. The `cmp` example shows that parameters of the same type can be declared together in one declaration, and that the parameters need not be declared in the same order in which they appear in the parameter list. Finally, the `mktree` example illustrates the convention of not specifying the return type for a function that does not return a value, if the type `void` is not supported by the compiler.

Function Call

In the original C, no declaration is required in the calling function for a function being called that returns an `int` . However, if a called function returns a value other than `int` and its declaration is not available, it must be explicitly declared in the calling function using a declaration of the form

    function-type   *function-name* () ;

Unlike ANSI C function prototypes, parameter names and their types are not specified in the declaration. The following example shows the declaration and call to the `cmp` function in ANSI C and the original C:

ANSI C	Original C
``char *scmp(char s[], char *t, int n)
{
    char *cmp(char [], int, char *);
    int safestr(char [], int);

    return safestr(s,n) ?
           cmp(s,n,t): NULL;
}``` | ```char *scmp(s, t, n)
    char s[], *t;
    int n;
{
    char *cmp();

    return safestr(s,n) ?
           cmp(s,n,t): NULL;
}``` |

In the original C version, it has been specified that `cmp` returns a `char *`, but the types of its parameters have not been specified. Also, no declaration has been given for `safestr`, as it returns an `int`.

Parameter Binding

The type conversion rules at the time of binding arguments to the parameters are different in ANSI and the original C. In the original C, when an expression appears as an argument in a function call, adjustments are made in the type of the value of the expression, using the unary conversion rules. In particular, arguments of type `float` are converted to `double`, and of type `char` or `short` to `int`, before being passed as arguments. Adjustments are also made to the types of the function's parameters, and parameters of type `char`, `short`, or `float` are implicitly promoted to `int`, `int`, and `double` respectively. No other conversions are performed automatically; appropriate casts must be used to effect necessary conversions. The following example illustrates this difference:

ANSI C	Original C
``double poly(int i, int j)
{
    double chebyshev(int, float);

    return chebyshev(i,j);
}``` | ```double poly(i, j)
    int i, j;
{
    double chebyshev();

    return chebyshev(i, (float) j);
}``` |

In ANSI C, when a function for which a prototype has been specified is called, the arguments to the function are converted, as if by assignment, to the declared types of the parameters. Thus, the call

```
chebyshev(i, j);
```

is equivalent to

```
chebyshev(i, (float) j);
```

and no explicit casting is necessary.

Since the original C does not have function prototypes, the function arguments are not checked for consistency with the parameters. Functions can potentially take an arbitrary number of arguments of arbitrary types. Thus, an original C compiler does not detect an error in the following call to cmp:

```
return safestr(s,n) ? cmp(s,t,n) : NULL;
```

in which t, a char *, is being passed to an int, and n, an int, to a char *. It also does not detect an error in the following call to safestr:

```
return safestr(s,t,n) ? cmp(s,t,n) : NULL;
```

in which there is an extra argument and the types of the second argument and parameter do not match. Similarly, the error that safestr has been provided one less argument in the following call:

```
return safestr(s) ? cmp(s,t,n) : NULL;
```

is also not detected. Mismatch in number and types of arguments and parameters is the most common error found in programs written in the original C, and you should always ensure that the caller provides the correct number of arguments of consistent types, and that the callee does not use an unsupplied argument.

C.2 WORK-AROUNDS

ANSI C provides some convenient features not available in the original C. However, you may get by in many instances by using alternative facilities.

Size of an Identifier

ANSI C permits a minimum of 31 significant characters in identifiers, whereas the original C specifies that only the first eight characters of an identifier are significant. Thus, variable names like average_weight and average_width may not be distinguishable in the original C, as they are identical up to the first eight characters. Use small variable names.

String Concatenation

The original C does not concatenate adjacent string constants. Write them as one constant and use a backslash at the end of a line to continue a long string onto the next line.

Automatic Type Conversion

The automatic type conversion rules in the original C are somewhat different. Keep in mind the following figure when writing expressions involving mixed types:

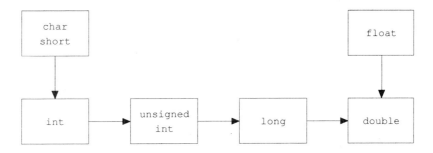

Predefined Data Types

The types `size_t` and `ptrdiff_t` are not standard in the original C. Use `int`, instead.

Generic Pointer

ANSI C uses the type `void *` as the proper type for a *generic* pointer. The type `char *` plays this role in the original C.

`switch` Statement

The `switch` statement control and case label expressions may only be of type `int` (not any integral type) in the original C. Use the `if` statement for other integral types.

Initialization of Automatic Arrays and Structures

ANSI C permits the initialization of automatic arrays and structures, a feature not permitted in the original C. You should replace initialization with explicit assignments in such cases, as shown in the following example:

ANSI C	Original C
| ```
void foo(void)
    {
        int a[2] = {0, 1};
        struct pt
            {
                float x, y;
            } p = {0, 0};
        ...

    }
``` | ```
foo()
    {
        int a[2];
        struct pt
            {
                float x, y;
            } p;
        a[0] = 0, a[1] = 1;
        p.x = p.y = 0;
        ...
    }
``` |

However, the original C does allow initialization of static arrays and structures. Therefore, if you do not need to subsequently change the elements of the arrays or structures to be initialized, you may declare them to be `static` and initialize them, as shown in the following example:

ANSI C	Original C

<pre>void foo(void)
  {
    int a[2] = {0, 1};
    struct pt
      {
        float x, y;
      } p = {0, 0};
    ...
  }</pre>
	<pre>foo()
	  {
	    static int a[2] = {0, 1};
	    static struct pt
	      {
	        float x, y;
	      } p = {0, 0};
	    ...
	  }</pre>

Initialization of Unions

ANSI C allows restricted initialization of union variables, whereas the original C does not allow any union variable (including `static`) to be initialized. Replace initializations with explicit assignments.

Structures and Unions in Assignments and Function Definitions

In ANSI C, a structure variable may be assigned to another structure variable, structures may be passed as function arguments, and functions may return structures. These features are not available in the original C. However, you may replace structure assignment by assignments to individual members; instead of passing a structure as argument, you may either pass structure members or a pointer to the structure; and a function may return a pointer to the structure, rather than returning the structure. The following example illustrates these work-arounds:

ANSI C	Original C

<pre>struct pt
  {
    float x, y;
  } p = {0, 0};
 	
void bar(void)
  {
    struct pt q, r;
    float dist(struct pt), f;
    struct pt polar(struct pt);
 	
    q = p;
    f = dist(q);
    r = polar(q);
    ...
  }</pre>
	<pre>struct pt
	  {
	    float x, y;
	  } p = {0, 0};
	
	bar()
	  {
	    struct pt q, *r;
	    float dist(/* int, int */);
	    struct pt *polar(/* struct pt * */);
	
	    q.x = p.x, q.y = p.y;
	    f = dist(q.x, q.y);
	    r = polar(&q);
	    ...
	  }</pre>

The preceding observations also hold for union types.

Enumeration Types

The original C does not provide enumeration types. However, their functionality can be partially simulated using `#defines` and `typedefs`, as shown in the following example:

ANSI C	Original C

`typedef enum {chablis,claret} wine;`	`#define chablis 0`
	`#define claret  1`
	`typedef int wine;`

`...` `wine bordeaux, *burgundy;`	`...` `wine bordeaux, *burgundy;`

`...`
`bordeaux = claret;`
`*burgundy = chablis;`
	`...`
	`bordeaux = claret;`
	`*burgundy = chablis;`

Standard Library

The "standard" library is not standard in the original C, and the functions present in one implementation may differ from those in another. However, you should be able to find most of the functions defined in the standard library by ANSI C in your implementation's library, although sometimes under different names.

C.3 IRRECONCILABLES

The following are some of the important ANSI C features for which there are no analogs in the original C:

- A standard and portable facility for writing functions that take a variable number of arguments.
- The type qualifiers `const` and `volatile` to indicate special properties of the objects being declared.
- The extra-precision type `long double`.
- The facility to explicitly specify the signedness of characters and other types by using the keywords `signed` and `unsigned`.
- The suffixes `U` or `L` for integers and `F` or `L` for reals, to make the types of constants explicit.
- The notation for expressing a hexadecimal constant by a bit pattern of the form `'\xhh'`.
- Trigraph sequences as alternative spellings of C characters not in the ASCII invariant code set, and the data type `wchar_t` for wide characters.
- The preprocessing operators `defined`, `#`, and `##`.

- Flexibility to allow whitespaces to precede or follow the directive-introducing character #.
- The preprocessing directives #elif and #pragma.
- The #include directive of the form

    #include *token-sequence*

- The special macro names __LINE__, __FILE__, __DATE__, __TIME__, and __STDC__.

✛ D Internal Representation

Consider the simple problem: 6 + 5 = ?. Almost all of you would say that the answer is 11 and, of course, you are right. However, certain computer scientists and inhabitants of the planet of Hex, who have 16 fingers and toes, may reply that the answer is 'b' and they are also perfectly right. Instead of counting 0, 1, 2, 3, 4, 5, 6, 7, 8, 9, 10, 11, 12, 13, 14, 15, 16, 17, 18, 19, 20, and so on like the rest of us, these people count 0, 1, 2, 3, 4, 5, 6, 7, 8, 9, a, b, c, d, e, f, 10, 11, 12, 13, 14, 15, 16, 17, 18, 19, 1a, 1b, 1c, 1d, 1e, 1f, 20, and so on. The point is that an entity can be represented in many ways as long as the meaning of the symbols used and the system of representation is well defined and understood. Computers are built using devices that can be at any time in one of the two states: 'on' and 'off', which represent 1 and 0 respectively. It is not surprising, therefore, that almost all present-day computers are based on the binary system of representation that uses only two symbols: 1 and 0. In this appendix, we first review some number systems and then see how numbers and characters are internally represented in a computer.

D.1 NUMBER SYSTEMS

The number system that we are accustomed to uses the ten digits 0, 1, 2, 3, 4, 5, 6, 7, 8, and 9, and is called the *decimal*, or *base-10*, number system. The significance of a digit in a number depends upon the *position* occupied by the digit. For example, the number 596 represents the number five hundred ninety-six and can be written in the expanded form as

$$(5 \times 100) + (9 \times 10) + (6 \times 1),$$

or

$$(5 \times 10^2) + (9 \times 10^1) + (6 \times 10^0).$$

Thus, the digits that appear in the various positions of a decimal number are coefficients of powers of 10, representing various positions.

In a decimal number representing a fraction, digits to the right of the decimal point also represent coefficients of powers of 10, but the powers appearing on the base 10 are negative integers. For example, the number 47.238 can be written in the expanded form as

$$(4 \times 10) + (7 \times 1) + (2 \times \frac{1}{10}) + (3 \times \frac{1}{100}) + (8 \times \frac{1}{1000}),$$

or

$$(4 \times 10^1) + (7 \times 1^0) + (2 \times 10^{-1}) + (3 \times 10^{-2}) + (8 \times 10^{-3}).$$

Other than decimal, the important positional number systems used in computing are binary, octal, and hexadecimal. These number systems differ in the *base* (also called the *radix*) used. Whereas the decimal system uses base 10, the binary system uses base 2, the octal system uses base 8, and the hexadecimal system uses base 16.

The *binary* number system is a *base-2* system and makes use of the binary digits 0 and 1. As in the case of the decimal system, the significance of a digit in a binary number is determined by its position. For example, the binary number 101.110 can be expanded as

$$(1 \times 2^2) + (0 \times 2^1) + (1 \times 2^0) + (1 \times 2^{-1}) + (1 \times 2^{-2}) + (0 \times 2^{-3}),$$

and thus has the decimal number value

$$4 + 0 + 1 + 1/2 + 1/4 + 0 = 5.75.$$

The *octal* number system is a *base-8* system and makes use of the eight digits 0, 1, 2, 3, 4, 5, 6, and 7. Again, the significance of a digit in an octal number is determined by its position. For example, the octal number 7.2 can be expanded as

$$(7 \times 8^0) + (2 \times 8^{-1}),$$

and thus has the decimal number value

$$7 + 2/8 = 7.25.$$

The *hexadecimal* number system is a *base-16* system and makes use of the sixteen digits 0, 1, 2, 3, 4, 5, 6, 7, 8, 9, a(10), b(11), c(12), d(13), e(14), and f(15). The significance of a digit in this system also depends on its position in the number. For example, the hexadecimal number 8.c can be expanded as

$$(8 \times 16^0) + (12 \times 16^{-1}),$$

and thus has the decimal number value

$$8 + 12/16 = 8.75.$$

To determine the decimal number value of a binary, octal, or hexadecimal number with a non-terminating fraction, we make use of the formula

$$1 + r + r^2 + r^3 + \cdots = \frac{1}{1-r}, \quad -1 < r < 1$$

for the sum of an infinite geometric series. For example, the binary number

$$0.1\ 0110\ 0110\ 0110\ \ldots$$

can be expanded as

$$1{\times}2^{-1} + (1{\times}2^{-3} + 1{\times}2^{-4}) + (1{\times}2^{-7} + 1{\times}2^{-8}) + (1{\times}2^{-11} + 1{\times}2^{-12}) + \ldots$$

and thus has the decimal number value

$$1 \times 2^{-1} + (1 \times 2^{-3} + 1 \times 2^{-4})(1 + 2^{-4} + 2^{-8} + \ldots)$$
$$= 1 \times 2^{-1} + (1 \times 2^{-3} + 1 \times 2^{-4})(1/(1 - 2^{-4}))$$
$$= 1/2 + (1/8 + 1/16)(16/15)$$
$$= 0.7$$

To avoid confusion about the base that is being used, we will enclose a nondecimal number within parentheses and write the base as a subscript. Thus, $(101.110)_2$ denotes a base-2 (binary) number, $(7.2)_8$ denotes a base-8 (octal) number, and $(8.c)_{16}$ denotes a base-16 (hexadecimal) number.

D.1.1 Conversion from Base-10 to Base-b

To convert the integer portion of a base-10 number to its base-b equivalent, the integer is divided repeatedly by b until a quotient of zero results. The successive remainders are the digits from right to left of the base-b representation. To convert the fractional part of a decimal number to its base-b equivalent, the fractional part is repeatedly multiplied by b till the derived fraction reduces to zero, or the derived fraction begins to repeat, or the derived fraction has enough digits for the required precision. The integer portions of the successive products are the digits from left to right of the base-b representation.

For example, the binary representation of $(25)_{10}$ is $(11001)_2$, since

		0	1
2	1		1
2	3		0
2	6		0
2	12		1
2	25		

The octal representation of $(25)_{10}$ is $(31)_8$, since

		0	3
8	3		1
8	25		

The hexadecimal representation of $(25)_{10}$ is $(19)_{16}$, since

		0	1
16	1		9
16	25		

The binary representation of $(.3125)_{10}$ is $(.0101)_2$, since

	.3125
	$\times$ 2
0	.625
	$\times$ 2
1	.25
	$\times$ 2
0	.5
	$\times$ 2
1	0

The binary representation of $(.7)_{10}$ is $(.1\ 0110\ 0110\ \ldots)_2$, where the pattern 0110 is repeated *ad infinitum*, since

	.7
	$\times$ 2
1	.4
	$\times$ 2
0	.8
	$\times$ 2
1	.6
	$\times$ 2
1	.2
	$\times$ 2
0	.4

This representation is commonly written as $(.1\overline{0110})_2$.

Finally, the binary representation of $(25.3125)_{10}$ is $(11001.0101)_2$, since the binary representation of $(25)_{10}$ is $(11001)_2$ and that of $(.3125)_{10}$ is $(.0101)_2$.

D.1.2 Conversion from Octal or Hexadecimal to Binary and Vice Versa

For conversion from octal or hexadecimal to binary, we need only replace each octal or hexadecimal digit by its binary equivalent. For example, to convert $(2705)_8$ to binary, replace 2 by 010, 7 by 111, 0 by 000, and 5 by 101 to obtain

$(010111000101)_2$, and to convert $(abc)_{16}$ to binary, replace a by 1010, b by 1011, and c by 1100 to obtain $(101010111100)_2$.

To convert a binary number to octal, group the digits in threes to the left and to the right of the radix point. If the number of digits left in the last group is less than three, the missing digits are made up by adding zeros. A similar procedure is followed for converting a binary number to a hexadecimal number, except that the groups now consist of four digits. For example:

$$
\begin{aligned}
(110010)_2 &= (110\ 010) &&= (62)_8 \\
(110010)_2 &= (0011\ 0010)_2 &&= (32)_{16} \\
(10101111)_2 &= (010\ 101\ 111)_2 &&= (257)_8 \\
(10101111)_2 &= (1010\ 1111)_2 &&= (af)_{16} \\
(1010.10101)_2 &= (001\ 010\ .\ 101\ 010)_2 &&= (12.52)_8 \\
(1010.10101)_2 &= (1010\ .\ 1010\ 1000)_2 &&= (a.a8)_{16}
\end{aligned}
$$

The conversion from octal or hexadecimal to binary and vice versa can also be effected via decimal equivalents. Thus, to convert the octal $(62)_8$ to binary, we first convert it to its decimal equivalent $(50)_{10}$ and then convert the decimal equivalent to its binary equivalent $(110010)_2$. Similarly, to convert the binary number $(1010.10101)_2$ to hexadecimal, we first convert it to its decimal equivalent $(10.65625)_{10}$ and then convert the decimal equivalent to its hexadecimal equivalent $(a.a8)_{16}$.

D.2 NUMBER REPRESENTATION

To store a decimal integer in a computer, it is first converted to its binary equivalent and then stored right-justified in a word. One bit of the word, usually the leftmost, is reserved to specify the sign of the integer. Typically, a 0 implies positive and 1 a negative sign. For example, the decimal integer 25 has the binary representation $(11001)_2$, and +25 is stored in a 16-bit word as

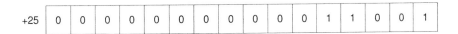

whereas −25 is stored as

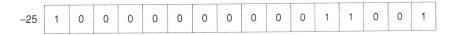

the difference in the two being in the leftmost sign bit.

The fixed size of the word imposes a limitation on the magnitude of the integers that can be stored internally. Thus, since the leftmost bit is used to represent the sign of the integer, the largest positive integer that can be stored in an 8-bit word is $(1111111)_2$, which is the binary representation of the decimal number

$$(1\times2^6) + (1\times2^5) + (1\times2^4) + (1\times2^3) + (1\times2^2) + (1\times2^1) + (1\times2^0)$$
$$= 2^6 + 2^5 + 2^4 + 2^3 + 2^2 + 2 + 1$$
$$= 2^7 - 1$$
$$= 127.$$

Similarly, the largest positive integer that can be stored in a 16-bit word is $2^{15} - 1 = 32767$, and in a 32-bit word the limit is $2^{31} - 1 = 2147483647$.

In many computers, *twos complement* is used to store integers, the advantage being that the arithmetic operation of subtraction can be realized by adding the twos complement of the subtrahend. In the binary system, the *complement* of 0 is 1, and that of 1 is 0. The *ones complement* of a binary number N, denoted by $\overline{N}$, is the number obtained by complementing each of the digits of N. For example, if

$$N = 00000000\ 01100101$$

then

$$\overline{N} = 11111111\ 10011010$$

The *twos complement* of a binary number N is the number resulting from adding 1 to the rightmost digit position (regardless of the position of the radix point) of its ones complement $\overline{N}$, that is, $\overline{N} + 1$. Thus, in the preceding example

$$\overline{N} + 1 = 11111111\ 10011011$$

and

$$N + (\overline{N} + 1) = 00000000\ 00000000$$

after deleting 1, which would be an overflow in a 16-bit word. Since the sum of any number and its negative is 0 in any number system, it follows that the twos complement of a binary number N can be used to represent the negative of N, i.e., $-N$. The following shows the representation of +25 and –25 in a twos complement machine:

+25	0	0	0	0	0	0	0	0	0	0	0	1	1	0	0	1

–25	1	1	1	1	1	1	1	1	1	1	1	0	0	1	1	1

If the twos complement form of representing negative integers is used, then the range of integer values that may be stored in a word is -2^{n-1} to $2^{n-1} - 1$, where n is the number of bits in a word.

The scheme used for storing *floating-point numbers* differs among various computers. A floating-point number has two parts: an *exponent* and a *fraction*. The fraction is often referred to as the *mantissa*. For example, in the floating-point number 0.8×10^2, the exponent is 2 and the mantissa is 0.8. In general, a floating-point number is of the form $m \times \beta^e$, where m is the mantissa, which is a signed fraction such that $-1 < m < 1$, e is the exponent, which is an integer, and β is the radix, which is 10 for decimal computers, 2 for binary computers, and 16 for hexadecimal computers.

A common scheme for storing floating-point numbers is to use one part of a word or some contiguous words to store a fixed number of bits of the mantissa and another part to store the exponent. In addition, a bit is used for storing the sign of the mantissa. No sign bit is provided for storing the sign of the exponent; instead, a large positive integer is added to the exponent to take care of a negative exponent. This adjusted exponent is often referred to as the *characteristic*. For example, 0.8×10^2 is stored in the short (single precision) format in IBM System/370 as

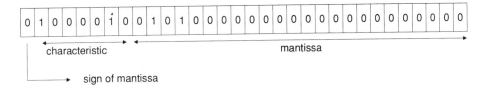

System/370 can be considered to be a hexadecimal machine. The twos complement discussed earlier is not used in representing floating-point numbers; instead, each four-bit (a hexadecimal digit) forms a basic unit. Thus, the magnitude of a floating-point number is the mantissa times a power of 16. The true exponent indicates this power. The characteristic is obtained by adding $(64)_{10} = (40)_{16}$ to the exponent. Therefore, the true exponent in the preceding figure is $(42)_{16} - (40)_{16} = 2$. The mantissa is $(.5)_{16}$. Thus, the number represented is

$$(5 \times 16^{-1}) \times 16^2 = 80.0$$

Observe that the number of bits available to store the mantissa determines the precision, and the number of bits available to store the exponent bounds the largest (smallest in the case of negative) floating-point number that can be represented.

An attempt to store an integer greater than the maximum permissible value results in what is known as *overflow*, *i.e.*, the loss of some of the bits of its binary representation. This limitation may be partially overcome by using more than one word to store an integer, but it does not solve the problem of overflow, as the range of representable integers is still finite. A similar problem arises when storing a fraction that does not have a terminating binary representation, or a floating-point number if the binary representation of its exponent or mantissa or both may require more than the available number of bits. For example, only a fixed number of bits of the mantissa of the floating-point number 0.7 that has a nonterminating representation can be stored, which results in loss of precision that can be reduced but not eliminated by using a larger number of bits.

D.3 CHARACTER REPRESENTATION

The internal representation of characters is based upon an assignment of numeric codes to characters. Using these numeric codes, characters are arranged in an order in which one character precedes another if its numeric code is less than the numeric code of the other. This ordering of characters based on their numeric codes is called the *collating sequence*, and varies from one computer to another. All that is guaranteed is as follows:

1. Blank (space) precedes all letters and digits.
2. Letters are in alphabetical order.
3. Digits are in numerical order.
4. Letters and digits are not intermingled; that is, either all the digits precede all the letters or vice versa.

Amongst the several coding schemes that have been developed, the two most popular are ASCII (American Standard Code for Information Interchange) and EBCDIC (Extended Binary Coded Decimal Interchange Code). A complete table of ASCII and EBCDIC character codes is given in Appendix E.

A character is internally represented by storing the binary equivalent of its numeric code in a byte. Character strings are represented by storing the numeric codes of the characters involved in adjacent bytes. The C compiler automatically puts a *null* character, whose numeric code is 0, at the end of each string. Thus, the string "TO" is stored in three bytes with the numeric code for the character T in the first byte, the code for the character O in the next byte, and the code for the null character in the last byte. The string then is represented in ASCII as

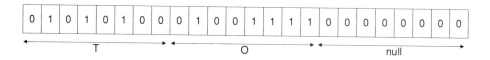

and in EBCDIC as

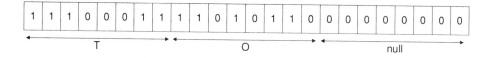

ASCII and EBCDIC Character Codes

E

Deci-mal	Binary	Octal	Hexa-deci-mal	ASCII	EBCDIC	Deci-mal	Binary	Octal	Hexa-deci-mal	ASCII	EBCDIC
0	0	0	0	NUL	NUL	1	1	1	1		
2	10	2	2			3	11	3	3		
4	100	4	4			5	101	5	5		
6	110	6	6			7	111	7	7		
8	1000	10	8			9	1001	11	9		
10	1010	12	a			11	1011	13	b		
12	1100	14	c			13	1101	15	d		
14	1110	16	e			15	1111	17	f		
16	10000	20	10			17	10001	21	11		
18	10010	22	12			19	10011	23	13		
20	10100	24	14			21	10101	25	15		
22	10110	26	16			23	10111	27	17		
24	11000	30	18			25	11001	31	19		
26	11010	32	1a			27	11011	33	1b		
28	11100	34	1c			29	11101	35	1d		
30	11110	36	1e			31	11111	37	1f		
32	100000	40	20	space		33	100001	41	21	!	
34	100010	42	22	"		35	100011	43	23	#	
36	100100	44	24	$		37	100101	45	25	%	
38	100110	46	26	&		39	100111	47	27	'	
40	101000	50	28	(		41	101001	51	29	)	
42	101010	52	2a	*		43	101011	53	2b	+	
44	101100	54	2c	,		45	101101	55	2d	-	
46	101110	56	2e	.		47	101111	57	2f	/	
48	110000	60	30	0		49	110001	61	31	1	
50	110010	62	32	2		51	110011	63	33	3	
52	110100	64	34	4		53	110101	65	35	5	
54	110110	66	36	6		55	110111	67	37	7	
56	111000	70	38	8		57	111001	71	39	9	
58	111010	72	3a	:		59	111011	73	3b	;	
60	111100	74	3c	<		61	111101	75	3d	=	
62	111110	76	3e	>		63	111111	77	3f	?	
64	1000000	100	40	@	space	65	1000001	101	41	A	
66	1000010	102	42	B		67	1000011	103	43	C	
68	1000100	104	44	D		69	1000101	105	45	E	
70	1000110	106	46	F		71	1000111	107	47	G	
72	1001000	110	48	H		73	1001001	111	49	I	
74	1001010	112	4a	J	¢	75	1001011	113	4b	K	.
76	1001100	114	4c	L	<	77	1001101	115	4d	M	(

Decimal	Binary	Octal	Hexadecimal	ASCII	EBCDIC	Decimal	Binary	Octal	Hexadecimal	ASCII	EBCDIC
78	1001110	116	4e	N	+	79	1001111	117	4f	O	|
80	1010000	120	50	P	&	81	1010001	121	51	Q	
82	1010010	122	52	R		83	1010011	123	53	S	
84	1010100	124	54	T		85	1010101	125	55	U	
86	1010110	126	56	V		87	1010111	127	57	W	
88	1011000	130	58	X		89	1011001	131	59	Y	
90	1011010	132	5a	Z	!	91	1011011	133	5b	[	$
92	1011100	134	5c	\	*	93	1011101	135	5d	]	)
94	1011110	136	5e	^	;	95	1011111	137	5f	_	~
96	1100000	140	60	`	-	97	1100001	141	61	a	/
98	1100010	142	62	b		99	1100011	143	63	c	
100	1100100	144	64	d		101	1100101	145	65	e	
102	1100110	146	66	f		103	1100111	147	67	g	
104	1101000	150	68	h		105	1101001	151	69	i	
106	1101010	152	6a	j		107	1101011	153	6b	k	,
108	1101100	154	6c	l	%	109	1101101	155	6d	m	
110	1101110	156	6e	n	>	111	1101111	157	6f	o	?
112	1110000	160	70	p		113	1110001	161	71	q	
114	1110010	162	72	r		115	1110011	163	73	s	
116	1110100	164	74	t		117	1110101	165	75	u	
118	1110110	166	76	v		119	1110111	167	77	w	
120	1111000	170	78	x		121	1111001	171	79	y	
122	1111010	172	7a	z	:	123	1111011	173	7b	{	#
124	1111100	174	7c	|	@	125	1111101	175	7d	}	'
126	1111110	176	7e	~	=	127	1111111	177	7f	DEL	"
128	10000000	200	80			129	10000001	201	81		a
130	10000010	202	82		b	131	10000011	203	83		c
132	10000100	204	84		d	133	10000101	205	85		e
134	10000110	206	86		f	135	10000111	207	87		g
136	10001000	210	88		h	137	10001001	211	89		i
138	10001010	212	8a			139	10001011	213	8b		
140	10001100	214	8c			141	10001101	215	8d		
142	10001110	216	8e			143	10001111	217	8f		
144	10010000	220	90			145	10010001	221	91		j
146	10010010	222	92		k	147	10010011	223	93		l
148	10010100	224	94		m	149	10010101	225	95		n
150	10010110	226	96		o	151	10010111	227	97		p
152	10011000	230	98		q	153	10011001	231	99		r
154	10011010	232	9a			155	10011011	233	9b		
156	10011100	234	9c			157	10011101	235	9d		
158	10011110	236	9e			159	10011111	237	9f		
160	10100000	240	a0			161	10100001	241	a1		
162	10100010	242	a2		s	163	10100011	243	a3		t
164	10100100	244	a4		u	165	10100101	245	a5		v
166	10100110	246	a6		w	167	10100111	247	a7		x
168	10101000	250	a8		y	169	10101001	251	a9		z
170	10101010	252	aa			171	10101011	253	ab		
172	10101100	254	ac			173	10101101	255	ad		
174	10101110	256	ae			175	10101111	257	af		
176	10110000	260	b0			177	10110001	261	b1		
178	10110010	262	b2			179	10110011	263	b3		
180	10110100	264	b4			181	10110101	265	b5		
182	10110110	266	b6			183	10110111	267	b7		
184	10111000	270	b8			185	10111001	271	b9		
186	10111010	272	ba			187	10111011	273	bb		
188	10111100	274	bc			189	10111101	275	bd		
190	10111110	276	be			191	10111111	277	bf		

Deci-mal	Binary	Octal	Hexa-deci-mal	ASCII	EBCDIC	Deci-mal	Binary	Octal	Hexa-deci-mal	ASCII	EBCDIC
192	11000000	300	c0		{	193	11000001	301	c1		A
194	11000010	302	c2		B	195	11000011	303	c3		C
196	11000100	304	c4		D	197	11000101	305	c5		E
198	11000110	306	c6		F	199	11000111	307	c7		G
200	11001000	310	c8		H	201	11001001	311	c9		I
202	11001010	312	ca			203	11001011	313	cb		
204	11001100	314	cc			205	11001101	315	cd		
206	11001110	316	ce			207	11001111	317	cf		
208	11010000	320	d0		}	209	11010001	321	d1		J
210	11010010	322	d2		K	211	11010011	323	d3		L
212	11010100	324	d4		M	213	11010101	325	d5		N
214	11010110	326	d6		O	215	11010111	327	d7		P
216	11011000	330	d8		Q	217	11011001	331	d9		R
218	11011010	332	da			219	11011011	333	db		
220	11011100	334	dc			221	11011101	335	dd		
222	11011110	336	de			223	11011111	337	df		
224	11100000	340	e0			225	11100001	341	e1		
226	11100010	342	e2		S	227	11100011	343	e3		T
228	11100100	344	e4		U	229	11100101	345	e5		V
230	11100110	346	e6		W	231	11100111	347	e7		X
232	11101000	350	e8		Y	233	11101001	351	e9		Z
234	11101010	352	ea			235	11101011	353	eb		
236	11101100	354	ec			237	11101101	355	ed		
238	11101110	356	ee			239	11101111	357	ef		
240	11110000	360	f0		0	241	11110001	361	f1		1
242	11110010	362	f2		2	243	11110011	363	f3		3
244	11110100	364	f4		4	245	11110101	365	f5		5
246	11110110	366	f6		6	247	11110111	367	f7		7
248	11111000	370	f8		8	249	11111001	371	f9		9
250	11111010	372	fa			251	11111011	373	fb		
252	11111100	374	fc			253	11111101	375	fd		
254	11111110	376	fe			255	11111111	377	ff		

A blank entry in the table indicates that the code either has not been assigned or is used for control.

F References

Draft Proposed American National Standard for Information Systems — Programming Language C. Document X3J11/88-090. The American National Standards Institute, December 1988. The description of the ANSI C standard.

Rationale for Draft Proposed American National Standard for Information Systems — Programming Language C. Document X3J11/88-151. The American National Standards Institute, November 1988. Summarizes the rationale for design of ANSI C.

O.J. Dahl, E.W. Dijkstra, and C.A.R. Hoare. *Structured Programming.* Academic Press, 1972. The classic book on the structured method of programming.

A. Feuer and N. Gehani (Editors). *Comparing and Assessing Programming Languages.* Prentice Hall, 1984. Contains papers comparing C to other languages.

S.P. Harbison and G.L. Steele Jr. *C: A Reference Manual*, Second Edition. Prentice Hall, 1987. An outstanding reference for finding the fine details of C.

B.W. Kernighan and P.J. Plauger. *The Elements of Programming Style.* Mc-Graw-Hill, 1974. Contains excellent tips on writing good programs.

B.W. Kernighan and D.M. Ritchie. *The C Programming Language*, First Edition. Prentice Hall, 1978. The original classic; contains "The C Reference Manual".

B.W. Kernighan and D.M. Ritchie. *The C Programming Language*, Second Edition. Prentice Hall, 1988. ANSI C version of the first edition.

B. Stroustrup. *The C++ Programming Language.* Addison Wesley, 1986. Describes C++ — an upwardly compatible, object-oriented extension of C.

N. Wirth. "Program Development by Stepwise Refinement". *Communications of the ACM*, Vol. 14, No. 3, 1971. The classic paper on program design.

Index

Companion Disk for Programming in ANSI C

A companion disk containing the source code for the illustrative examples in the book can be ordered from *Informatix*. Programs are organized into sub-directories, one for each chapter.

To order, please specify 5.25 inch or 3.5 inch diskette. Price: $9.95, California residents add 8.25% sales tax. Shipping and Handling: United States, Canada, and Mexico: $3 for 1st diskette, $1 for each additional diskette. Other Countries: $5 for 1st diskette, $1 for each additional diskette. Additional $12 for Express delivery. All prices in U.S. dollars. Prices subject to change without notice.

Make check or Money Order payable to *Informatix*. Send your order to: *Informatix*, 1290 Quail Creek Circle, San Jose, CA 95120.